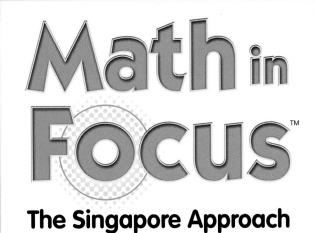

Math in Focus™

The Singapore Approach

Teacher's Edition

1A

Consultant and Author
Dr. Fong Ho Kheong

Authors
Chelvi Ramakrishnan and Bernice Lau Pui Wah

U.S. Consultants
Dr. Richard Bisk, Andy Clark
and Patsy F. Kanter

Marshall Cavendish
Education

GREAT★SOURCE®

HOUGHTON MIFFLIN HARCOURT
Supplemental Publishers

© 2009 Marshall Cavendish International (Singapore) Private Limited

Published by Marshall Cavendish Education
An imprint of Marshall Cavendish International (Singapore) Private Limited
A member of Times Publishing Limited

Marshall Cavendish International (Singapore) Private Limited
Times Centre, 1 New Industrial Road
Singapore 536196
Tel: +65 6411 0820
Fax: +65 6266 3677
E-mail: fps@sg.marshallcavendish.com
Website: www.marshallcavendish.com/education

Distributed by
Great Source
A division of Houghton Mifflin Harcourt Publishing Company
181 Ballardvale Street
P.O. Box 7050
Wilmington, MA 01887-7050
Tel: 1-800-289-4490
Website: www.greatsource.com

First published 2009

Math in Focus™ is a trademark of Marshall Cavendish Education.

Great Source® is a registered trademark of Houghton Mifflin Harcourt Publishing Company.

Math in Focus™ Grade 1 Teacher's Edition Book A
ISBN 978-0-669-01315-3

Printed in China
1A 2 3 4 5 6 7 8 MCI 16 15 14 13 12 11 10 09

Program Overview

*Your Teacher's Edition is key to the successful implementation of any mathematics program. The next few pages will help you understand and appreciate the unique attributes of the **Math in Focus** program.*

You will learn how your students will gain depth of understanding, fluency with skills, and confidence in problem solving. You will learn how to use the Workbook in conjunction with the Student Book, how to prepare students for formal assessments, and how to remediate and enrich to meet all your students' needs.

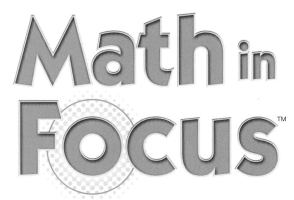

Math in Focus: The Singapore Approach *is an elementary mathematics program for Kindergarten through Grade 5 created specifically to address the recommendations for instructional materials agreed upon by national and international panels of mathematics education specialists.*

Meeting the Needs of U.S. Classrooms...

Top performing countries have gained ground on and now surpass the U.S. in mathematics education, as shown by the Trends in International Math and Science Study (TIMSS)[1]. Efforts to reverse this trend have led to a large body of solid research. Analysis of the research base has led the National Council of Teachers of Mathematics (NCTM)[2], the National Math Advisory Panel[3], the American Institutes for Research[4], and the National Research Council[5] to make several undisputed key recommendations.

1 Above all, a focused, coherent curriculum, without significant repitition year after year

2 An equal emphasis on conceptual understanding, and fluency with skills

3 Use of concrete and pictorial representations

4 Multi-step and non-routine problem-solving

...by Drawing on Success in Singapore

Singapore students have been top performers in the TIMSS assessment since 1995. Their success can be largely attributed to the mathematics curriculum revision implemented by the Singapore Ministry of Education[6] in the 1980s.

Key requirements of their instructional materials as described that parallel the recommendations of U.S. specialists are:

- **Precise framework** of concepts and skills (specifics of what to exclude as well as what to include provides hierarchy and linkage)

- **Skills and concepts** taught in depth to allow for mastery (consolidation of concepts and skills)

- **Use of a concrete to visual to abstract development** of concepts using model drawings to connect visual representation to problem solving

- **Emphasis on problem solving** considered central to all mathematics study

Footnotes

1. Gonzales, Patrick, Juan Carlos Guzmán, Lisette Partelow, Erin Pahlke, Leslie Jocelyn, David Kastberg, and Trevor Williams. *Highlights From the Trends in International Mathematics and Science Study:* TIMSS 2003. U.S. Department of Education, National Center for Education Statistics, 2004.

2. National Council of Teachers of Mathematics. *Curriculum Focal Points for Prekindergarten through Grade 8 Mathematics*, 2006.

3. National Mathematics Advisory Panel. *Foundations for Success.* U.S. Department of Education, 2008.

4. American Institutes for Research® *What the United States Can Learn from Singapore's World-Class Mathematics System.* U. S. Department of Education Policy and Program Studies Services, 2005.

5. National Research Council. *Adding It Up: Helping Children Learn Mathematics.* Washington, DC, National Academy Press, 2001.

6. Ministry of Education, Singapore. *Mathematics Syllabus: Primary*, 2007.

Math in Focus is the Solution

Math in Focus: The Singapore Approach *uses the world-class Singaporean curriculum and instructional materials adapted to meet the unique needs of American teachers and students.*

● A Focused, Coherent Syllabus

Answering the call for a "focused, coherent progression of mathematics learning, with an emphasis on proficiency with key topics," *Math in Focus* authors created a strategic, articulated sequence of topics to be developed in depth to allow true mastery. (*see* Scope and Sequence Introduction, p. T24)

● Integrated Concepts and Skills

Math in Focus helps students build a solid conceptual understanding through use of manipulative materials and visual models. Computational skills develop from this conceptual understanding and are reinforced through practice. As skills fluency increases, understanding is **reinforced in turn.** (*see* Learning and Consolidating Skills and Concepts, p. T8–T11)

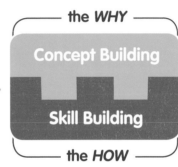

● Concrete to Pictorial to Abstract

The *Math in Focus: The Singapore Approach* series consistently employs the Concrete ▶ Pictorial ▶ Abstract pedagogy. Clear and engaging visuals that present concepts and model solutions allow all students regardless of language skills to focus on the math lesson.

Market research for *Math in Focus* included multiple rounds of research including focus group testing and discussions with experienced educators. Regional and national studies ensured that the student books and teacher support meet the current needs of students and teachers across the U.S.

For more details, visit www.greatsource.com/mathinfocus

● Extensive Problem Solving

The creators of *Math in Focus: The Singapore Approach* believe not only that all children can learn math but that they can also enjoy math. Students learn to use model drawings to visualize and solve problems through mathematical reasoning and critical thinking. (*see* Applying Concepts and Skills, pp. T12–T13)

National and International Research Recommendations

▶ Focus and Depth

National Council of Teachers of Mathematics

"A curriculum is more than a collection of activities: it must be coherent, focused on important mathematics, and well articulated across the grades."

—*Curriculum Focal Points for Prekindergarten through Grade 8 Mathematics*, 2006.

Math in Focus

addresses fewer topics in greater depth at each level.

- Knowledge is built carefully and thoroughly with both *multi-page* lessons and *multi-day* lessons.

- Time is built into the program to develop understanding with *hands-on activities* with manipulatives as well as *extensive skills practice*.

Grade 1, Chapter 3, Lesson 1

▶ Interlocking Concepts and Skills

National Math Advisory Panel

"Use should be made of what is clearly known from rigorous research about how children learn, especially by recognizing the mutually-reinforcing benefits of conceptual understanding, procedural fluency, and automatic (i.e., quick and effortless) recall of facts."

—*Foundations for Success*, 2008.

Math in Focus

develops concepts and skills in tandem.

- Manipulatives and visual representations provide a conceptual backbone.

- *Skills are connected to concepts* through visual representations.

- Extensive problem solving *merges conceptual understanding with computational skills.*

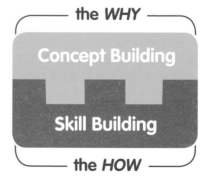

the *WHY*

Concept Building

Skill Building

the *HOW*

▶ Clear Visuals and Use of Models

National Research Council

"Opportunities should involve connecting symbolic representations and operations with physical or pictorial representations, as well as translating between various symbolic representations."

—*Adding It Up: Helping Children Learn Mathematics*, 2001.

Math in Focus

uses clear and engaging visuals that present concepts and model solutions.

- *Minimal text* and simple, direct visuals allow all students regardless of language skills to focus on the math lesson.

- The use of *model drawings* offer a visual representation of word problems, leading to symbolic solutions of rich and complex problems.

- Consistent use of the *concrete–pictorial–abstract pedagogy* repeatedly "models" the model-drawing problem-solving strategy.

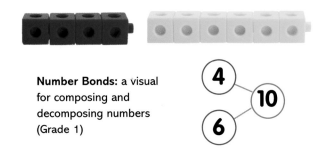

Number Bonds: a visual for composing and decomposing numbers (Grade 1)

▶ Emphasis on Problem Solving

Singapore Ministry of Education

"Mathematical problem solving is central to mathematics learning. It involves the acquisition and application of mathematics concepts and skills in a wide range of situations, including non-routine, open-ended, and real-world problems."

—*Mathematics Syllabus: Primary*, 2006.

Math in Focus

uses a scaffolded approach to solving word problems, focusing on model drawing to build success and confidence.

- The visual representation of word problems leads to symbolic solutions of *rich and complex problems.*

- Students draw on prior knowledge as well as recently acquired concepts and skills as they combine *problem-solving strategies with critical thinking skills.*

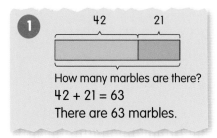

Bar Model: a visual representation of a word problem (Grade 2)

Instructional Pathway
Learning, Consolidating and Applying Grades 1–5

Math in Focus *Student Books and Workbooks follow an instructional pathway of:*

- *learning concepts and skills through visual lessons and teacher instruction*
- *consolidating concepts and skills through practice, activities, and math journals, and*
- *applying concepts and skills with extensive problem-solving practice and challenges*

Learning Concepts and Skills
Understanding the **How** *and the* **Why**

Each lesson in the Student Book is introduced with a ***Learn*** *element. Mathematical concepts are presented in a straightforward visual format, with specific and structured learning tasks.*

Scaffolded, coherent instruction promotes deep math understanding for all students with:

- clearly explained thought processes
- carefully selected visuals
- minimal text
- focus on both the *how* and the *why*

Building a Solid Foundation at Each Level

Concrete

Manipulatives are used to explain abstract mathematical concepts.

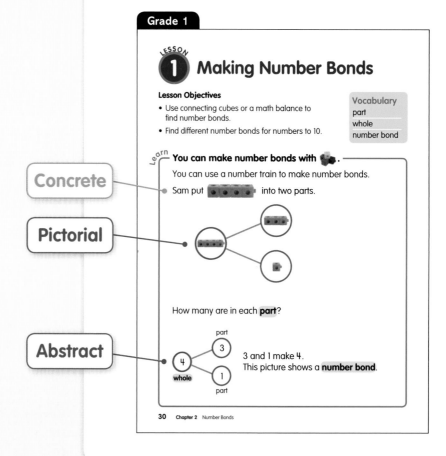

❝ Increase the number, variety, and overall use of pictorial representations directly tied to concepts in textbooks. **❞**

— National Math Advisory Panel

Within each lesson, from chapter to chapter, and from year to year, instruction follows the concrete to pictorial to abstract sequence.

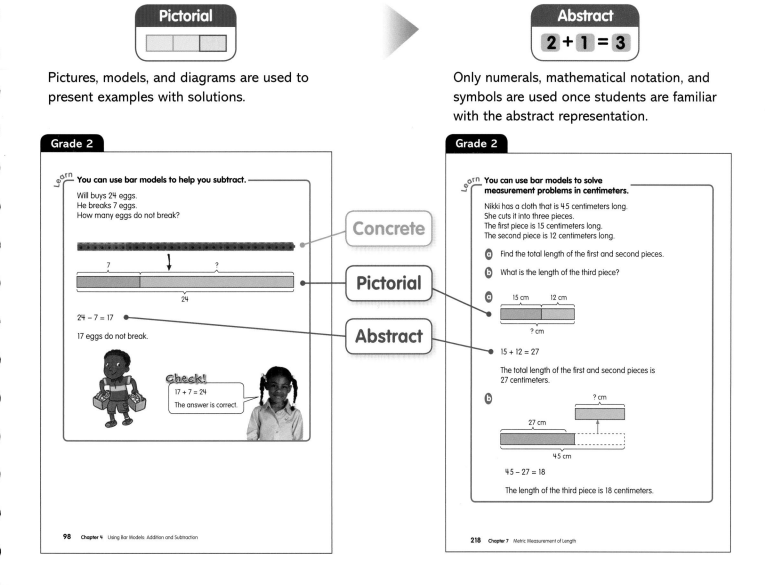

Pictorial

Pictures, models, and diagrams are used to present examples with solutions.

Abstract

2 + 1 = 3

Only numerals, mathematical notation, and symbols are used once students are familiar with the abstract representation.

Grade 2

Learn **You can use bar models to help you subtract.**

Will buys 24 eggs.
He breaks 7 eggs.
How many eggs do not break?

7 ↓ ?

24

24 – 7 = 17

17 eggs do not break.

Concrete

Pictorial

Abstract

Check!
17 + 7 = 24
The answer is correct.

Grade 2

Learn **You can use bar models to solve measurement problems in centimeters.**

Nikki has a cloth that is 45 centimeters long.
She cuts it into three pieces.
The first piece is 15 centimeters long.
The second piece is 12 centimeters long.

ⓐ Find the total length of the first and second pieces.

ⓑ What is the length of the third piece?

ⓐ 15 cm   12 cm

? cm

15 + 12 = 27

The total length of the first and second pieces is 27 centimeters.

ⓑ

? cm

27 cm

45 cm

45 – 27 = 18

The length of the third piece is 18 centimeters.

Consolidating Concepts and Skills
for Deep Math Understanding

Extensive Practice

Each **Learn** element of the lesson is followed by opportunities to develop deeper understanding through these features:

- carefully crafted skills practice in the lesson using Guided Practice and Let's Practice
- real-world problems
- independent practice in the Workbook
- additional practice problems in the Extra Practice Book

> **Guided Practice** allows students to check their understanding while working with some guidance.

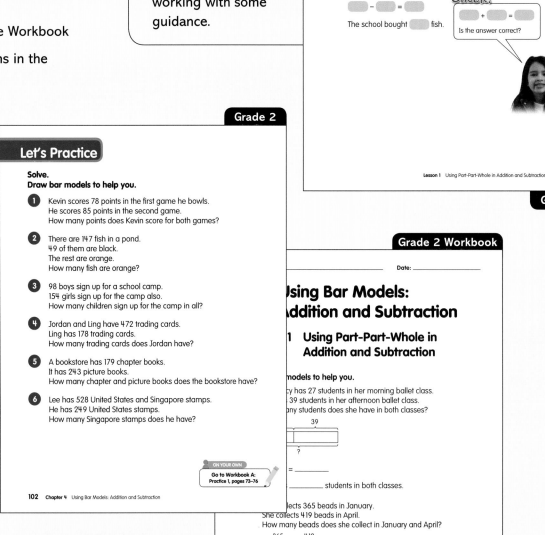

Let's Practice

> **Let's Practice**
> consolidates learning and checks all prerequisite skills needed before students work independently in the Workbook.

Solve.
Draw bar models to help you.

1. Kevin scores 78 points in the first game he bowls.
   He scores 85 points in the second game.
   How many points does Kevin score for both games?

2. There are 147 fish in a pond.
   49 of them are black.
   The rest are orange.
   How many fish are orange?

3. 98 boys sign up for a school camp.
   154 girls sign up for the camp also.
   How many children sign up for the camp in all?

4. Jordan and Ling have 472 trading cards.
   Ling has 178 trading cards.
   How many trading cards does Jordan have?

5. A bookstore has 179 chapter books.
   It has 243 picture books.
   How many chapter and picture books does the bookstore have?

6. Lee has 528 United States and Singapore stamps.
   He has 249 United States stamps.
   How many Singapore stamps does he have?

ON YOUR OWN
Go to Workbook A:
Practice 1, pages 73–76

102 **Chapter 4** Using Bar Models: Addition and Subtraction

> **ON YOUR OWN** directs students to Workbook pages for independent practice.

Hands-On Work in Pairs and Small Groups

Students develop concepts and explore connections as they practice skills and reasoning processes.

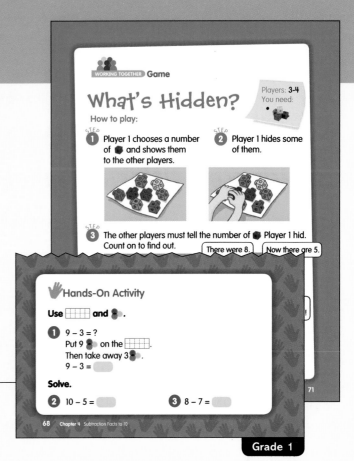

> **Hands-On Activity** and **Game** reinforce skills, concepts, and problem-solving strategies in small group or partner settings.

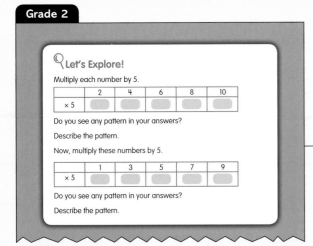

> **Let's Explore!** provides opportunities for students to carry out investigative activities and to discus alternate solutions to open-ended questions.

Communication and Reflection

Students communicate with each other, discuss their thinking, and reflect on the math they are practicing.

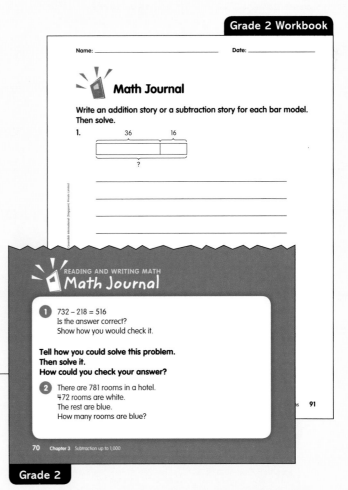

> **Math Journal** offers opportunities for students to reflect on mathematical learning.

Applying Concepts and Skills
Builds Real-World Problem Solvers

Frequent Exposure

Math in Focus: The Singapore Approach embeds problem solving throughout a lesson.

Learn elements use models to explain computation concepts. Students become accustomed to seeing and using visual models to form mental images of mathematical ideas.

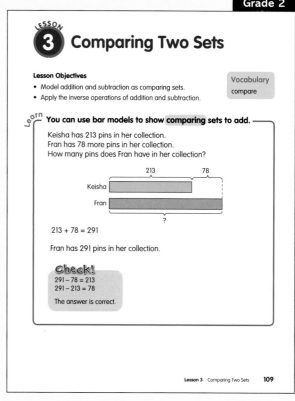

Frequent Practice

Practice pages in the Workbook include both computation and problem-solving sections.

- Each set of problems encompasses previous skills and concepts.

- Word problems progress in complexity from 1-step to 2-step to multi-step.

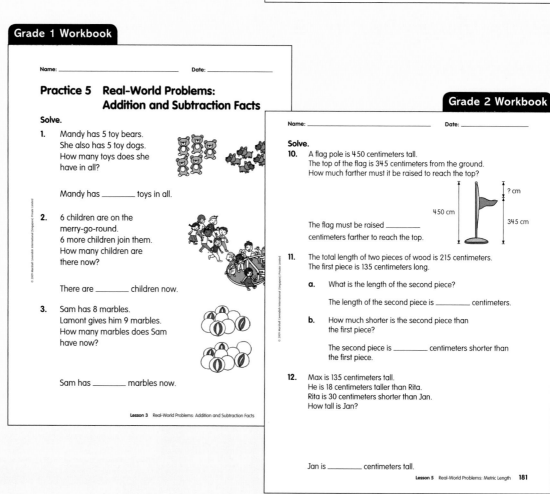

Model-Drawing Strategies

Using bar models as a problem-solving tool is taught explicitly in Grades 2–5. Students become familiar with this systematic way to translate complex word problems into mathematical equations, and avoid the common issue with not knowing where to start.

Model Drawing

- helps children solve simple and complex word problems
- develops algebraic thinking
- follows the introduction of operational skills
- helps visualize the part-whole structure of the problem
- develops operational sense
- fosters proportional reasoning

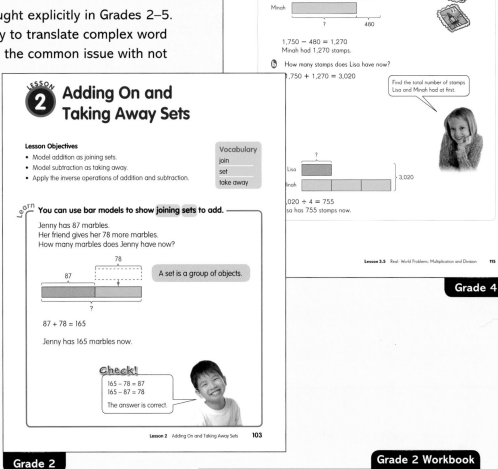

Challenging Problems

Each *Math in Focus* chapter concludes with **Put on Your Thinking Cap!** which challenges students to solve non-routine questions.

These problems ask children to draw on *deep prior knowledge* as well as recently acquired concepts, combining problem-solving strategies with *critical thinking skills*.

Critical thinking skills students develop with *Math in Focus* include:

- classifying
- comparing
- sequencing
- analyzing parts and whole
- identifying patterns and relationships
- induction (from specific to general)
- deduction (from general to specific)
- spatial visualization

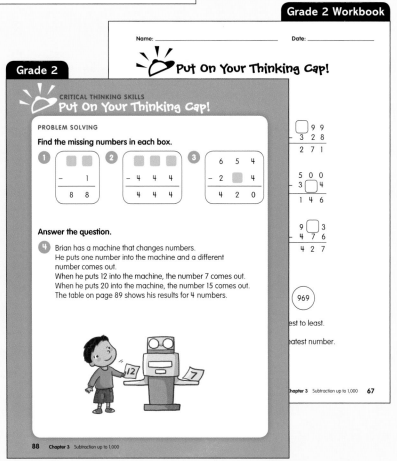

Extensive Teacher Support

Step-by-Step Support
and Embedded Professional Development

Math in Focus *Teacher's Editions provide comprehensive lesson plans with pacing suggestions, step-by-step instructional support, and embedded professional development including math background discussions and classroom management tips.*

> **Math Background** clearly outlines the mathematical significance of key concepts.

> **Skills Trace** shows concepts and skills learned in the previous level that this chapter is based on, as well as concepts and skills in the following level that this chapter will lead to.

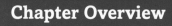

CHAPTER **4**

Chapter Overview

Subtraction Facts to 10

Math Background

Children have learned the part-whole concept and addition of numbers to 10. These two concepts are related to subtraction skills and concepts.

In this chapter, children will learn different methods of subtraction, the most basic of which is the taking-away strategy. The addition concept is the inverse of subtraction, and one of the ways to subtract involves counting on. Other strategies are counting on, counting back, and using number bonds.

All the subtraction strategies can be taught using the part-whole concept. If you know one part and the whole amount, and need to know the other part, you use subtraction. The subtraction strategy that builds and reinforces this concept most effectively involves the use of number bonds, which relate parts with the whole, and relate addition with subtraction.

As is found in addition, there is an Identity Property of Subtraction. This property states that zero subtracted from any number is equal to that number. Another property of subtraction states that any number subtracted from itself equals zero.

This chapter also requires children to use problem-solving skills to solve simple real-world word problems that involve subtraction. Children solve problems by writing subtraction sentences from number bonds.

Cross-Curricular Connections

Reading/Language Arts Read aloud *Subtraction Action* by Loreen Leedy (Holiday House, © 2002) about Miss Prime and her students' subtraction adventures at the fair. As a class, brainstorm subtraction story ideas. Choose one of them to be the setting for your own illustrated class book about subtraction.

Skills Trace

Grade K	Represent subtraction stories with small whole numbers. (Chap. 18)
Grade 1	Subtract 2-digit numbers up to 100. (Chap. 4, 8, 13, 14 and 17)
Grade 2	Subtract 3-digit numbers up to 1000. (Chap. 3, 4, and 10)

EVERY DAY COUNTS®
Calendar Math

The October activities provide...

Preview of geometric patterns and attributes of rectangles (skills and concepts taught at depth in Chapter 5)

Review of number patterns (Chapter 1) and length comparisons using *longer, shorter,* and the *same length as* (Kindergarten skill)

Practice of sums and differences involving the number 6 (see Lessons 1 and 2 of this chapter) and writing addition and subtraction sentences (see Lessons 3 and 4)

> **Every Day Counts®** is an interactive bulletin board companion piece for grades K–5 to encourage classroom discussion through all the strands.

> **Cross-Curricular Connections** provide suggestions for tying the chapter topics to other parts of the student's day.

CHAPTER 4: OVERVIEW **64A**

Each chapter begins with a day of guiding children to recall prior knowledge and a quick check to assess children's readiness to proceed.

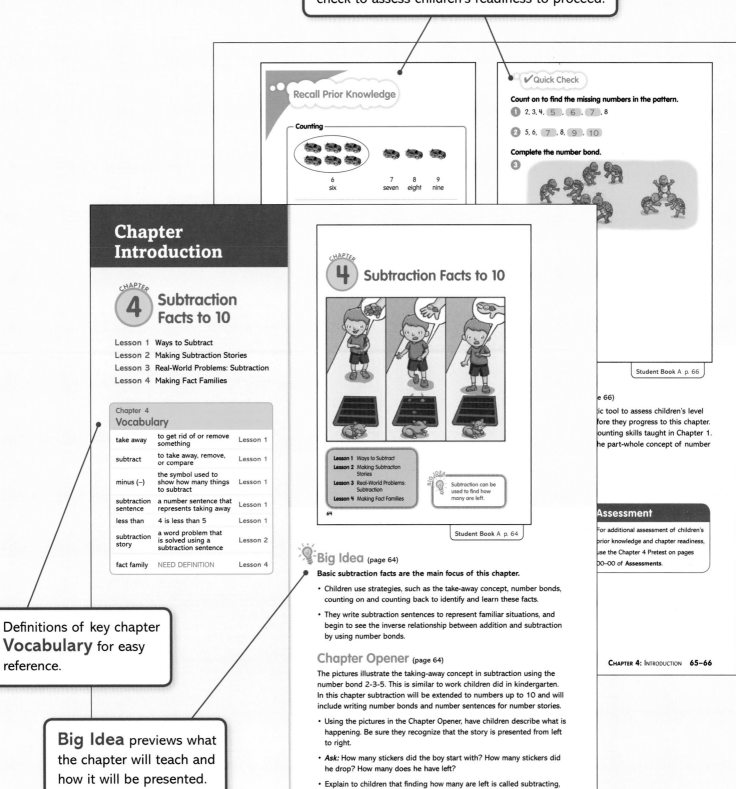

Recall Prior Knowledge

Counting

6 seven eight nine
six 7 8 9

✔ **Quick Check**

Count on to find the missing numbers in the pattern.

1 2, 3, 4, 5 , 6 , 7 , 8

2 5, 6, 7 , 8, 9 , 10

Complete the number bond.

3

Student Book A p. 66

(e 66)

tic tool to assess children's level
fore they progress to this chapter.
ounting skills taught in Chapter 1.
he part-whole concept of number

Chapter Introduction

CHAPTER 4 Subtraction Facts to 10

Lesson 1 Ways to Subtract
Lesson 2 Making Subtraction Stories
Lesson 3 Real-World Problems: Subtraction
Lesson 4 Making Fact Families

Chapter 4
Vocabulary

take away	to get rid of or remove something	Lesson 1
subtract	to take away, remove, or compare	Lesson 1
minus (–)	the symbol used to show how many things to subtract	Lesson 1
subtraction sentence	a number sentence that represents taking away	Lesson 1
less than	4 is less than 5	Lesson 1
subtraction story	a word problem that is solved using a subtraction sentence	Lesson 2
fact family	NEED DEFINITION	Lesson 4

CHAPTER 4 Subtraction Facts to 10

Lesson 1 Ways to Subtract
Lesson 2 Making Subtraction Stories
Lesson 3 Real-World Problems: Subtraction
Lesson 4 Making Fact Families

BIG IDEA Subtraction can be used to find how many are left.

64

Student Book A p. 64

Definitions of key chapter Vocabulary for easy reference.

Big Idea (page 64)

Basic subtraction facts are the main focus of this chapter.

• Children use strategies, such as the take-away concept, number bonds, counting on and counting back to identify and learn these facts.

• They write subtraction sentences to represent familiar situations, and begin to see the inverse relationship between addition and subtraction by using number bonds.

Chapter Opener (page 64)

The pictures illustrate the taking-away concept in subtraction using the number bond 2-3-5. This is similar to work children did in kindergarten. In this chapter subtraction will be extended to numbers up to 10 and will include writing number bonds and number sentences for number stories.

• Using the pictures in the Chapter Opener, have children describe what is happening. Be sure they recognize that the story is presented from left to right.

• *Ask:* How many stickers did the boy start with? How many stickers did he drop? How many does he have left?

• Explain to children that finding how many are left is called subtracting, and that they will learn many ways of subtracting in this chapter.

Assessment

For additional assessment of children's
prior knowledge and chapter readiness,
use the Chapter 4 Pretest on pages
00–00 of **Assessments**.

CHAPTER 4: INTRODUCTION 65–66

Big Idea previews what the chapter will teach and how it will be presented.

64 CHAPTER 4: INTRODUCTION

Extensive Teacher Support

For Deep Understanding

Math in Focus: The Singapore Approach is designed for deep understanding through:

- multi-page lessons
- multi-day lessons
- support for learners
- support for teachers

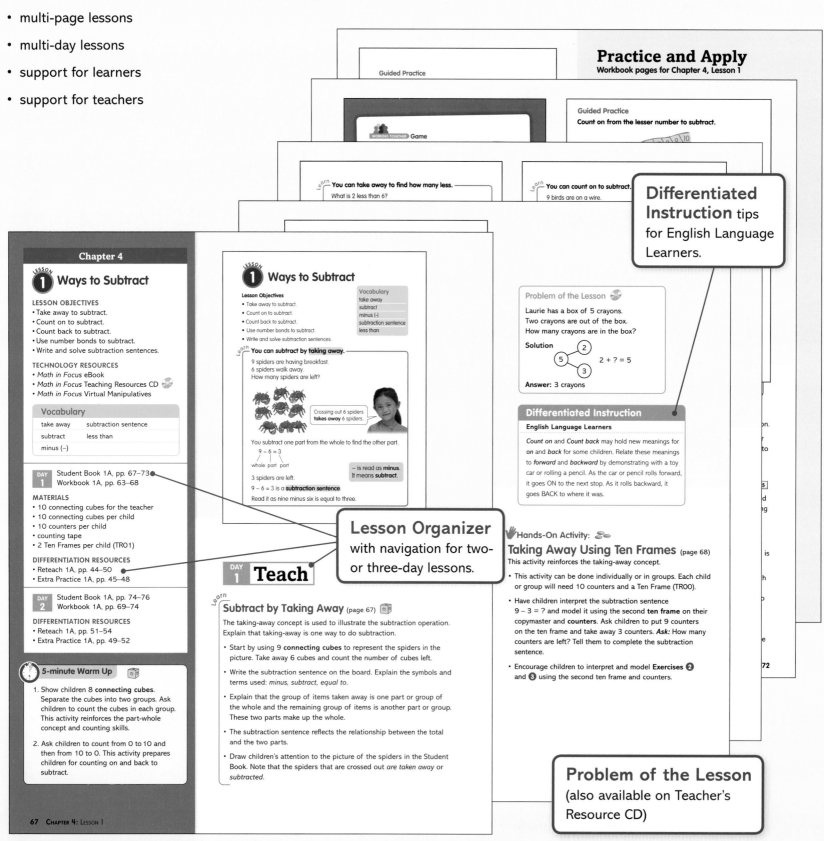

Differentiated Instruction tips for English Language Learners.

Lesson Organizer with navigation for two- or three-day lessons.

Problem of the Lesson (also available on Teacher's Resource CD)

Practice and Apply
Workbook pages for Chapter 4, Lesson 1

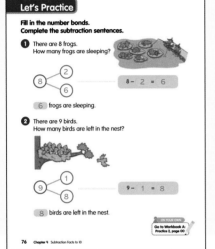

Name: _____ Date: _____

Practice 2 Ways To Subtract
Fill in the nu___
Complete t___

Name: _____ Date: _____

Complete the number bonds.

Let's Practice

Fill in the number bonds.
Complete the subtraction sentences.

1 There are 8 frogs.
How many frogs are sleeping?

8 → 2, 6

8 – 2 = 6

6 frogs are sleeping.

2 There are 9 birds.
How many birds are left in the nest?

9 → 1, 8

9 – 1 = 8

8 birds are left in the nest.

ON YOUR OWN
Go to Workbook A:
Practice 2, page 00

76 Chapter 4 Subtraction Facts to 10

Student Book A p. 76

Fill in the nu___
Complete th___

3.
4.
5.

8 Chapter ___

76A CHAPTER 4: LESSO___

✔ **Guided Practice** (page 75)
14 This exercise provides practice using the taking-away concept and number bond strategy in subtraction.

• Ask children to identify the two parts: the seahorses swimming away and the seahorses not swimming away. Have students use the number bond strategy to complete the subtraction sentence 10 – 3 = 7.

Let's Practice (page 76)

This practice reinforces the subtraction strategies. Exercise **1** uses the part-whole concept and number bond strategy. Exercise **2** uses the taking-away concept and number bond strategy.

Best Practices You may want to have students work in pairs to complete the Guided Practice and/or Let's Practice exercises. Then have them share their results with the class.

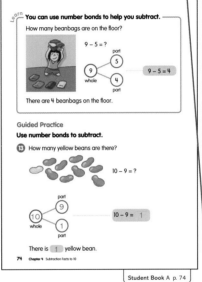

Learn **You can use number bonds to help you subtract.**
How many beanbags are on the floor?

9 – 5 = ?

9 (whole) → 5 (part), 4 (part)

9 – 5 = 4

There are 4 beanbags on the floor.

Guided Practice
Use number bonds to subtract.

13 How many yellow beans are there?

10 – 9 = ?

10 (whole) → 9 (part), 1 (part)

10 – 9 = 1

There is 1 yellow bean.

74 Chapter 4 Subtraction Facts to 10

Student Book A p. 74

Learn **You can use number bonds to help you subtract.**
How many strawberries are left on the plate?

5 (whole) → 1 (part), 4 (part)

5 – 1 = 4

4 strawberries are left on the plate.

Guided Practice
Use number bonds to subtract.

14 How many seahorses do not swim away?

10 (whole) → 3 (part), 7 (part)

10 – 3 = 7

7 seahorses do not swim away.

Lesson 1 Ways to Subtract 75

Student Book A p. 75

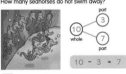

DAY
2 **Teach**   See lesson launch on page 67 for Day 2 resources.

Learn **Use Number Bonds to Subtract** (page 74)

This example illustrates the part-whole concept and the use of number bonds for subtraction. Children use number bonds to see the connection between the parts and the whole and to complete a subtraction sentence.

• Help children recognize that the picture shows two parts: the bean bags on the girl's head and the bean bags on the floor. The number 5 represents the bean bags on the girl's head. The total number is 9 and taking 5 away gives the number of bags on the floor.

• Children can recall the number bond 4-5-9 to complete the subtraction sentence 9 – 5 = 4. In Chapter 2, children created the number bonds for 9, so they should see the connection and then complete the subtraction sentence.

✔ **Guided Practice** (page 74)
13 This exercise provides practice using the part-whole concept and number bond strategy in subtraction.

74–75 CHAPTER 4: LESSON 1

• Guide children to identify the two parts: 1 yellow bean and 9 green beans. Help them use the number bond strategy to complete the subtraction sentence 10 – 9 = 1.

Common Error Some students may confuse the two subtraction sentences for a given number bond. If they write the sentence 5 – 4 = 1, have them reread the question that was asked. Be sure they understand that the answer to the question should be the answer to the subtraction problem.

Learn **Use Number Bonds to Subtract** (page 75)

This example illustrates the use of the taking-away concept and number bond strategy in subtraction.

• Ask the children to identify the two parts: the number of strawberries taken away and the strawberries left. The total number is 5 and taking away 1 gives the number of strawberries left on the plate.

• Use the number bond 1-4-5 to complete the subtraction sentences.

Core Components

The direct correlation of Student Books and Workbooks provides the full program of learning, consolidating and practicing. Student Books and Workbooks are designed to work together. The Student Books focus on learning, classroom teaching, and discussion. The Workbook problems are assigned for individual work.

Student Book

Workbook

Teacher's Edition

Student Book

Workbook

Teacher's Edition

Differentiation Resources

English Language Learners

The clear drawings and visual aspect of *Math in Focus: The Singapore Approach* means the entire program is inherently accessible to English language learners. Additionally, the *Math in Focus* Teacher's Edition provides lesson-specific suggestions for facilitating instruction for English language learners.

For Struggling Learners

Reteach pages provide more exposure to concepts for those students who need more time to master new skills or concepts. Additionally, the *Math in Focus* Teacher's Edition provides tips for helping struggling students at point of use.

For On-Level Students

Extra Practice pages correlate directly to the Workbook practices. Here again, Put on Your Thinking Cap! questions provide more practice on both non-routine and strategy-based questions.

For Advanced Students

Enrichment exercises of varying complexity provide advanced students opportunities to extend the concepts, skills, and strategies they have learned in the Student Book and Workbook.

The *Math in Focus* Kindergarten program has a unique instructional pathway with special Kindergarten components. For more information visit www.greatsource.com/mathinfocus

Program Components

Assessment Opportunities

Assessment opportunities in *Math in Focus* offer a complete picture of student progress. The Student Book, the Workbook, the Assessments Book and the Teacher's Edition all work in concert to provide both short-term and long-term assessment options.

Prior Knowledge

- **Recall Prior Knowledge** in the Student Book: At the start of each chapter, students review related prior knowledge, then try Quick Check questions to ensure they are ready for the new chapter.

- **Pre-Test** in the Assessments Book: A paper and pencil pretest is also available for a more formal diagnostic assessment.

Ongoing Diagnostic

- **Guided Practice** in the Student Book: After each Learn element students work out Guided Practice examples with either peer or teacher input. Tips in the Teacher's Edition help in assessing student understanding.

- **Common Errors** in the Teacher's Edition. Common Error alerts help teachers recognize and correct potential misconceptions before students practice on their own.

Formal Assessment

- **Chapter Review/Test** in the Workbook: This can be used as either review exercises or formal assessment.

- **Chapter Assessment** (Test Prep) in the Assessments Book: This can be used as an alternate chapter test.

- **Cumulative and Mid-Year Assessments** in the Workbook: These Assessments provide opportunities for consolidation of concepts and skills from small chunks of chapters.

- **Benchmark Tests** in the Assessments Book: Midway through each book, these assessments provide further test-prep practice combined with the opportunity to consolidate concepts and skills acquired over a period of time.

- **Mid-Year and End-of-Year Tests** in the Assessments Book: These end-of book assessments in test-prep format provide cumulative assessment for each book.

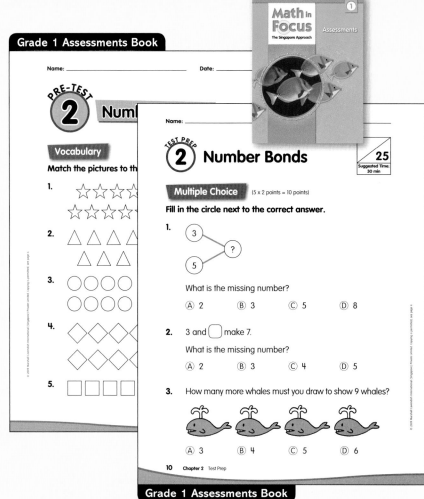

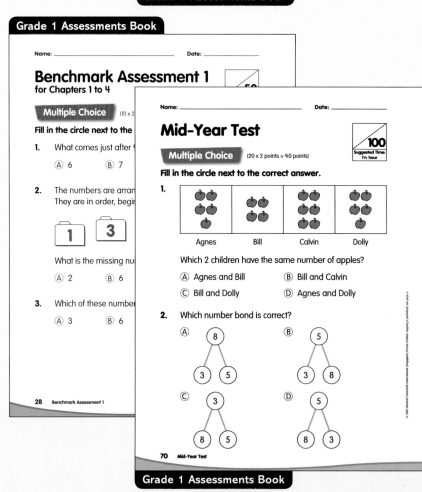

Classroom Manipulatives Kit for Grade 1

Manipulative use plays a key role in the concrete-pictorial-abstract learning sequence.
The following materials are included in the Grade 1 Math in Focus Classroom Manipulatives Kit.

Grade 1 Manipulatives Kit	Suggested Alternatives
Attribute blocks, classroom kit	Seashells, pasta, buttons
Blank number cubes with labels	Number cards, spinners
Coin and bill combination set	Real coins and bills made from construction paper
Connecting cubes	Paper clips, beads and string
Counters, at least 4 colors	Buttons, coins, beans
Counting tape	Strips of paper cut and taped
Craft sticks (bag of 1000)	Marker sets, unused pencils
Demonstration clock	Cardboard clock face with hands attached with brad
Geometric solids	Cans, boxes, balls, or shapes made from modeling clay
Math balance	Virtual manipulatives math balance
Number cubes	Number cards, spinners
Pan balance	Ruler, paper clips, and string
Place value blocks	Grid paper cutouts
Transparent spinners	Construction paper, paper clip, and pencil

Technology Resources

Convenient, practical, technology-based resources available online
and on CD-ROMs to facilitate class instruction and discussions.

eBooks CD-ROM (Student Book pages,) for use
with projection technology

Math in Focus
Virtual Manipulatives CD-ROM for use with
interactive whiteboard technology or other projection
technology

Teacher Resources CD-ROM with Problem
of the Lessons, Reteach, Extra Practice, Enrichment,
and Assessments and additional blackline masters in
printable pdf format

Online Resources
Visit www.greatsource.com/mathinfocus
for additional resources.

Program Authors and Consultants

Dr. Fong Ho Kheong

Dr. Fong Ho Kheong is an Associate Professor and the Head of Math and Science Department of the Emirates College for Advanced Education in Abu Dhabi, United Arab Emirates. He was involved in training Mathematics teachers in the National Institute of Education, Nanyang Technological University, Singapore, for 25 years. He is the Founding President of the Association of the Mathematics Educators, Singapore.

Dr. Fong specializes in teaching both high-ability children and children who have problems in mathematics. His research work includes diagnosing children with mathematical difficulties, teaching thinking to solve mathematical problems, and applying psychological theories for the teaching and learning of mathematics. His experience in curriculum development has led him to innovate the use of the model-drawing approach to tackle challenging problems. He is the consultant and principal author of Marshall Cavendish's *My Pals are Here!* math series, which is currently being used by 80% of the primary schools in Singapore.

Dr. Pamela Sharpe

Dr. Pamela Sharpe has been involved in training teachers in both Singapore and the United Kingdom for 38 years and has also played a major role in setting up early childhood programs in Singapore. She was formerly an associate professor at the National Institute of Education, Nanyang Technological University, Singapore. She is currently a part time lecturer there, as well as a consultant for early childhood programs and early childhood intervention programs.

Dr. Sharpe specializes in teaching both high-ability children and children who have problems in mathematics at the preschool level. Her research work includes studying the adjustment patterns of children in transition from preschool to primary school, as well as identifying and assessing preschool children with special needs. Dr. Sharpe has also been deeply involved in the development of the preschool mathematics curriculum in Singapore.

Chelvi Ramakrishnan

Chelvi Ramakrishnan is currently the Head of the Mathematics Department in a primary school in Singapore. She has been teaching for 25 years and has authored primary mathematics books since 1997.

Bernice Lau Pui Wah

Bernice Lau Pui Wah is currently the Head of the Mathematics Department in a primary school in Singapore. She has been teaching for 36 years in primary and secondary schools. She has authored primary mathematics books since 1997.

Michelle Choo

Michelle Choo has been teaching in Singapore for 20 years, including 5 years in the Gifted Education Program. She has been writing primary mathematics books for the past 12 years and also conducts math review classes and workshops on the use of problem-solving skills and strategies.

Gan Kee Soon

Gan Kee Soon has been an Inspector of Schools, a Principal of a secondary school and a Lecturer at the National Institute of Education, Nanyang Technological University, Singapore. There, for 22 years, he trained and supervised primary mathematics teachers.

U.S. Consultants

Andy Clark

Andy Clark was the Math Coordinator for Portland Public Schools in Portland, Oregon, where he was previously an elementary and middle school teacher. Andy is coauthor of *Every Day Counts® Calendar Math, Every Day Counts® Algebra Readiness, Partner Games,* and *Summer Success®: Math* published by Great Source Education Group.

Patsy F. Kanter

Patsy F. Kanter is an author, teacher, and math consultant. Until 1997, Patsy was the Lower School Math Coordinator and Assistant Principal at Isidore Newman School in New Orleans, Louisiana, for 13 years where she developed and implemented a hands-on activity-based math program. Patsy is the senior author of numerous supplemental math programs including *Afterschool Achievers: Math Club K-5, Summer Success®: Math K-8,* co-author of *Every Day Counts® Calendar Math Grades K-6,* and *Every Day Counts® Partner Games* K-6, published by Great Source Education Group.

Teacher Reviewers

Judy Chambers, Educational Consultant
Fayetteville, GA

Carolyn Goodnight, Grade 4 Teacher
Helen Carr Castello Elementary School
Elk Grove, CA

Shelly Gufert, Grade 5 Special Education
PS/MS 95X
Bronx, NY

Karin Hanson, Math Curriculum Chair
St. Robert School
Shorewood, WI

Diane Popp, Middle School Teacher
St. Rita of Cascia School
Dayton, OH

Lorianne Rotz, Assistant Principal
St. Margaret Mary Catholic School
Winter Park, FL

Roslyn Rowley-Penk, Lead Science Teacher
Maplewood Heights Elementary
Renton, WA

Elizabeth Sher, Curriculum Coordinator
Gwyneed-Mercy Academy Elementary
Spring House, PA

Nadine Solomon, Elementary Math &
Science Specialist
City of Arlington
Arlington, MA

Kathryn Tobon, Curriculum Program
Specialist
Broward County
Broward Country, FL

Jeanette Valore, Grade 4 Math and
Science Teacher
St. Anthony of Padua Catholic School
The Woodlands, TX

Melissa Walsh, Elementary Math Coach
Baldwin-Whitehall School District
Pittsburgh, PA

Key Differences
and Distinguishing Characteristics

Articulated Sequence

Math in Focus answers the call for a coherent sequence of topics giving students time to master foundational topics, so that little repetition is required the next year. Thus, each grade level covers fewer topics but in more depth, and you will not find all topics in every grade level.

- **"Missing topics"** When a topic appears to be "missing," you can be assured that it is found in either an earlier or later grade level. For example you will find calendar concepts in grades K and 1, but not repeated in grade 2.

- **More advanced** As a result of not repeating topics year after year, students who use *Math in Focus* will advance faster than students in other programs. As a result, you may find topics that seem to be "too advanced." However, you will find your students easily able to handle the challenge as long as they have had the appropriate preliminary instruction.

Preparation for Algebra

Math in Focus answers the call to prepare students for Algebra. As recommended by the National Math Panel, the *Math in Focus* sequence of topics emphasizes:

- **Number sense, basic facts, and computation** An early understanding of composition and decomposition of numbers is developed in tandem with mastery of basic facts and computation algorithms in Grades K–2.

- **Fractions and proportional reasoning** Significant time is allocated for in-depth work with fractions in Grades 3–5.

- **Problem-solving** Challenging problem-solving is built into each chapter in every grade level.

Developmental Continuum

Kindergarten	Grades 1–2	Grades 3–5

Foundational concepts through songs, rhymes, hands-on activities

- counting
- sorting
- number sense

Concept and skill development through hands-on instruction and practice

- basic facts
- place value
- mental math
- geometry concepts

Emphasis on problem-solving, skill consolidation, and a deep understanding in preparation for algebra

- fractions
- decimals
- ratios
- model drawing
- expressions, equations, and inequalities

> View the complete K–5 Scope and Sequence at
> **www.greatsource.com/mathinfocus**

	Kindergarten	Grade 1	Grade 2
Number and Operations			
Sets and Numbers	Use concrete models to create a set with a given number of objects. (Up to 20)	Use concrete and pictorial models to create a set with a given number of objects. (Up to 100) Group objects in tens and ones. Numbers up to 100.	Use concrete and pictorial models to create a set with a given number of objects. (Up to 1,000) Group objects into hundreds, tens, and ones. Group objects into equal sized groups.
	Use cardinal and ordinal numbers.	Use cardinal and ordinal numbers up to 10th.	
Number Representation	Use numbers to represent quantities up to 20.	Use number bonds to represent number combinations. Represent numbers to 100 on a number line.	Use place value models to create equivalent representations of numbers. Represent numbers to 1,000 on a number line.
Count	Count up to 20 objects in a set. Count on and back to 20. Count by 2s and 5s up to 20.	Count to 100. Count by 1s, 2s, 5s, and 10s forward and backward to 100.	Count to 1,000. Count by multiples of ones, tens, and hundreds.
Compare and Order	Compare and order sets and numbers up to 20. Compare and order using the terms *fewer, more, less.*	Compare and order whole numbers to 100. Compare and order using the terms *same, more, fewer, greater than, less than, equal to, greatest, least.*	Compare and order whole numbers to 1,000. Use <, >, = to compare numbers.
Place Value		Use place-value models and place-value charts to represent numbers to 100. Express numbers to 100 in standard and word forms.	Use base-ten models and place-value charts to represent numbers to 1,000. Express numbers to 1,000 in terms of place value. Compose and decompose multi-digit numbers (including expanded form).

Scope and Sequence Kindergarten–Grade 2

	Kindergarten	Grade 1	Grade 2
Number and Operations (continued)			
Fraction Concepts			Connect geometric concepts with unit fractions halves, thirds, and fourths. Understand the relationship between a fraction and a whole. Compare and order halves, thirds, and fourths using bar models.
Decimal Concepts			Use the dollar sign and decimal point.
Money	Identify and relate coin values (penny, nickel, dime, quarter). Count and make coin combinations.	Identify and relate coin values (penny, nickel, dime, quarter). Count and make coin combinations.	Identify $1, $5, $10, $20 bills. Count and make combinations of coins and bills. Compare money amounts.
Whole Number Computation: Addition and Subtraction	Model joining and separating sets. Use +, -, and = to write number sentences for addition and subtraction stories.	Model addition and subtraction situations. Use models, numbers, and symbols for addition and subtraction facts to 20. Use the order, grouping, and zero properties to develop addition and subtraction fact strategies. Add and subtract up to 2-digit numbers with and without regrouping.	Model addition and subtraction with place value. Recall addition and subtraction facts. Use different methods to develop fluency in adding and subtracting multi-digit numbers.
Whole Number Computation: Addition and Subtraction Real-World Problems	Represent addition and subtraction stories.	Formulate addition and subtraction stories. Solve addition and subtraction problems using basic facts.	Solve multi-digit addition and subtraction problems by using a bar model.

	Kindergarten	Grade 1	Grade 2
Number and Operations (continued)			
Whole Number Computation: Multiplication and Division Concepts	Count by 2s and 5s up to 20.	Count by 2s, 5s, and 10s. Add the same number to multiply. Represent sharing equally and making equal groups.	Multiply and divide with 2, 3, 4, 5, and 10. Represent multiplication as repeated addition. Represent division as repeated subtraction. Use the ×, ÷, and = symbols to represent multiplication and division situations.
Whole Number Computation: Multiplication and Division Real-World Problems			Use bar models to represent multiplication and division situations. Solve multiplication and division fact problems.
Fraction Computation			Add and subtract like fractions.
Decimal Computation		Add and subtract money.	Solve addition and subtraction money problems.
Estimation and Mental Math		Use mental math strategies to add and subtract. Estimate quantity by using referents.	Use mental math strategies to add and subtract. Round to the nearest ten to estimate sums and differences.
Algebra			
Patterns	Describe and extend repeating shape patterns. Count by 2s and 5s. Describe a rule for sorting objects. Find missing terms in repeating patterns.	Identify, describe and extend two- and three-dimensional shape patterns. Skip count by 2s, 5s, and 10s. Identify a rule for sorting objects. Identify and extend growing and repeating patterns. Find missing terms in growing and repeating patterns.	Describe, extend and create two-dimensional shape patterns. Skip count by 2s, 3s, 4s, 5s, and 10s. Identify rules for number patterns. Find missing terms in table patterns.
Properties		Identify 0 as the identity element for addition and subtraction. Use the Associative and Commutative Properties of Addition.	Understand that addition and subtraction are inverse operations. Apply properties of addition. Use the Distributive Property as a multiplication strategy.

Scope and Sequence Kindergarten–Grade 2

	Kindergarten	Grade 1	Grade 2
Algebra (continued)			
Number Theory	Identify odd and even numbers.		
Functional Relationships		Understand the relationships between the numbers in fact families.	Recognize how bar models show the relationship between bar models and number patterns.
Models		Use a variety of concrete, pictorial, and symbolic models for addition and subtraction.	Use a variety of concrete, pictorial, and symbolic models for addition, subtraction, multiplication, and division.
Number Sentences and Equations	Model addition and subtraction stories with addition and subtraction number sentences.	Model addition and subtraction situations by writing addition and subtraction number sentences.	Model multiplication and division situations by writing multiplication and division number sentences. Use bar models and number sentences to represent real-world problems. Determine the value of missing quantities in number sentences.
Equality and Inequality	Understand the meaning of the = sign in number sentences.	Understand the difference between equality and inequality.	Use and create models that demonstrate equality or inequality. Use <, >, and = to write number sentences.
Geometry (continued)			
Size and Position	Understand *big, middle-sized,* and *small.* Describe and compare objects by position.	Describe position with *left* and *right.* Use positional words to describe location.	
Two-Dimensional Shapes	Identify similarities and differences. Name flat shapes that make up real-world objects. Identify, describe, sort, and classify two-dimensional shapes.	Identify real-world two-dimensional shapes. Identify and describe attributes and properties of two-dimensional shapes.	Identify, describe, sort, and classify two-dimensional shapes.

	Kindergarten	Grade 1	Grade 2
Geometry (continued)			
Two-Dimensional Shapes (continued)	Make flat shape pictures. Compare areas using non-standard units.	Sort and classify two-dimensional shapes. Compose and decompose two-dimensional shapes.	Identify parts of lines and curves. Compose and decompose two-dimensional shapes. Develop foundations for understanding area.
Three-Dimensional Shapes	Name and sort solid shapes. Understand that three-dimensional shapes are made up of two-dimensional shapes. Make shape patterns.	Identify real-world three-dimensional shapes. Identify two-dimensional shapes in three-dimensional shapes. Sort and classify three-dimensional shapes. Recognize shapes from different perspectives. Compose and decompose three-dimensional shapes.	Identify, describe, sort, and classify three-dimensional shapes. Identify surfaces that slide, stack, and roll.
Congruence and Symmetry		Develop initial understanding of congruence and symmetry.	
Measurement			
Length and Distance	Compare lengths and heights using non-standard units. Compare and order lengths (long, short, longest, shortest). Develop a background for measurement using non-standard units.	Compare two lengths by comparing each with a third length (transitivity). Use a start line to measure length. Measure lengths, using non-standard units. Explain the need for equal-length units to measure. Count length units in groups of tens and ones. Compare measurements made using different units. Understand the inverse relationship between the size of a unit and the number of units.	Demonstrate linear measure as an iteration of units. Use rulers to measure length. Measure lengths in meters, centimeters, feet, and inches. Compare and measure lengths using customary and metric units. Demonstrate partitioning and transitivity in relation to length. Solve problems involving estimating, measuring, and computing length.

Scope and Sequence Kindergarten–Grade 2

	Kindergarten	Grade 1	Grade 2
Measurement (continued)			
Weight/Mass	Order objects by weight.	Compare and measure weights using non-standard units.	Compare and measure masses.
	Compare weights using non-standard units.	Compare two massess by comparing eah with a third mass (transitivity).	Solve mass problems.
Capacity/Volume	Compare capacities.		Measure volume (capacity) in liters.
			Solve volume problems.
Time	Name and order the days of the week and the months of the year.	Identify the days of the week and months of the year.	
		Recognize the correct way to write the date.	Tell time to five minutes. Use A.M. and P.M.
	Compare durations of events.	Tell time to the hour and half hour.	Find elapsed time.
Data Analysis			
Classifying and Sorting	Understand similarities and differences in objects and shapes.	Sort and classify geometric shapes.	Sort and classify two- and three-dimensional shapes by properties.
	Sort and classify objects using one or two attributes.	Sort and classify data in order to make graphs.	Collect and organize data in picture graphs.
Collect and Organize Data	Organize data for a picture graph.	Collect and organize data in different ways.	Collect, sort, and organize data in different ways.
Represent Data	Represent data in picture graphs.	Represent measurements and data in picture graphs and bar graphs.	Represent data in picture graphs.
Interpret/Analyze Data	Interpret data in tally charts and bar graphs.	Interpret data in picture graphs, tally charts, and bar graphs.	Interpret picture graphs with scales.
		Solve problems involving data.	Solve real-world problems using picture graphs.
Problem Solving			
Build Skills Through Problem Solving	Build skills in addition and subtraction through problem solving.	Build skills in addition, subtraction, and measurement through problem solving.	Build skills in addition, subtraction, multiplication, division, and measurement through problem solving.
Solve Real-World Problems	Solve real-world problems involving addition and subtraction.	Solve real-world problems involving addition and subtraction.	Solve real-world problems involving addition, subtraction, multiplication, division, and measurement.

	Kindergarten	Grade 1	Grade 2
Problem Solving (continued)			
Use Appropriate Strategies and Thinking Skills to Solve Problems		Apply problem-solving strategies in Put on Your Thinking Cap! and Problem Solving activities.	Apply problem-solving strategies in Put on Your Thinking Cap! and Problem Solving activities.
Apply and Explain Problem Solving	Solve real-world problems.	Apply and explain problem-solving processes in Put on Your Thinking Cap! and other activities.	Apply and explain problem-solving processes in Put on Your Thinking Cap! and other activities.
Reasoning and Proof			
Explore Concepts	Use models to explain reasoning.	Explore concepts more deeply and justify reasoning in Let's Explore and Hands-On activities. Apply Thinking Skills in Put on Your Thinking Cap!, Challenging Practice, and Problem Solving activities.	Explore concepts more deeply and justify reasoning in Let's Explore and Hands-On activities. Apply Thinking Skills in Put on Your Thinking Cap!, Challenging Practice, and Problem Solving activities.
Investigate Mathematical Ideas	Investigate ideas with two- and three-dimensional shapes.	Further investigate mathematical ideas by completing critical thinking skills activities.	Further investigate mathematical ideas by completing critical thinking skills activities.
Identify, Demonstrate, and Explain Mathematical Proof	Demonstrate that only a few big things fit into small spaces and many small things fit into big spaces. Describe, sort, and classify two- and three-dimensional shapes. Interpret data in tally charts and bar graphs. Identify and extend repeating shape patterns.	Explore transitivity by comparing lengths and weights of three different objects. Identify and describe attributes and properties of two- and three-dimensional shapes. Interpret picture graphs, tally charts, and bar graphs. Identify and extend growing number patterns and repeating shape patterns.	Demonstrate the inverse relationship between the size of a unit and the number of units. Identify, describe, sort, and classify two- and three-dimensional shapes. Interpret picture graphs with scales. Identify rules for number patterns.
Use a Variety of Reasoning Skills	Sort and classify using attributes. Identify similarities and differences.	Recognize shapes from different perspectives. Use the Commutative and Associative Properties and tens and ones to solve two-digit addition and subtraction problems.	Identify surfaces that slide, stack, and roll. Explore the inverse relationship between addition and subtraction.

Scope and Sequence Kindergarten–Grade 2

	Kindergarten	Grade 1	Grade 2
Communication			
Consolidate Mathematical Thinking	Consolidate thinking in independent activities.	Present mathematical thinking through Math Journal activities.	Present mathematical thinking through Math Journal activities.
Communicate with Peers, Teachers, and Others	Discuss mathematical ideas in paired and small group activities.	Discuss mathematical ideas in Let's Explore activities. Work together in pairs or groups in Let's Explore, Games, and other activities.	Discuss mathematical ideas in Let's Explore activities. Work together in pairs or groups in Let's Explore, Games, and other activities.
Share Mathematical Thinking	Share mathematical ideas in paired and small group activities.	Share mathematical ideas with others during Let's Explore and Hands-On activities.	Share mathematical ideas with others during Let's Explore and Hands-On activities.
Express Mathematics Ideas	Express ideas in paired and small group activities.	Express ideas in Math Journal activities, using lesson vocabulary. Use chapter and lesson vocabulary correctly.	Express ideas in Math Journal activities, using lesson vocabulary. Use chapter and lesson vocabulary correctly.
Connections			
Recognize Connections in Mathematical Ideas	Understand the connection between quantities and written numerals.	Understand the relationship between counting and addition and subtraction. Understand the relationships between the numbers in fact families. Connect addition and multiplication (repeated addition). Recognize and apply different strategies for adding and subtracting 1-and 2-digit numbers.	Examine and apply the inverse relationship between addition and subtraction. Connect geometric concepts with halves, thirds, and fourths. Connect subtraction and division (repeated subtraction). Recognize and apply different strategies for multiplication and division facts.
Understand How Concepts Build on One Another	Explore relationships among counting, ordering, and ordinal numbers.	Learn how place-value concepts apply to regrouping in addition and subtraction.	Understand how patterns can be described using numbers, operations, and data displays. Recognize the relationship between bar models, number sentences, and number patterns.

	Kindergarten	Grade 1	Grade 2
Connections (continued)			
Solve Real-World Problems in Contexts Outside of Mathematics	Solve real-world problems involving *more* and *less*.	Solve real-world problems involving addition, subtraction, and measurement.	Solve real-world problems involving addition, subtraction, multiplication, division, and measurement and data analysis.
Representation			
Use Representations to Model, Organize, and Record	Use concrete models to create a set with a given number of objects. (Up to 20)	Use concrete and pictorial models to create a set with a given number of objects. (Up to 100)	Use concrete and pictorial models to create a set with a given number of objects. (Up to 1,000)
	Use numbers and numerals to represent quantities up to 20.	Represent numbers to 100 on a number line.	Represent numbers to 1,000 on a number line.
	Use picture cards to communicate understanding of comparisons *(bigger, taller, smaller)*.		Use symbolic notation (<, >) to compare numbers.
	Understand the meaning of the = sign in number sentences.	Use the +, −, and = symbols to represent addition and subtraction situations.	Use bar models to represent addition and subtraction situations.
	Model addition and subtraction stories with addition and subtraction number sentences.	Represent numerical data using picture graphs, tally charts and bar graphs.	Represent numerical data using picture graphs with scales, tally charts, and bar graphs.
	Represent addition and subtraction stories.	Represent sharing equally making equal groups.	Use the ×, ÷, and = symbols to represent multiplication and division situations.
			Represent multiplication with skip counting, dot paper arrays, and bar models.
			Represent division as repeated subtraction.
	Describe and extend shape patterns.	Identify, describe and extend two- and three-dimensional shape patterns.	Describe, extend and create two-dimensional shape patterns.
	Describe a rule for sorting objects.	Identify a rule for sorting objects.	

Scope and Sequence Kindergarten–Grade 2

	Kindergarten	Grade 1	Grade 2
Representation (continued)			
Use Representations to Model, Organize, and Record (continued)		Identify and extend growing and repeating patterns.	Identify rules for number and table patterns.
Select and Apply Representations to Model Problems	Represent quantities with objects, number cubes, and numerals.	Use number bonds to represent number combinations. Use a variety of concrete, pictorial, and symbolic models for addition and subtraction.	Use place-value models to create equivalent representations of numbers. Use a variety of concrete, pictorial, and symbolic models for addition, subtraction, multiplication, and division.
Interpret Phenomena Through Representations	Show understanding of *big, middle-sized, small,* and *same size.* Describe and compare objects by position. Name flat shapes that make up real-world objects. Represent measurements and data in picture graphs and bar graphs. Order a number of objects according to length, height, or weight. Use one-to-one correspondence.	Measure and compare lengths and weights using non-standard units. Use positional words to describe location. Identify real-world two- and three-dimensional shapes. Represent data in picture graphs. Solve problems about sharing equally and making equal groups. Use a variety of models for adding and subtracting. Use technology (virtual manipulatives and computers) to model and draw.	Use metric and customary units to measure length, volume (capacity), weight and mass. Represent data in bar graphs and picture graphs. Solve real-world problems about social phenomena. Use bar models to represent addition, subtraction, multiplication, and division situations. Use technology (virtual manipulatives and computers) to model and draw.

Table of Contents

CHAPTER 2 Number Bonds

1 Making Number Bonds 2 DAY Lesson

Learn Make number bonds with connecting cubes • Make number bonds using a math balance

Hands-On Activities Make number bonds using connecting cubes • Make number bonds using a math balance

Let's Explore! Number bonds with three numbers • Making number trains with connecting cubes (Associative Property)

Look for Assessment Opportunities

Student Book A and Student Book B	Workbook A and Workbook B
• Quick Check at the beginning of every chapter to assess chapter readiness	• Chapter Review/Test in every chapter to review or test chapter material
• Guided Practice after every example or two to assess readiness to continue	• Cumulative Reviews eight times during the year
	• Mid-Year and End-of-Year Reviews to assess test readiness

Look for Practice and Problem Solving

Student Book A and Student Book B	Workbook A and Workbook B
• **Let's Practice** in every lesson	• **Independent Practice** for every lesson
• Put on Your Thinking Cap! in every chapter	• Put on Your Thinking Cap! in every chapter

Math in Focus: The Singapore Approach

CHAPTER 4 Subtraction Facts to 10

1 Ways to Subtract [2 DAY Lesson] 67

Learn Subtract by taking away • Take away to find how many less • Count on to subtract • Count back to subtract • Use number bonds to subtract

Hands-On Activity Taking away using ten frames

Game What's Hidden?

2 Making Subtraction Stories 77

Learn Tell subtraction stories about a picture

Hands-On Activity Zero concept

3 Real-World Problems: Subtraction 82

Learn Read and understand a word problem • Subtract to solve word problems by taking away

4 Making Fact Families 85

Learn Addition and subtraction are related • Use related addition facts to solve subtraction sentences • Use related subtraction facts to solve addition sentences

Let's Explore! Use cards to make number sentences

Shapes and Patterns

1 Exploring Plane Shapes [3 DAY Lesson] 98

Learn Get to know shapes • Sides and corners • Sort shapes in many ways • Shapes can be alike and different • Use folding to make shapes that are alike

Hands-On Activities Sort shapes • Fold paper to make shapes that are alike

Let's Explore! Fold paper to make two new shapes

2 Exploring Solid Shapes 110

Learn Get to know solid shapes • Name and compare solid shapes • Move solid shapes in different ways

Hands-On Activity Find how to move solid shapes

3 Making Pictures and Models with Shapes [2 DAY Lesson] 116

Learn Combine plane shapes • Build models with solid shapes

Hands-On Activities Combine shapes to make a picture • Make a picture with shapes on a computer • Combine shapes to make a new shape • Make a model with solid shapes

Let's Explore! Make a picture using cut-out shapes

4 Seeing Shapes Around Us. 124

Learn See shapes in things around you

Hands-On Activities Find plane and solid shapes around you • Draw around solid shapes to find plane shapes

CHAPTER
6 Ordinal Numbers and Position

CHAPTER 7 Numbers to 20

1 Counting to 20 165

Learn Count on from 10 • Make a ten, then count on

Game Roll the Number Cube!

2 Place Value 171

Learn Use place value to show numbers to 20 • Use models to show numbers to 20

Hands-On Activities Show numbers by grouping connecting cubes
into a ten and ones and drawing place-value charts

3 Comparing Numbers 2 DAY Lesson 175

Learn Compare sets and numbers • Use place value to find out how much greater or how
much less • Use place value to compare three numbers

Let's Explore! Understand greatest and least using number trains

CHAPTER

(8) Addition and Subtraction Facts to 20

CHAPTER

9 Length

CHAPTER 1

Chapter Overview

Numbers to 10

Math Background

As children begin their formal math education, they use numbers in their cardinal sense, to tell how many. In this chapter, children will learn how to count, read and write within 10. Countable items are used to develop the association between the physical representation of the number, the number symbol and the number-word. As they learn to say each number name, children must also learn to account for each item in a collection.

In learning to represent and use numbers in different contexts, they will encounter number relationships. Children are shown different representations of sets with the same number of items while using the word *same* to describe the sets. These sets are modified using different number of items. Children are encouraged to compare and verbally describe the sets using the terms *more* and *less*. In preparation for skills needed in computation, children will be taught to recognize relationships between numbers, such as *1 more* or *1 less*, without the concrete representations. Children need to understand the sequential order of the counting numbers and their relative magnitudes. Hence, they will learn to identify and complete growing and reducing number patterns, where each number in a given sequence is 1 more or 1 less than the number before.

Cross-Curricular Connections

Reading/Language Arts Put children into groups of two or three and assign each group a number 1 through 10. Have groups draw a picture and write a sentence for their number. For example, *The spider has 8 long legs.* After each group presents their work to the class, collect the drawings. Put them together to make a class counting book.

Art Tell children that the colors of the color wheel are yellow, orange, red, violet, blue, and green. Have children draw a number pattern with these six colors. They might draw one yellow triangle, two orange triangles, three red triangles, and so on. Encourage children to use both increasing and decreasing patterns. Tell them to write the numeral or number word with each element of the pattern.

Skills Trace

Grade K	Count and write numbers 0 to 20. (Chaps. 1, 2, 4, and 6)
Grade 1	Count and compare numbers to 100. (Chaps. 1, 7, 12, and 16)
Grade 2	Count and compare numbers to 1,000. (Chap. 1)

EVERY DAY COUNTS® Calendar Math

The August/September activities provide...

Review of counting and reading numbers and writing numerals (Kindergarten)

Preview of part and whole relationships for different numbers (Chapter 2)

Practice of counting and comparing numbers (Lessons 1 and 2 in this chapter)

Differentiation Resources

Differentiation for Special Populations

	English Language Learners	Struggling Reteach 1A	On Level Extra Practice 1A	Advanced Enrichment 1A
Lesson 1	p. 15	pp. 1–8	pp. 1–6	Enrichment pages can be used to challenge advanced children.
Lesson 2	p. 14	pp. 9–16	pp. 7–14	
Lesson 3	pp. 21–22	pp. 17–20	pp. 15–18	

Additional Support

For English Language Learners

Select activities that reinforce the chapter vocabulary and the connections among these words, such as having children

- create a Word Wall that includes terms, definitions, and examples
- create and practice with flash cards that have number words on one side and the number on the other
- draw and label pictures with terms they represent
- discuss the Chapter Wrap Up, encouraging children to use the chapter vocabulary

For Struggling Learners

Select activities that go back to the appropriate stage of the Concrete-Pictorial-Abstract spectrum, such as having children

- act out number words and comparison terms
- use manipulatives to model patterns
- identify and tell about classroom objects that represent and compare numbers
- draw pictures to illustrate number words and patterns

For Advanced Learners

See suggestions on pages 8–9.

Assessment and Remediation

Chapter 1 Assessment

Prior Knowledge

	Resource	Page numbers
Quick Check	Student Book 1A	p. 3
Pre-Test	Assessments 1	p. 1

Ongoing Diagnostic

Guided Practice	Student Book 1A	pp. 7, 8, 9, 15, 16, 17, 20, 21, 22, 23, 24
Common Error	Teacher's Edition 1A	pp. 12, 17–18, 25

Formal Evaluation

Chapter Review/Test	Workbook 1A	pp. 19–20
Chapter 1 Test Prep	Assessments 1	pp. 2–6

Remediation Options

Problems with these items...   Can be remediated with...

Objective	Review/Test Items Workbook 1A pp. 19–20	Chapter Assessment Items Assessments 1 pp. 2–6	Reteach Reteach 1A	Student Book Student Book 1A
Use chapter vocabulary correctly.	1–9	Not assessed	pp. 2–20	pp. 4, 13, 20
Count from 0 to 10 objects.	5–9	1	pp. 2–5, 8	Lesson 1
Read and write numbers (0–10) for a group of objects.	5–6	2, 6–7	pp. 2–8	Lesson 1
Compare two sets of objects by using one-to-one correspondence.	8–9		pp. 9–15	Lesson 2
Identify the set that has more, fewer, or the same number of objects.	7–9	4, 8–9, 11–13	pp. 9–16	Lesson 2
Identify the number that is greater than or less than another number.	10–11, 13–14	5, 14–15	pp. 12–16	Lesson 2
Make number patterns.	12	3, 10	pp. 17–20	Lesson 3

Chapter Planning Guide

CHAPTER 1 Numbers to 10

Lesson	Pacing	Instructional Objectives	Vocabulary
Chapter Opener pp. 1–3 Recall Prior Knowledge Quick Check	*1 day	**Big Idea** Count and compare numbers to 10.	
Lesson 1, pp. 4–12 Counting to 10	2 days	• Count from 0 to 10 objects • Read and write 0 to 10 in numbers and words	• zero • six • one • seven • two • eight • three • nine • four • ten • five
Lesson 2, pp. 13–19 Comparing Numbers	2 days	• Compare two sets of objects by using one-to-one correspondence • Identify the set that has more, fewer, or the same number of objects • Identify the number that is greater than or less than another number	• same • more • fewer • greater than • less than
Lesson 3, pp. 20–26 Making Number Patterns	1 day	• Make number patterns	• pattern • more than • less than
Problem Solving p. 26 Put on Your Thinking Cap!	1 day	Thinking Skills • Comparing, Classifying Problem Solving Strategies • Looking for patterns and relationships	
Chapter Wrap Up p. 27	1 day	• Reinforce and consolidate chapter skills and concepts	
Chapter Assessment	1 day		

*Assume that 1 day is a 45–55 minute period.

Resources	Materials	NCTM Focal Points	NCTM Process Standards
Student Book 1A, pp. 1–3 **Assessments 1**, p. 1			
Student Book 1A, pp. 4–12 **Workbook 1A**, pp. 1–6 **Extra Practice 1A**, pp. 1–6 **Reteach 1A**, pp. 1–8	• 10 connecting cubes per child • 10 counters per child • 1 Ten Frame per child (TRO1)	***Number and Operations*** Understand the sequential order of the counting numbers	Communication Connections Representation
Student Book 1A, pp. 13–19 **Workbook 1A**, pp. 7–12 **Extra Practice 1A**, pp. 7–14 **Reteach 1A**, pp. 9–16	• 15 connecting cubes per child • 10 counters per child • 2 Horizontal Ten Frames per child (TRO2) • 1 set of Shoes and Socks Cut-Out per child (TRO2) • scissors • paste or glue stick	***Number and Operations*** Compare and order whole numbers	Problem Solving Reasoning/Proof Representation
Student Book 1A, pp. 20–26 **Workbook 1A**, pp. 13–16 **Extra Practice 1A**, pp. 15–18 **Reteach 1A**, pp. 17–20	• 10 connecting cubes per child • 10 counters per child • 1 Ten Frame per child (TRO1)	***Number and Operations*** Understand the connections between counting and the operations of addition and subtraction	Problem Solving Communication Reasoning/Proof
Student Book 1A, p. 26 **Workbook 1A**, pp. 17–18 **Extra Practice 1A**, pp. 19–20 **Enrichment 1A**, pp. 1–8		***Number and Operations and Algebra*** Solve non-routine problems involving number and patterns	Problem Solving Reasoning/Proof
Student Book 1A, p. 27 **Workbook 1A**, pp. 19–20			
Assessments 1, pp. 2–6			

> **Technology Resources for easy classroom management**
> • *Math in Focus*™ eBook
> • *Math in Focus*™ Teaching Resources CD
> • *Math in Focus*™ Virtual Manipulatives
> • On-Line Web Resources

Chapter Introduction

CHAPTER 1 Numbers to 10

Lesson 1 Counting to 10
Lesson 2 Comparing Numbers
Lesson 3 Making Number Patterns

Chapter 1 Vocabulary

zero	0	Lesson 1
one	1	Lesson 1
two	2	Lesson 1
three	3	Lesson 1
four	4	Lesson 1
five	5	Lesson 1
six	6	Lesson 1
seven	7	Lesson 1
eight	8	Lesson 1
nine	9	Lesson 1
ten	10	Lesson 1
same	equal to	Lesson 2
more	4 eggs is *more* than 3 eggs	Lesson 2
fewer	3 eggs is *fewer* than 4 eggs	Lesson 2
greater than	4 is *greater than* 3	Lesson 2
less than	3 is *less than* 4	Lesson 2
pattern	sequence that is repeated	Lesson 3
more than	4 is 1 *more than* 3	Lesson 3

Student Book A p. 1

Big Idea (page 1)

Counting and comparing numbers to 10 are the main focus of this chapter.

- Children use countable objects to develop the association between the physical representation of the number, the number symbol, and the number word.

- Besides counting the objects in a set, and creating a set with a given number of objects, children also differentiate between numbers of objects in sets, a skill that forms a basis for number comparison.

- They learn to recognize relationships between numbers, such as 1 *more than* and 1 *less than*.

Chapter Opener (page 1)

This picture illustrates 10 children with 10 balls. Children learned to count in Kindergarten. This page provides countable items for children to count. In this chapter, children will count and compare numbers of objects.

- Show children the picture without the poem. *Ask:* Where is this place? Show the picture with the poem. Read the poem aloud for the children.

- Reread the poem, asking children to read along with you. *Ask:* How many children are in the picture? (10) Count aloud and encourage children to count along with you.

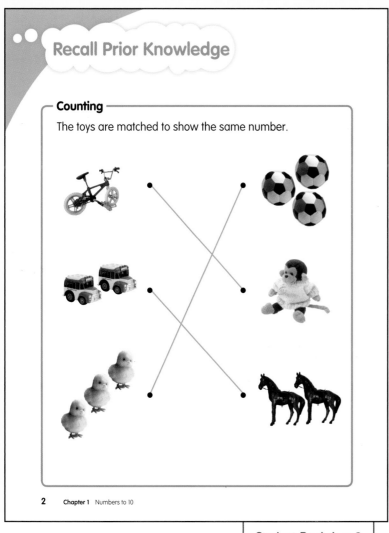

Student Book A p. 2

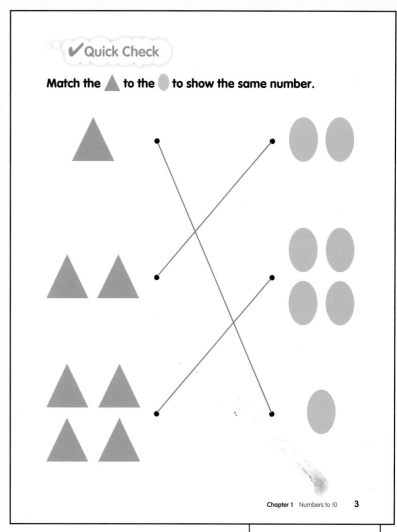

Student Book A p. 3

- *Ask:* How many balls can you see in the picture? (10) Count aloud and encourage children to count along with you. You may have to help children find the ball held by the girl in green. Have children recognize that each child has a ball.

Recall Prior Knowledge (page 2)

Counting

Children learned in Kindergarten to count objects in a small set.

- Have children count the objects in each set on the left of the page. *Ask:* How many objects are in each set? (1 bicycle, 2 toy trucks, 3 chicks)

- Have children find a matching set on the right with the same number of objects.

- Help children to see that the number is the same in each matched pair.

✔Quick Check (page 3)

Use this section as a diagnostic tool to assess children's level of prerequisite knowledge before they progress to this chapter. The exercise on this page assesses counting and matching skills. Remind children that they are not writing in the Student Book. You may want to have them match by tracing the lines with their fingers or by projecting the page on the board.

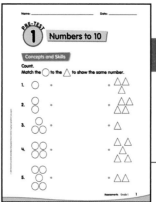

Assessments 1 p. 1

Assessment

For additional assessment of children's prior knowledge and chapter readiness, use the Chapter 1 Pre-Test on page 1 of **Assessments** 1.

1 Counting to 10

LESSON OBJECTIVES
- Count from 0 to 10 objects.
- Read and write 0 to 10 in numbers and words.

TECHNOLOGY RESOURCES
- *Math in Focus* eBook
- *Math in Focus* Teaching Resources CD
- *Math in Focus* Virtual Manipulatives

Vocabulary

zero	three	six	nine
one	four	seven	ten
two	five	eight	

DAY 1 Student Book 1A, pp. 4–9

MATERIALS
- 10 connecting cubes per child
- 10 counters per child
- 1 Ten Frame per child (TRO1)

DAY 2 Student Book 1A, pp. 10–12
Workbook 1A, pp. 1–6

DIFFERENTIATION RESOURCES
- Reteach 1A, pp. 1–8
- Extra Practice 1A, pp. 1–6

5-minute Warm Up

Have children count their fingers on one hand along with you, from 0 to 5. Begin with a closed fist then the thumb. Repeat with the fingers on the other hand. This activity prepares them for counting objects.

Problem of the Lesson

Count the number of stars on the flag.

Answer: 6 stars

---

1 Counting to 10

Lesson Objectives
- Count from 0 to 10 objects.
- Read and write 0–10 in numbers and words.

Vocabulary

zero	one	two
three	four	five
six	seven	eight
nine	ten	

Point with your finger and count.

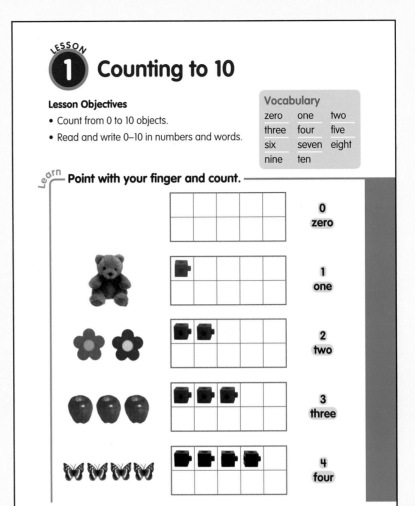

4   **CHAPTER 1** Numbers to 10

Student Book A p. 4

DAY 1 **Teach**

Point with Your Finger and Count (pages 4 and 5)

Explain that the index finger is often used in counting objects in a set.

- Have children look at the pictures on the page and count the number of objects along with you beginning from zero. *Say:* 0, 0 things; 1, 1 bear; 2, 2 flowers; 3, 3 apples, …

- After each count, repeat counting the same number as you place **connecting cubes** on the **Ten Frame** (TRO1) one at a time to model the diagrams on the page.

- Associate each numeral and number word with the actual number of cubes and the number of corresponding objects.

- Say a number from 1 to 10. Have children point to the corresponding number in the Student Book. Ask them to say aloud the number and the name of the object, for example, 6 paper clips. Then, count the cubes together on the ten frame: 1, 2, 3, …, 6.

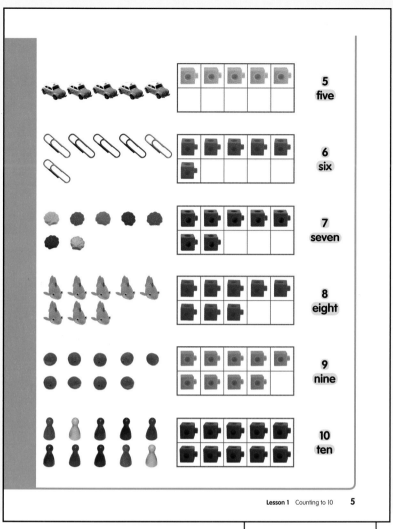

Student Book A p. 5

Differentiated Instruction

English Language Learners

Children may have difficulty matching the numerals to the number words. Introduce each number with a picture. Count as you point to each object in the picture. Next, write and say the numeral. Finally, write and say the number word. Have children repeat this procedure with you as you point to the objects in the picture, then to the numeral, and finally to the number word.

Best Practices Many of the activities in this lesson and in other lessons in the chapter use counters, such as connecting cubes. To minimize preparation time, you may wish to create packages of 10 counters before starting the chapter. Use plastic sandwich bags, and keep the packages in a convenient place. Children can quickly pick up a bag at the beginning of the math lesson.

Best Practices Discuss examples from the Student Book using a variety of methods, depending on the technology in your classroom. For example, you might project pages from the Interactive eBook, use an opaque projector, or have children follow along in the Student Book.

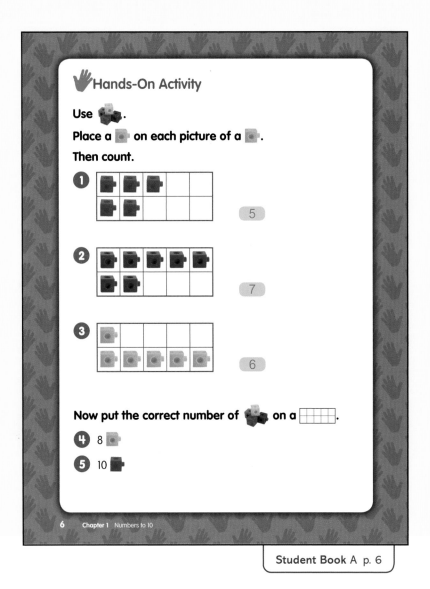

Student Book A p. 6

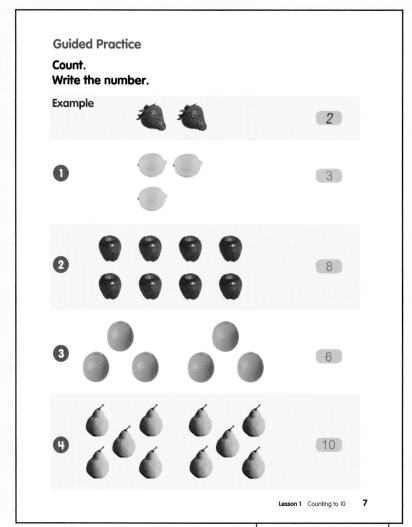

Student Book A p. 7

Hands-On Activity:

Show a Number in a Ten Frame, Then Count (page 6)

This activity helps children practice counting different numbers of connecting cubes.

• This activity can be done in pairs. Each child in the pair will need 10 **connecting cubes** of assorted colors and a copy of a **Ten Frame** (TRO1).

• Have children place the cubes on all the pictures of cubes on the page in Exercises ❶ to ❸. Remind children not to write in their books. You may want to have them say the answers out loud or write the answers on the board.

• In Exercises ❹ and ❺, have each child place 8 or 10 cubes on their ten frames and count them. They show their partners the filled ten frames. Encourage children to model cubes using the same colors shown on page 6.

Check for Understanding
✓ Guided Practice (page 7)

Have children count the objects in the Example and say the number *two*. Guide them to say 2 strawberries. Ask children to write the number 2 in the air with their fingers.

❶ to ❹ Repeat the process of counting, saying the number word and then writing the numeral in the air or on the board.

Best Practices An effective way to use the Guided Practice exercises is to have children work in pairs. Then have pairs share their ideas with the class. Children might also work on the exercises individually and share their work using white boards.

Point to the bugs and count.
Write in numbers and in words.

Example

3 three

5 2 two

6 1 one

7 0 zero

Student Book A p. 8

How many are there?
Count. Write the number.

8 🍄 0

✿ 10

🐰 3

🐝 6

🧚 5 🦆 2 🐸 4 🦋 7

Student Book A p. 9

✔ **Guided Practice** (pages 8 and 9) 🎲

5 to **7** Use objects to help children practice counting back to zero. Hold 3 **connecting cubes** in your hand. Ask children to count the number of cubes aloud.

• Remove 1 cube and have children count the remaining cubes. Repeat this until there are no cubes left. Reinforce the concept of '0' and the number word *zero*.

• Have children look at the Example on the page. *Say:* There are 3 bugs. 1 bug flies away. Look at Exercise **5**. *Ask:* How many bugs are there now? Have children count and write the numeral 2 and word *two*. Repeat for Exercises **6** and **7**.

8 Have children count each of the items in the picture and write the number on the board or on a piece of paper. Check that children are able to count and write to complete the exercise.

For Advanced Learners For further practice, encourage children to count given types of objects around them. For example, have children count the number of chairs in each row in the classroom, or the number of lights in the classroom.

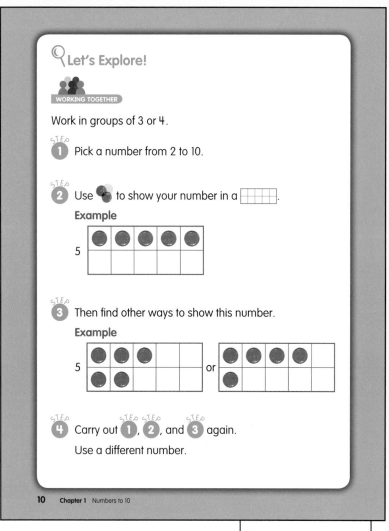

Student Book A p. 10

Student Book A p. 11

DAY 2 | **Teach**   See the Lesson Organizer on page 4 for Day 2 resources.

WORKING TOGETHER

 Let's Explore!

Show Numbers in Different Ways Using a Ten Frame (page 10)

This exploration helps children see and handle different representations of the same number of objects in a set. Encourage children to find different ways to show the same number on a ten frame using different arrangements of the counters.

- Children may work in small groups. Each group will need 10 **counters** and a blank **Ten Frame** (TRO1).

WORKING TOGETHER Game:

Land on 10! (page 11)

This game provides practice with using fingers to count on from 1 to 10.

- Arrange children in groups of three. Explain the game to children.

- A child starts counting from 1. This child has to show the corresponding number of fingers while counting. He or she can only use 1 to 3 fingers for each turn. The rest of the children take turns counting on aloud from the number given by the previous child. Likewise they can only use 1 to 3 fingers in their turns. The aim is to be the first to reach 10.

Example:

Child A (starts): 1, 2 (using 2 fingers)

Child B (counts on): 3, 4, 5 (using 3 fingers)

Child C (counts on): 6, 7, 8 (using 3 fingers)

Child A (counts on to win): 9, 10 (using 2 fingers)

- Offer the hint that a good strategy is to vary the number of fingers used.

Let's Practice

What is the number? Count.
Write the number.

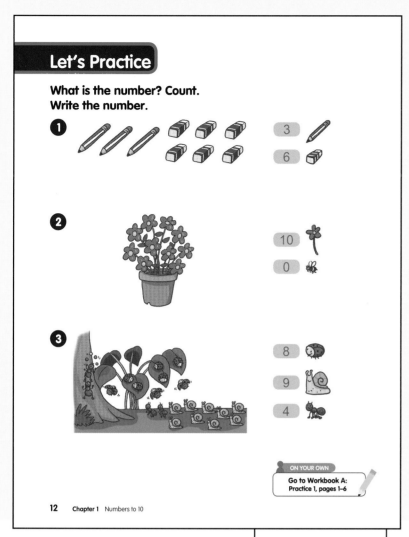

1 [pencils and erasers] — 3 [pencil], 6 [eraser]

2 [flowers in pot] — 10 [flower], 0 [bee]

3 [leaves scene] — 8 [ladybug], 9 [snail], 4 [ant]

ON YOUR OWN

Go to Workbook A:
Practice 1, pages 1–6

12   **Chapter 1** Numbers to 10

Student Book A p. 12

Practice and Apply
Workbook pages for Chapter 1, Lesson 1

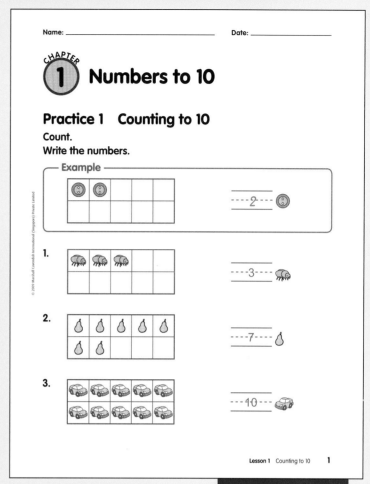

Name: _____   Date: _____

CHAPTER 1 Numbers to 10

Practice 1   Counting to 10

Count.
Write the numbers.

Example
[ten-frame with 2 buttons] — 2 [button]

1. [ten-frame with 3 flies] — 3 [fly]

2. [ten-frame with 7 pears] — 7 [pear]

3. [ten-frame with 10 cars] — 10 [car]

Lesson 1 Counting to 10   1

Workbook A p. 1

Let's Practice (page 12)

This practice reinforces locating and counting different types of objects within a mixed set. Exercises **1** and **2** require children to count two different types of objects while Exercise **3** requires children to count three different types of objects. Have children say the number while you write the number on the board.

Common Error   Children may not understand that the activity calls for counting the number of objects in different groups. In Exercise **1**, children may count the pencils and erasers together to get 9. Direct their attention to the pictures on the right and explain that they have to count the pencils, then the erasers, and so on.

ON YOUR OWN

Children practice counting in Practice 1, pp. 1–6 of **Workbook 1A**. These pages (with the answers) are shown at the right and on page 12A.

Differentiation Options   Depending on children's success with the Workbook pages, use these materials as needed.
Struggling: Reteach 1A, pp. 1–8
On Level: Extra Practice 1A, pp. 1–6

Count.
Write the numbers.

4.

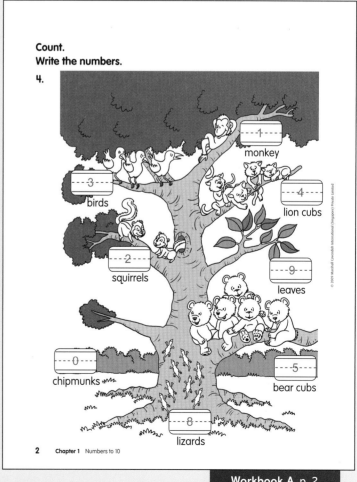

1 monkey
3 birds
4 lion cubs
2 squirrels
9 leaves
0 chipmunks
5 bear cubs
8 lizards

2   **Chapter 1** Numbers to 10

Workbook A p. 2

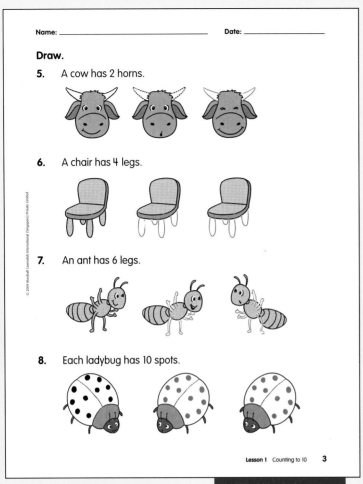

Name: _____   Date: _____

Draw.

5. A cow has 2 horns.

6. A chair has 4 legs.

7. An ant has 6 legs.

8. Each ladybug has 10 spots.

Workbook A p. 3

Name: _____   Date: _____

Count the things on the snowman.
Circle the correct words.

10.		two	three	four	five	(zero)
11.		zero	(one)	two	three	four
12.		six	seven	(eight)	nine	ten
13.		one	two	three	(four)	five
14.		nine	six	(one)	eight	three

Workbook A p. 5

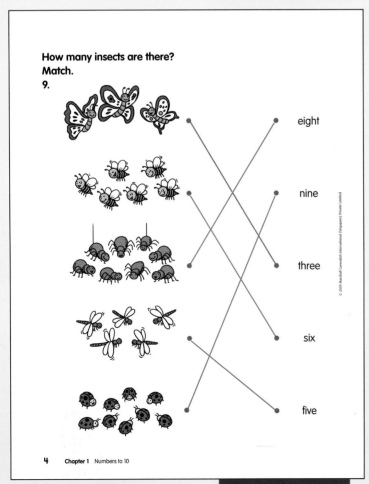

How many insects are there?
Match.

9.

eight

nine

three

six

five

Workbook A p. 4

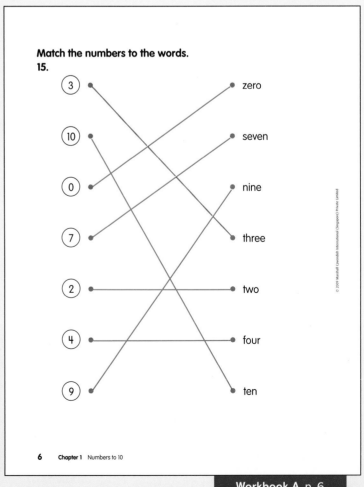

Match the numbers to the words.

15.

3   zero

10   seven

0   nine

7   three

2   two

4   four

9   ten

Workbook A p. 6

LESSON 2 Comparing Numbers

LESSON OBJECTIVES

- Compare two sets of objects by using one-to-one correspondence.
- Identify the set that has more, fewer, or the same number of objects.
- Identify the number that is greater than or less than another number.

TECHNOLOGY RESOURCES

- *Math in Focus* eBook
- *Math in Focus* Teaching Resources CD
- *Math in Focus* Virtual Manipulatives

Vocabulary

same	fewer	less than
more	greater than	

DAY 1 Student Book 1A, pp. 13–16

MATERIALS

- 15 connecting cubes per child
- 10 counters per child
- 2 Horizontal Ten Frames per child (TR02)
- 1 set of Shoes and Socks Cut-Outs per child (TR02)
- scissors
- paste or glue sticks or Blu-Tack®

DAY 2 Student Book 1A, pp. 16–19
Workbook 1A, pp. 7–12

DIFFERENTIATION RESOURCES

- Reteach 1A, pp. 9–16
- Extra Practice 1A, pp. 7–14

 5-minute Warm Up

- Have children work in pairs. One child draws a set with 1 to 10 objects. The other child draws a set that has a different number of objects. This activity prepares children for comparing sets using *more* or *fewer*.

LESSON 2 Comparing Numbers

Lesson Objectives

- Compare two sets of objects by using one-to-one correspondence.
- Identify the set that has more, fewer, or the same number of objects.
- Identify the number that is greater than or less than another number.

Vocabulary
same
more
fewer
greater than
less than

Learn **Match and compare.**

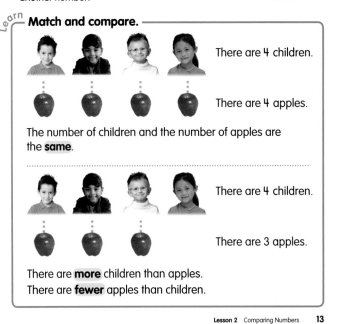

There are 4 children.

There are 4 apples.

The number of children and the number of apples are the **same**.

There are 4 children.

There are 3 apples.

There are **more** children than apples.
There are **fewer** apples than children.

Lesson 2 Comparing Numbers **13**

Student Book A p. 13

DAY 1 # Teach

Learn **Match and Compare** (page 13)

Two sets of objects can be compared using the one-to-one correspondence strategy.

- Have 6 children volunteer to stand in front of the class. Show 6 **counters**. Have children count the volunteers and the counters. Help children see that each volunteer has a counter because the number of volunteers and counters are the same.

- Have children look at the pictures in the Student Book. Guide children to see that the number of children and apples are the same.

- Collect the counters from the volunteers. Then, have one more volunteer join the original group. Re-distribute the counters. There will be one volunteer without a counter.

- Ask children if every volunteer has a counter. Use the words *more than* and *fewer than* to describe the situation.

- Discuss the next example in the Student Book.

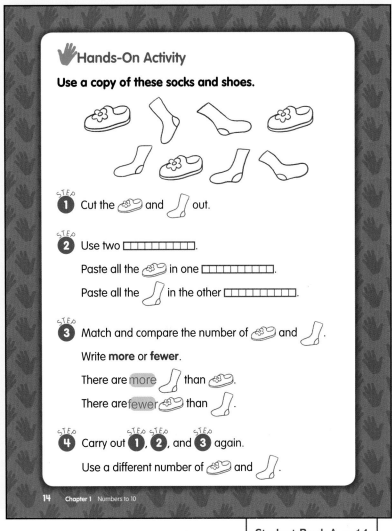

Hands-On Activity

Use a copy of these socks and shoes.

STEP 1 Cut the 👟 and 🧦 out.

STEP 2 Use two ▭▭▭▭▭.

Paste all the 👟 in one ▭▭▭▭▭.

Paste all the 🧦 in the other ▭▭▭▭▭.

STEP 3 Match and compare the number of 👟 and 🧦.

Write **more** or **fewer**.

There are more 🧦 than 👟.

There are fewer 👟 than 🧦.

STEP 4 Carry out **STEP 1**, **STEP 2**, and **STEP 3** again.

Use a different number of 👟 and 🧦.

14 Chapter 1 Numbers to 10

Student Book A p. 14

Student Book A p. 14

Problem of the Lesson

There are six chairs in a room.
These circles show the chairs.

Five children enter the room.
Each child sits on a chair.
How many chairs will be empty?

Solution:

⬤⬤⬤⬤⬤◯

Answer: One chair will be empty.

Differentiated Instruction

English Language Learners

Children may need more practice using the comparative language in this lesson. Write the terms *more*, *fewer*, *less than*, and *greater than* on index cards. Place the cards facedown on a table along with counters. Pick up a card, and model making a comparison statement with numbers or objects through 10. Have children repeat after you. Model several situations, and then have children practice creating their own comparison statements. Reinforce the different usage of the terms, one is for sets of objects and the other for numbers.

👋 Hands-On Activity: ▭▭▭▭▭
Count and Compare Using Cut-outs and Ten Frames (page 14)

This activity helps children match and compare the numbers of two different types of objects using the **Shoes and Socks Cut-Outs** (TR02) and two **Horizontal Ten Frames** (TR02).

- Each child needs a set of Shoes and Socks Cut-Outs and two ten frames. Have children cut out all the 👟 and 🧦. Then guide children to paste all the 👟 in one ten frame and all the 🧦 in the other. You may wish to use Blu-Tack® instead of glue so that the cut-outs can be re-used in **STEP 4**.

- Guide them to match and compare the objects one-to-one by placing the ten frames one above the other.

- Help children recall the concepts of *more* and *fewer* and complete the statements in **STEP 3**.

- Arrange the children in pairs. Then ask one child in each pair to take away any cut-out from the other child. Have children carry out the pasting and matching activity again.

Best Practices In this lesson, the concepts *more* and *fewer* are introduced and practiced before the terms *greater than* and *less than*. You may wish to informally introduce *greater than* and *less than* while teaching *more* and *fewer*. For example, *say:* There are more children than apples. Four is greater than three. There are fewer apples than children. Three is less than four.

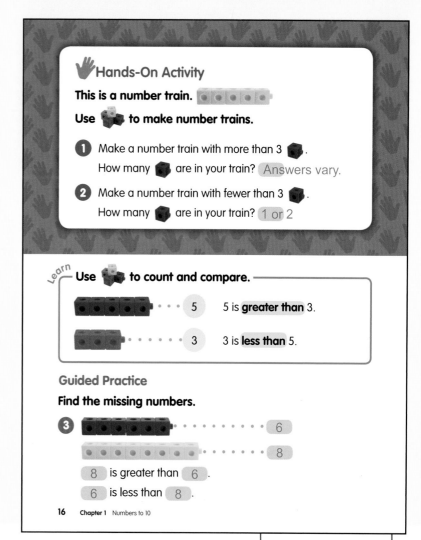

Student Book A p. 15

Student Book A p. 16

Check for Understanding

✔ **Guided Practice** (page 15)

❶ Have children draw matching lines with their fingers to match each butterfly to a flower. Check if children are able to use *more* and *fewer* appropriately.

❷ Have children match the number of cats and ducks to the fish. Help them compare the three sets of objects and complete the sentences by saying *more* or *fewer*.

✋ **Hands-On Activity:**

Make Number Trains Using Connecting Cubes (page 16)

This activity requires children to make **connecting-cube** number trains with more or fewer cubes than a given number.

• In Exercise ❶, guide children to see that they can make number trains with different numbers of cubes, as long as there are more than 3.

• In Exercise ❷, help children see that they can have 1 or 2 cubes in their number train.

DAY 2 **Teach** See the Lesson Organizer on page 13 for Day 2 resources.

Count and Compare (page 16)

Children have learned on page 13 to compare sets using the one-to-one correspondence strategy. In this section, they learn to count the **connecting cubes** before comparing the numbers. Then, introduce them to the terms *greater than* and *less than*. Tell children that the terms *greater than* and *less than* are used to compare numbers while the terms *more* and *fewer* are used when talking about sets of objects.

• Help children relate the numbers and concrete objects. *Say:* 5 cubes are more than 3 cubes, so 5 is greater than 3. 3 cubes are fewer than 5 cubes, so 3 is less than 5.

✔ **Guided Practice** (pages 16 and 17)

These exercises provide children with practice using the terms *greater than* and *less than* when comparing numbers.

❸ Children need to count the cubes in the number trains first. Then they show their understanding of *greater than* and *less than* by completing the sentences correctly.

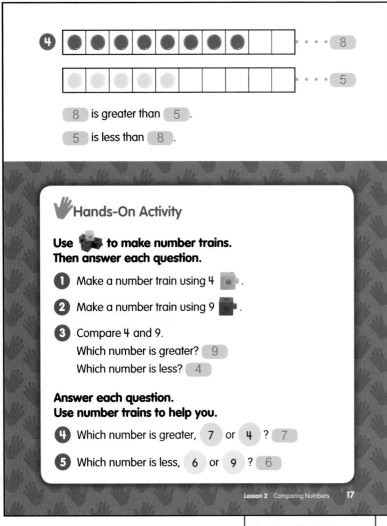

8 is greater than 5.

5 is less than 8.

✋Hands-On Activity

Use 🧊 to make number trains.
Then answer each question.

1 Make a number train using 4 🟦.

2 Make a number train using 9 🟦.

3 Compare 4 and 9.
Which number is greater? 9
Which number is less? 4

**Answer each question.
Use number trains to help you.**

4 Which number is greater, 7 or 4 ? 7

5 Which number is less, 6 or 9 ? 6

Lesson 2 Comparing Numbers **17**

Student Book A p. 17

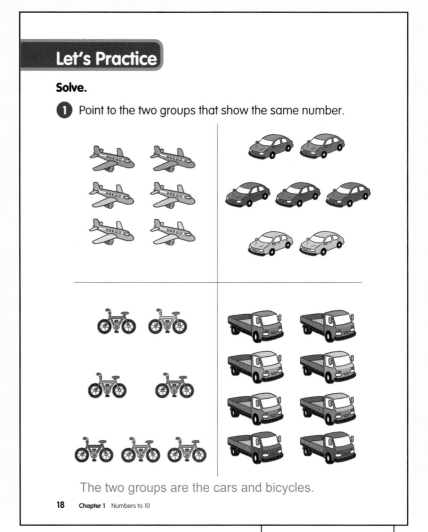

Let's Practice

Solve.

1 Point to the two groups that show the same number.

The two groups are the cars and bicycles.

18 Chapter 1 Numbers to 10

Student Book A p. 18

✔ Guided Practice (page 17)

4 This exercise is a repeat of Exercise **3** using counters on a horizontal ten frame.

✋ Hands-On Activity:

Make Number Trains Using Connecting Cubes (page 17)

1 to **3** This activity reinforces the skills of counting and comparing, and provides further practice in the use of *greater than* and *less than* in number comparison.

• Have children make two number trains using 4 **connecting cubes** and 9 connecting cubes respectively.

• *Ask:* Which train has more (or fewer) cubes? Then ask children to tell you which number is greater or lesser.

• For Exercises **4** and **5**, encourage children to make number trains to compare the given numbers.

Let's Practice (pages 18 and 19)

These exercises provide a review and practice of the vocabulary used in number comparison. Exercise **1** requires children to count and compare 4 groups, and then to apply the concept of *same*. Exercises **2** and **3** review the use of *more* and *fewer* when comparing sets of objects. Exercises **4** to **7** check if children can apply the concepts of *greater* and *less* in comparing the magnitude of two numbers from the numerals alone.

Common Error Children may confuse the terms *greater than* and *less than*. Make a visual display that shows two sets of objects. Include the word *greater* with the larger set and *less* and with the smaller set. You may also wish to provide a mnemonic device, such as the fact that *greater* has more letters than *less*.

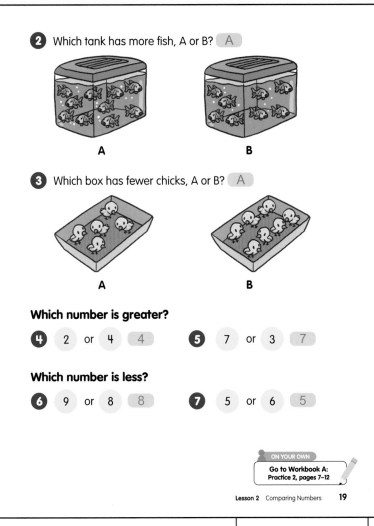

2 Which tank has more fish, A or B? A

A   B

3 Which box has fewer chicks, A or B? A

A   B

Which number is greater?

4 2 or 4 4   **5** 7 or 3 7

Which number is less?

6 9 or 8 8   **7** 5 or 6 5

ON YOUR OWN
Go to Workbook A:
Practice 2, pages 7–12

Lesson 2 Comparing Numbers **19**

Student Book A p. 19

ON YOUR OWN

Children practice comparing numbers in Practice 2, pp. 7–12 of **Workbook 1A**. These pages (with the answers) are shown at the right and on page 19A.

Differentiation Options Depending on children's success with the Workbook pages, use these materials as needed.
Struggling: Reteach 1A, pp. 9–16
On Level: Extra Practice 1A, pp. 7–14

Practice and Apply
Workbook pages for Chapter 1, Lesson 2

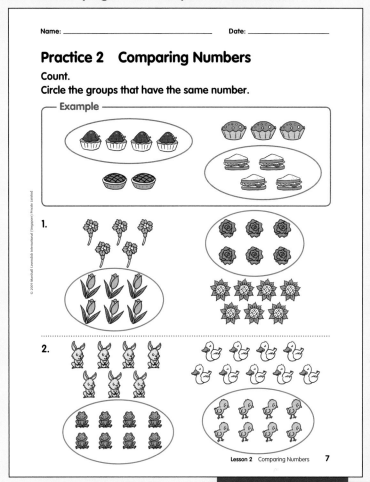

Name: _____ Date: _____

Practice 2   Comparing Numbers
Count.
Circle the groups that have the same number.

Example

1.

2.

Lesson 2 Comparing Numbers **7**

Workbook A p. 7

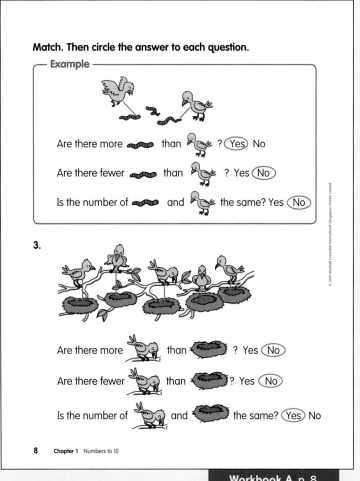

Match. Then circle the answer to each question.

Example

Are there more 🪱 than 🐦 ? (Yes) No

Are there fewer 🪱 than 🐦 ? Yes (No)

Is the number of 🪱 and 🐦 the same? Yes (No)

3.

Are there more 🐦 than 🪺 ? Yes (No)

Are there fewer 🐦 than 🪺 ? Yes (No)

Is the number of 🐦 and 🪺 the same? (Yes) No

8 Chapter 1 Numbers to 10

Workbook A p. 8

Name: _____ **Date:** _____

Match. Then circle the answer.

4.
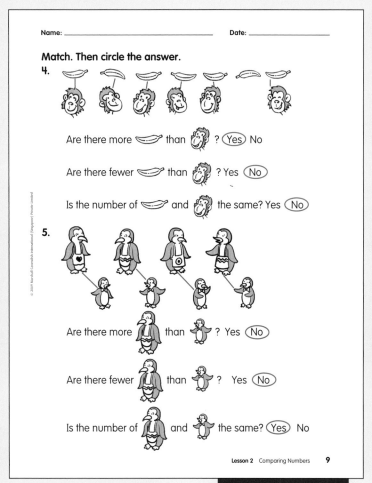

Are there more 🍌 than 🐵 ? (Yes) No

Are there fewer 🍌 than 🐵 ? Yes (No)

Is the number of 🍌 and 🐵 the same? Yes (No)

5.

Are there more 🐧 than 🐧 ? Yes (No)

Are there fewer 🐧 than 🐧 ? Yes (No)

Is the number of 🐧 and 🐧 the same? (Yes) No

Workbook A p. 9

Name: _____ **Date:** _____

Count and write the number.
Then answer each question by coloring the correct box.

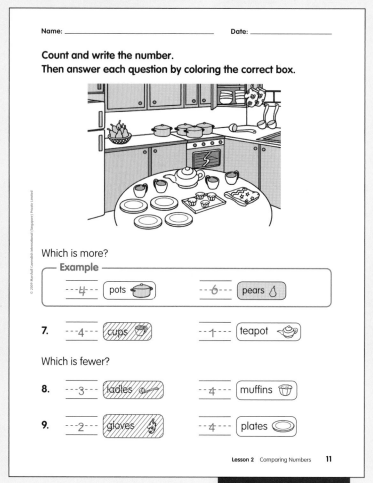

Which is more?

┌─ **Example** ─────────────────────────┐
│ --4-- [pots 🍲]   --6-- [pears 🍐] │
└────────────────────────────────────┘

7. --4-- [cups ☕]   --1-- [teapot 🫖]

Which is fewer?

8. --3-- [ladles 🥄]   --4-- [muffins 🧁]

9. --2-- [gloves 🧤]   --4-- [plates 🍽]

Workbook A p. 11

Which two groups have the same number of things?

Join them to a -·-·-·-.

Then write the number in each -·-·-·-.

6.
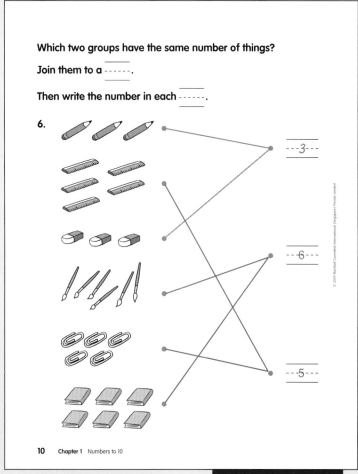

--3--

--6--

--5--

Workbook A p. 10

Color the correct signs.
Which number is greater?

10.
5   8

11.
10   9

Which number is less?

12.
7   3

13.
1   6

Write the numbers in the blanks.

14.
2   0

15.
9   3

--2-- is greater than --0--.   --3-- is less than --9--.

Color the flags with the same number.

16.
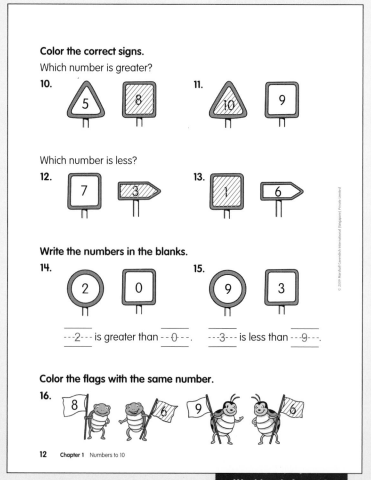
8   6   9   6

Workbook A p. 12

Chapter 1

LESSON 3 Making Number Patterns

LESSON OBJECTIVE
• Make number patterns.

TECHNOLOGY RESOURCES
• *Math in Focus* eBook
• *Math in Focus* Teaching Resources CD
• *Math in Focus* Virtual Manipulatives

Vocabulary
pattern
more than
less than

DAY 1 Student Book 1A, pp. 20–26
Workbook 1A, pp. 13–16

MATERIALS
• 10 connecting cubes per child
• 10 counters per child
• 1 Ten Frame per child (TR01)

DIFFERENTIATION RESOURCES
• Reteach 1A, pp. 17–20
• Extra Practice 1A, pp. 15–18

 5-minute Warm Up

Use different color counters or connecting cubes to make at least two AB repeating patterns. Include at least three repetitions of the pattern unit. Show children the patterns and ask volunteers to tell what comes next.

Problem of the Lesson

Jane has 4 beads.
Her sister, Joy, has 1 bead less than Jane has.
How many beads does Joy have?

Solution:

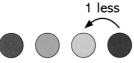

1 less than 4 is 3.

Answer: Joy has 3 beads.

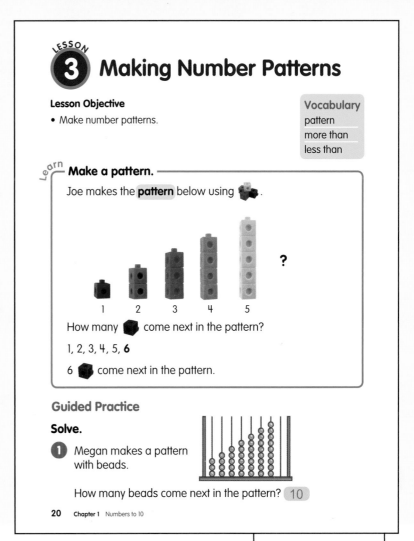

Student Book A p. 20

DAY 1 Teach

Make a Pattern (page 20)

Connecting cubes are used to form a growing or increasing pattern. Explain that each set of cubes is part of a pattern or sequence.

• Show children a set of **connecting cubes** arranged in the pattern as shown in the Student Book. Have children compare the number of cubes in the first tower on the left with those in the second tower. *Ask:* What is the difference in number? (There is 1 more cube in the second tower.)

• Have children compare the number of cubes in the second and third towers, third and fourth towers, and fourth and fifth towers. Point out that there is one more cube in each tower.

• Finally, show children the number sequence and show them that the next tower should have 6 cubes.

Check for Understanding
✓ Guided Practice (page 20)

❶ Have children count the beads in each column and write the number on the board. Then, have children say aloud the numbers from left to right: 3, 4, 5, 6, 7, 8, 9. Then have them say the missing number.

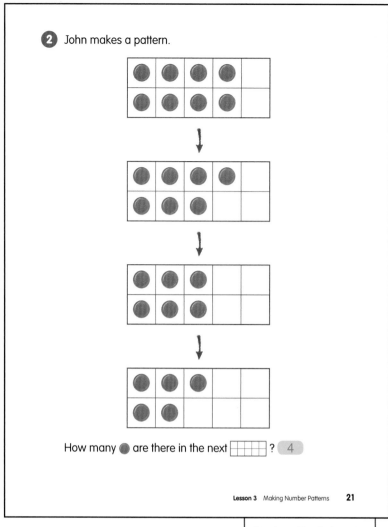

2 John makes a pattern.

How many 🔵 are there in the next ▦ ? 4

Student Book A p. 21

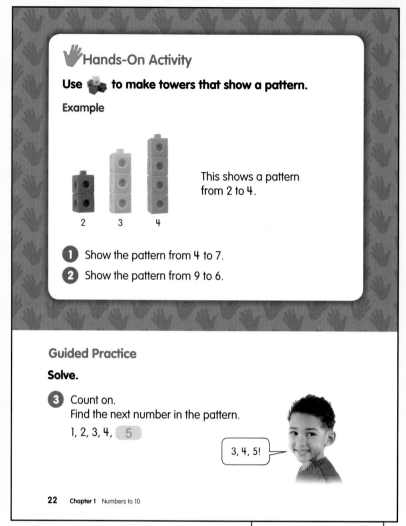

✋**Hands-On Activity**

Use 🧱 to make towers that show a pattern.

Example

This shows a pattern from 2 to 4.

2   3   4

1 Show the pattern from 4 to 7.

2 Show the pattern from 9 to 6.

Guided Practice

Solve.

3 Count on.
Find the next number in the pattern.

1, 2, 3, 4, 5

3, 4, 5!

Student Book A p. 22

✔**Guided Practice** (page 21)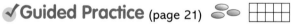

2 This requires children to count back from 8 to 4. Have children place 8 **counters** on a **Ten Frame** (TR01) as shown in the first picture on the page. Ask children to remove one counter at a time and count back from 8 as they do so: 8, 7, 6, 5. Have children remove one more and say the number: 4. Then have them say it.

✋**Hands-On Activity:** 🎲

Make Tower Patterns Using Connecting Cubes (page 22)

In this activity, children practice making patterns that do not begin at 1.

• Show children a set of **connecting cube** towers arranged in sequence from 2 to 4. Lead them to see that the sets of cube towers show an increasing or growing pattern of *one more*.

1 Arrange children in groups of 3 or 4 with 30 **connecting cubes**. Have each group make towers to show an increasing pattern from 4 to 7. Help children see they have to add 1 more to make up the next tower.

2 Have children arrange cubes to show a decreasing pattern from 9 to 6 cubes. Help children see they have to take away one cube to make up the next tower.

✔**Guided Practice** (pages 22 and 23)

3 Have children count on aloud from 1 to 4, and then to 5.
4 This provides practice counting on from a number other than 0 or 1. Have children count on from 4 to 10, and fill in the missing numbers as they do so. Then, have them count back from 10 to 5, and fill in the missing numbers.

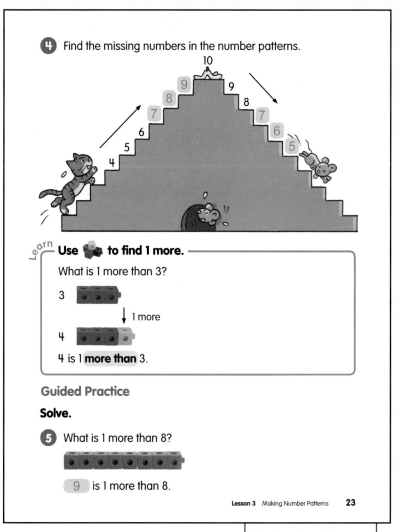

Student Book A p. 23

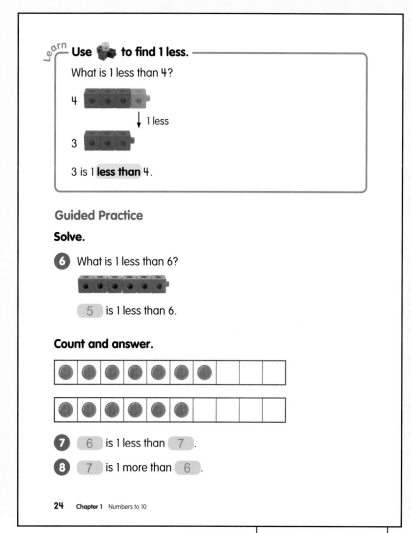

Student Book A p. 24

Use Connecting Cubes to Find 1 More

(page 23)

This activity uses **connecting cube** trains to demonstrate the meaning of *1 more than*.

• Have children make a train of 3 **connecting cubes**. Model and ask them to add 1 cube of another color to the train. Say and ask children to repeat after you: 4 is 1 more than 3.

• Model and have children add 1 more cube to the train. *Ask:* What is 1 more than 4? Lead children to say: 5 is 1 more than 4. Repeat this activity by adding cubes one at a time, if necessary.

✓ Guided Practice (page 23)

5 This exercise checks that children have grasped the concept of *1 more than*.

Best Practices Children may need to use different methods to internalize the concepts *one more* and *one less*. Building sets of connecting cubes may work for some, while counting tapes are better for other children. Blank counting tapes can be found in the Teaching Resources section. Counting up and back may be the preferred method for verbal learners.

Use Connecting Cubes to Find 1 Less

(page 24)

This activity uses **connecting cube** trains to demonstrate the meaning of *1 less than*.

• Have children make a train of 4 **connecting cubes**, 3 of one color and 1 of another. Model and ask them to remove the cube of another color. Say and ask children to repeat after you: 3 is 1 less than 4.

• Model and have children remove 1 more cube from the train. *Ask:* What is 1 less than 3? Lead children to say: 2 is 1 less than 3.

• Repeat this by removing one cube at a time.

✓ Guided Practice (page 24)

6 Have children look at the number train on the page and count the cubes. *Ask:* What is 1 less than 6? Lead children to complete the sentence on the page.

7 and **8** Have children read the sentences before writing the numbers.

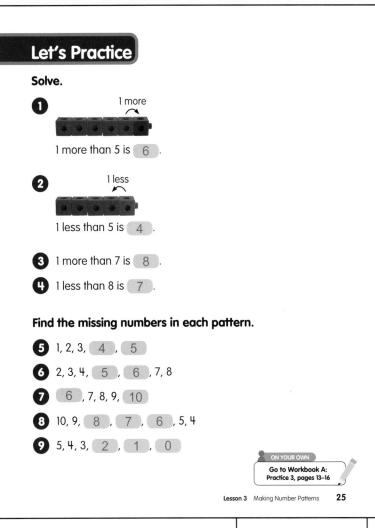

Student Book A p. 25

Let's Practice (page 25)

This practice reinforces skills for identifying and continuing number patterns with *1 more* or *1 less*. Exercises ❶ and ❷ require children to count the number of cubes. Exercises ❸ and ❹ check that children can apply the concepts of *1 more than* and *1 less than* without counting the objects. Encourage children to use the cubes to check their answers.

Exercises ❺ to ❼ are more challenging, and require children to complete the number patterns in increasing sequence. Exercises ❽ and ❾ require children to count back to complete the patterns.

Common Error Children may confuse *1 more* and *1 less*. It may be helpful to provide a visual clue to help with this issue. On the board, make a counting tape by drawing a horizontal ten frame as shown on Student Book page 17. Label the squares from 1 to 10. Draw an arrow from 1 to 10 above the counting tape and label it *more*. Draw an arrow from 10 to 1 below the counting tape and label it *less*.

Differentiated Instruction

English Language Learners

Demonstrate the meaning of *1 more* and *1 less*. Display a group of five counters. Count the objects and add 1 more. **Say:** There are five counters. One more makes six. Six is one more than five. Invite children to repeat your actions and language. Continue by modeling *1 less*. Write the following on the board: _ *is 1 _ than* _. Say different numbers and have children fill in the blanks with appropriate numbers and the words *more* and *less*.

ON YOUR OWN

Children practice making number patterns in Practice 3, pp. 13–16 of **Workbook 1A**. These pages (with the answers) are shown on page 25A.

Differentiation Options Depending on children's success with the Workbook pages, use these materials as needed.
Struggling: Reteach 1A, pp. 17–20
On Level: Extra Practice 1A, pp. 15–18

Practice and Apply

Workbook pages for Chapter 1, Lesson 3

Name: _____ Date: _____

Practice 3 Making Number Patterns

What comes next in each pattern?
Write the number.

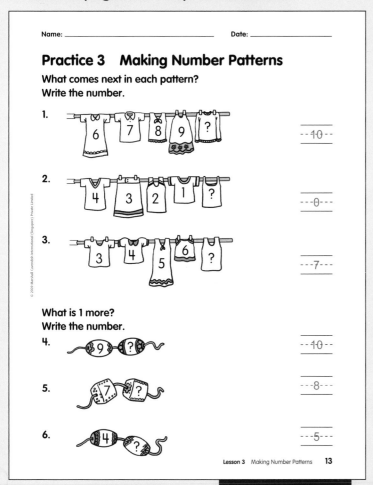

1. 6 7 8 9 ? — — 10 — —

2. 4 3 2 1 ? — — 0 — —

3. 3 4 5 6 ? — — 7 — —

What is 1 more?
Write the number.

4. 9 ? — — 10 — —

5. 7 ? — — 8 — —

6. 4 ? — — 5 — —

Lesson 3 Making Number Patterns **13**

Workbook A p. 13

What is 1 less?
Write the number.

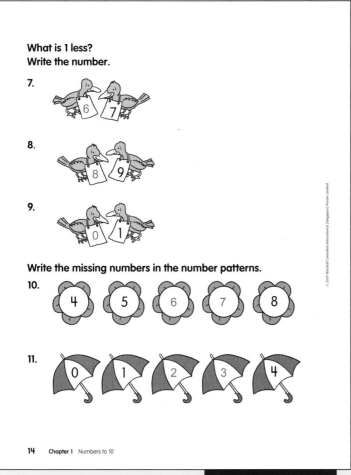

7. 6 7

8. 8 9

9. 0 1

Write the missing numbers in the number patterns.

10. 4 5 6 7 8

11. 0 1 2 3 4

14 Chapter 1 Numbers to 10

Workbook A p. 14

Name: _____ Date: _____

Write the missing numbers in the number patterns.

12. 6 7 8 9 10

13. 6 5 4 3 2

14. 3 2 1 0

15. 9 8 7 6 5

Lesson 3 Making Number Patterns **15**

Workbook A p. 15

Fill in the blanks.

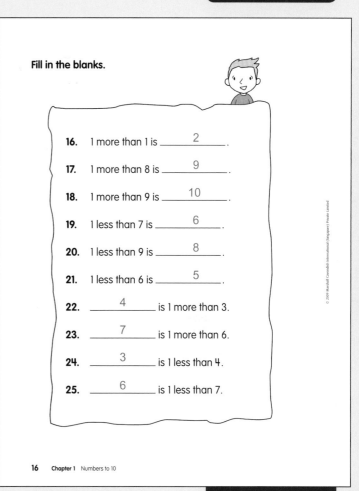

16. 1 more than 1 is _____2_____.

17. 1 more than 8 is _____9_____.

18. 1 more than 9 is _____10_____.

19. 1 less than 7 is _____6_____.

20. 1 less than 9 is _____8_____.

21. 1 less than 6 is _____5_____.

22. _____4_____ is 1 more than 3.

23. _____7_____ is 1 more than 6.

24. _____3_____ is 1 less than 4.

25. _____6_____ is 1 less than 7.

16 Chapter 1 Numbers to 10

Workbook A p. 16

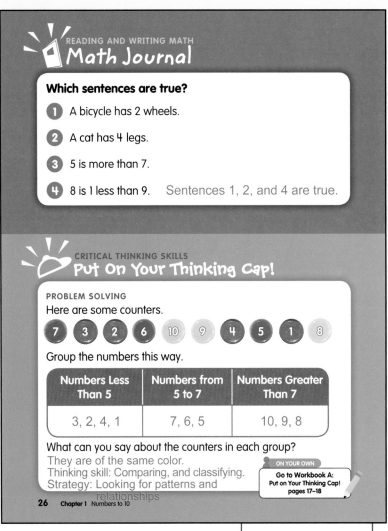

READING AND WRITING MATH
Math Journal

Which sentences are true?

1 A bicycle has 2 wheels.

2 A cat has 4 legs.

3 5 is more than 7.

4 8 is 1 less than 9.   Sentences 1, 2, and 4 are true.

CRITICAL THINKING SKILLS
Put On Your Thinking Cap!

PROBLEM SOLVING

Here are some counters.

7 3 2 6 10 9 4 5 1 8

Group the numbers this way.

Numbers Less Than 5	Numbers from 5 to 7	Numbers Greater Than 7
3, 2, 4, 1	7, 6, 5	10, 9, 8

What can you say about the counters in each group?
They are of the same color.
Thinking skill: Comparing, and classifying.
Strategy: Looking for patterns and
relationships

ON YOUR OWN
Go to Workbook A:
Put on Your Thinking Cap!
pages 17–18

26 Chapter 1 Numbers to 10

Student Book A p. 26

READING AND WRITING MATH
Math Journal (page 26)

This section allows children to reflect on their observations and understanding.

For sentences **1** and **2**, have children think about the number of items on these everyday things. Encourage children to make similar sentences from their observations of other things, for example, an insect has 6 legs. For sentences **3** and **4**, have children check their own understanding of *more than* and *less than* by evaluating the truth of the given statements.

CRITICAL THINKING AND PROBLEM SOLVING
Put on Your Thinking Cap! (page 26)

This problem-solving exercise involves the use of comparing and classifying skills.

- Copy the table from page 26 on to the board.

- Guide children to focus their attention on the first column, *Numbers Less Than 5*. Help them to decide which counters belong in that column.

- Repeat for the next column and the last column until all the counters have been sorted.

- Then, lead children to observe that the counters have also been sorted by color.

Thinking Skills

- Comparing
- Classifying

Problem Solving Strategy

- Looking for patterns and relationships

ON YOUR OWN

Because all children should be challenged, have all children try the Challenging Practice and Problem-Solving pages in **Workbook 1A**, pp. 17–18. These pages (with the answers) are shown on page 26A.

Differentiation Options Depending on children's success with the Workbook pages, use these materials as needed.

On Level: Extra Practice 1A, pp. 19–20

Advanced: Enrichment 1A, pp. 1–8

Practice and Apply

Workbook pages for Put on Your Thinking Cap!

Name: _____ Date: _____

Put On Your Thinking Cap!

Challenging Practice

Mother Hen's eggs have numbers that are greater than 2 and less than 8.
Color the eggs that belong to Mother Hen.

Workbook A p. 17

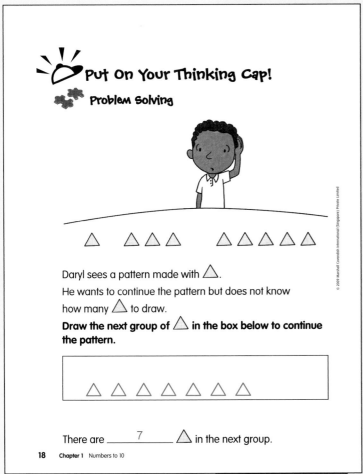

Put On Your Thinking Cap!

Problem Solving

△   △ △ △   △ △ △ △ △

Daryl sees a pattern made with △.
He wants to continue the pattern but does not know how many △ to draw.
Draw the next group of △ in the box below to continue the pattern.

△ △ △ △ △ △ △

There are ____7____ △ in the next group.

Workbook A p. 18

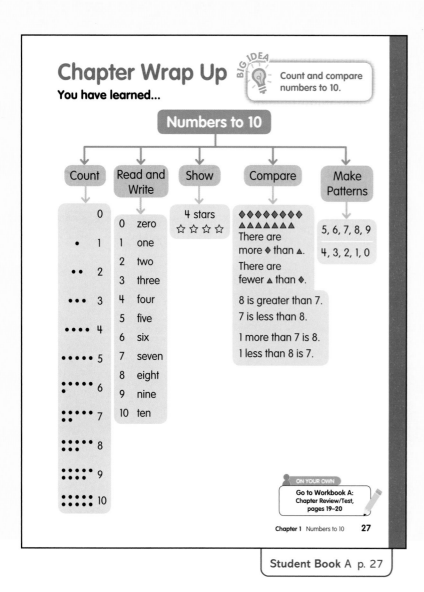

Student Book A p. 27

Chapter Wrap Up (page 27)

Review reading and writing by having children read the numerals and words at random from a display, on the board, or from cards. Have children count from 0 to 10. You may want to make different number trains and have children count the number of cubes. Use the examples from *Compare* and *Make Patterns* on the page to review the concepts. As you work through the examples, encourage children to use the chapter vocabulary:

• zero	• six	• more
• one	• seven	• fewer
• two	• eight	• greater than
• three	• nine	• pattern
• four	• ten	• more than
• five	• same	• less than

ON YOUR OWN

Have children review the vocabulary, concepts, and skills from Chapter 1 with the Chapter Review/Test in **Workbook 1A** pp. 19–20. These pages (with the answers) are shown on page 27A.

Assessment

Use the Chapter 1 Test Prep on pages 2–6 of **Assessments 1** to assess how well children have learned the material of this chapter. This assessment is appropriate for reporting results to parents and administrators. This test is shown on page 27B.

Assessments 1 pp. 2–6

Workbook pages for Chapter Review/Test

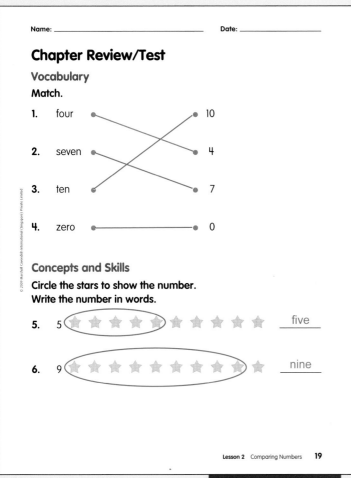

Name: _____ Date: _____

Chapter Review/Test

Vocabulary
Match.

1. four   •   • 10

2. seven •   • 4

3. ten   •   • 7

4. zero •   • 0

Concepts and Skills
Circle the stars to show the number.
Write the number in words.

5. 5   ☆☆☆☆☆ ☆☆☆☆☆   _five_

6. 9   ☆☆☆☆☆☆☆☆☆ ☆   _nine_

Lesson 2 Comparing Numbers   **19**

Workbook A p. 19

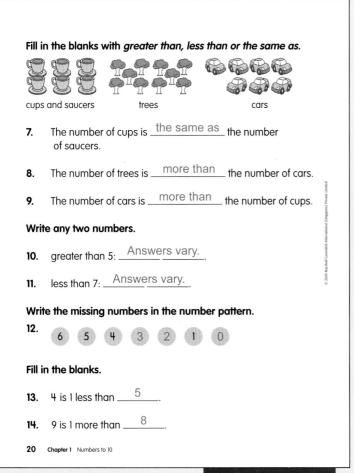

Fill in the blanks with *greater than, less than or the same as.*

cups and saucers   trees   cars

7. The number of cups is __the same as__ the number of saucers.

8. The number of trees is __more than__ the number of cars.

9. The number of cars is __more than__ the number of cups.

Write any two numbers.

10. greater than 5: __Answers vary.__

11. less than 7: __Answers vary.__

Write the missing numbers in the number pattern.

12. 6   5   4   3   2   1   0

Fill in the blanks.

13. 4 is 1 less than ___5___.

14. 9 is 1 more than ___8___.

20   Chapter 1   Numbers to 10

Workbook A p. 20

Notes

Assessments Book pages for Chapter 1 Test Prep
Answer key appears in Assessments Book.

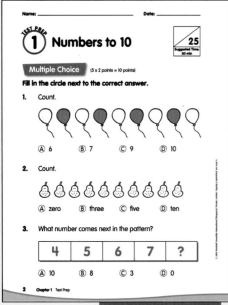

Name: _____ Date: _____

TEST PREP 1 Numbers to 10 □ 25
Suggested Time: 30 min

Multiple Choice (5 x 2 points = 10 points)

Fill in the circle next to the correct answer.

1. Count.

   Ⓐ 6   Ⓑ 7   Ⓒ 9   Ⓓ 10

2. Count.

   Ⓐ zero   Ⓑ three   Ⓒ five   Ⓓ ten

3. What number comes next in the pattern?

   | 4 | 5 | 6 | 7 | ? |

   Ⓐ 10   Ⓑ 8   Ⓒ 3   Ⓓ 0

2   Chapter 1   Test Prep

Assessments p. 2

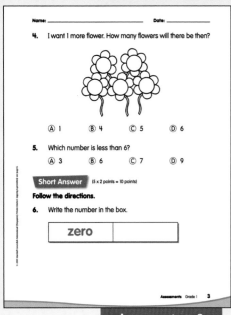

Name: _____ Date: _____

4. I want 1 more flower. How many flowers will there be then?

   Ⓐ 1   Ⓑ 4   Ⓒ 5   Ⓓ 6

5. Which number is less than 6?
   Ⓐ 3   Ⓑ 6   Ⓒ 7   Ⓓ 9

Short Answer (5 x 2 points = 10 points)

Follow the directions.

6. Write the number in the box.

   | zero | |

   Assessments   Grade 1   **3**

Assessments p. 3

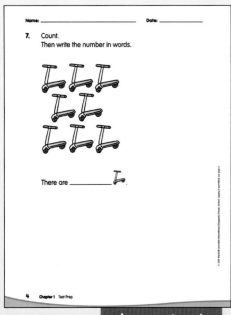

Name: _____ Date: _____

7. Count.
   Then write the number in words.

   There are _____.

   4   Chapter 1   Test Prep

Assessments p. 4

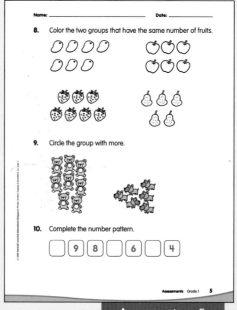

Name: _____ Date: _____

8. Color the two groups that have the same number of fruits.

9. Circle the group with more.

10. Complete the number pattern.

    | | 9 | 8 | | 6 | | 4 |

    Assessments   Grade 1   **5**

Assessments p. 5

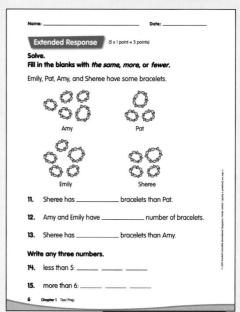

Name: _____ Date: _____

Extended Response (5 x 1 point = 5 points)

Solve.
Fill in the blanks with *the same, more,* or *fewer.*

Emily, Pat, Amy, and Sheree have some bracelets.

Amy   Pat

Emily   Sheree

11. Sheree has _____ bracelets than Pat.

12. Amy and Emily have _____ number of bracelets.

13. Sheree has _____ bracelets than Amy.

Write any three numbers.

14. less than 5: _____ _____ _____

15. more than 6: _____ _____ _____

6   Chapter 1   Test Prep

Assessments p. 6

Chapter Overview

Number Bonds

Math Background

Number bonds form an important foundation for the learning of the concept of addition, which will be introduced in the next chapter. In fact, number bonding is closely related to both addition and subtraction. When children understand the concept of number bonds, it will be easier when they do addition and subtraction with regrouping at a later stage. Number bonding is widely regarded as one of the necessary tools to do well at mental arithmetic, especially when regrouping is involved. In this chapter, children are led to investigate all possible sets of two numbers that make a given number up to 10.

Children are first taught to identify the parts and whole of a set. They are then led to separate a set of objects into two parts. Hence, children will realize that they can make different number bonds for a given number. This part-whole concept forms the basis for addition and subtraction strategies. Recognizing the relationships between the parts and the whole will also help children to understand formal number relationships such as the commutative property of addition.

Cross-Curricular Connections

Reading/Language Arts The word *bond* has multiple meanings, so give children definitions and examples that they will understand. Explain that a bond is a joining, a close relationship, or a material that holds parts together. A child might have a strong bond with a pet. Point out that in a number bond, two numbers are joined together to form another number.

Science Tell children that some materials bond together to make a mixture. Solids and liquids can be mixed together. Sometimes the solid dissolves into the liquid, so it can no longer be seen. Use a glass of water and salt to demonstrate the meaning of dissolve. Use number bond diagrams to represent some common mixtures. (lemon juice, water, sugar → lemonade; salt, water → saltwater; syrup, milk → chocolate milk)

Skills Trace

Grade K	Find parts and wholes in addition and subtraction stories. (Chaps. 17 and 18)
Grade 1	Show parts and whole using number bonds. (Chaps. 2, 3, 4, and 8)
Grade 2	Use part-part-whole bar models in addition and subtraction. (Chap. 4)

EVERY DAY COUNTS®
Calendar Math

The August/September activities provide...

Review of reading and writing numbers (Chapter 1)

Preview of addition strategies and number stories (Chapter 2)

Practice of part and whole relationships for different numbers (Lesson 1 in this chapter)

Differentiation Resources

Differentiation for Special Populations

	English Language Learners	Struggling Reteach 1A	On Level Extra Practice 1A	Advanced Enrichment 1A
Lesson 1	p. 31	pp. 21–28	pp. 21–30	Enrichment pages can be used to challenge advanced children.

Additional Support

For English Language Learners

Select activities that reinforce the chapter vocabulary and the connections among these words, such as having children

- add terms, definitions, and examples to the Word Wall
- use manipulatives to show examples of each term
- retell meanings of each term in children's own words and give examples
- discuss the Chapter Wrap Up, encouraging children to use the chapter vocabulary

For Struggling Learners

Select activities that go back to the appropriate stage of the Concrete-Pictorial-Abstract spectrum, such as having children

- act out terms first and then having other children orally identifying the term
- use manipulatives to model whole and parts
- tell stories that describe number bonds
- create and solve new number bond problems using problems in the chapter as models

See also pages 36 and 37.

If necessary, review:

- Chapter 1 (Numbers to 10)

Assessment and Remediation

Chapter 2 Assessment

Prior Knowledge		
	Resource	**Page numbers**
Quick Check	Student Book 1A	p. 29
Pre-Test	Assessments 1	pp. 7–9
Ongoing Diagnostic		
Guided Practice	Student Book 1A	pp. 31–32
Common Error	Teacher's Edition 1A	pp. 32–33
Formal Evaluation		
Chapter Review/Test	Workbook 1A	pp. 33–34
Chapter 2 Test Prep	Assessments 1	pp. 10–14
Cumulative Review for Chapters 1 and 2	Workbook 1A	pp. 35–40

Problems with these items...   Can be remediated with...

Remediation Options

	Review/Test Items	Chapter Assessment Items	Reteach	Student Book
Objective	**Workbook 1A pp. 33–34**	**Assessments 1 pp. 10–14**	**Reteach 1A**	**Student Book 1A**
Use chapter vocabulary correctly.	1–2	Not assessed	22–28	p. 30
Use connecting cubes or a math balance to find number bonds.	5	Not assessed	22–24	Lesson 1
Find different number bonds for numbers to 10.	3–4, 6	1–11	22–24, 27–28	Lesson 2

Chapter Planning Guide

2 Number Bonds

Lesson	Pacing	Instructional Objectives	Vocabulary
Chapter Opener pp. 28–29 Recall Prior Knowledge Quick Check	*1 day	**Big Idea** Number bonds can be used to show parts and whole.	
Lesson 1, pp. 30–36 Making Number Bonds	2 days	• Use connecting cubes or a math balance to find number bonds • Find different number bonds for numbers to 10	• part • whole • number bond
Problem Solving p. 37 Put on Your Thinking Cap!	1 day	Thinking Skills: • Analyzing parts and whole, Deduction Problem Solving Strategies: • Act it out • Guess and check	
Chapter Wrap Up p. 38	1 day	• Reinforce and consolidate chapter skills and concepts	
Chapter Assessment	1 day		
Review			

*Assume that 1 day is a 45–55 minute period.

Resources	Materials	NCTM Focal Points	NTCM Process Standards
Student Book 1A, p. 28–29 **Assessments 1,** pp. 7–9	• math balance • 4 connecting cubes for the teacher		
Student Book 1A, pp. 30–36 **Workbook 1A,** pp. 21–30 **Extra Practice 1A,** pp. 21–30 **Reteach 1A,** pp. 21–28	• 10 connecting cubes per child • 1 math balance per group • 10 weights per group	***Number and Operations*** Model part-whole, adding to, taking away from, and comparing situations.	Problem Solving Reasoning/Proof Connections Representation
Student Book 1A, p. 37 **Workbook 1A,** pp. 31–32 **Extra Practice 1A,** pp. 31–32 **Enrichment 1A,** pp. 9–18			
Student Book 1A, p. 38 **Workbook 1A,** pp. 33–34			
Assessments 1, pp. 10–14			
Workbook 1A, pp. 35–40			

Technology Resources for easy classroom management
• *Math in Focus* eBook
• *Math in Focus* Teaching Resources CD
• *Math in Focus* Virtual Manipulatives
• On-Line Web Resources

Chapter Introduction

Lesson 1 Making Number Bonds

Chapter 2
Vocabulary

part	one of two or more smaller units that make up a whole	Lesson 1
whole	a complete unit	Lesson 1
number bond	a number relationship between parts and the whole	Lesson 1

part **3**
     8 whole
part **5**

Student Book A p. 28

Big Idea (page 28)

Children use number bonds to show the parts and whole for a given number.

- Using countable objects and a **math balance**, children are led to see how a given number can be made from two smaller numbers.

- This part-whole analysis forms the basis for the concept of adding two numbers to give another number in the next chapter.

Chapter Opener (page 28)

The picture illustrates the part-whole concept, with ten kittens, some of which are in a basket and the others outside. Children learned to count in Kindergarten and in Chapter 1. In this chapter, children will count the number of items in the parts that make up a whole and relate them in the form of number bonds.

- Show children the picture without the poem and *ask:* What do you see? (kittens)

- Show the picture with the poem. Read the poem aloud for the children. Reread the poem, asking children to read along with you.

- Have children count the kittens in and outside the basket, counting along with them. Write 3 and 7 on the board respectively.

- *Ask:* How many kittens are there? (10) Complete the number bond on the board, as shown on the Student Book page.

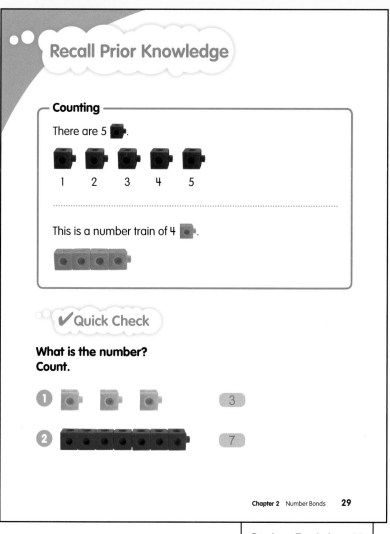

Recall Prior Knowledge

Counting

There are 5 ⬛.

1　2　3　4　5

This is a number train of 4 ⬛.

✔ **Quick Check**

What is the number?
Count.

① 　　　　　　　　③

② 　　　　　　　　⑦

Chapter 2　Number Bonds　**29**

Student Book A p. 29

Recall Prior Knowledge (page 29)

Counting 🎲

Children learned in Kindergarten and Chapter 1 to count objects to 10.

• Have children count the connecting cubes in each set on the page. *Ask:* How many objects are in each set?

• Model counting the cubes when separated as well as when linked to other cubes. This prepares children for part-whole analysis.

✔ Quick Check (page 29)

Use this section as a diagnostic tool to assess children's level of prerequisite knowledge before they progress to this chapter. The exercises on this page assess counting skills taught in Chapter 1.

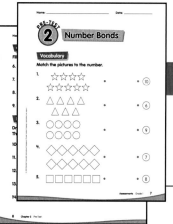

Assessments 1 pp. 7–9

Assessment

For additional assessment of children's prior knowledge and chapter readiness, use the Chapter 2 Pre-Test on pages 7–9 of **Assessments 1**.

LESSON 1 Making Number Bonds

LESSON OBJECTIVES

- Use connecting cubes or a math balance to find number bonds.
- Find different number bonds for numbers to 10.

TECHNOLOGY RESOURCES

- *Math in Focus* eBook
- *Math in Focus* Teaching Resources CD
- *Math in Focus* Virtual Manipulatives

Vocabulary

part	whole	number bond

 DAY 1 Student Book 1A, pp. 30–32

MATERIALS

- 10 connecting cubes per child
- 1 math balance per group
- 10 weights per group

 DAY 2 Student Book 1A, pp. 33–36
Workbook 1A, pp. 21–30

DIFFERENTIATION RESOURCES

- Reteach 1A, pp. 21–28
- Extra Practice 1A, pp. 21–30

 5-minute Warm Up

Give each child 10 **connecting cubes**. Say a number and have children form a number train with the cubes to make the given number. This sharpens their counting skills and introduces them to the concept of using units to make a whole.

LESSON 1 Making Number Bonds

Lesson Objectives

- Use connecting cubes or a math balance to find number bonds.
- Find different number bonds for numbers to 10.

Vocabulary
part
whole
number bond

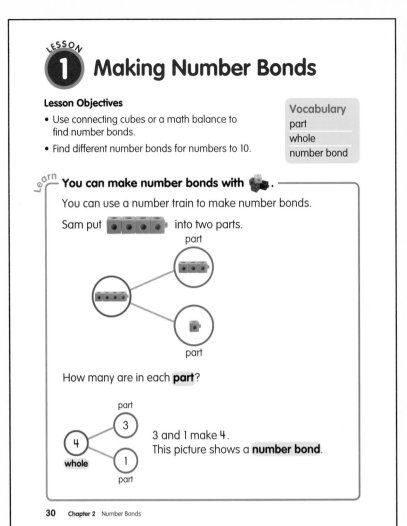

Student Book A p. 30

DAY 1 # Teach

Learn Make Number Bonds with Connecting Cubes
(page 30)

Connecting cubes are used to help children understand the part-whole concept.

- Make a number train with 4 **connecting cubes**. Count aloud the number of cubes. Then, separate 1 cube from the train to make two groups of cubes. Ask children to count aloud the number of cubes in each group. For each group of cubes, *ask:* How many are in this part?

- If children encounter difficulties, use 3 cubes of one color and 1 cube of another color when making the 4-cube train.

- Write the number bond 3-1—4 on the board. Lead children to see that the two number bonds 3-1—4 and 1-3—4, are the same. Explain that number bonds are different combinations of numbers that make up a number. Each number bond represents a part-whole relationship between numbers.

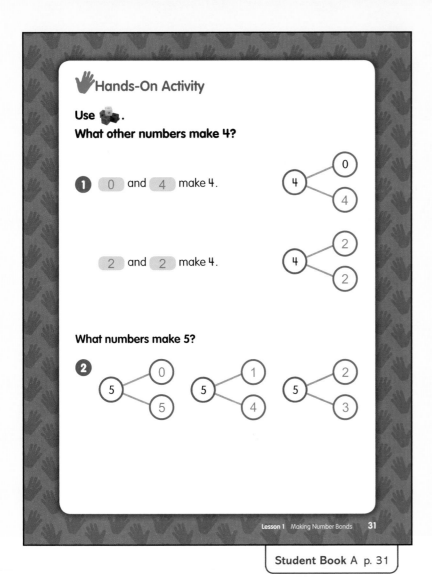

Hands-On Activity

Use 🎲.

What other numbers make 4?

1 0 and 4 make 4.

2 and 2 make 4.

What numbers make 5?

2

Student Book A p. 31

- Show that this relationship is the same regardless of the arrangement of the circles, (i.e. the following are all the same).

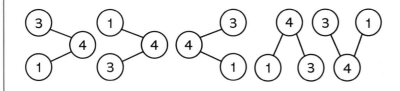

Hands-On Activity:
Make Number Bonds Using Connecting Cubes (page 31)

For Exercise **1**, encourage children to find other ways to make 4.

- Give each child 10 **connecting cubes**.

- Ask children to experiment with other possible ways to make 4 by varying the number of cubes in each part. Write the number bonds on the board.

- You could place the connecting cubes on an overhead projector to show a bigger image.

Problem of the Lesson

Mr. Jones has 2 sons and 1 daughter.

How many children does Mr. Jones have?

Solution: **Answer:** 3 children

Differentiated Instruction

English Language Learners

Children may need help with the directions to the Let's Explore! activity on page 36. Read Step 1 aloud and demonstrate what to do with the cubes. Ask the child to repeat your actions, and explain what he or she did, if possible. Move to Step 2, reading the directions and modeling the actions. Make sure the children record the appropriate answers. Continue providing support as necessary until the activity has been completed.

For Exercise **2**, you could have children work in groups of 4 to 6.

- Have them find all the possible combinations of numbers that make 5.

- Have groups of children present their answers to the class.

- Write the number bonds on the board.

Best Practices You may find it helpful to introduce the number bonds concept in two different ways. Demonstrate breaking apart different trains of connecting cubes, counting and recording the number of cubes in each part, joining the parts back together, and counting the total number of cubes. Also put two parts of a cube train on one side of a pan balance and a whole train on the other side to demonstrate equality.

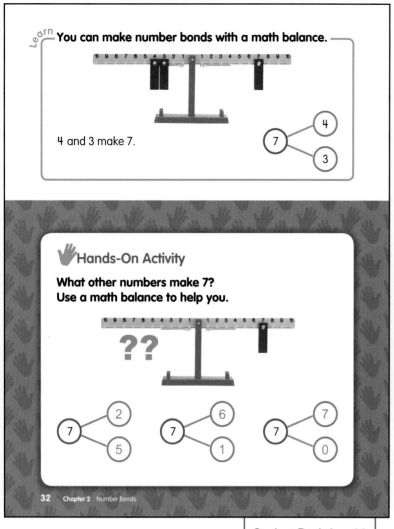

Learn You can make number bonds with a math balance.

4 and 3 make 7.

7 — 4
7 — 3

Hands-On Activity

What other numbers make 7?
Use a math balance to help you.

??

7 — 2 / 5
7 — 6 / 1
7 — 7 / 0

32 Chapter 2 Number Bonds

Student Book A p. 32

Make number bonds for these numbers.
Use or a math balance to help you.

1
6 — 0 / 6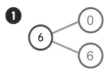
6 — 1 / 5
6 — 2 / 4
6 — 3 / 3

2
8 — ○ / ○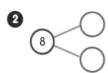

3
9 — ○ / ○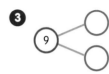

Accept 0 and 8;
1 and 7; 2 and 6;
3 and 5; 4 and 4.

Accept 0 and 9; 1 and 8;
2 and 7; 3 and 6; 4 and 5.

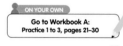
ON YOUR OWN
Go to Workbook A:
Practice 1 to 3, pages 21–30

Lesson 1 Making Number Bonds **33**

Student Book A p. 33

Learn

Make Number Bonds Using a Math Balance (page 32)

- Display the **math balance**. Explain to children that when three weights (two weights on one side and one weight on the other side) are placed on the balance and it is level, it means that the three numbers form a number bond.

- Show children how to obtain a number bond for 7 (3-4 —7) by placing weights at 3 and 4 on one side, and at 7 on the other side. Write the number bond on the board.

✋Hands-On Activity:
Make Number Bonds Using a Math Balance (page 32)

- Remove the weights from the balance at 3 and 4 but keep the other weight at 7.

- Ask children to think of other numbers that can make the balance level.

- Ask for volunteers to use the math balance to check their answers.

- Write the number bonds on the board.

32–33 **CHAPTER 2: LESSON 1**

DAY 2 Teach See the Lesson Organizer on page 30 for Day 2 resources.

Let's Practice (page 33)

This provides children more practice with making number bonds using **connecting cubes**. Exercise **1** lets children investigate all the possible number bonds that make 6. Exercises **2** and **3** have children provide any one number bond for 8 and 9.

Common Error Children may confuse the parts of the number bond and record numbers in the wrong places. Draw a bond on the board, and explain that the lines join the parts together to form the whole. To demonstrate further, tear apart a piece of paper and then join the parts together.

ON YOUR OWN

Children practice making number bonds within 10 in Practice 1 to 3, pp. 21–30 of **Workbook 1A**. These pages (with the answers) are shown on pages 33A–33C.

Differentiation Options Depending on children's success with the Workbook pages, use these materials as needed.
Struggling: Reteach 1A, pp. 21–28
On Level: Extra Practice 1A, pp. 21–30

Practice and Apply
Workbook pages for Chapter 2, Lesson 1

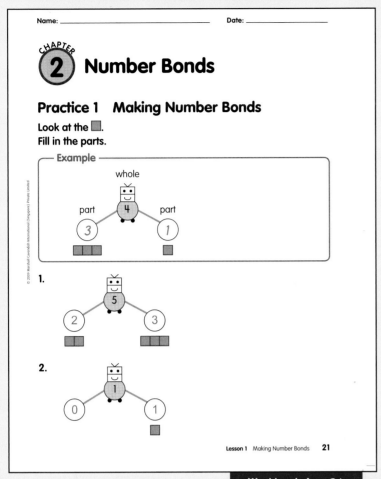

Name: _____   Date: _____

CHAPTER 2 Number Bonds

Practice 1   Making Number Bonds

Look at the ☐.
Fill in the parts.

Example

whole

part 4 part

3   1

☐☐   ☐

1.

5

2   3

☐   ☐☐

2.

1

0   1

☐

Workbook A p. 21

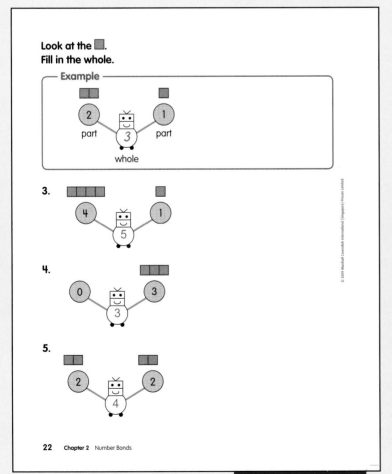

Look at the ☐.
Fill in the whole.

Example

☐☐   ☐

2   3   1

part 3 part

whole

3.

☐☐☐   ☐

4   5   1

4.

☐☐☐

0   3   3

5.

☐☐   ☐☐

2   4   2

Workbook A p. 22

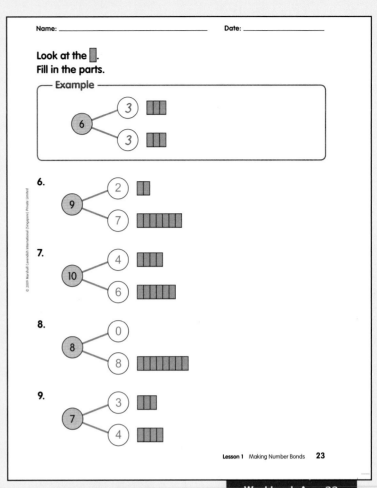

Look at the ☐.
Fill in the parts.

Example

6   3   ☐☐

3   ☐☐

6.

9   2   ☐

7   ☐☐☐☐☐

7.

10   4   ☐☐☐

6   ☐☐☐☐☐☐

8.

8   0

8   ☐☐☐☐☐☐☐☐

9.

7   3   ☐☐☐

4   ☐☐☐☐

Workbook A p. 23

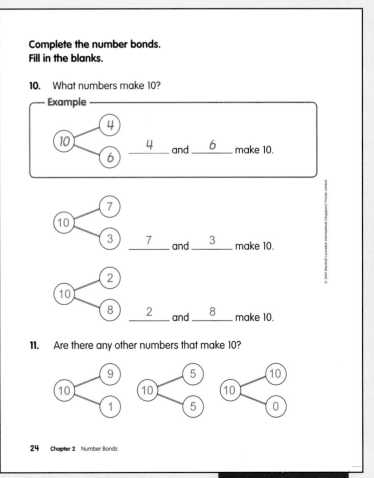

Complete the number bonds.
Fill in the blanks.

10.   What numbers make 10?

Example

10   4

6

____4____ and ____6____ make 10.

10   7

3

____7____ and ____3____ make 10.

10   2

8

____2____ and ____8____ make 10.

11.   Are there any other numbers that make 10?

10   9   10   5   10   10

1   5   0

Workbook A p. 24

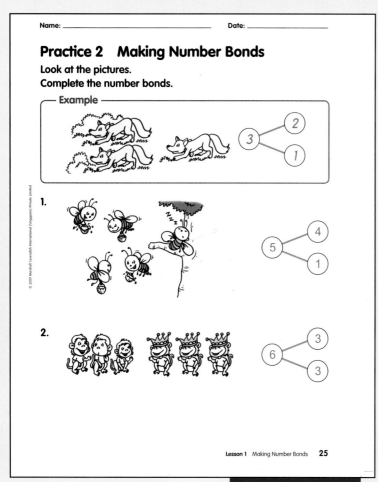

Practice 2   Making Number Bonds
Look at the pictures.
Complete the number bonds.

— Example —

1.

2.

Workbook A p. 25

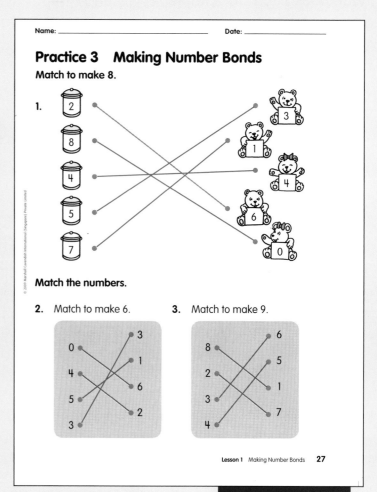

Practice 3   Making Number Bonds
Match to make 8.

1.

Match the numbers.

2.   Match to make 6.

3.   Match to make 9.

Workbook A p. 27

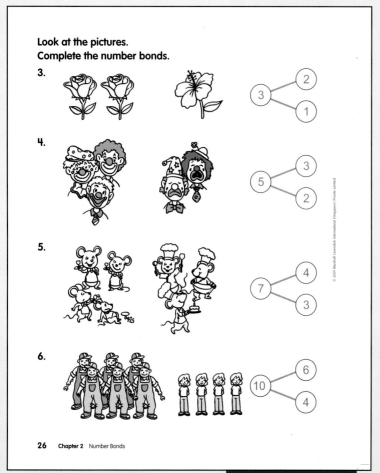

Look at the pictures.
Complete the number bonds.

3.

4.

5.

6.

Workbook A p. 26

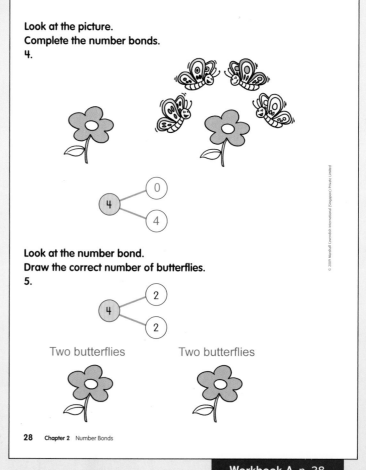

Look at the picture.
Complete the number bonds.
4.

Look at the number bond.
Draw the correct number of butterflies.
5.

Two butterflies   Two butterflies

Workbook A p. 28

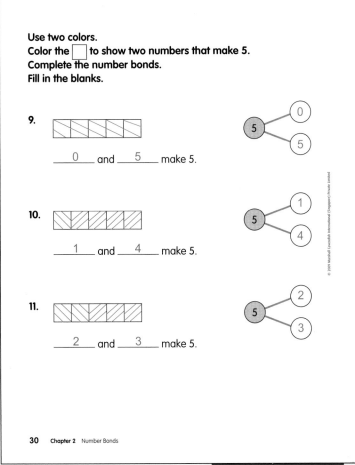

Name: _____ **Date:** _____

Use two colors. Color the ☐ to show two numbers
that make the number in ⬤.
Complete the number bonds.
Fill in the blanks.

Example

_5_ and _2_ make 7.

6.

_____ and _____ make 10.
Accept 0 and 10; 1 and 9; 2 and 8; 3 and 7;
4 and 6; 5 and 5.

7.

_____ and _____ make 6.
Accept 0 and 6; 1 and 5; 4 and 2; 3 and 3.

8.

_____ and _____ make 8.
Accept 0 and 8; 1 and 7; 2 and 6; 3 and 5; 4 and 4.

Lesson 1 Making Number Bonds **29**

Workbook A p. 29

Use two colors.
Color the ☐ to show two numbers that make 5.
Complete the number bonds.
Fill in the blanks.

9.

_0_ and _5_ make 5.

10.

_1_ and _4_ make 5.

11.

_2_ and _3_ make 5.

30 **Chapter 2** Number Bonds

Workbook A p. 30

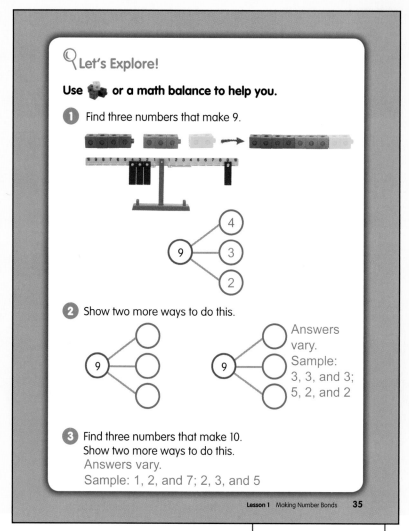

READING AND WRITING MATH
Math Journal (page 34)

This section allows children to reflect on their observations and understanding.

- Lead children to relate the picture with number bonds.

- Help them verbalize statements involving stools of different colors, boys and girls, and so on, to make different number bonds. For example,

  - 1 red stool and 5 blue stools make 6 stools.

  - 3 boys and 4 girls make 7 children.

- Write, or invite volunteers to write, the different number bonds on the board.

Let's Explore!
Number Bonds with Three Numbers (page 35)

In this exploration, children are introduced to the concept of 3 parts making up one whole.

- For Exercises ❶ and ❷, have children work in groups of 4 to 6 on the **math balance**. Have each group of children investigate all possible combinations of three numbers that make 9 with the help of a math balance.

- For Exercise ❸, have children work on all the possible number bonds for 10. Encourage children to use **connecting cubes** or the math balance to help them. Have children write their number bonds on the board and demonstrate with the connecting cubes or math balance how they arrive at the number bonds.

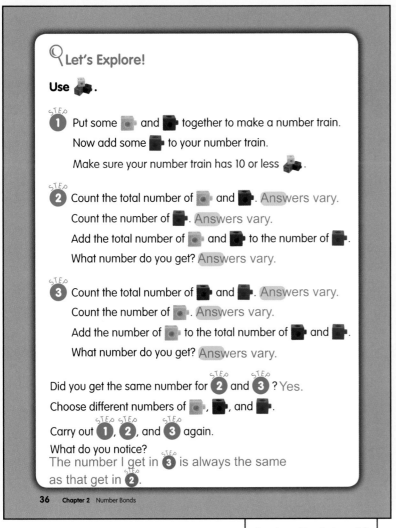

Student Book A p. 36

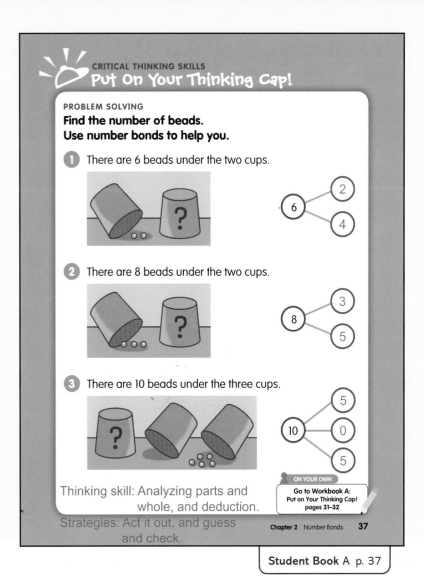

Student Book A p. 37

Let's Explore!
Making Number Trains with Connecting Cubes (Associative Property) (page 36)

- In this exploration, children are introduced to the *associative property* of addition. Using **connecting cubes**, lead children to see that (2 + 3) + 4 is the same as 2 + (3 + 4). Even though children have not yet been taught formal addition, they should be able to understand that the parts in the number bond can be grouped in different ways.

- Model **1** to **3** using connecting cubes and explain to children that the answers in **2** and **3** are always the same.

CRITICAL THINKING SKILLS
Put on Your Thinking Cap! (page 37)

In this problem-solving activity, children relate number bonds with covered and uncovered cups.

- For each exercise from **1** to **3**, *ask*: How many beads are there under the two/three cups?

- *Ask:* How many beads do you see? *Ask:* How many beads are there under the cup?

- Encourage children to recall the number bonds they have done.

For Struggling Learners Have children work in pairs. One child gets a set of counters with not more than 10. He/she tells his/her partner the number of counters. Next, he/she puts some counters under a cup and shows the rest to the partner. He/she asks the partner to tell how many counters are under the cup. Partners switch roles and repeat.

Thinking Skills
- Analyzing parts and whole
- Deduction

Problem Solving Strategies
- Act it out
- Guess and check

 **ON YOUR OWN**

Because all children should be challenged, have all children try the Challenging Practice and Problem-Solving pages in **Workbook 1A**, pp. 31–32. These pages (with the answers) are shown on page 37A.

Differentiation Options Depending on children's success with the Workbook pages, use these materials as needed.
On Level: Extra Practice 1A, pp. 31–32
Advanced: Enrichment 1A, pp. 9–18

Practice and Apply
Workbook pages for Put on Your Thinking Cap!

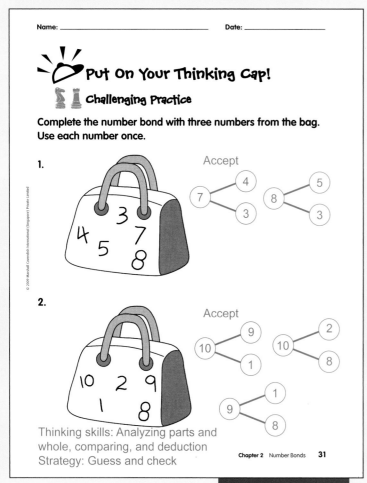

Put On Your Thinking Cap!

Challenging Practice

Complete the number bond with three numbers from the bag.
Use each number once.

1. Accept

2. Accept

Thinking skills: Analyzing parts and
whole, comparing, and deduction
Strategy: Guess and check

Chapter 2   Number Bonds   **31**

Workbook A p. 31

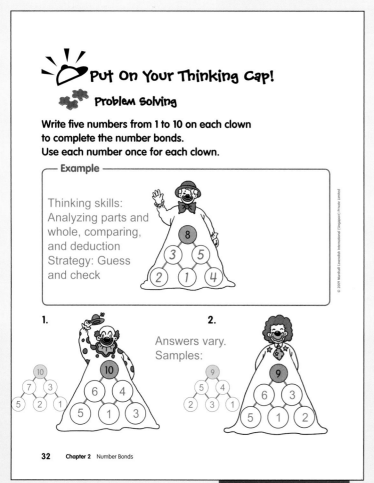

Put On Your Thinking Cap!

Problem Solving

Write five numbers from 1 to 10 on each clown
to complete the number bonds.
Use each number once for each clown.

— Example —

Thinking skills:
Analyzing parts and
whole, comparing,
and deduction
Strategy: Guess
and check

1.   2.

Answers vary.
Samples:

32   Chapter 2   Number Bonds

Workbook A p. 32

Notes

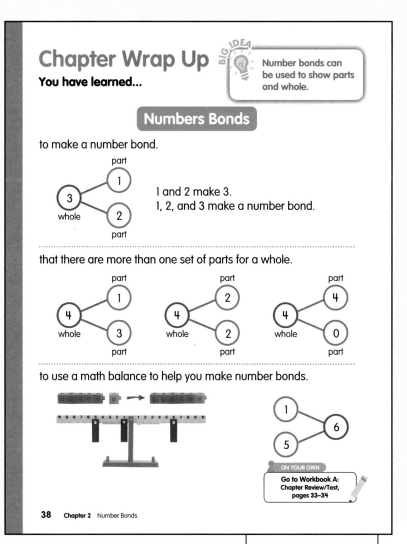

Chapter Wrap Up

BIG IDEA Number bonds can be used to show parts and whole.

You have learned...

Numbers Bonds

to make a number bond.

1 and 2 make 3.
1, 2, and 3 make a number bond.

that there are more than one set of parts for a whole.

to use a math balance to help you make number bonds.

ON YOUR OWN
Go to Workbook A:
Chapter Review/Test,
pages 33–34

38   **Chapter 2**   Number Bonds

Student Book A p. 38

Chapter Wrap Up (page 38)

Review the key concept of using number bonds to show part-whole relationships. Lead children to recognize that a given number may be made of more than one combination of parts. As you work through the examples, encourage children to use the chapter vocabulary:

- part
- whole
- number bond

ON YOUR OWN

Have children review the vocabulary, concepts, and skills from Chapter 2 with the Chapter Review/Test in **Workbook 1A**, pp. 33–34. These pages (with the answers) are shown on page 38A.

You may also wish to use the Cumulative Review for Chapters 1 and 2 from **Workbook 1A**, pp. 35–40. These pages (with the answers) are shown on pages 38B and 38C.

Assessment

Use the Chapter 2 Test Prep on pages 10–14 of **Assessments 1** to assess how well children have learned the material of this chapter. This assessment is appropriate for reporting results to adults at home and administrators. This test is shown on pages 38A and 38B.

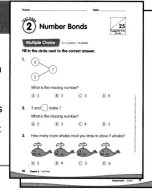

Assessments 1 pp. 10–14

Workbook pages for Chapter Review/Test

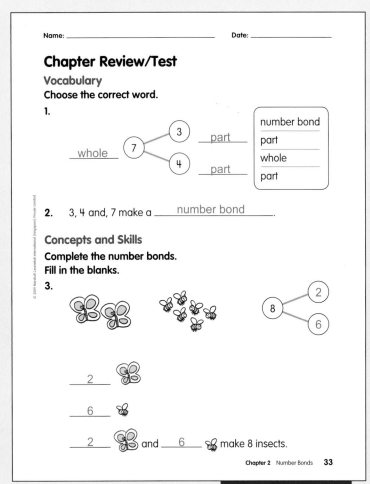

Name: _____ Date: _____

Chapter Review/Test
Vocabulary
Choose the correct word.

1.

| number bond |
| part |
| whole |
| part |

whole — 7 — 3 — _part_
7 — 4 — _part_

2. 3, 4 and, 7 make a ___number bond___.

Concepts and Skills
Complete the number bonds.
Fill in the blanks.

3.

8 — 2
8 — 6

___2___ 🦋

___6___ 🐝

___2___ 🦋 and ___6___ 🐝 make 8 insects.

Chapter 2 Number Bonds **33**

Workbook A p. 33

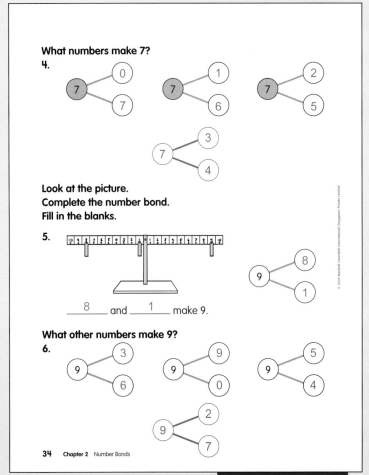

What numbers make 7?

4.

7 — 0
7 — 7

7 — 1
7 — 6

7 — 2
7 — 5

7 — 3
7 — 4

Look at the picture.
Complete the number bond.
Fill in the blanks.

5.

9 — 8
9 — 1

___8___ and ___1___ make 9.

What other numbers make 9?

6.

9 — 3
9 — 6

9 — 9
9 — 0

9 — 5
9 — 4

9 — 2
9 — 7

34 Chapter 2 Number Bonds

Workbook A p. 34

Assessments Book pages for Chapter 2 Test Prep
Answer key appears in Assessments Book.

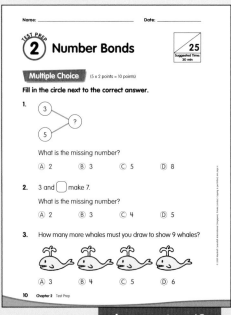

Name: _____ Date: _____

(2) **Number Bonds** ⬜ 25
Suggested Time 30 min

Multiple Choice (5 x 2 points = 10 points)

Fill in the circle next to the correct answer.

1.

3 — ?
5

What is the missing number?
Ⓐ 2   Ⓑ 3   Ⓒ 5   Ⓓ 8

2. 3 and ⬜ make 7.
What is the missing number?
Ⓐ 2   Ⓑ 3   Ⓒ 4   Ⓓ 5

3. How many more whales must you draw to show 9 whales?

🐋 🐋 🐋 🐋

Ⓐ 3   Ⓑ 4   Ⓒ 5   Ⓓ 6

10 Chapter 2 Test Prep

Assessments p. 10

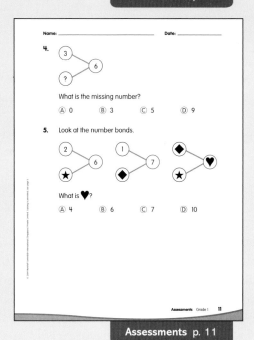

Name: _____ Date: _____

4.

3 — 6
?

What is the missing number?
Ⓐ 0   Ⓑ 3   Ⓒ 5   Ⓓ 9

5. Look at the number bonds.

2 — 6
★

1 — 7
◆

◆ — ♥
★

What is ♥?
Ⓐ 4   Ⓑ 6   Ⓒ 7   Ⓓ 10

Assessments Grade 1 **11**

Assessments p. 11

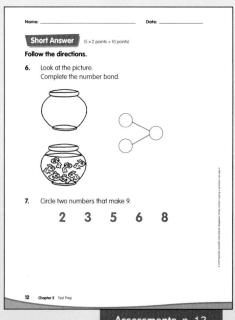

Name: _____ Date: _____

Short Answer (5 x 2 points = 10 points)

Follow the directions.

6. Look at the picture.
Complete the number bond.

7. Circle two numbers that make 9.

2   3   5   6   8

12 Chapter 2 Test Prep

Assessments p. 12

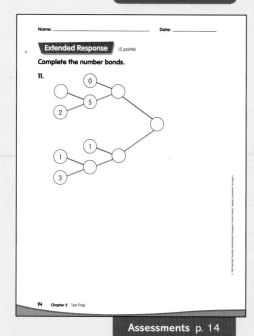

Name: _____ **Date:** _____

8. Fill in the missing number.

   5 and _____ make 8.

9. Complete the number bond with three numbers from the box.

   | 3 9 4 |
   | 7 2 |

10. Complete the number bond.

Assessments Grade 1 **13**

Assessments p. 13

Name: _____ **Date:** _____

Extended Response (5 points)

Complete the number bonds.

11.

14 Chapter 2 Test Prep

Assessments p. 14

Cumulative Review for Chapters 1 and 2

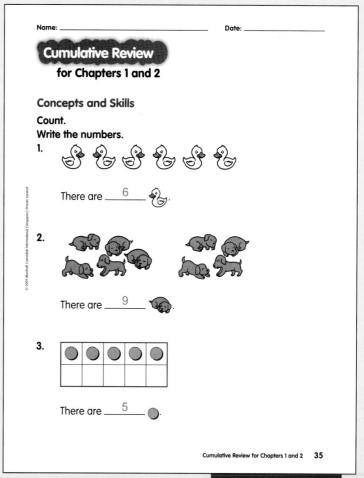

Name: _____ **Date:** _____

Cumulative Review
for Chapters 1 and 2

Concepts and Skills

Count.
Write the numbers.

1.

   There are ___6___ 🦆.

2.

   There are ___9___ 🐕.

3.

   There are ___5___ 🔵.

Cumulative Review for Chapters 1 and 2 **35**

Workbook A p. 35

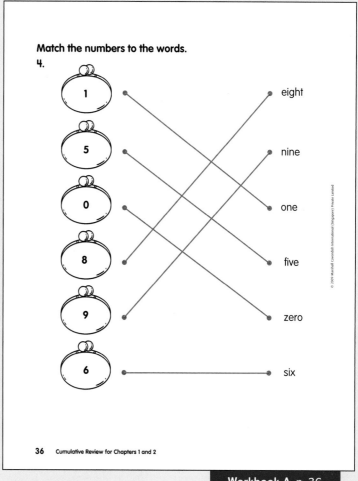

Match the numbers to the words.

4.

1	— eight
5	— nine
0	— one
8	— five
9	— zero
6	— six

36 Cumulative Review for Chapters 1 and 2

Workbook A p. 36

CHAPTERS 1 AND 2: ASSESSMENT ANCILLARY AND **CHAPTERS 1 AND 2:** CUMULATIVE REVIEW **38B**

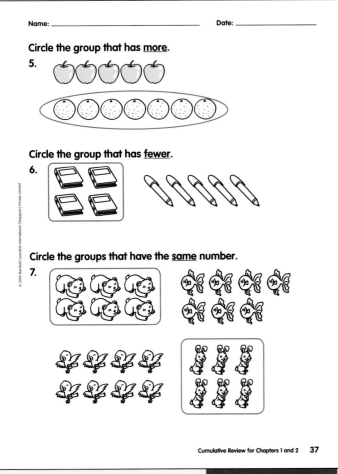

Circle the group that has <u>more</u>.

5.

Circle the group that has <u>fewer</u>.

6.

Circle the groups that have the <u>same</u> number.

7.

Workbook A p. 37

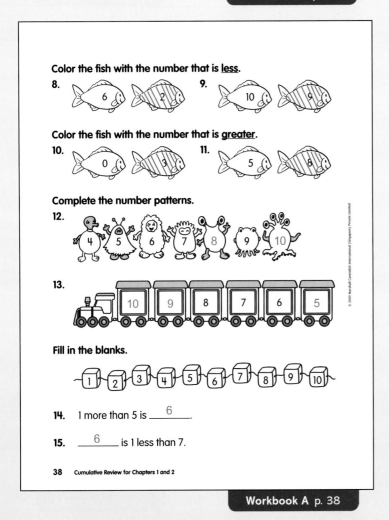

Color the fish with the number that is <u>less</u>.

8.   9.

Color the fish with the number that is <u>greater</u>.

10.   11.

Complete the number patterns.

12.   4 5 6 7 8 9 10

13.   10 9 8 7 6 5

Fill in the blanks.

1 2 3 4 5 6 7 8 9 10

14.   1 more than 5 is ___6___.

15.   ___6___ is 1 less than 7.

Workbook A p. 38

Count and complete each number bond.
Then fill in the blanks.

16.   5
2   7

___5___ and ___2___ make 7.

17.   5
3   8

___5___ and ___3___ make 8.

18.   5
4   9

___5___ and ___4___ make 9.

19.   6
4   10

___6___ and ___4___ make 10.

Workbook A p. 39

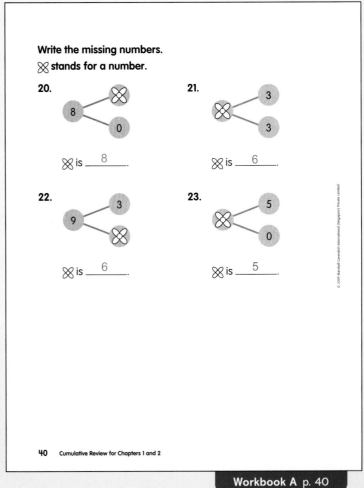

Write the missing numbers.
✗ stands for a number.

20.   8
✗   0

✗ is ___8___.

21.   ✗   3
3

✗ is ___6___.

22.   9   3
✗

✗ is ___6___.

23.   ✗   5
0

✗ is ___5___.

Workbook A p. 40

Chapter Overview

Addition Facts to 10

Math Background

Children have learned counting skills as well as the part-whole concept in number bonds of numbers within 10. These form an important basis for the learning of addition skills, which is introduced in this chapter. Addition is one of the four basic operations that form the foundation of arithmetic and is an essential part of the computation work in elementary school. The general form of an addition sentence is written as a + b = c, where a, b, and c are whole numbers.

Children's counting skills are utilized in counting on, one of the basic strategies of addition. They are led to see and understand the connection between counting and addition. Another addition strategy introduced is associated with the part-whole concept involving number bonds. Furthermore, addition stories are constructed about countable items in pictures to help children write addition sentences. This strategy is subsequently applied in solving real-world addition problems.

One of the properties of addition introduced in this chapter is the Commutative Property of Addition, which states that numbers can be added in any order and the sum will be the same. This property not only makes computation easier, but also lays the foundation for the study of algebra.

Cross-Curricular Connections

Reading/Language Arts Review with children that a sentence is a group of words that expresses an idea and makes a statement. Explain that sentences include some kind of action. Connect these ideas to addition sentences. An addition sentence makes a statement, but it uses numbers and symbols. Point out that the action

in an addition sentence is to add. Ask children to give examples of sentences and addition sentences.

Social Studies Apply the part-whole relationship to geography concepts. Discuss the relationships below and others that children may know.

Whole	Part
World→	The 7 continents
North America→	Canada, United States, Mexico
United States→	The 50 states

Skills Trace

Grade K	Represent addition stories with small whole numbers. (Chap. 17)
Grade 1	Add 2-digit to 2-digit numbers to 100. (Chaps. 3, 8, 13, and 17)
Grade 2	Add 3-digit to 3-digit numbers to 1,000. (Chaps. 2 and 10)

EVERY DAY COUNTS®
Calendar Math
The October activities provide...

Review of part and whole relationships for different numbers (Chapter 2)

Preview of subtraction concepts and the relationship between addition and subtraction (Chapter 4)

Practice of addition strategies and number stories (Lessons 1, 2, and 3 in this chapter)

Differentiation Resources

Differentiation for Special Populations

	English Language Learners	Struggling Reteach 1A	On Level Extra Practice 1A	Advanced Enrichment 1A
Lesson 1	p. 43	pp. 29–36	pp. 33–38	Enrichment pages can be used to challenge advanced children.
Lesson 2	p. 54	pp. 37–40	pp. 39–40	
Lesson 3	p. 58	pp. 41–42	pp. 41–42	

Additional Support

For English Language Learners

Select activities that reinforce the chapter vocabulary and the connections among these words, such as having children

- add terms, definitions, and examples to the Word Wall
- use manipulatives to show the meaning of terms
- draw and label a picture for each new term
- discuss the Chapter Wrap Up, encouraging children to use the chapter vocabulary

For Struggling Learners

Select activities that go back to the appropriate stage of the Concrete-Pictorial-Abstract spectrum, such as having children

- act out addition stories within the chapter
- use manipulatives to act out addition stories
- draw pictures of addition stories
- create addition stories for given addition sentences

See also pages 44, 45 and 59

If necessary, review:
- Chapter 1 (Numbers to 10)
- Chapter 2 (Number Bonds)

For Advanced Learners

See suggestions on pages 43 and 50–51.

Assessment and Remediation

Chapter 3 Assessment

Prior Knowledge		
	Resource	**Page numbers**
Quick Check	Student Book 1A	pp. 40–41
Pre-Test	Assessments 1	pp. 15–16
Ongoing Diagnostic		
Guided Practice	Student Book 1A	pp. 43, 44, 45, 48, 50, 52, 54–55, 58, 59
Common Error	Teacher's Edition 1A	pp. 46–47, 55–56, 61
Formal Evaluation		
Chapter Review/Test	Workbook 1A	pp. 59–62
Chapter 3 Test Prep	Assessments 1	pp. 17–20

Problems with these items...   Can be remediated with...

Remediation Options

Objective	Review/Test Items Workbook 1A pp. 59–62	Chapter Assessment Items Assessments 1 pp. 17–20	Reteach Reteach 1A	Student Book Student Book 1A
Use chapter vocabulary correctly.	1–5, 15–18	Not assessed	pp. 30–42	pp. 42, 53
Count on to add.	6, 9, 10–12	1–5, 8	pp. 30–32	Lesson 1
Use number bonds to add in any order.	14	12	pp. 33–36	Lesson 1
Write addition stories.	13	Not assessed	pp. 37–40	Lesson 2
Write and solve addition sentences.	13–14	6–7, 10–12	pp. 37–42	Lesson 2 and 3
Solve real-world problems.	15–16	9, 11–12	pp. 41–42	Lesson 3

Chapter Planning Guide

3 Addition Facts to 10

Lesson	Pacing	Instructional Objectives	Vocabulary
Chapter Opener pp. 39–41 *Recall Prior Knowledge* *Quick Check*	*1 day	💡**Big Idea** Addition can be used to find how many in all.	
Lesson 1, pp. 42–52 Ways to Add	3 days	• Count on to add • Use number bonds to add in any order • Write and solve addition sentences	• add • plus (+) • equal to (=) • addition sentence • more than
Lesson 2, pp. 53–56 Making Addition Stories	1 day	• Tell addition stories about pictures • Write addition sentences	• addition story
Lesson 3, pp. 57–60 Real-World Problems: Addition	1 day	• Write addition stories • Solve real-world problems	
Problem Solving p. 61 Put on Your Thinking Cap!	1 day	Thinking Skills • Analyzing parts and whole, Deduction Problem Solving Strategies • Act it out • Draw a diagram	
Chapter Wrap Up pp. 62–63	1 day	• Reinforce and consolidate chapter skills and concepts	
Chapter Assessment	1 day		

*Assume that 1 day is a 45–55 minute period.

Resources	Materials	NCTM Focal Points	NCTM Process Standards
Student Book 1A, pp. 39–41 **Assessments 1,** pp. 15–16			
Student Book 1A, pp. 42–52 **Workbook 1A,** pp. 41–50 **Extra Practice 1A,** pp. 33–38 **Reteach 1A,** pp. 29–36	• 10 connecting cubes per child • 20 counters per child, 10 of each color • 20 counters for the teacher, 10 of each color • 1 Ten Frame per child (TRO1) • Number Cards (TRO3) • 1 paper cup per child	***Number and Operations*** Develop strategies for adding and subtracting whole numbers.	Problem Solving Reasoning/Proof Communication Representation
Student Book 1A, pp. 53–56 **Workbook 1A,** pp. 51–54 **Extra Practice 1A,** pp. 39–40 **Reteach 1A,** pp. 37–40	• 10 connecting cubes per child	***Number and Operations and Algebra*** Create and use strategies to solve addition and subtraction problems involving basic facts.	Problem Solving Communication Representation
Student Book 1A, pp. 57–60 **Workbook 1A,** pp. 55–56 **Extra Practice 1A,** pp. 41–42 **Reteach 1A,** pp. 41–42	• 20 connecting cubes per child, 10 of each color	***Number and Operations and Algebra*** Create and use strategies to solve addition and subtraction problems involving basic facts.	Problem Solving Reasoning/Proof Connections
Student Book 1A, p. 61 **Workbook 1A,** pp. 57–58 **Extra Practice 1A,** pp. 43–44 **Enrichment 1A,** pp. 19–25		***Number and Operations and Algebra*** Use addition sentences to solve both routine and non-routine problems.	Problem Solving
Student Book 1A, pp. 62–63 **Workbook 1A,** pp. 59–62			
Assessments 1, pp. 17–20			

> **Technology Resources for easy classroom management**
> • *Math in Focus* eBook
> • *Math in Focus* Teaching Resources CD
> • *Math in Focus* Virtual Manipulatives
> • On-Line Web Resources

Chapter Introduction

Chapter 3 Vocabulary

add	put together two or more parts to make a whole	Lesson 1
plus (+)	the symbol used to show add	Lesson 1
equal to (=)	having the same amount or number	Lesson 1
addition sentence	arithmetic expression involving the addition operation	Lesson 1
more than	added on to	Lesson 1
addition story	a real-world situation represented by one or more addition sentences	Lesson 2

Student Book A p. 39

Big Idea (page 39)

Basic addition facts and strategies are introduced in this chapter.

- Children add by counting on and by using number bonds.

- Children learn to construct addition stories from pictures and solve real-world problems by writing addition sentences.

Chapter Opener (page 39)

The picture illustrates children riding on a school bus and two children waiting at the traffic lights. Children have learned to count and add in Kindergarten. Together with the poem, the picture can be used to tell simple addition stories.

- Show the picture with the poem. Read the poem aloud for the children. *Ask:* How many children are on the bus at the start of the poem? (1) Have children hold up one finger. Write the numeral and the number word on the board.

- Read the first stanza and then *ask:* How many children are on the bus after this? (2). Have children hold up one more finger to make 2. Write the numeral and the number word on the board.

- Repeat this until the poem is completed.

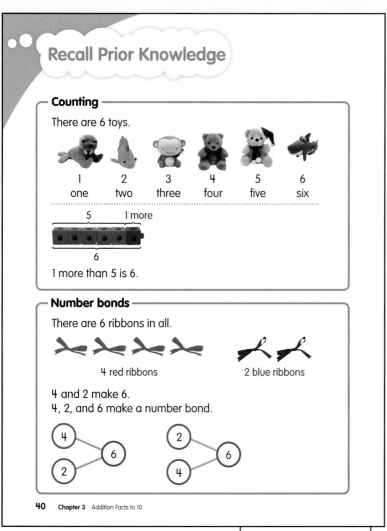

Recall Prior Knowledge

Counting

There are 6 toys.

1	2	3	4	5	6
one	two	three	four	five	six

5 — 1 more

6

1 more than 5 is 6.

Number bonds

There are 6 ribbons in all.

4 red ribbons   2 blue ribbons

4 and 2 make 6.
4, 2, and 6 make a number bond.

4
2 — 6

2
4 — 6

Student Book A p. 40

✔ Quick Check

Count.

1 1, 2, 3, **4**, **5**, **6**

2 There are **7** flowers.
1 more than 6 is **7**.

3 There are 7 butterflies in all.

5 white butterflies   **2** black butterflies

Complete the number bonds.

4 5 and 2 make 7.
What other numbers make 7?

0
7 — 7

1
6 — 7

3
4 — 7

Student Book A p. 41

Recall Prior Knowledge (page 40)

Counting

Children learned in Chapter 1 to count objects up to 10.

- Have children count the objects on the page. *Ask:* How many toys are there? (6)

- Have children count the red connecting cubes in the number train. (5) Help children to see that 1 more than 5 is 6.

- Draw the number bond 5-1—6 on the board.

Number bonds

Children learned number bonds in Chapter 2.

- Have children count the red ribbons and the blue ribbons. *Say:* 4 and 2 make 6. Draw the number bond on the board.

- *Say:* 2 and 4 also make 6. Draw the number bond on the board.

- Have children provide all possible number bonds for 6.

✔ Quick Check (page 41)

Use this section as a diagnostic tool to assess children's level of prerequisite knowledge before they progress to this chapter. Exercise **1** checks that children can complete a number pattern by counting on. Exercises **2** and **3** check counting skills and ability to find 1 more. Exercise **4** checks that children can write number bonds for 7.

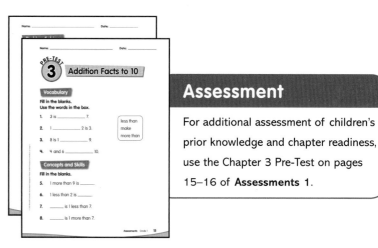

Assessment

For additional assessment of children's prior knowledge and chapter readiness, use the Chapter 3 Pre-Test on pages 15–16 of **Assessments** 1.

Assessments 1 pp. 15–16

LESSON 1 Ways to Add

LESSON OBJECTIVES
- Count on to add.
- Use number bonds to add in any order.
- Write and solve addition sentences.

TECHNOLOGY RESOURCES
- *Math in Focus* eBook
- *Math in Focus* Teaching Resources CD
- *Math in Focus* Virtual Manipulatives

Vocabulary

add	addition sentence
plus (+)	more than
equal to (=)	

DAY 1 Student Book 1A, pp. 42–45

MATERIALS
- 10 connecting cubes per child
- 20 counters per child, 10 of each color
- 20 counters for the teacher, 10 each of each color
- 1 Ten Frame per child (TR01)
- Number cards (TR03)
- 1 paper cup per child

DAY 2 Student Book 1A, pp. 46–47
Workbook 1A, pp. 41–44

DIFFERENTIATION RESOURCES
- Reteach 1A, pp. 29–32
- Extra Practice 1A, pp. 33–34

DAY 3 Student Book 1A, pp. 48–52
Workbook 1A, pp. 45–50

DIFFERENTIATION RESOURCES
- Reteach 1A, pp. 33–36
- Extra Practice 1A, pp. 35–38

 5-minute Warm Up

Prepare a set of number trains for numbers 1 through 5 using different colored connecting cubes. Join the 1-4 trains and 2-3 trains. Have children count the cubes in each part and the whole as you write the number bonds 1-4—5, 2-3—5, and 5-0—5 on the board.

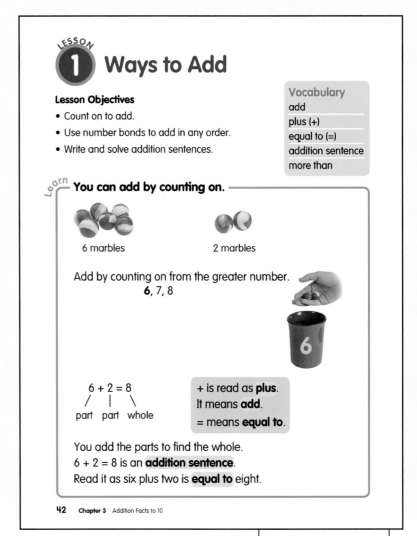

LESSON 1 Ways to Add

Lesson Objectives
- Count on to add.
- Use number bonds to add in any order.
- Write and solve addition sentences.

Vocabulary
add
plus (+)
equal to (=)
addition sentence
more than

Learn You can add by counting on.

6 marbles   2 marbles

Add by counting on from the greater number.
6, 7, 8

$6 + 2 = 8$
part part whole

+ is read as **plus**.
It means **add**.
= means **equal to**.

You add the parts to find the whole.
$6 + 2 = 8$ is an **addition sentence**.
Read it as six plus two is **equal to** eight.

42 Chapter 3 Addition Facts to 10

Student Book A p. 42

DAY 1 # Teach

Learn

Add by Counting On (page 42)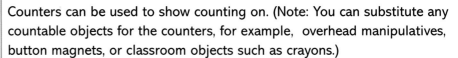

Counters can be used to show counting on. (Note: You can substitute any countable objects for the counters, for example, overhead manipulatives, button magnets, or classroom objects such as crayons.)

- Make a group of 5 **counters**. Have children count them. Then, place 2 more counters of a different color in a separate group. **Ask:** What is $5 + 2$? (7)

- Model counting on from the greater number, 5. **Say:** 5, 6, 7, as you shift each of the 2 counters to join the first group.

- Write on the board: $5 + 2 = 7$. Explain the symbols used.

- Emphasize to children that to find $5 + 2$, they should always start counting on from the greater number.

- Put 6 counters in a paper cup. Write '6' on the paper cup. **Say:** I'm going to add 2 counters to the cup to find out what is $6 + 2$. Now drop 2 more counters into the cup as you count aloud from 6: 6, 7, 8.

- Write the addition sentence on the board and explain the symbols used.

- Help children see the part-whole relationship among the three numbers in a number sentence.

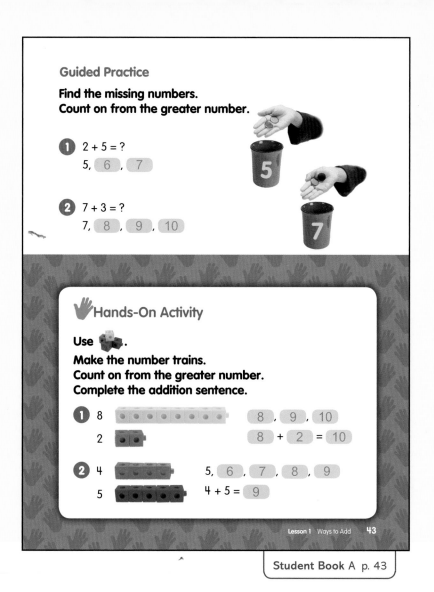

Guided Practice

Find the missing numbers.
Count on from the greater number.

1 2 + 5 = ?
5, 6 , 7

2 7 + 3 = ?
7, 8 , 9 , 10

Hands-On Activity

Use 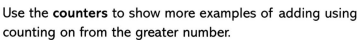.
Make the number trains.
Count on from the greater number.
Complete the addition sentence.

1 8
2
8 , 9 , 10
8 + 2 = 10

2 4
5
5, 6 , 7 , 8 , 9
4 + 5 = 9

Lesson 1 Ways to Add   **43**

Student Book A p. 43

Problem of the Lesson

Problem of the Lesson

Amy has 3 crackers.
Bert gives her 3 crackers.
How many crackers does Amy have now?

Solution 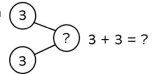 3 + 3 = ?

Answer: 6; Amy has 6 crackers now.

Differentiated Instruction

English Language Learners

Use the pictures on the pages to introduce words that children need to know. Point to and say *lemon, paper clip, monkey, bee*. Ask children to say the words a few times and correct pronunciation as necessary. To further develop meaning, use each word in a sentence or ask a question, for example, "A lemon is a fruit."

For Advanced Learners When children are familiar with the counting on strategy, provide other addition sentences, and encourage them to take turns to form number trains and demonstrate counting on to each other.

Check for Understanding
✓Guided Practice (page 43)

Use the **counters** to show more examples of adding using counting on from the greater number.

1 Lead children to see that this strategy can be used even if the addition sentence begins with a smaller number: 2 + 5 =?

2 This reinforces the strategy by adding 3 to 7.

Hands-On Activity:
Count On To Add Using Connecting Cubes
(page 43)

This activity reinforces the counting on strategy.
- For Exercise **1**, have children count the connecting cubes in the longer number train first, then count on to add 2 cubes. Write the sequence and addition sentence on the board. Count all the cubes from 1 again.

- For Exercise **2**, model counting the cubes in the longer number train first. Then count on to add cubes from the other train. Write the number sequence: 5, 6, 7, 8, 9 and the addition sentence on the board. Have children count all the cubes in the two trains again.

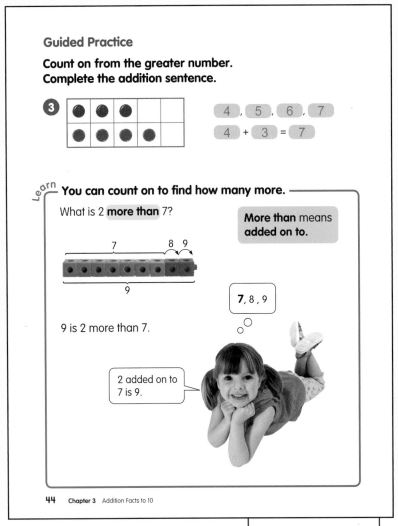

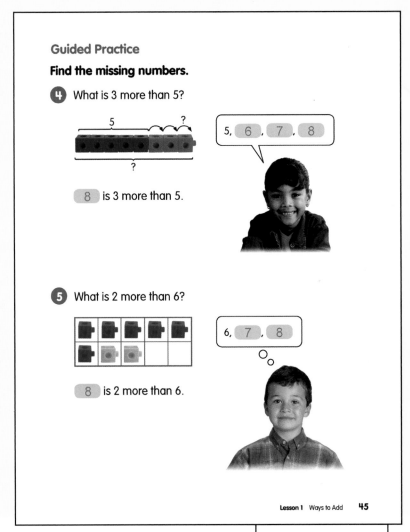

✓ **Guided Practice** (page 44) ⬤⬤ ▦

③ Using a **Ten Frame** (TRO1) and **counters**, model the picture on the Student Book page and have children count on from the greater number to add. Write the sequence and addition sentence on the board.

ᴸᵉᵃʳⁿ
Count On to Find How Many More

(page 44) 🎲

- Show children a 7-cube number train. Ask them to count along with you the cubes in the train.

- **Ask:** What is 2 more than 7? (9) Write this on the board.

- **Say:** There are 7 cubes in this number train.

- Add two cubes of another color to the train, and as you do so, count on from 7 to 9.

- Lead children to see that 2 more than 7 means 2 added on to 7. **Say:** 2 more than 7 is 9.

✓ **Guided Practice** (page 45) 🎲

Encourage children to find the answers by using **connecting cubes** to practice counting on and using the term *more than* in adding.

④ Have children build a 5-cube number train and add 3 cubes to it. Lead children to count on and *say:* 8 is 3 more than 5.

⑤ Place **connecting cubes** on the **Ten Frame** (TRO1) before counting.

For Struggling Learners You might want to display a counting tape for the numbers 1 through 10 for children to use to count on. Blank Counting Tapes can be found in the Teaching Resources section.

Student Book A p. 46

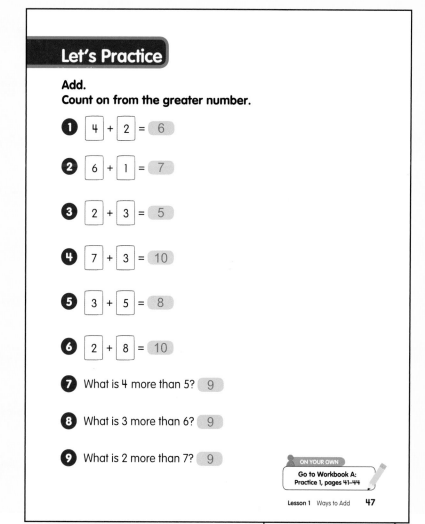

Student Book A p. 47

Teach

See the Lesson Organizer on page 42 for Day 2 resources.

 **Game:**

Card Fun! (page 46)

Play this game with children to reinforce the strategy of counting on for addition.

- Distribute the two packs of **Number Cards** (TR03) to groups of 3 children. Explain the instructions in the Student Book. Children take turns to play.

- Encourage children to use the counting on strategy to find the answer. Have Player 3 do the counting on aloud before giving the answer.

- Check that children use the counting on strategy to do the addition.

Let's Practice (page 47)

This activity provides children more practice with adding by counting on.

- Remind children to begin counting on from the greater number, regardless of which number comes first in the addition sentence.

- For Exercises **7** to **9**, show children that finding a number more than another number involves counting on from the greater number.

Common Error Some children may lose track of the numbers when they count on. First have them record the number they are counting on from. Suggest that they physically keep track of the numbers they have counted, using counters, tally marks, or their fingers.

ON YOUR OWN

Children practice adding by counting on in Practice 1, pp. 41–44 of **Workbook 1A**. These pages (with the answers) are shown on page 47A.

Differentiation Options Depending on children's success with the Workbook pages, use these materials as needed.
Struggling: Reteach 1A, pp. 29–32
On Level: Extra Practice 1A, pp. 33–34

Practice and Apply
Workbook pages for Chapter 3, Lesson 1

Name: _____ Date: _____

CHAPTER 3 Addition Facts to 10

Practice 1   Ways to Add
Add. Count on from the greater number.

Example

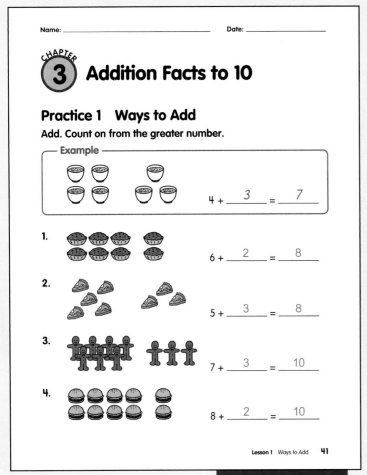

$4 + \underline{3} = \underline{7}$

1. $6 + \underline{2} = \underline{8}$

2. $5 + \underline{3} = \underline{8}$

3. $7 + \underline{3} = \underline{10}$

4. $8 + \underline{2} = \underline{10}$

Lesson 1   Ways to Add   **41**

Workbook A p. 41

Name: _____ Date: _____

Count on to add.

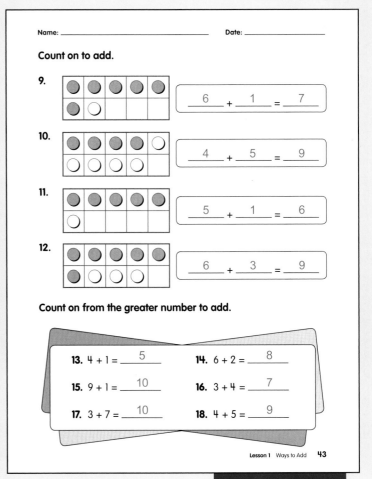

9. $\underline{6} + \underline{1} = \underline{7}$

10. $\underline{4} + \underline{5} = \underline{9}$

11. $\underline{5} + \underline{1} = \underline{6}$

12. $\underline{6} + \underline{3} = \underline{9}$

Count on from the greater number to add.

13. $4 + 1 = \underline{5}$ 14. $6 + 2 = \underline{8}$

15. $9 + 1 = \underline{10}$ 16. $3 + 4 = \underline{7}$

17. $3 + 7 = \underline{10}$ 18. $4 + 5 = \underline{9}$

Lesson 1   Ways to Add   **43**

Workbook A p. 43

Look at the pictures.
Add. Count on from the greater number.

Example

$\underline{1} + \underline{3} = \underline{4}$

5. $\underline{4} + \underline{4} = \underline{8}$

6. $\underline{2} + \underline{3} = \underline{5}$

7. $\underline{3} + \underline{7} = \underline{10}$

8. $\underline{9} + \underline{1} = \underline{10}$

42   Chapter 3   Addition Facts to 10

Workbook A p. 42

Name: _____ Date: _____

Complete.
Write the answer in each ☐.

Example

| 1 more than 1 | → | 1 + 1 | → | 2 |

19. | 2 more than 6 | → | 6 + 2 | → | 8 |

20. | 4 more than 5 | → | 5 + 4 | → | 9 |

21. | 3 more than 7 | → | 7 + 3 | → | 10 |

22. | 2 more than 8 | → | 8 + 2 | → | 10 |

44   Chapter 3   Addition Facts to 10

Workbook A p. 44

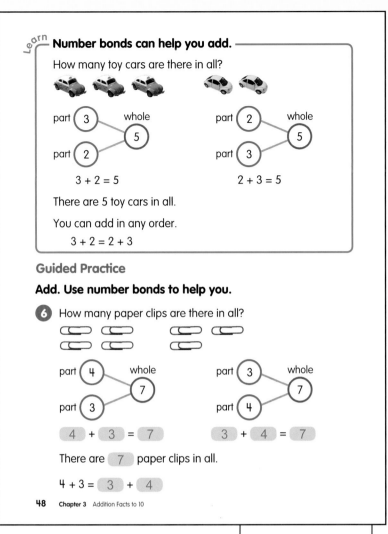

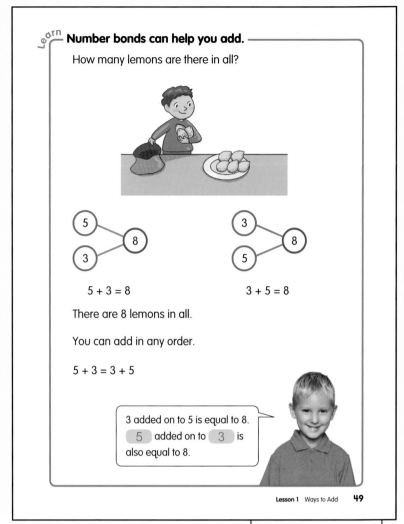

DAY 3 Teach

See the Lesson Organizer on page 42 for Day 2 resources.

Learn

Add Using Number Bonds (page 48)

This part of the lesson relates the part-whole concept in number bonds to addition. The Commutative Property of Addition (2 + 3 = 3 + 2) is highlighted in this and subsequent sections as well.

- Have children count the green toy cars and yellow toy cars separately.

- Lead children to see that 3 green cars and 2 yellow cars make 5 toy cars.

- Have children see that 3 and 2 are parts where 5 is the whole in both the number bonds as well as the addition sentence.

- Remind children that just as 3-2—5 and 2-3—5 are the same, 3 + 2 is the same as 2 + 3. Since you can add in any order, you can write 3 + 2 = 2 + 3.

✓ Guided Practice (page 48)

6 This exercise helps children to relate number bonds to addition sentences.

- Have children count the red and blue paper clips separately.

- Lead them to see that 4 red clips and 3 blue clips make 7 clips in all.

- Guide children to complete the addition sentences and reiterate that they can add in any order.

Learn

Add Using Number Bonds (page 49)

- Use the part-whole strategy using two groups of lemons to explain the concept of adding on.

- Have children recall that the parts and whole in number bonds are the same in addition sentences, and that they add in any order.

- Write the addition sentence 5 + 3 = 8 on the boa[rd] children to see that the sentence can be read as equal to 8, or 3 added on to 5 is equal to 8 o[r] 3 is equal to 8.

C[H]

Add.
Use number bonds to help you.

7 How many monkeys are there in all?

3 + 4 = 7   4 + 3 = 7

There are 7 monkeys in all.

You can add in any order.

3 + 4 = 4 + 3

> 4 added on to 3 is equal to 7.
> 3 added on to 4 is also equal to 7.

Student Book A p. 50

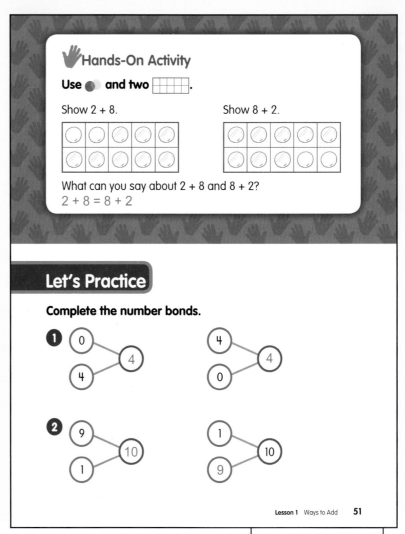

✋**Hands-On Activity**

Use ● and two ▭.

Show 2 + 8.   Show 8 + 2.

What can you say about 2 + 8 and 8 + 2?
2 + 8 = 8 + 2

Let's Practice

Complete the number bonds.

1
0, 4 → 4   4, 0 → 4

2
9, 1 → 10   1, 9 → 10

Student Book A p. 51

Best Practices This lesson provides two strategies for adding: counting on and using number bonds. You may want to teach one method at a time and follow with Workbook practice. After children are familiar with both strategies, ask which method they prefer. Suggest that they use the preferred method later in the chapter to solve story problems.

✓**Guided Practice** (page 50)

7 Explain the adding on strategy using a group of monkeys playing and another group of monkeys going to join them.

• **Say**: There are two groups of monkeys; one group is joining the other group. Remind children that they can add in any

✋**Hands-On Activity:**

Use Ten Frames To Add (Commutative Property) (page 51)

• Have children work in pairs and give each child a **Ten Frame** (TR01) and 20 **counters** of two different colors.

• Ask one child to show 2 + 8 using different colored counters, and the other child to show 8 + 2.

• Lead them to see that 2 + 8 = 8 + 2.

For Advanced Learners Have children use their ten frames and counters to find other examples of the Commutative Property using other facts for 10, such as 0, 10 and 10, 0; 1, 9 and 9, 1; 3, 7 and 7, 3; 4, 6 and 6, 4.

Let's Practice (pages 51 and 52)

1 to **4** Through this exercise set, children will see the direct relationship between number bonds and addition. Furthermore, children will encounter more examples that show the Commutative Property of Addition.

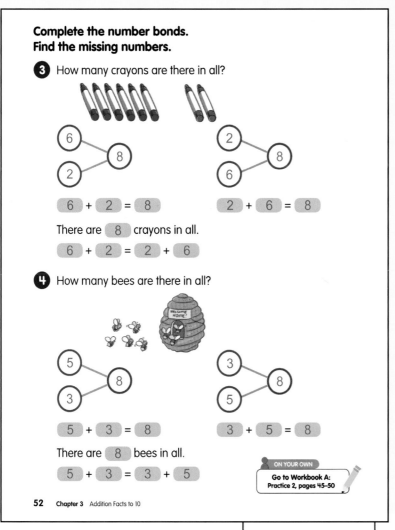

Complete the number bonds.
Find the missing numbers.

3 How many crayons are there in all?

6 + 2 = 8

2 + 6 = 8

There are 8 crayons in all.

6 + 2 = 2 + 6

4 How many bees are there in all?

5 + 3 = 8

3 + 5 = 8

There are 8 bees in all.

5 + 3 = 3 + 5

ON YOUR OWN

Go to Workbook A:
Practice 2, pages 45–50

52 Chapter 3 Addition Facts to 10

Student Book A p. 52

ON YOUR OWN

Children practice adding with number bonds in Practice 2, pp. 45–50 of **Workbook 1A**. These pages (with the answers) are shown at the right and on page 52A.

Differentiation Options Depending on children's success with the Workbook pages, use these materials as needed.
Struggling: Reteach 1A, pp. 33–36
On Level: Extra Practice 1A, pp. 35–38

Practice and Apply
Workbook pages for Chapter 3, Lesson 1

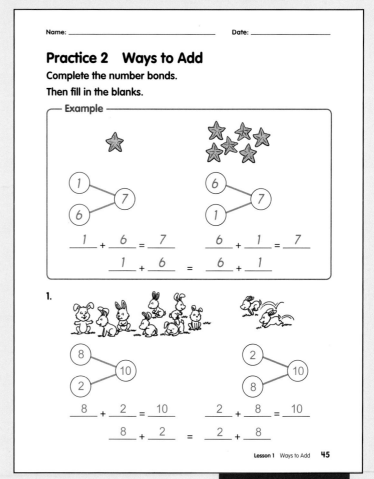

Name: _____   Date: _____

Practice 2   Ways to Add
Complete the number bonds.
Then fill in the blanks.

— Example —

1 + 6 = 7

6 + 1 = 7

1 + 6 = 6 + 1

1.

8 + 2 = 10

2 + 8 = 10

8 + 2 = 2 + 8

Lesson 1 Ways to Add 45

Workbook A p. 45

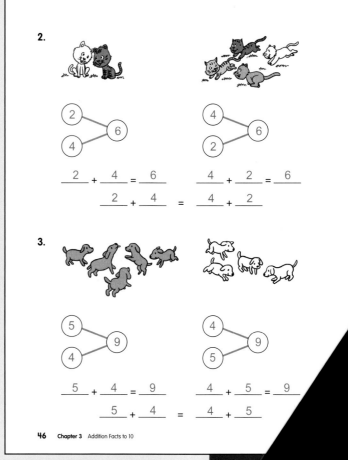

2.

2 + 4 = 6

4 + 2 = 6

2 + 4 = 4 + 2

3.

5 + 4 = 9

4 + 5 = 9

5 + 4 = 4 + 5

46 Chapter 3 Addition Facts to 10

Work

Workbook A p. 47

Complete the number bonds.
Then fill in the blanks.

4. $1 + \underline{4} = 5$ ☺ ☺☺☺☺

5. $4 + \underline{1} = 5$ ☺☺☺☺ ☺

6. $\underline{3} + 5 = 8$ ☺☺ ☺☺ ☺☺☺

7. $\underline{5} + 3 = 8$ ☺☺☺ ☺☺ ☺☺☺

8. $10 + \underline{0} = 10$ ☺☺☺☺☺ ☺☺☺☺☺

9. $\underline{0} + 10 = 10$ ☺☺☺☺☺ ☺☺☺☺☺

Lesson 1 Ways to Add   **47**

Workbook A p. 49

Add.
You can draw number bonds to help you.

15.

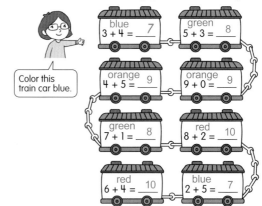

Color this train car blue.

blue $3 + 4 = \underline{7}$ green $5 + 3 = \underline{8}$

orange $4 + 5 = \underline{9}$ orange $9 + 0 = \underline{9}$

green $7 + 1 = \underline{8}$ red $8 + 2 = \underline{10}$

red $6 + 4 = \underline{10}$ blue $2 + 5 = \underline{7}$

Now color the train cars above.
Then fill in the table with your answers.

16.

If your answer is	Color	Number of train cars
7	blue	2
8	green	2
9	orange	2
10	red	2

Lesson 1 Ways to Add   **49**

Workbook A p. 48

Help each Momma Butterfly find her babies!
Color the small butterflies that match her number.

10. 5 $1+4$ $4+1$ $3+3$

11. 8 $2+7$ $3+5$ $5+3$

12. 7 $7+0$ $0+7$ $3+5$

 $3+2$ $5+1$

 $1+8$ $4+5$

Workbook A p. 50

Solve.

17. A ball falls into the number machine.
Which ball is it?
Write the correct number on the ball below.

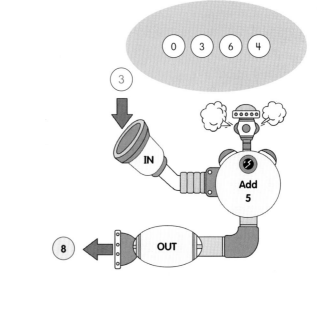

0 3 6 4

3

IN

Add 5

8 OUT

50 Chapter 3 Addition Facts to 10

LESSON 2 Making Addition Stories

LESSON OBJECTIVES
- Tell addition stories about pictures.
- Write addition sentences.

TECHNOLOGY RESOURCES
- *Math in Focus* eBook
- *Math in Focus* Teaching Resources CD
- *Math in Focus* Virtual Manipulatives

Vocabulary
addition story

DAY 1 | Student Book 1A, pp. 53–56
Workbook 1A, pp. 51–54

MATERIALS
- 10 connecting cubes per child

DIFFERENTIATION RESOURCES
- Reteach 1A, pp. 37–40
- Extra Practice 1A, pp. 39–40

 5-minute Warm Up

Have children work in pairs.

- Ask one child to hold up any number of fingers in one hand.
- Ask the other child to do the same.
- Have children add the two numbers to find the total.

Problem of the Lesson

There are 3 birds in a tree.
4 more birds fly to the tree.
How many birds are in the tree in all?

Solution

$$3 \quad 7 \quad 4$$

Answer: 7; There are 7 birds in all.

LESSON 2 Making Addition Stories

Lesson Objectives
- Tell addition stories about pictures.
- Write addition sentences.

Vocabulary
addition story

Learn **You can tell addition stories about a picture.**

5 🦆 are in a pond.
4 🦆 join them.

$5 + 4 = 9$

There are 9 🦆 in all.

Student Book A p. 53

DAY 1 **Teach**

Learn **Tell Addition Stories about a Picture** (page 53)

- Tell a story about the ducklings in the Student Book. Use connecting cubes to represent the ducklings and write the addition sentence on the board.

Best Practices You may wish to put children in pairs to complete this lesson. Children can take turns describing the pictures and telling stories orally then partners discuss and agree upon numbers to be used in the story. Finally, they complete the number stories.

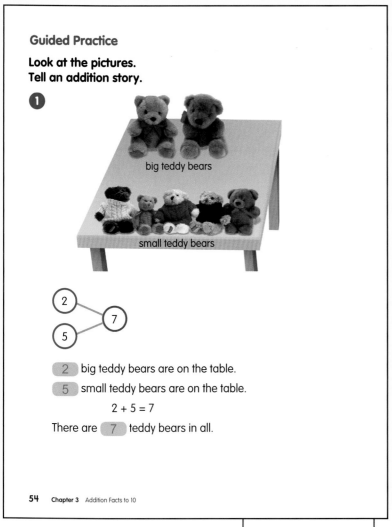

Guided Practice

Look at the pictures.
Tell an addition story.

1

big teddy bears

small teddy bears

Number bond: 2, 5 → 7

[2] big teddy bears are on the table.

[5] small teddy bears are on the table.

2 + 5 = 7

There are [7] teddy bears in all.

Student Book A p. 54

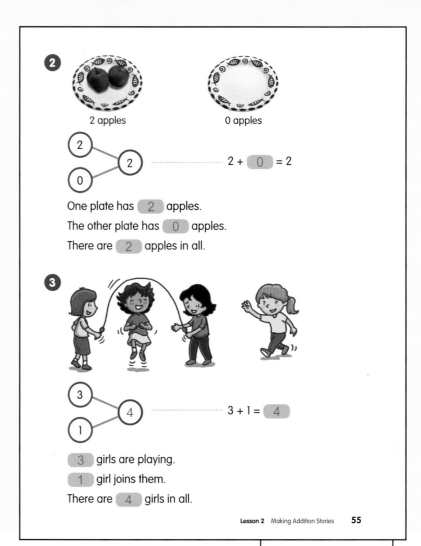

2

2 apples   0 apples

Number bond: 2, 0 → 2   2 + [0] = 2

One plate has [2] apples.

The other plate has [0] apples.

There are [2] apples in all.

3

Number bond: 3, 1 → 4   3 + 1 = [4]

[3] girls are playing.

[1] girl joins them.

There are [4] girls in all.

Student Book A p. 55

Check for Understanding

✓ Guided Practice (pages 54 and 55)

1 to **3** Have children study the pictures. Encourage them to tell a story from each picture.

• Lead children to see how number bonds are related to the addition sentences. Write the number bonds and the addition sentences on the board.

• Read with children the statements used in telling the story and relate them to the concepts learnt such as *adding on* and *part* and *whole*.

Let's Practice

Look at the picture.
Tell an addition story about each thing.

1 the birds

2 the bicycles

3 the turtles

Answers vary.

ON YOUR OWN
Go to Workbook A:
Practice 3, pages 51–54

56 Chapter 3 Addition Facts to 10

Student Book A p. 56

Differentiated Instruction

English Language Learners

Some children may need help with vocabulary and sentence structure before writing story problems. Using the picture on page 56, ask children to find: birds (in the nest/flying) red/blue bicycles, turtles (on the rocks/swimming). Record these words on the board along with *There are/is* _____. Model writing a problem for children and help them as necessary with the other two story problems.

Let's Practice (page 56)

This activity allows children to practice constructing addition stories when given a picture.

- Encourage children to name the objects in the picture. Lead them to count the objects that they see.

- *Ask:* How many baby birds are in the nest? (4) How many birds fly to join the baby birds? (1) How many birds are there in all? (5)

- As children answer your questions, write the answers on the board in the form of number bonds and addition sentences.

- Encourage volunteers to tell addition stories about the bicycles and turtles, and to write the number bonds and addition sentences on the board.

Common Error Some children may correctly identify the numbers to use in the story problems, but incorrectly add. Review how to use objects or count on to add. Remind them to check their answers.

ON YOUR OWN

Children practice adding with number bonds in Practice 3, pp. 51–54 of **Workbook 1A**. These pages (with the answers) are shown on page 56A.

Differentiation Options Depending on children's success with the Workbook pages, use these materials as needed.
Struggling: Reteach 1A, pp. 37–40
On Level: Extra Practice 1A, pp. 39–40

Practice and Apply
Workbook pages for Chapter 3, Lesson 2

Name: _____ Date: _____

Practice 3   Making Addition Stories
Use the pictures to make addition stories.
Use number bonds to help you.

Example

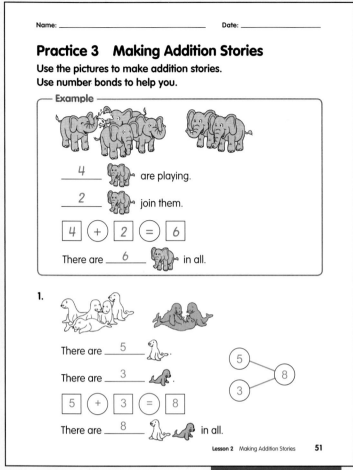

_____4_____ 🐘 are playing.

_____2_____ 🐘 join them.

| 4 | + | 2 | = | 6 |

There are _____6_____ 🐘 in all.

1.

There are _____5_____ 🦭 .

There are _____3_____ 🦭 .

| 5 | + | 3 | = | 8 |

5, 3 → 8

There are _____8_____ 🦭🦭 in all.

Name: _____ Date: _____

4.

Sonia has _____2_____ 🍪 .

She buys _____2_____ ⭐ .

| 2 | + | 2 | = | 4 |

Sonia has _____4_____ ⭐ in all.

5.

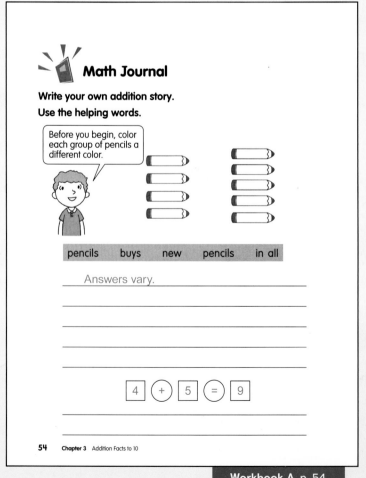

There are _____5_____ 🐟 .

There are _____0_____ 🐟 .

| 5 | + | 0 | = | 5 |

There are _____5_____ 🐟 in all.

2.

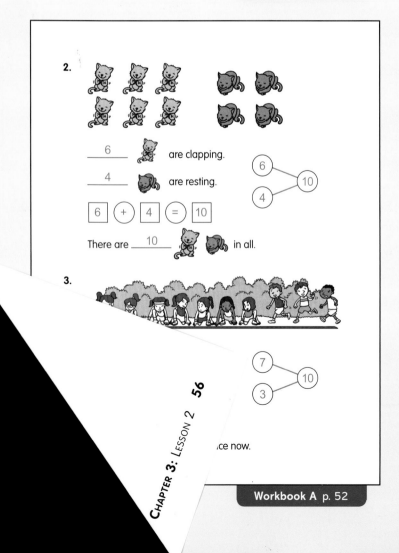

_____6_____ 🐱 are clapping.

_____4_____ 🐶 are resting.

6, 4 → 10

| 6 | + | 4 | = | 10 |

There are _____10_____ 🐱🐶 in all.

3.

7, 3 → 10

...ce now.

📓 Math Journal

Write your own addition story.
Use the helping words.

Before you begin, color each group of pencils a different color.

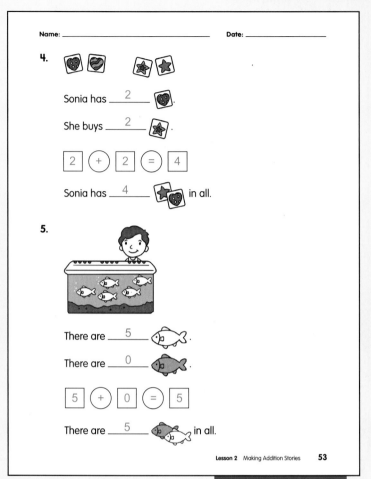

| pencils | buys | new | pencils | in all |

_____Answers vary._____

_____

_____

_____

_____

| 4 | + | 5 | = | 9 |

_____

LESSON 3 Real-World Problems: Addition

LESSON OBJECTIVES
- Write addition sentences.
- Solve real-world problems.

TECHNOLOGY RESOURCES
- *Math in Focus* eBook
- *Math in Focus* Teaching Resources CD
- *Math in Focus* Virtual Manipulatives

DAY 1 Student Book 1A, pp. 57–60
Workbook 1A, pp. 55–56

MATERIALS
- 20 connecting cubes per child, 10 of each color

DIFFERENTIATION RESOURCES
- Reteach 1A, pp. 41–42
- Extra Practice 1A, pp. 41–42

5-minute Warm Up

- Connect 5 **connecting cubes** of the same color and place them as a tower on a table. Connect 4 cubes of another color and place them as another tower on the table. *Ask:* How many cubes are there in all? (9)

- Write the number bond and number sentence on the board.

- Repeat, asking a child to make the two towers of different colors for the other children to see and answer.

LESSON 3 Real-World Problems: Addition

Lesson Objectives
- Write addition sentences.
- Solve real-world problems.

Learn Read and understand a word problem.

6 girls are playing.
3 boys are playing with them.
How many children are playing in all?

$6 + 3 = 9$ ....

9 children are playing in all.

Student Book A p. 57

DAY 1 # Teach

Learn

Read and Understand a Word Problem
(page 57)

Children have learned to write addition stories and addition sentences. In this lesson, children will interpret real-world addition problems with the help of pictures, to solve part-whole and adding on problems using number bonds.

- Display the picture without the problem.

- Encourage children to construct an addition story. If necessary, *ask:* How many girls are playing? (3) How many boys are playing? (6)

- Read aloud the word problem for children.

- *Ask:* How many children are playing in all? (9)

- Write the addition sentence and number bond on the board.

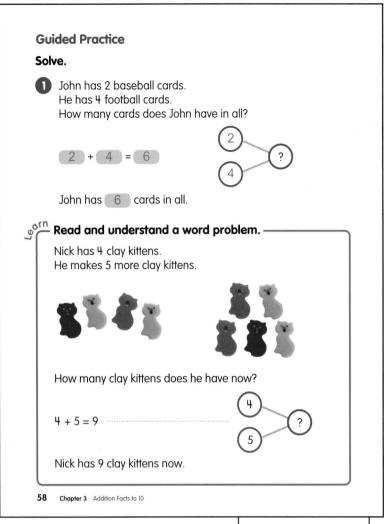

Guided Practice

Solve.

1 John has 2 baseball cards.
He has 4 football cards.
How many cards does John have in all?

2 + 4 = 6

John has 6 cards in all.

Learn **Read and understand a word problem.**

Nick has 4 clay kittens.
He makes 5 more clay kittens.

How many clay kittens does he have now?

4 + 5 = 9

Nick has 9 clay kittens now.

Student Book A p. 58

Problem of the Lesson

There are 4 children at a party.
2 more children join the party.
Mrs. Long gives each child a hat.
How many hats does Mrs. Long give away?

Solution

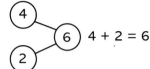

4 + 2 = 6

Answer: Mrs. Long gives away 6 hats.

Differentiated Instruction

English Language Learners

You may want to take advantage of the opportunity to introduce words that relate to zero. Write **zero** and **O** on the board. **Say:** Mary has **no** apples on her plate. She has **zero** apples. Demonstrate the use of other words that indicate zero, such as **nothing** and **no one**. Use examples such as, "Nothing is on the table." or "No one is at the playground."

Check for Understanding
✓ **Guided Practice** (page 58)

1 Help children read and understand the part-whole word problem.

• Read aloud the problem once.

• Read each sentence again, and guide children to fill in the number bond and addition sentence as each sentence of the word problem is read.

For Struggling Learners You may want to write number sentences with word labels on the board to help students see how the story translates to a number sentence. For example, in Exercise **1**, you might write *2 baseball cards and 4 football cards make how many cards in all?* before writing 2 + 4 = 6.

Best Practices Since this lesson requires children to read story problems, you may want to pair more fluent readers with those who are less fluent. Provide counters for those who want them. Allow partners to work together to solve the problems and share the strategies they use to add.

Learn
Read and Understand a Word Problem
(page 58)

Building on what has been learned in the previous part of the lesson, this learn focuses on the concept of addition being *more*.

• Read aloud the first two sentences of the word problem.

• Direct children's attention to the additional 5 kittens added to the 4 clay kittens.

• Lead children to solve the problem using the number bond and the addition sentence.

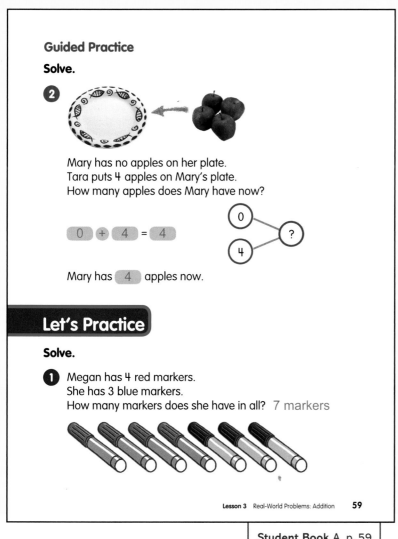

Guided Practice

Solve.

2

Mary has no apples on her plate.
Tara puts 4 apples on Mary's plate.
How many apples does Mary have now?

0 + 4 = 4

Mary has 4 apples now.

Let's Practice

Solve.

1 Megan has 4 red markers.
She has 3 blue markers.
How many markers does she have in all? 7 markers

Student Book A p. 59

2 2 children are dancing.
7 children join them.
How many children are dancing now? 9 children

3

Jar A   Jar B

Jar A has 5 marbles.
Jar B has 0 marbles.
How many marbles are there in all? 5 marbles

ON YOUR OWN

Go to Workbook A:
Practice 4, pages 55–56

Student Book A p. 60

✓ Guided Practice (page 59)

2 Help children recall that *no apples* is the same as *0 apples*.

• Lead children to solve the problem using the number bond and addition sentence.

Let's Practice (pages 59 and 60)

In these exercises, children are free to use either the strategies of **counting on** or **number bonds** to solve the problems.
1 Tests the part-whole concept, **2** Tests the adding on concept and **3** 0 as an identity element for addition.

• Have children attempt to solve Exercises **1** to **3** individually.

• Then ask children how they found their answers.

ON YOUR OWN

Children practice solving real-world problems in Practice 4, pp. 55–56 of **Workbook 1A**. These pages (with the answers) are shown on page 61.

Differentiation Options Depending on children's success with the Workbook pages, use these materials as needed.
Struggling: Reteach 1A, pp. 41–42
On Level: Extra Practice 1A, pp. 41–42

Practice and Apply

Workbook pages for Chapter 3, Lesson 3

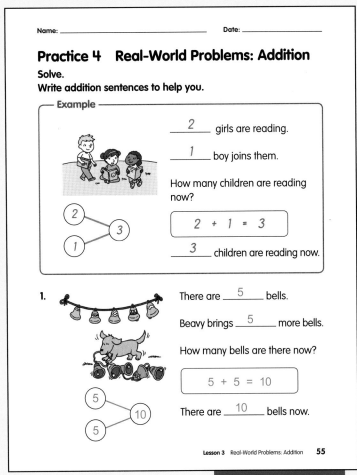

Name: _____   Date: _____

Practice 4   Real-World Problems: Addition

Solve.
Write addition sentences to help you.

Example

_____2_____ girls are reading.

_____1_____ boy joins them.

How many children are reading now?

2 — 3 — 1

| 2 + 1 = 3 |

_____3_____ children are reading now.

1.

There are __5__ bells.

Beavy brings __5__ more bells.

How many bells are there now?

| 5 + 5 = 10 |

5 — 10 — 5

There are __10__ bells now.

Workbook A p. 55

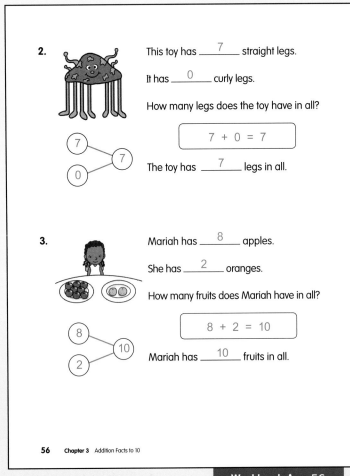

2.

This toy has __7__ straight legs.

It has __0__ curly legs.

How many legs does the toy have in all?

| 7 + 0 = 7 |

7 — 7 — 0

The toy has __7__ legs in all.

3.

Mariah has __8__ apples.

She has __2__ oranges.

How many fruits does Mariah have in all?

| 8 + 2 = 10 |

8 — 10 — 2

Mariah has __10__ fruits in all.

Workbook A p. 56

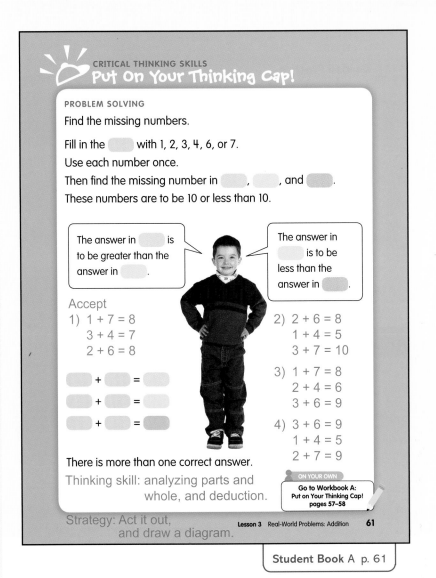

CRITICAL THINKING SKILLS
Put On Your Thinking Cap!

PROBLEM SOLVING

Find the missing numbers.

Fill in the ▢ with 1, 2, 3, 4, 6, or 7.
Use each number once.
Then find the missing number in ▢, ▢, and ▢.
These numbers are to be 10 or less than 10.

The answer in ▢ is to be greater than the answer in ▢.

The answer in ▢ is to be less than the answer in ▢.

Accept
1) $1 + 7 = 8$
$3 + 4 = 7$
$2 + 6 = 8$

▢ + ▢ = ▢

▢ + ▢ = ▢

▢ + ▢ = ▢

2) $2 + 6 = 8$
$1 + 4 = 5$
$3 + 7 = 10$

3) $1 + 7 = 8$
$2 + 4 = 6$
$3 + 6 = 9$

4) $3 + 6 = 9$
$1 + 4 = 5$
$2 + 7 = 9$

There is more than one correct answer.

Thinking skill: analyzing parts and whole, and deduction.

Strategy: Act it out, and draw a diagram.

ON YOUR OWN
Go to Workbook A:
Put on Your Thinking Cap!
pages 57–58

Lesson 3   Real-World Problems: Addition   **61**

Student Book A p. 61

CRITICAL THINKING AND PROBLEM SOLVING
Put on Your Thinking Cap! (page 61)

- Read and explain the steps to children, paying attention to 'Use each number once.' and the concepts of *greater than* and *less than*.

- Model the problem-solving process strategies of Act it out and Draw a diagram.

- Write the three number sentences containing blanks on the board.

- Ask a volunteer to give three numbers that form the first addition sentence. Have other children use number bonds or counting on to check if the sentence is correct.

- Have another child give three other numbers (different from the first two numbers) to form the second addition sentence. Have the other children check again.

- Guide children to check if the answer in the first sentence is greater than the second. If so, go on to guess three more numbers for the third sentence. If not, switch the first and second addition sentences.

- Encourage children to try out other combinations of numbers that are possible answers to the problem.

Practice and Apply

Workbook pages for Put on Your Thinking Cap!

Name: _____   Date: _____

Put On Your Thinking Cap!
Challenging Practice

Solve.

Ivy and Reena have 10 prizes in all.
They do not have the same number of prizes.
How many prizes can Reena have?

There is more than one correct answer!

Reena can have _____ prizes.

Accept 1; 2; 3; 4; 6; 7; 8; 9.

Thinking skills: Analyzing parts and whole, and deduction
Strategy: Make suppositions

Workbook A p. 57

Thinking Skills

• Analysing parts and whole   • Deduction

Problem Solving Strategies

• Act it out   • Draw a diagram

Common Error Some children may not understand the directions in the Put on Your Thinking Cap! activity. Demonstrate a possible answer, and then have children find a different answer. Show the following: 1 + 7 = 8; 3 + 4 = 7; 2 + 6 = 8. Point out that none of the addends are the same and that the first sum is greater than the second, and the second sum is less than the third.

ON YOUR OWN

Because all children should be challenged, have all children try the Challenging Practice and Problem Solving pages in **Workbook 1A**, pp. 57–58. These pages (with the answers) are shown at the right.

Differentiation Options Depending on children's success with the Workbook pages, use these materials as needed.

On Level: Extra Practice 1A, pp. 43–44
Advanced: Enrichment 1A, pp. 19–25

Put On Your Thinking Cap!
Problem Solving

Solve.

Lilian has these candles.
Help her choose the correct number candle for her friend's birthday.

● Cross out two numbers that add up to 5.
● Cross out two numbers that add up to 10.
● Look at the two numbers that are left.
  Cross out the number that is the less.

The correct number candle is ___7___.

Thinking skill: Analizing parts and whole,
                and deduction
Strategy: Act it out

Workbook A p. 58

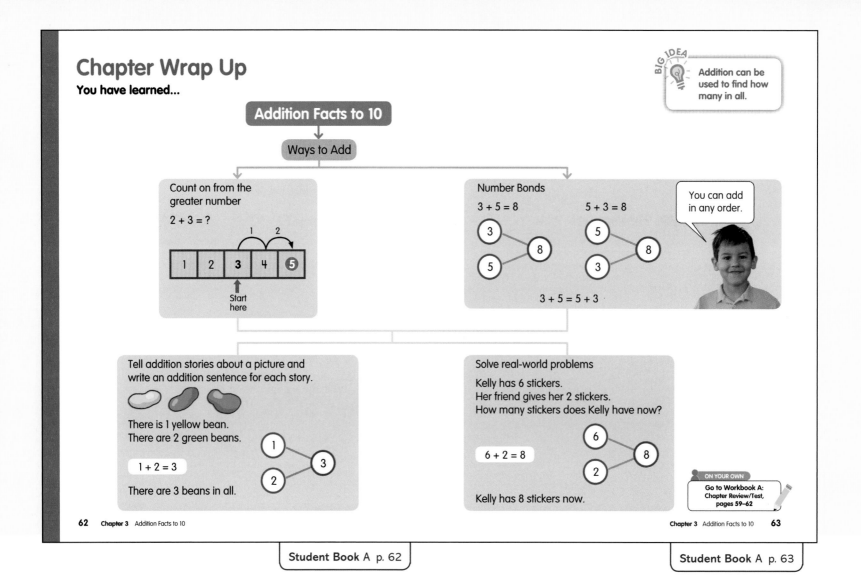

Chapter Wrap Up
You have learned...

Addition Facts to 10

Ways to Add

Count on from the greater number

$2 + 3 = ?$

| 1 | 2 | **3** | 4 | ⑤ |

↑ Start here

Number Bonds

$3 + 5 = 8$ $5 + 3 = 8$

$3 + 5 = 5 + 3$

You can add in any order.

BIG IDEA Addition can be used to find how many in all.

Tell addition stories about a picture and write an addition sentence for each story.

There is 1 yellow bean.
There are 2 green beans.

$1 + 2 = 3$

There are 3 beans in all.

Solve real-world problems

Kelly has 6 stickers.
Her friend gives her 2 stickers.
How many stickers does Kelly have now?

$6 + 2 = 8$

Kelly has 8 stickers now.

ON YOUR OWN
Go to Workbook A:
Chapter Review/Test,
pages 59–62

62   Chapter 3 Addition Facts to 10

Chapter 3 Addition Facts to 10   **63**

Student Book A p. 62

Student Book A p. 63

Chapter Wrap Up (pages 62 and 63)

Review addition strategies of counting on and number bonds using the examples at the top of pages 62 and 63. Review addition stories and solving real-world problems by going through the examples on the bottom half of the pages. As you work through the examples with the children, encourage them to use the chapter vocabulary:

- add
- plus (+)
- equal to (=)
- addition sentence
- more than
- addition story

ON YOUR OWN

Have children review the vocabulary, concepts and skills from Chapter 3 with the Chapter Review/Test in **Workbook 1A**, pp. 59–62. These pages (with the answers) are shown on page 63A.

Assessment

Use the Chapter 3 Test Prep on pages 17–20 of **Assessments 1** to assess how well children have learned the material of this chapter. This assessment is appropriate for reporting results to adults at home and administrators. This test is shown on page 63B.

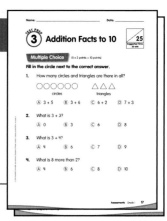

Assessments 1 pp. 17–20

Workbook pages for Chapter Review/Test

Name: _____ Date: _____

Chapter Review/Test

Vocabulary

Choose the correct word.

plus
add
equal to
more than
addition sentence

1. You can ___add___ by counting on from the greater number.

2. 2 + 3 = 5 is an ___addition sentence___.

3. 3 plus 4 is ___equal to___ 7.

4. "+" is read as ___plus___.

5. 6 is 2 ___more than___ 4.

Concepts and Skills

Add by counting on from the greater number.

6. 3 + 6 = ___9___   7. 7 + 1 = ___8___

8. 2 + 8 = ___10___   9. 1 + 9 = ___10___

Fill in the blanks.

10. ___9___ is 3 more than 6.

11. ___7___ is 2 more than 5.

12. ___8___ is 4 more than 4.

Chapter 3 Addition Facts to 10   **59**

Workbook A p. 59

Look at the pictures.
Fill in the blanks.

13.

There are ___2___ big 🦋.

There are ___5___ small 🦋.

2	+	5	=	7

There are ___7___ 🦋 in all.

Complete the number bonds.
Fill in the blanks.

14.

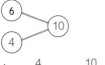

6 + ___4___ = ___10___   4 + ___6___ = ___10___

6 + 4 = 4 + ___6___

60   Chapter 3 Addition Facts to 10

Workbook A p. 60

Name: _____ Date: _____

Problem Solving

Solve.

15. Carlos has 3 brown belts.
He has 2 black belts.
How many belts does he have in all?

3 + 2 = ___5___

Carlos has ___5___ belts in all.

16. Jane has 4 bows.
She gets 3 more bows.
How many bows does she have now?

4 + 3 = ___7___

Jane has ___7___ bows now.

Chapter 3 Addition Facts to 10   **61**

Workbook A p. 61

Draw ⬭.
Then solve.

17. How many toys are there in all?

3 + ___5___ = ___8___

There are ___8___ toys in all.

Look at the [ ] in question 17 to answer the questions.

Circle the correct answer.

18. **a.** Are there more or more ?

There are more .

b. How many more?

5 is 3 ② more than 3.

62   Chapter 3 Addition Facts to 10

Workbook A p. 62

Assessments Book pages for Chapter 3 Test Prep
Answer key appears in Assessments Book.

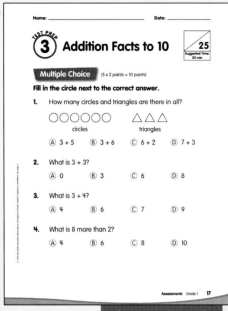

Assessments p. 17

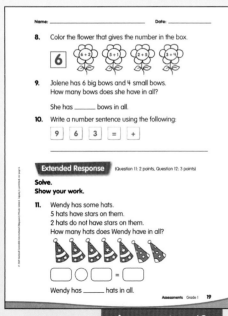

Assessments p. 18

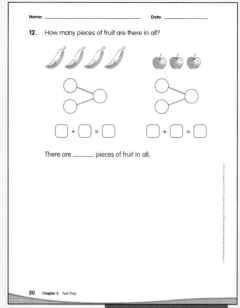

Assessments p. 20

Assessments p. 19

Chapter Overview

Subtraction Facts to 10

Math Background

Children have learned the part-whole concept and addition of numbers to 10. These two concepts are related to subtraction skills and concepts.

In this chapter, children will learn different methods of subtraction, the most basic of which is the taking-away strategy. The addition concept is the inverse of subtraction, and one of the ways to subtract involves counting back. Other strategies are counting on, and using number bonds.

All the subtraction strategies can be taught using the part-whole concept. If you know one part and the whole amount, and need to know the other part, you use subtraction. The subtraction strategy that builds and reinforces this concept most effectively involves the use of number bonds, which relate parts with the whole, and relate addition with subtraction.

As is found in addition, there is an Identity Property of Subtraction. This property states that zero subtracted from any number is equal to that number. Another property of subtraction states that any number subtracted from itself equals zero.

This chapter also requires children to use problem-solving skills to solve simple real-world subtraction problems. Children solve problems by writing subtraction sentences from number bonds.

Cross-Curricular Connections

Reading/Language Arts Read aloud **Subtraction Action** by Loreen Leedy (Holiday House, © 2002) about Miss Prime and her students' subtraction adventures at the fair. As a class, brainstorm subtraction story ideas. Choose one of them to be the setting for your own illustrated class book about subtraction.

Skills Trace

Grade K	Represent subtraction stories with small whole numbers. (Chap. 18)
Grade 1	Subtract 2-digit numbers to 100. (Chaps. 4, 8, 13, 14, and 17)
Grade 2	Subtract 3-digit numbers to 1,000. (Chaps. 3, 4, and10)

EVERY DAY COUNTS® Calendar Math

The October activities provide...

Preview of geometric patterns and attributes of rectangles (skills and concepts taught at depth in Chapter 5)

Review of number patterns (Chapter 1) and length comparisons using *longer*, *shorter*, and the *same length as* (Kindergarten skill)

Practice of sums and differences involving the number 6 (Lessons 1 and 2 in this chapter) and writing addition and subtraction sentences (Lessons 3 and 4 in this chapter)

Differentiation Resources

Differentiation for Special Populations

	English Language Learners	Struggling Reteach 1A	On Level Extra Practice 1A	Advanced Enrichment 1A
Lesson 1	p. 68	pp. 44–54	pp. 45–52	Enrichment pages can be used to challenge advanced children.
Lesson 2	p. 78	pp. 55–58	pp. 53–54	
Lesson 3	p. 83	pp. 59–60	pp. 55–58	
Lesson 4	p. 86	pp. 61–66	pp. 59–60	

Additional Support

For English Language Learners

Select activities that reinforce the chapter vocabulary and the connections among these words, such as having children

- create a Word Wall that includes terms, definitions, and examples
- draw pictures and write problems to illustrate subtraction
- discuss the Chapter Wrap Up, encouraging children to use the chapter vocabulary

For Struggling Learners

Select activities that go back to the appropriate stage of the Concrete-Pictorial-Abstract spectrum, such as having children

- act out subtraction in a skit
- represent subtraction with manipulatives
- tell subtraction stories
- draw pictures to illustrate subtraction
- try similar problems using smaller numbers

See also pages 71–72 and 77.

If necessary, review:
- Counting (Chapter 1), or
- Number Bonds (Chapter 2)

For Advanced Learners

See suggestions on page 86.

Assessment and Remediation

Chapter 4 Assessment

Prior Knowledge		
	Resource	**Page numbers**
Quick Check	Student Book 1A	p. 66
Pre-Test	Assessments 1	pp. 21–22
Ongoing Diagnostic		
Guided Practice	Student Book 1A	pp. 68, 69, 72, 73, 74, 75, 76, 77, 78, 83, 86, 87, 88
Common Error	Teacher's Edition 1A	pp. 73, 74–75, 80–81
Best Practices	Teacher's Edition 1A	pp. 69–70, 71–72
Formal Evaluation		
Chapter Review/Test	Workbook 1A	pp. 85–88
Chapter 4 Test Prep	Assessments 1	pp. 23–27
Cumulative Review for Chapters 3 and 4	Workbook 1A	pp. 89–92
Test Prep for Chapters 1 to 4	Extra Practice 1A	pp. 63–70
Benchmark Assessment 1 for Chapters 1 to 4	Assessments 1	pp. 28–37

Problems with these items...   **Can be remediated with...**

Remediation Options

	Review/Test Items	Chapter Assessment Items	Reteach	Student Book
Objective	**Workbook 1A pp. 85–88**	**Assessments 1 pp. 23–27**	**Reteach 1A**	**Student Book 1A**
Use chapter vocabulary correctly.	1–4	Not assessed	pp. 44–66	pp. 67, 69–70, 77, 85
Subtract using the taking away, counting on, counting back, or number bonds strategies.	5–7, 8–9, 10–11, 12–13	1–4, 9	pp. 44–54	Lesson 1
Write subtraction stories.	18	Not assessed	pp. 55–58	Lesson 2
Write and solve subtraction sentences.	14–17, 20–21	5–7, 10–11	pp. 59–60	Lesson 3
Write fact families.	19	8, 12	pp. 61–66	Lesson 4
Solve real-world problems.	20–21	3, 4, 7, 11, 12	pp. 55–60, 64, 66	Lesson 3 and 4

Chapter Planning Guide

CHAPTER 4 Subtraction Facts to 10

Lesson	Pacing	Instructional Objectives	Vocabulary
Chapter Opener pp. 64–66 Recall Prior Knowledge Quick Check	*1 day *26*	💡 **Big Idea** Subtraction can be used to find how many are left.	
Lesson 1, pp. 67–76A Ways to Subtract	2 days *27* *28*	• Take away to subtract • Count on to subtract • Count back to subtract • Use number bonds to subtract • Write and solve subtraction sentences	• take away • subtract • minus (−) • subtraction sentence • less than
Lesson 2, pp. 77–81A Making Subtraction Stories	1 day *29*	• Tell subtraction stories about pictures • Write subtraction sentences	• subtraction story
Lesson 3, pp. 82–84 Real-World Problems: Subtraction	1 day *30*	• Write subtraction sentences • Solve real-world word problems	
Lesson 4, pp. 85–89 Making Fact Families	1 day *31*	• Recognize related addition and subtraction sentences • Write fact families • Use fact families to solve real-world problems	• fact family
Problem Solving pp. 90–91A 👐 Put on Your Thinking Cap!	1 day *32*	Thinking Skill • Analyzing parts and whole Problem Solving Strategy • Guess and check	
Chapter Wrap Up pp. 92–93	1 day *33*	• Reinforce and consolidate chapter skills and concepts	
Chapter Assessment	1 day *34*		
Review	*35*		

*Assume that 1 day is a 45–55 minute period.

Resources	Materials	NCTM Focal Points	NCTM Process Standards
Student Book 1A, pp. 64–66 **Assessments 1,** pp. 21–22	• 10 connecting cubes for the teacher		Communication
Student Book 1A, pp. 67–76 **Workbook 1A,** pp. 63–74 **Extra Practice 1A,** pp. 45–52 **Reteach 1A,** pp. 44–54	• 10 connecting cubes for the teacher • 10 connecting cubes per child • 10 counters per child • counting tape • 1 Ten Frame per child (TRO1)	***Number and Operations*** and ***Algebra*** Develop strategies for subtracting whole numbers, including counting on, counting back, and part-whole	Communication Problem Solving Reasoning/Proof Representation
Student Book 1A, pp. 77–81 **Workbook 1A,** pp. 75–78 **Extra Practice 1A,** pp. 53–54 **Reteach 1A,** pp. 55–58	• 10 counters for the teacher • math balance and weights • counting tape • 10 counters per child • *Subtraction Action* by Loreen Leedy	***Number and Operations*** and ***Algebra*** Develop strategies for subtracting whole numbers, including counting on, counting back, and part-whole	Communication Problem Solving Reasoning/Proof Representation
Student Book 1A, pp. 82–84 **Workbook 1A,** pp. 79–80 **Extra Practice 1A,** pp. 55–58 **Reteach 1A,** pp. 59–60	• 10 counters for the teacher	***Number and Operations*** and ***Algebra*** Develop strategies for subtracting whole numbers, including counting on, counting back, and part-whole	Problem Solving Representation
Student Book 1A, pp. 85–89 **Workbook 1A,** pp. 81–82 **Extra Practice 1A,** pp. 59–60 **Reteach 1A,** pp. 61–66	• 20 connecting cubes in 10 of each color for the teacher • 1 set of Number/Symbol Cards (TRO4) per group • clear plastic container	***Number and Operations*** and ***Algebra*** Relate addition and subtraction as inverse operations and use this understanding to solve problems	Problem Solving Reasoning/Proof Representation
Student Book 1A, pp. 90–91 **Workbook 1A,** pp. 83–84 **Extra Practice 1A,** pp. 61–62 **Enrichment 1A,** pp. 26–32	• 1 Problem-Solving Grid per child (TRO5)	***Number and Operations*** and ***Algebra*** Solve both routine and non-routine problems	Problem Solving Reasoning/Proof
Student Book 1A, pp. 92–93 **Workbook 1A,** pp. 85–88			
Assessments 1, pp. 23–27			
Workbook 1A, pp. 89–92 **Extra Practice 1A,** pp. 63–70 **Assessments 1,** pp. 28–37			

Technology Resources for easy classroom management
• *Math in Focus* eBook
• *Math in Focus* Teaching Resources CD
• *Math in Focus* Virtual Manipulatives
• On-Line Web Resources

Subtraction Facts to 10

Lesson 1 Ways to Subtract
Lesson 2 Making Subtraction Stories
Lesson 3 Real-World Problems: Subtraction
Lesson 4 Making Fact Families

Chapter 4
Vocabulary

take away	remove, subtract	Lesson 1
subtract	take away, or remove	Lesson 1
minus (−)	the symbol used to show subtract	Lesson 1
subtraction sentence	a number sentence that represents taking away	Lesson 1
less than	4 is less than 5	Lesson 1
subtraction story	a word problem that is solved using a subtraction sentence	Lesson 2
fact family	a group of addition and subtraction sentences that have the same parts and whole	Lesson 4

Lesson 1 Ways to Subtract
Lesson 2 Making Subtraction Stories
Lesson 3 Real-World Problems: Subtraction
Lesson 4 Making Fact Families

BIG IDEA Subtraction can be used to find how many are left.

64

Student Book A p. 64

Big Idea (page 64)

Basic subtraction facts are the main focus of this chapter.

- Children use strategies, such as the take-away concept, number bonds, counting on, and counting back, to identify and learn subtraction facts.

- They write subtraction sentences to represent familiar situations, and begin to see the inverse relationship between addition and subtraction by using number bonds.

Chapter Opener (page 64)

The pictures illustrate the taking-away concept in subtraction using the number bond 2-3—5. This is similar to work children did in Kindergarten. In this chapter, subtraction will be extended to numbers up to 10 and will include writing number bonds and number sentences for subtraction stories.

- Using the pictures in the Chapter Opener, have children describe what is happening. Be sure they recognize that the story is presented from left to right.

- *Ask:* How many stickers did the boy start with? (5) How many stickers did he drop? (3) How many does he have left? (2)

- Explain to children that finding how many are left is called *subtracting*, and that they will learn many ways of subtracting in this chapter.

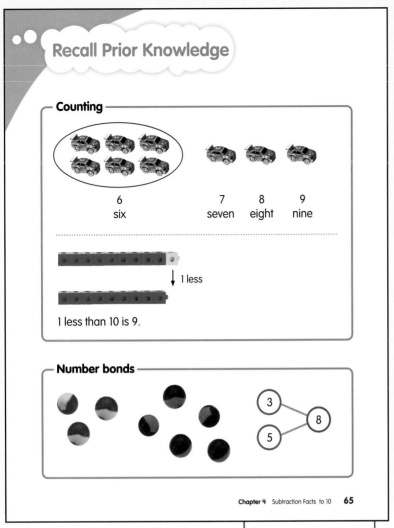

Student Book A p. 65

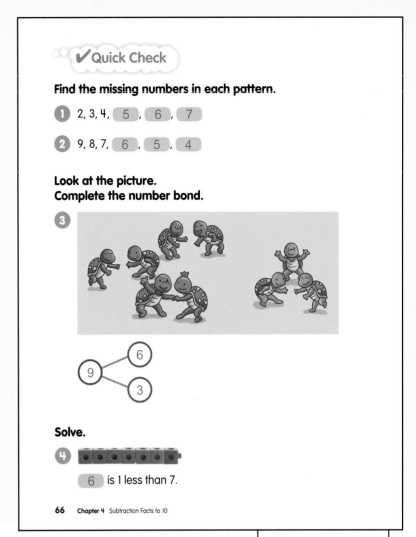

Student Book A p. 66

Recall Prior Knowledge (page 65)

Counting 🎲
Children learned to count from 0 to 10 in Chapter 1.

- Show children different numbers of objects, such as pencils or crayons, and ask them to say the number.

- Use **connecting cubes** to make a number train. *Ask:* How many cubes are there? Take away 1 cube. *Ask:* How many is 1 less than this?

Number bonds
Number bonds form the fundamental concept in addition and subtraction. They are the basis for the formal definition of the subtraction model $y - x = z$.

- Show children two groups of objects. Write the related number bond on the board.

- Help children recall other number bonds for addition. Indicate that they can also use number bonds for subtraction.

✔Quick Check (page 66)

Use this section as a diagnostic tool to assess children's level of prerequisite knowledge before they progress to this chapter. Exercises ❶ and ❷ assess counting skills taught in Chapter 1. Exercises ❸ and ❹ assess the part-whole concept of number bonds taught in Chapter 2.

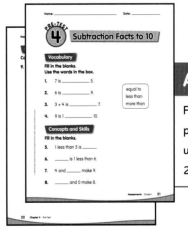

Assessment

For additional assessment of children's prior knowledge and chapter readiness, use the Chapter 4 Pre-Test on pages 21–22 of **Assessments 1**.

Assessments 1 pp. 21–22

LESSON 1 Ways to Subtract

LESSON OBJECTIVES
- Take away to subtract.
- Count on to subtract.
- Count back to subtract.
- Use number bonds to subtract.
- Write and solve subtraction sentences.

TECHNOLOGY RESOURCES
- *Math in Focus* eBook
- *Math in Focus* Teaching Resources CD
- *Math in Focus* Virtual Manipulatives

Vocabulary

take away	subtraction sentence
subtract	less than
minus (–)	

DAY 1	Student Book 1A, pp. 67–73
	Workbook 1A, pp. 63–68

MATERIALS
- 10 connecting cubes for the teacher
- 10 connecting cubes per child
- 10 counters per child
- counting tape
- 2 Ten Frames per child (TR01)

DIFFERENTIATION RESOURCES
- Reteach 1A, pp. 44–50
- Extra Practice 1A, pp. 45–48

DAY 2	Student Book 1A, pp. 74–76
	Workbook 1A, pp. 69–74

DIFFERENTIATION RESOURCES
- Reteach 1A, pp. 51–54
- Extra Practice 1A, pp. 49–52

5-minute Warm Up

1. Show children 8 **connecting cubes**. Separate the cubes into two groups. Ask children to count the cubes in each group. This activity reinforces the part-whole concept and counting skills.

2. Ask children to count from 0 to 10 and then from 10 to 0. This activity prepares children for counting on and back to subtract.

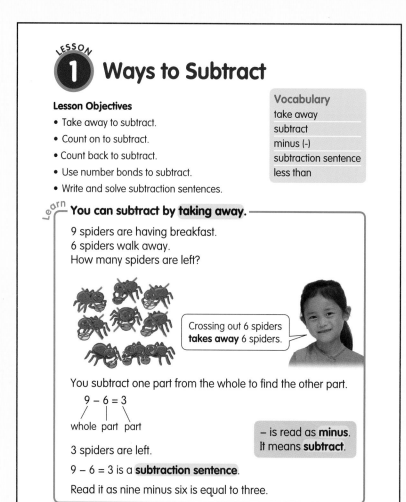

LESSON 1 Ways to Subtract

Lesson Objectives
- Take away to subtract.
- Count on to subtract.
- Count back to subtract.
- Use number bonds to subtract.
- Write and solve subtraction sentences.

Vocabulary
take away
subtract
minus (-)
subtraction sentence
less than

Learn **You can subtract by taking away.**

9 spiders are having breakfast.
6 spiders walk away.
How many spiders are left?

Crossing out 6 spiders **takes away** 6 spiders.

You subtract one part from the whole to find the other part.

$9 - 6 = 3$
whole part part

– is read as **minus**. It means **subtract**.

3 spiders are left.

$9 - 6 = 3$ is a **subtraction sentence**.

Read it as nine minus six is equal to three.

Lesson 1 Ways to Subtract **67**

Student Book A p. 67

DAY 1 Teach

Learn Subtract by Taking Away (page 67)

The taking-away concept is used to illustrate the subtraction operation. Explain that taking-away is one way to do subtraction.

- Start by using 9 **connecting cubes** to represent the spiders in the picture. Take away 6 cubes and count the number of cubes left.

- Write the subtraction sentence on the board. Explain the symbols and terms used: *minus, subtract, equal to.*

- Explain that the group of items taken away is one part or group of the whole and the remaining group of items is another part or group. These two parts make up the whole.

- The subtraction sentence reflects the relationship between the total and the two parts.

- Draw children's attention to the picture of the spiders in the Student Book. Note that the spiders that are crossed out *are taken away* or *subtracted*.

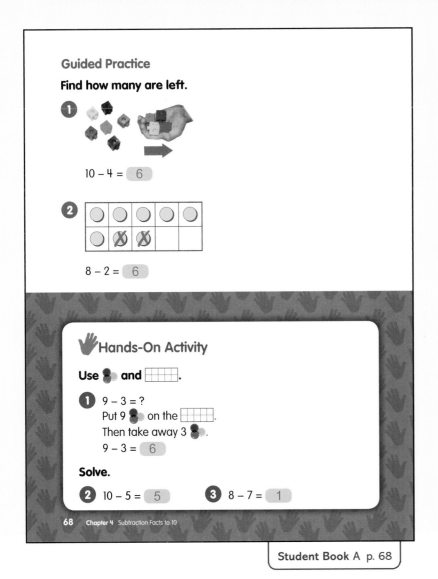

Guided Practice

Find how many are left.

1. $10 - 4 = \boxed{6}$

2. $8 - 2 = \boxed{6}$

Hands-On Activity

Use 🔵 and ⬛.

1. $9 - 3 = ?$
    Put 9 🔵 on the ⬛.
    Then take away 3 🔵.
    $9 - 3 = \boxed{6}$

Solve.

2. $10 - 5 = \boxed{5}$ 3. $8 - 7 = \boxed{1}$

68 Chapter 4 Subtraction Facts to 10

Student Book A p. 68

Problem of the Lesson

Laurie has a box of 5 crayons.
Two crayons are out of the box.
How many crayons are in the box?

Solution

$2 + ? = 5$

Answer: 3 crayons

Differentiated Instruction

English Language Learners

Count on and *Count back* may hold new meanings for *on* and *back* for some children. Relate these meanings to *forward* and *backward* by demonstrating with a toy car or rolling a pencil. As the car or pencil rolls forward, it goes ON to the next stop. As it rolls backward, it goes BACK to where it was.

Check for Understanding

✓ Guided Practice (page 68)

1. Use **connecting cubes** to help children practice the taking-away concept. Have them say the number they are taking away and then count the remaining cubes before they complete the subtraction sentence.

2. Use **Ten Frames** (TRO1) to help children to relate the concepts of taking away and subtraction and to have them practice the taking-away concept.

    - Give each child a ten frame. Have them draw 8 circles and then cross out 2. After they count the circles that are not crossed out, guide them in completing the subtraction sentence.

Best Practices You may want to teach this day's lesson as a series of three mini-lessons, focusing each on one of the three strategies of subtracting: taking away, counting on, and counting back. Two pages of independent practice in the Workbook correlate to each strategy.

Hands-On Activity:

Taking Away Using Ten Frames (page 68)

This activity reinforces the taking-away concept.

- This activity can be done individually or in groups. Each child or group will need 10 **counters** and a **Ten Frame** (TRO1).

- Have children interpret the subtraction sentence $9 - 3 = ?$ and model it using counters on the ten frame. Ask children to put 9 counters on the ten frame and take away 3 counters. *Ask:* How many counters are left? (6) Have them complete the subtraction sentence.

- Encourage children to interpret and model Exercises 2 and 3 using the ten frame and counters.

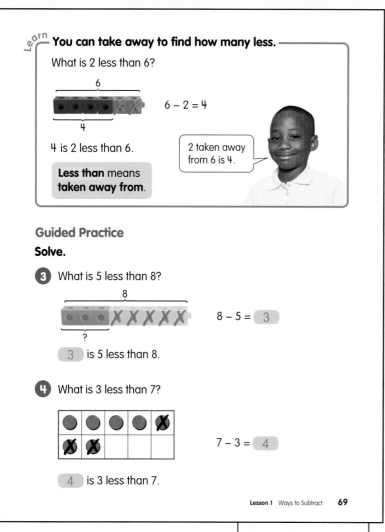

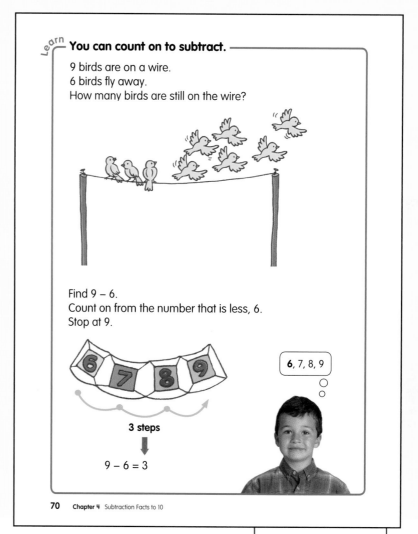

Take Away to Find How Many Less

(page 69)

This concept builds on the taking-away concept in the previous Learn element. The taking-away concept is used to illustrate the meaning of the sentence *What is x less than y?* Explain that *less than* means *taken away from*. In the given example,

2 *less than* 6 means
2 *is taken away* from 6.

- Using **connecting cubes**, model the *less than* concept. Show 6 connecting cubes and then take away 2 with 4 remaining. Explain that 2 less than 6 is 4. Guide children in using this concept to solve problems.

✓ Guided Practice (page 69)

❸ Using **connecting cubes**, have children model 5 *less than* 8. Have them first show 8 connecting cubes and then **say**: *Take 5 away from 8. 3 are left.* Guide them in completing the missing numbers in the number sentence.

❹ Using a **Ten Frame**, have the children draw 7 circles and then cross out 3. Have them count the circles that are not crossed out. Then ask them to fill in the missing numbers.

Count On to Subtract (page 70) 1 2 3 4 5

Children will count on from the *subtrahend* (the lesser number, 6) and stop at the *minuend* (9). This is the second important strategy for subtraction. You will need to make a **counting tape** for the numbers 1 to 10. Blank Counting Tapes can be found in the Teaching Resources section.

- Using a counting tape, show children how to count on from 6 until they reach 9. Explain that since they took 3 steps to reach 9, the answer is 3.

- Children may also use their fingers to count on. Have each child show 6 fingers, and then show one more finger at a time until they reach 9. **Ask**: How many more fingers did you put up after the first 6? (3) Help children see that this is the answer to 9 – 6.

Best Practices Check that children know how to identify the number which is less and to count on from there.

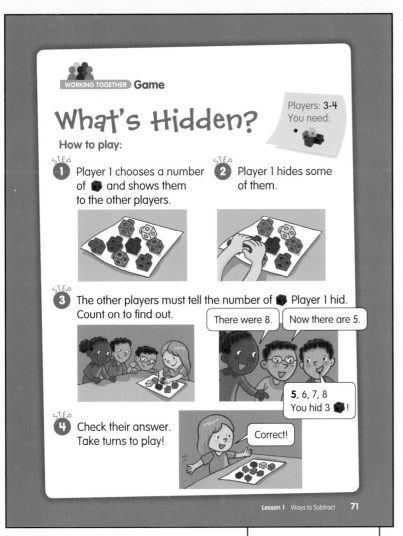

Student Book A p. 71

WORKING TOGETHER Game

Guided Practice

Count on from the number that is less to subtract.

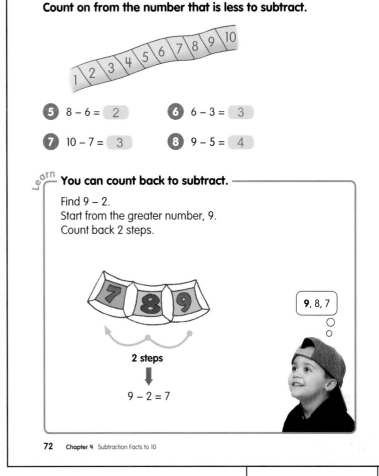

5 8 – 6 = 2   **6** 6 – 3 = 3

7 10 – 7 = 3   **8** 9 – 5 = 4

You can count back to subtract.

Find 9 – 2.
Start from the greater number, 9.
Count back 2 steps.

2 steps

9 – 2 = 7

9, 8, 7

Student Book A p. 72

WORKING TOGETHER Game:

What's Hidden? (page 71)

This game helps reinforce the counting-on strategy in subtraction. Children should recognize that the number of **connecting cubes** displayed at the beginning (8) is the minuend (or whole) and the number of counters covered is the answer to 8 – 5 = __. The number of unit cubes not covered is the subtrahend (or one part).

- Arrange children in groups of 3 or 4.

- Player 1 puts 2 to 10 cubes on the desk and shows the rest of the players. Player 1 then covers some of the cubes with their hands.

- The other players try to find out the number of hidden cubes. They can count the number of cubes that are not hidden, count on to the original number of cubes and state the number of hidden cubes.

- Next, Player 1 uncovers the cubes and the other players check the answer.

- Have children take turns playing the game.

- Encourage children to write the subtraction sentences modeled.

✓ Guided Practice **5** to **8** (page 72)

These exercises practice the counting-on strategy in subtraction.

For Struggling Learners A counting tape may be useful for children who have difficulty counting on. Have children point to the initial number and count on from it.

Count Back to Subtract (page 72) 1 2 3 4 5

Children will count back from the minuend (9). The subtrahend (2) is the number of steps to count back. Explain that counting back is yet another way to subtract.

- Using a **counting tape**, show children how to start by counting back from 9. Have children count back 2 steps to get an answer of 7.

- Children may also use their fingers to count back. Have each child put up 9 fingers. Ask children to put down two fingers, one at a time. *Ask:* How many fingers are up now? Guide children to see that the answer to 9 – 2 is 7.

Best Practices Check that children know how to identify the greater number and how to count back from there and the number of steps to be counted.

Guided Practice

Count back from the greater number to subtract.

9 7 − 2 = 5   **10** 9 − 3 = 6

11 8 − 4 = 4   **12** 10 − 3 = 7

Let's Practice

Solve.

1 What is 3 less than 5? 2

2 What is 4 less than 10? 6

Count on from the number that is less to subtract.

3 5 − 3 = 2   **4** 7 − 3 = 4

5 10 − 6 = 4   **6** 9 − 4 = 5

Count back from the greater number to subtract.

7 9 − 6 = 3   **8** 7 − 4 = 3

9 8 − 6 = 2   **10** 10 − 9 = 1

> **ON YOUR OWN**
> Go to Workbook A:
> Practice 1, pages 63–68

Lesson 1 Ways to Subtract **73**

Student Book A p. 73

✔ Guided Practice **9** to **12** (page 73)

These exercises provide practice using the counting-back strategy in subtraction. Guide children in identifying the number to begin counting from and the number of steps to be counted.

Let's Practice (page 73)

This practice reinforces subtraction strategies. Exercises **1** and **2** require children to use the taking-away strategy. Exercises **3** to **6** require them to count on to subtract. Exercises **7** to **10** require them to count back to subtract.

ON YOUR OWN

Children practice the taking-away, counting on and counting back strategies to subtract in Practice 1, pp. 63–68 of **Workbook 1A**. These pages (with the answers) are shown at the right and on page 73A.

Differentiation Options Depending on children's success with the Workbook pages, use these materials as needed.

Struggling: Reteach 1A, pp. 44–50

On Level: Extra Practice 1A, pp. 45–48

Practice and Apply
Workbook pages for Chapter 4, Lesson 1

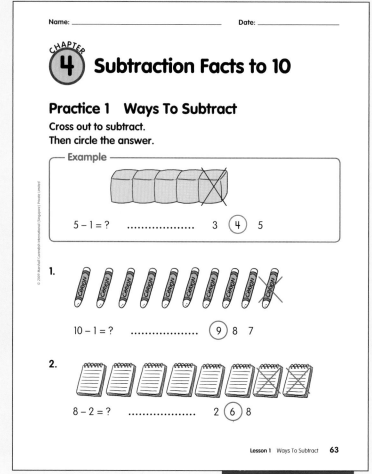

Name: _____   Date: _____

CHAPTER 4 Subtraction Facts to 10

Practice 1   Ways To Subtract

Cross out to subtract.
Then circle the answer.

Example

5 − 1 = ? .... 3 **④** 5

1. 10 − 1 = ? .... **⑨** 8 7

2. 8 − 2 = ? .... 2 **⑥** 8

Lesson 1 Ways To Subtract **63**

Workbook A p. 63

Write a subtraction sentence for each picture.

Example

9 − __1__ = __8__

3. 5 − __3__ = __2__

4. 9 − __3__ = __6__

5. 10 − __2__ = __8__

6. 6 − __0__ = __6__

64 Chapter 4 Subtraction Facts to 10

Workbook A p. 64

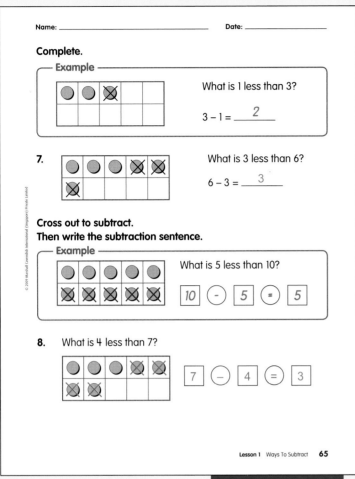

Complete.

Example

What is 1 less than 3?

$3 - 1 = \underline{2}$

7.

What is 3 less than 6?

$6 - 3 = \underline{3}$

**Cross out to subtract.
Then write the subtraction sentence.**

Example

What is 5 less than 10?

$10 \;\ominus\; 5 \;=\; 5$

8. What is 4 less than 7?

$7 \;\ominus\; 4 \;=\; 3$

Workbook A p. 65

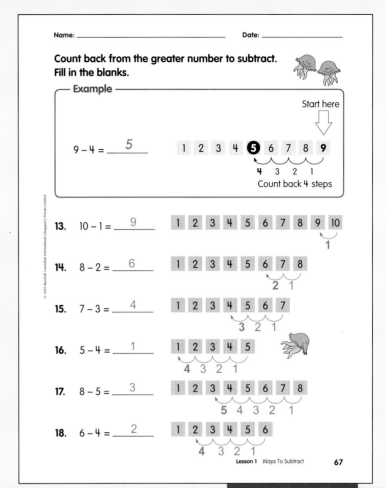

**Count back from the greater number to subtract.
Fill in the blanks.**

Example

Start here

$9 - 4 = \underline{5}$ 1 2 3 4 **5** 6 7 8 **9**

4 3 2 1

Count back 4 steps

13. $10 - 1 = \underline{9}$ 1 2 3 4 5 6 7 8 9 10

1

14. $8 - 2 = \underline{6}$ 1 2 3 4 5 6 7 8

2 1

15. $7 - 3 = \underline{4}$ 1 2 3 4 5 6 7

3 2 1

16. $5 - 4 = \underline{1}$ 1 2 3 4 5

4 3 2 1

17. $8 - 5 = \underline{3}$ 1 2 3 4 5 6 7 8

5 4 3 2 1

18. $6 - 4 = \underline{2}$ 1 2 3 4 5 6

4 3 2 1

Workbook A p. 67

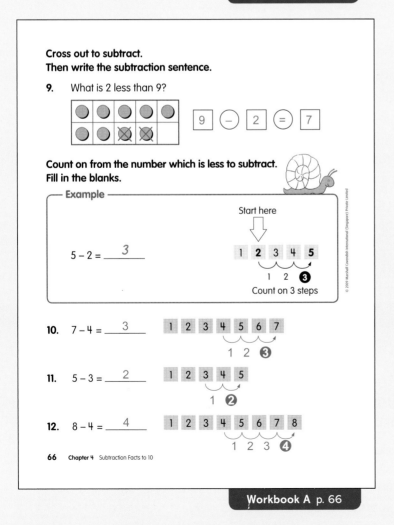

**Cross out to subtract.
Then write the subtraction sentence.**

9. What is 2 less than 9?

$9 \;\ominus\; 2 \;=\; 7$

**Count on from the number which is less to subtract.
Fill in the blanks.**

Example

Start here

$5 - 2 = \underline{3}$ 1 **2** 3 4 **5**

1 2 **3**

Count on 3 steps

10. $7 - 4 = \underline{3}$ 1 2 3 4 5 6 7

1 2 **3**

11. $5 - 3 = \underline{2}$ 1 2 3 4 5

1 **2**

12. $8 - 4 = \underline{4}$ 1 2 3 4 5 6 7 8

1 2 3 **4**

Workbook A p. 66

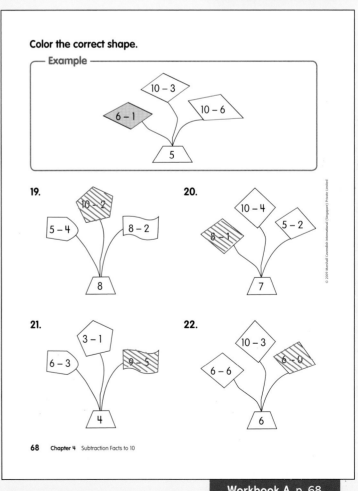

Color the correct shape.

Example

10 – 3

6 – 1

10 – 6

5

19.

10 – 2

5 – 4

8 – 2

8

20.

10 – 4

8 – 1

5 – 2

7

21.

3 – 1

6 – 3

9 – 5

4

22.

10 – 3

6 – 6

6 – 0

6

Workbook A p. 68

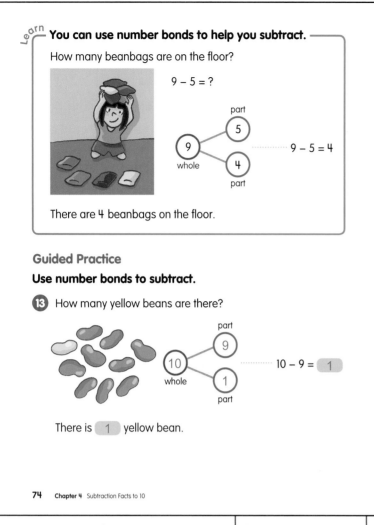

How many beanbags are on the floor?

9 – 5 = ?

9 – 5 = 4

There are 4 beanbags on the floor.

Guided Practice

Use number bonds to subtract.

13 How many yellow beans are there?

10 – 9 = 1

There is 1 yellow bean.

Student Book A p. 74

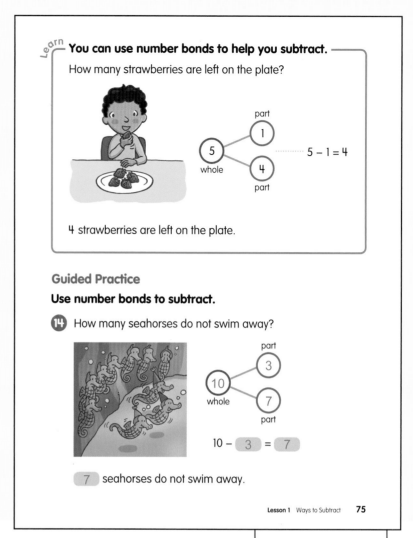

Learn **You can use number bonds to help you subtract.**

How many strawberries are left on the plate?

5 – 1 = 4

4 strawberries are left on the plate.

Guided Practice

Use number bonds to subtract.

14 How many seahorses do not swim away?

10 – 3 = 7

7 seahorses do not swim away.

Student Book A p. 75

DAY 2 Teach

See Lesson Organizer on page 67 for Day 2 resources.

Learn
Use Number Bonds to Subtract (page 74)

This example illustrates the part-whole concept and the use of number bonds for subtraction. Children use number bonds to see the connection between the parts and the whole and to complete a subtraction sentence.

• Help children recognize that the picture shows two parts: the 5 bean bags on the girl's head and the bean bags on the floor. The total number is 9 and taking 5 away gives the number of bags on the floor.

• Help children recall the number bond 5-4—9 and use that to complete the subtraction sentence 9 – 5 = 4.

✔ **Guided Practice** (page 74)
13 This exercise provides practice using the part-whole concept and number bond strategy in subtraction.

• Guide children to identify the two parts: 1 yellow bean and 9 green beans. Help them use the number bond strategy to complete the subtraction sentence 10 – 9 = 1.

Learn
Use Number Bonds to Subtract (page 75)

This example illustrates the use of the taking-away concept and number bond strategy in subtraction.

• Ask the children to identify the two parts: the number of strawberries taken away and the strawberries left. The total number is 5 and taking away 1 gives the number of strawberries left on the plate.

• Use the number bond 5—1-4 to complete the subtraction sentence.

Common Error Some children may confuse the two subtraction sentences for a given number bond. If they write the sentence 5 – 4 = 1, have them reread the question that was asked. Be sure they understand that the answer to the question should be the answer to the subtraction problem.

✔ **Guided Practice** (page 75)
14 This exercise provides practice using the taking-away concept and number bond strategy in subtraction.

• Guide children to identify the two parts: the seahorses swimming away and the seahorses not swimming away. Have children use the number bond strategy to complete the subtraction sentence 10 – 3 = 7.

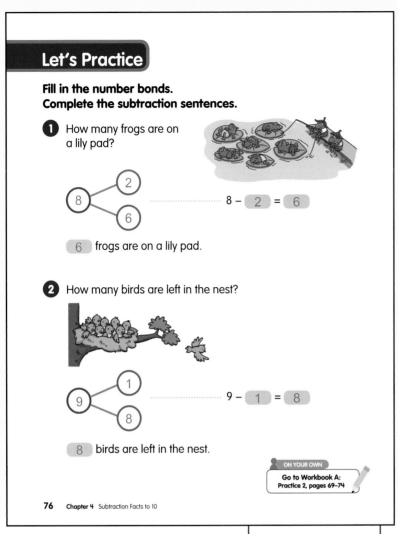

Let's Practice

Fill in the number bonds.
Complete the subtraction sentences.

1 How many frogs are on a lily pad?

8 – 2 = 6

6 frogs are on a lily pad.

2 How many birds are left in the nest?

9 – 1 = 8

8 birds are left in the nest.

ON YOUR OWN

Go to Workbook A:
Practice 2, pages 69–74

76 Chapter 4 Subtraction Facts to 10

Student Book A p. 76

Practice and Apply
Workbook pages for Chapter 4, Lesson 1

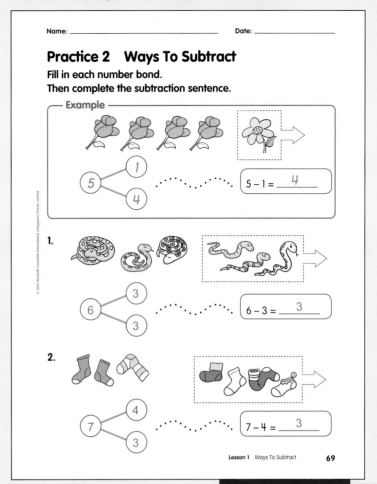

Name: _____   Date: _____

Practice 2   Ways To Subtract
Fill in each number bond.
Then complete the subtraction sentence.

Example

5 – 1 = 4

1.

6 – 3 = 3

2.

7 – 4 = 3

Lesson 1 Ways To Subtract   **69**

Workbook A p. 69

Let's Practice (page 76)

This practice reinforces the subtraction strategies. Exercise **1** uses the part-whole concept and number bond strategy. Exercise **2** uses the taking-away concept and number bond strategy.

Best Practices You may want to have children work in pairs to complete the Guided Practice and/or Let's Practice exercises. Then have them share their answers with the class.

ON YOUR OWN

Children practice the subtraction strategies in Practice 2, pp. 69–74 of **Workbook 1A**. These pages (with the answers) are shown at the right and on page 76A.

Differentiation Options Depending on children's success with the Workbook pages, use these materials as needed.
Struggling: Reteach 1A, pp. 51–54
On Level: Extra Practice 1A, pp. 49–52

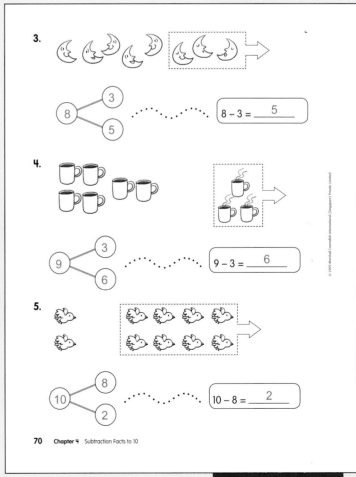

3.

8 – 3 = 5

4.

9 – 3 = 6

5.

10 – 8 = 2

70 Chapter 4 Subtraction Facts to 10

Workbook A p. 70

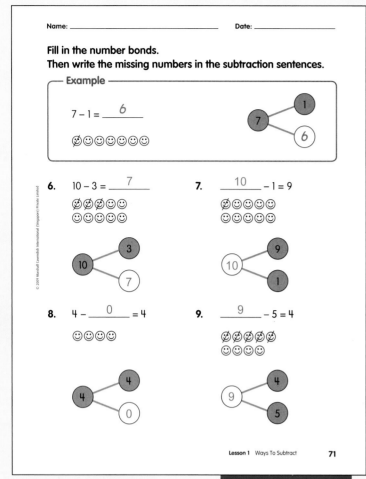

Name: _____ Date: _____

Fill in the number bonds.
Then write the missing numbers in the subtraction sentences.

┌─ Example ──────────────────────────────────┐
│ 7 – 1 = ___6___   ●7   │
│   ╱ ╲   │
│ Ø☺☺☺☺☺☺   ●1   ○6   │
└───┘

6. 10 – 3 = ___7___

ØØØ☺☺
☺☺☺☺

10 ● ╱ ● 3
     ╲ ○ 7

7. ___10___ – 1 = 9

Ø☺☺☺☺
☺☺☺☺

10 ○ ╱ ● 9
      ╲ ● 1

8. 4 – ___0___ = 4

☺☺☺☺

4 ● ╱ ● 4
     ╲ ○ 0

9. ___9___ – 5 = 4

ØØØØØ
☺☺☺☺

9 ○ ╱ ● 4
     ╲ ● 5

Lesson 1 Ways To Subtract   71

Workbook A p. 71

Name: _____ Date: _____

Subtract.
Then match the answers to show where each animal lives.

13.

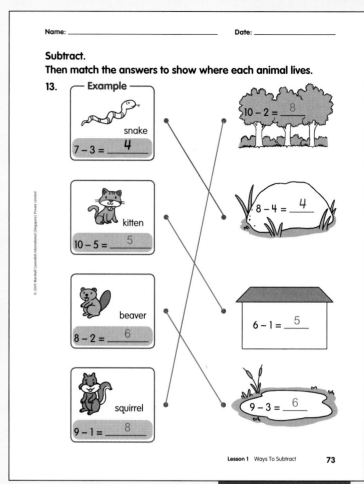

┌─ Example ─────┐
│ snake   │
│ 7 – 3 = __4__│
└───────────────┘

│ kitten   │
│ 10 – 5 = __5__│

│ beaver   │
│ 8 – 2 = __6__│

│ squirrel   │
│ 9 – 1 = __8__│

10 – 2 = __8__

8 – 4 = __4__

6 – 1 = __5__

9 – 3 = __6__

Lesson 1 Ways To Subtract   73

Workbook A p. 73

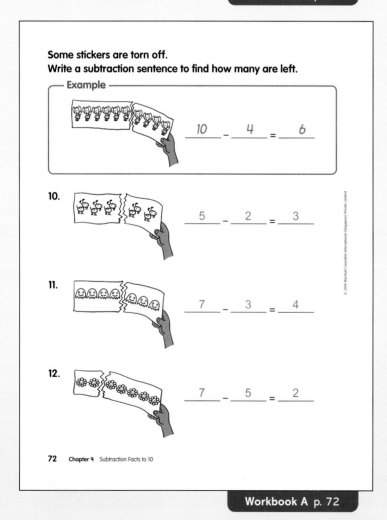

Some stickers are torn off.
Write a subtraction sentence to find how many are left.

┌─ Example ──────────────────────────────────┐
│   10 – 4 = 6   │
└───┘

10.   5 – 2 = 3

11.   7 – 3 = 4

12.   7 – 5 = 2

72   Chapter 4   Subtraction Facts to 10

Workbook A p. 72

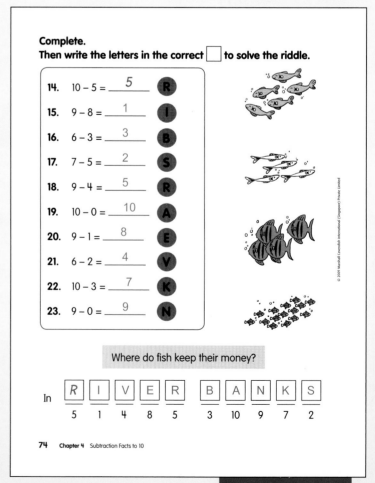

Complete.
Then write the letters in the correct ☐ to solve the riddle.

14. 10 – 5 = __5__ **R**
15. 9 – 8 = __1__   **I**
16. 6 – 3 = __3__   **B**
17. 7 – 5 = __2__   **S**
18. 9 – 4 = __5__   **R**
19. 10 – 0 = __10__ **A**
20. 9 – 1 = __8__   **E**
21. 6 – 2 = __4__   **V**
22. 10 – 3 = __7__ **K**
23. 9 – 0 = __9__   **N**

Where do fish keep their money?

In | R | I | V | E | R | | B | A | N | K | S |
      5   1   4   8   5   3   10 9   7   2

74   Chapter 4   Subtraction Facts to 10

Workbook A p. 74

LESSON 2 Making Subtraction Stories

LESSON OBJECTIVES
- Tell subtraction stories about pictures.
- Write subtraction sentences.

TECHNOLOGY RESOURCES
- *Math in Focus* eBook
- *Math in Focus* Teaching Resources CD
- *Math in Focus* Virtual Manipulatives

Vocabulary

subtraction story

DAY 1 Student Book 1A, pp. 77–81
Workbook 1A, pp. 75–78

MATERIALS
- 10 counters for the teacher (at least 2 red and 5 blue)
- 10 connecting cubes for the teacher
- math balance and weights for the teacher
- counting tape
- 10 counters per child

DIFFERENTIATION RESOURCES
- Reteach 1A, pp. 55–58
- Extra Practice 1A, pp. 53–54

 5-minute Warm Up

Use counters to help children tell take away and part-whole subtraction stories. Show a subtraction sentence such as 7−2 = ?

- Hold 7 counters and *say*: I have 7 balloons. Take away 2 counters. Lead children to finish the story to match the sentence. *Sample story*: 2 balloons pop. How many balloons do I have left?

- Then hold 5 blue counters and 2 red counters and *say*: I have 7 balloons. *Sample story*: 2 balloons are red. The rest are blue. How many blue balloons do I have?

LESSON 2 Making Subtraction Stories

Lesson Objectives
- Tell subtraction stories about pictures.
- Write subtraction sentences.

Vocabulary
subtraction story

Learn You can tell subtraction stories about a picture.

There are 7 animals.
4 are squirrels.

7 − 4 = 3

3 are hamsters.

Guided Practice

Look at the picture.
Tell a subtraction story.
Complete the subtraction sentence.

1

4 − 2 = 2

Lesson 2 *Making Subtraction Stories* **77**

Student Book A p. 77

DAY 1 Teach

Learn Tell Subtraction Stories About a Picture (page 77)

This example illustrates the part-whole concept in subtraction.

- Tell a story about the squirrels and hamsters shown. Use **connecting cubes** to represent the animals. Guide children to see that the whole (7 animals) comprises 2 parts (4 squirrels and 3 hamsters).

- Link the number of each animal to the number bond and then to the subtraction sentence.

For Struggling Learners Use a **math balance** to help children subtract if necessary. Put weights at 7 and 4 on opposite arms of the balance. Then find where to add another weight to make the arms level.

Check for Understanding

✓ **Guided Practice** (page 77)

1 Guide children to see that the children in the picture comprise two genders (parts): boys and girls. Ask children to make up a subtraction story using the part-whole concept of subtraction. Relate this story to a number bond and subtraction sentence.

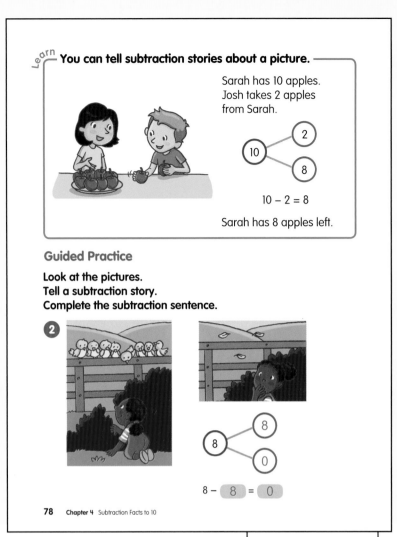

Learn You can tell subtraction stories about a picture.

Sarah has 10 apples.
Josh takes 2 apples from Sarah.

$$10 - 2 = 8$$

Sarah has 8 apples left.

Guided Practice

Look at the pictures.
Tell a subtraction story.
Complete the subtraction sentence.

2

$$8 - 8 = 0$$

78   **Chapter 4** Subtraction Facts to 10

Student Book A p. 78

Write a number bond and a number sentence for this story.

Five birds are sitting on a fence.
Three birds are in the tree.
How many birds are there in all?

Solution   **Number sentence**

5
8        $5 + 3 = 8$
3

Differentiated Instruction

English Language Learners

Some children may need guidance to help them interpret the pictures. Tell a story orally and have children act it out using counters. **Say**: There are 4 children in a group. Two of the children are boys. How many are girls? Have children record the appropriate subtraction sentence and repeat or rephrase the problem.

Learn

Tell Subtraction Stories About a Picture

(page 78)

This example illustrates the taking-away concept in subtraction.

• Ask children to tell a story about the picture. Guide them to identify the two groups of apples: a group of 2 apples taken away and another of 8 left over.

• Then relate the numbers of apples to the number bond and to the subtraction sentence.

✔ **Guided Practice** (page 78)

2 This exercise practices telling a subtraction story using the taking-away concept of subtraction.

• Ask children to make up a subtraction story about the picture. Help them to identify the number of birds in each picture: 8 and 0.

• Then have children write a story, a number bond, and the related subtraction sentence.

Best Practices In this lesson, children tell stories about pictures and then write subtraction sentences. Consider asking two or three children to present a story orally for each picture. This activity will promote oral language practice and learning from other's mathematical ideas.

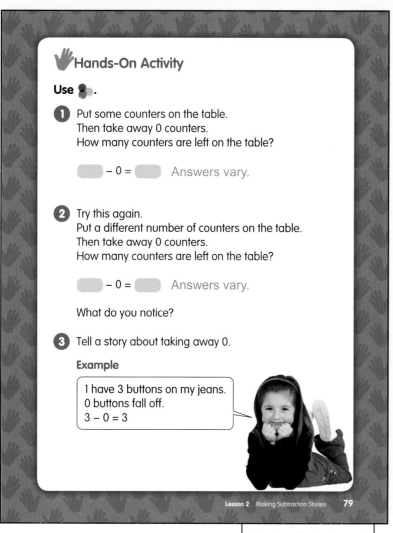

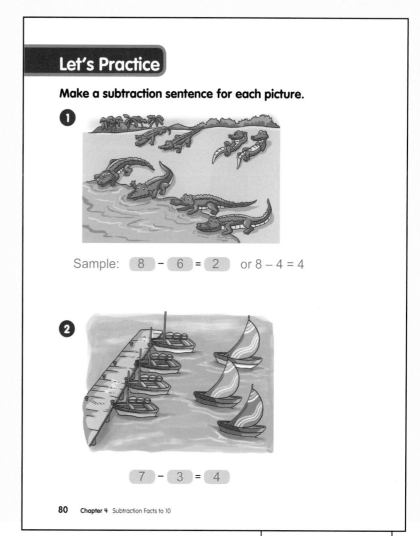

Hands-On Activity:
Zero Concept (page 79)

This activity further reinforces the concept of zero as an identity element for subtraction. Zero in subtraction acts as an identity in that $n - 0 = n$ for any number n. It is not a true identity because it is not true that $n - 0 = 0 - n = n$. The order in which you subtract the two numbers is important, unlike in addition and multiplication.

- Three different situations are used to illustrate this zero concept. Children may need help identifying 0 as a part.

- Children may work in small groups, with partners, or alone. Each group or child will need 10 **counters**.

Let's Practice (page 80)

This practice reinforces subtraction concepts and subtraction strategies introduced in this lesson.

Exercise **1** shows 4 crocodiles on land and another 4 in the water. This is a part-whole situation for which children may write the subtraction sentence $8 - 4 = 4$.

- Some children may notice that 2 of the crocodiles on the sand are also headed to the water. They may write the sentence $8 - 6 = 2$ or $8 - 2 = 6$.

Exercise **2** shows 7 boats, with 3 of them sailing away. This is a taking-away situation, which can also be represented by using a subtraction sentence $7 - 3 = 4$.

Common Error Some children may have difficulty seeing the subtraction situations in the pictures. For example, in Exercise **1** you may need to ask leading questions to help with this problem. For example, *ask*: How many crocodiles are there in all? Listen as children describe one group of crocodiles. What is this group of crocodiles doing? What is the other group of crocodiles doing?

Look at the picture.
Tell subtraction stories about it.
Make a subtraction sentence for each story.

3

ON YOUR OWN

Go to Workbook A:
Practice 3, pages 75–78

Lesson 2 Making Subtraction Stories **81**

Student Book A p. 81

Differentiated Instruction

For Struggling Learners

Some children may benefit from acting out subtraction stories as they complete number bonds and then write number sentences. Provide **cups** and **counters**. *Ask* children to place the number of counters represented by the *whole* in a cup, then take out the number or counters shown as a *part*. Help children understand that the number of counters that remain in the cup represent the other *part*.

Let's Practice (page 81)

Exercise ❸ provides many opportunities for telling subtraction stories. Have children summarize each of their stories with a subtraction sentence.

ON YOUR OWN

Children practice writing subtraction sentences in Practice 3, pp. 75–78 of **Workbook 1A**. These pages (with the answers) are shown on page 81A.

Differentiation Options Depending on children's success with the Workbook pages, use these materials as needed.
Struggling: Reteach 1A, pp. 55–58
On Level: Extra Practice 1A, pp. 53–54

Practice and Apply
Workbook pages for Chapter 4, Lesson 2

Name: _____   Date: _____

Practice 3   Making Subtraction Stories
Look at the pictures.
Make subtraction stories.
Write subtraction sentences for each story.

Example

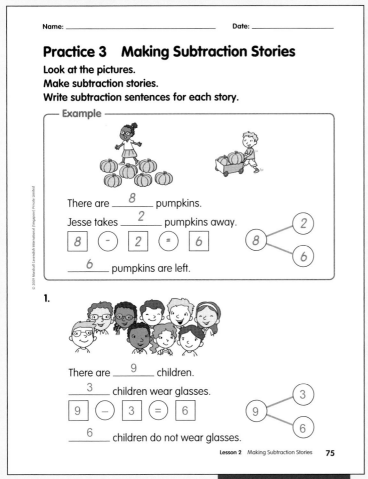

There are ___8___ pumpkins.
Jesse takes ___2___ pumpkins away.

| 8 | − | 2 | = | 6 |

(8)
  ／＼
(2)
(6)

___6___ pumpkins are left.

1.

There are ___9___ children.
___3___ children wear glasses.

| 9 | − | 3 | = | 6 |

(9)
  ／＼
(3)
(6)

___6___ children do not wear glasses.

Workbook A p. 75

Name: _____   Date: _____

4.

Lola has ___9___ crayons.

She gives ___7___ crayons to Pete.

| 9 | − | 7 | = | 2 |

Lola has ___2___ crayons left.

Workbook A p. 77

2.

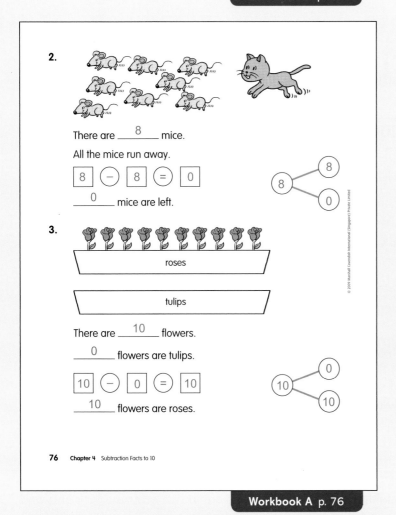

There are ___8___ mice.

All the mice run away.

| 8 | − | 8 | = | 0 |

(8)
  ／＼
(8)
(0)

___0___ mice are left.

3.

roses

tulips

There are ___10___ flowers.

___0___ flowers are tulips.

| 10 | − | 0 | = | 10 |

(10)
  ／＼
(0)
(10)

___10___ flowers are roses.

Workbook A p. 76

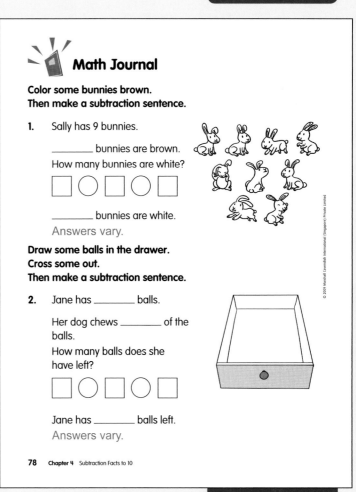

Math Journal

Color some bunnies brown.
Then make a subtraction sentence.

1.   Sally has 9 bunnies.

_____ bunnies are brown.
How many bunnies are white?

| □ | ◯ | □ | ◯ | □ |

_____ bunnies are white.
Answers vary.

Draw some balls in the drawer.
Cross some out.
Then make a subtraction sentence.

2.   Jane has _____ balls.

Her dog chews _____ of the balls.

How many balls does she have left?

| □ | ◯ | □ | ◯ | □ |

Jane has _____ balls left.
Answers vary.

Workbook A p. 78

LESSON 3 Real-World Problems: Subtraction

LESSON OBJECTIVES
- Write subtraction sentences.
- Solve real-world word problems.

TECHNOLOGY RESOURCES
- *Math in Focus* eBook
- *Math in Focus* Teaching Resources CD
- *Math in Focus* Virtual Manipulatives

DAY 1
Student Book 1A, pp. 82–84
Workbook 1A, pp. 79–80

MATERIALS
- 10 counters for the teacher

DIFFERENTIATION RESOURCES
- Reteach 1A, pp. 59–60
- Extra Practice 1A, pp. 55–58

5-minute Warm Up

- Reinforce writing subtraction number sentences by drawing 10 circles on the board. Ask a volunteer to color any number of circles red. Ask another child to say how many circles are *not* red. Write the subtraction sentence and number bond on the board.

- Repeat, asking another child to color another number of circles red.

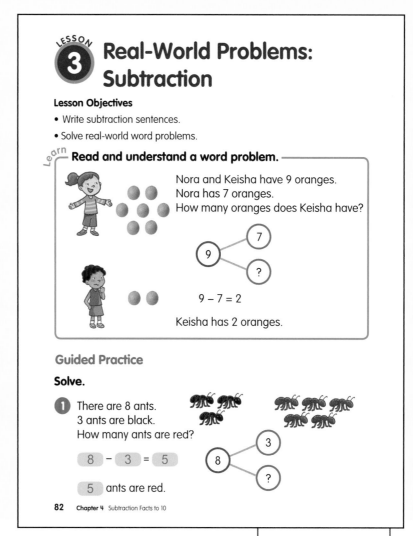

Student Book A p. 82

DAY 1 **Teach**

Read and Understand a Word Problem (page 82)

This example shows how children can apply the part-whole concept in solving real-world subtraction problems.

- Explain that the problem involves the part-whole concept. Help children identify the two *parts* or groups of fruit: one part of 7 oranges for Nora and the other part of unknown number for Keisha. The total or *whole* is 9.

- Then relate the numbers of fruit to the number bond and to the subtraction sentence.

Best Practices At this point, children may be at varying levels and prefer different subtraction strategies. You may wish to review these strategies before beginning the lesson. Make available a variety of manipulatives and suggest that children gather those they want to use for this lesson.

Check for Understanding
✓ **Guided Practice** (page 82)
① Guide children to see that the ants are in two groups: black ants and red ants.

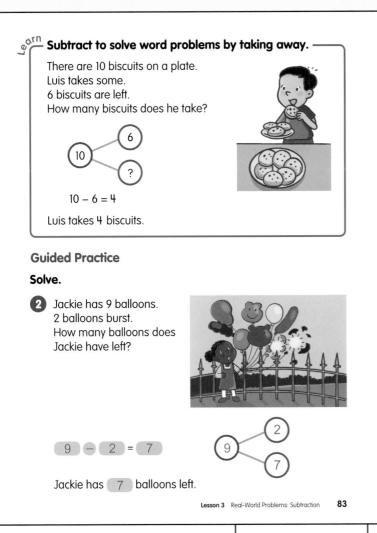

Learn — Subtract to solve word problems by taking away.

There are 10 biscuits on a plate.
Luis takes some.
6 biscuits are left.
How many biscuits does he take?

$10 - 6 = 4$

Luis takes 4 biscuits.

Guided Practice

Solve.

2 Jackie has 9 balloons.
2 balloons burst.
How many balloons does
Jackie have left?

$9 - 2 = 7$

Jackie has 7 balloons left.

Lesson 3   Real-World Problems: Subtraction   83

Student Book A p. 83

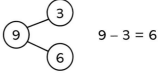

Problem of the Lesson

There are 9 eggs.
Three eggs hatch into chicks.
How many eggs are left?

Solution

$9 - 3 = 6$

Answer: 6 eggs are left.

Differentiated Instruction

English Language Learners

In this lesson, children can use the pictures to help them understand the vocabulary in the word problems. For example, in Exercise ❶ on page 84, point to the picture of the lemons on the tree as you **say**: A tree has 7 lemons. Point to the yellow lemons and **say**: Two of the lemons are yellow. Point to each of the green lemons and **ask**: How many lemons are green? (5) Use similar procedures to help with as many problems as necessary.

• Ask children to relate the problem to a number bond and subtraction sentence.

Learn — Subtract to Solve Word Problems by Taking Away (page 83)

This example shows how children can apply the taking-away strategy in solving real-world subtraction problems.

• Use **counters** to illustrate the 10 biscuits in the example. Place the counters on a table.

• Have a volunteer act out the problem in the example. Ask the volunteer to count 6 for leaving behind, and then take away the remaining counters. **Ask**: How many counters are left? (6) How many counters did he (or she) take away? (4)

• Draw the number bond 10—6-4 and the subtraction sentence on the board.

• Explain that if the volunteer takes away 6 counters, 4 will be left. This reinforces the part-whole concept of subtraction.

✔ Guided Practice (page 83)

❷ Check children's understanding in applying the taking-away strategy to solve the problem. Ask children to relate the problem to a number bond and subtraction sentence.

Let's Practice

Solve.

1

A tree has 7 lemons.
2 of the lemons are yellow.
How many lemons are green? 5 lemons

2

There are 10 muffins.
Hector takes some.
3 muffins are left.
How many muffins does Hector take?
7 muffins

> **ON YOUR OWN**
> Go to Workbook A:
> Practice 4, pages 79–80

84 Chapter 4 Subtraction Facts to 10

> Student Book A p. 84

Practice and Apply
Workbook pages for Chapter 4, Lesson 3

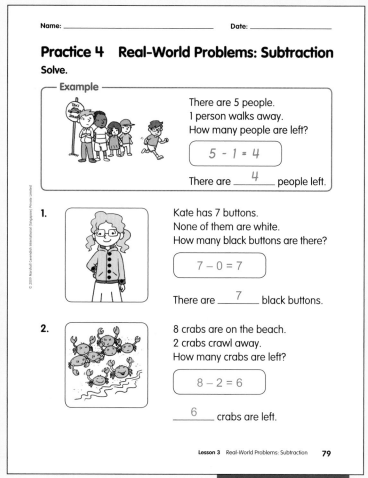

Name: _____ Date: _____

Practice 4   Real-World Problems: Subtraction
Solve.

Example

There are 5 people.
1 person walks away.
How many people are left?

$5 - 1 = 4$

There are ____4____ people left.

1.

Kate has 7 buttons.
None of them are white.
How many black buttons are there?

$7 - 0 = 7$

There are ____7____ black buttons.

2.

8 crabs are on the beach.
2 crabs crawl away.
How many crabs are left?

$8 - 2 = 6$

____6____ crabs are left.

Lesson 3 Real-World Problems: Subtraction 79

> Workbook A p. 79

Let's Practice (page 84)

These exercises let children practice writing subtraction sentences based on real-world problems. Exercise **1** requires children to apply the part-whole concept of subtraction and Exercise **2** requires children to apply the taking-away concept to solve real-world problems.

Common Error Children may be able to correctly identify the numbers to be subtracted, but still make errors in subtracting. Suggest that they use counters or draw a picture and cross out to subtract.

ON YOUR OWN

Children practice using subtraction sentences to solve real-world problems in Practice 4, pp. 79–80 of **Workbook 1A**. These pages (with the answers) are shown at the right.

Differentiation Options Depending on children's success with the Workbook pages, use these materials as needed.
Struggling: Reteach 1A, pp. 59–60
On Level: Extra Practice 1A, pp. 55–58

Solve.

3.

Brian has 9 toys.
6 of them are cars and the rest are bears.
How many bears does Brian have?

$9 - 6 = 3$

Brian has ____3____ bears.

4.

There are 10 eggs in a basket.
3 eggs roll out.
How many eggs are left?

$10 - 3 = 7$

____7____ eggs are left.

5.

Abby blows 4 soap bubbles.
She pops all of them.
How many bubbles are left?

$4 - 4 = 0$

____0____ bubbles are left.

80 Chapter 4 Subtraction Facts to 10

> Workbook A p. 80

84 CHAPTER 4: LESSON 3

Chapter 4

LESSON 4 Making Fact Families

LESSON OBJECTIVES
- Recognize related addition and subtraction sentences.
- Write fact families.
- Use fact families to solve real-world problems.

TECHNOLOGY RESOURCES
- *Math in Focus* eBook
- *Math in Focus* Teaching Resources CD
- *Math in Focus* Virtual Manipulatives

Vocabulary
fact family

DAY 1 Student Book 1A, pp. 85–89
Workbook 1A, pp. 81–82

MATERIALS
- 20 connecting cubes, 10 of each color for the teacher
- Number/Symbol Cards (TR04) – 1 set per group
- clear plastic container

DIFFERENTIATION RESOURCES
- Reteach 1A, pp. 61–66
- Extra Practice 1A, pp. 59–60

 5-minute Warm Up

- Make a number train with 5 red and 3 blue **connecting cubes**. Ask children to make an addition sentence and related number bond.

- Remove the 3 blue cubes from the number train, and *ask*: How many cubes are left? (5) Ask children to make a subtraction sentence.

- Repeat using another combination of red and blue cubes.

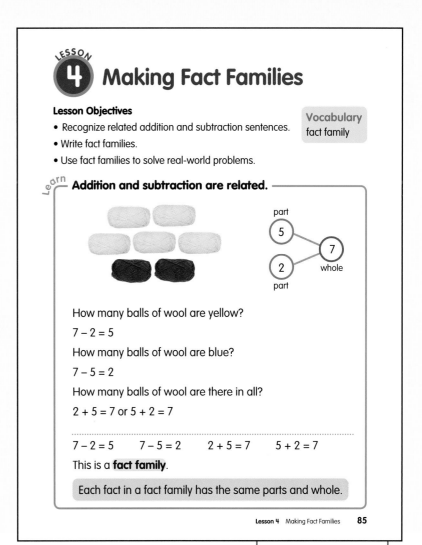

DAY 1 Teach

Addition and Subtraction Are Related
(page 85)

Children have learned to write addition and subtraction sentences to solve real-world problems. This example shows how addition and subtraction facts may be related in a fact family.

- Show children 5 red and 2 blue **connecting cubes**. *Ask*: How many cubes are red? (5) How many are blue? (2) How many cubes are there in all? (7). Have children say the related number bond, 5-2—7 and write it on the board. Ask them to make an addition sentence. Accept 2 + 5 = 7 or 5 + 2 = 7.

- Ask children to construct two subtraction sentences from the same number bond. Accept 7 − 5 = 2 or 7 − 2 = 5

- Explain that all the sentences have the same three numbers (5, 2, 7) and they make up a family of number sentences. Point to all four number sentences and *say*: These sentences form a fact family. They have the same parts and whole.

- Have children read the example in the Student Book.

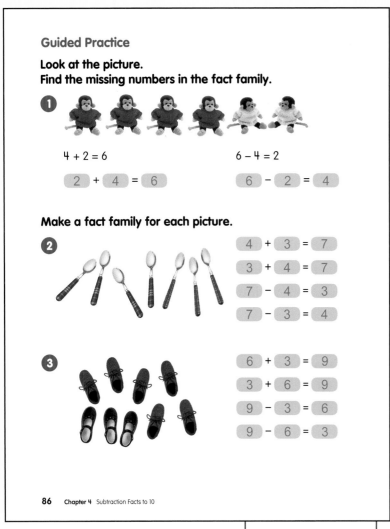

Guided Practice

Look at the picture.
Find the missing numbers in the fact family.

1

$4 + 2 = 6$ $6 - 4 = 2$

$2 + 4 = 6$ $6 - 2 = 4$

Make a fact family for each picture.

2

$4 + 3 = 7$
$3 + 4 = 7$
$7 - 4 = 3$
$7 - 3 = 4$

3

$6 + 3 = 9$
$3 + 6 = 9$
$9 - 3 = 6$
$9 - 6 = 3$

86   **Chapter 4** Subtraction Facts to 10

Student Book A p. 86

Problem of the Lesson

Ling has some stamps.
She puts 4 of them in an album.
She gives 2 to Lucy.
How many stamps does Ling have?

Solution

$? - 4 = 2$

$4 + 2 = 6$

Answer: Ling has 6 stamps.

Differentiated Instruction

English Language Learners

Activate children's prior knowledge to bring meaning to the term *fact family*. Ask children to describe a family and name some parts of a family. Explain that brothers, sisters, parents, grandparents, and so on are all *related*. They are part of the same family. Write a fact family on the board. Show that like a regular family, a fact family has the same parts and the same whole. The number sentences in a fact family are related.

Check for Understanding

✓**Guided Practice** (page 86)

1 Guide children to recognize that there are four toy monkeys in red shirts and two toy monkeys in white shirts. Have them write addition and subtraction sentences related to this picture of monkeys.

2 and **3** Guide children to identify two parts making a whole in each exercise and write related addition and subtraction sentences to show the relationships.

For Advanced Learners Ask children to use the numbers 4, 4, and 8 to write a fact family. *Ask*: How many sentences are there in the fact family? (2) Children draw pictures to show there are only 2 related sentences in the fact family. Have children make fact families with these numbers: 1, 1, 2 and 3, 3, 6. Ask them what they notice. (There are only two sentences in the fact family and not four.)

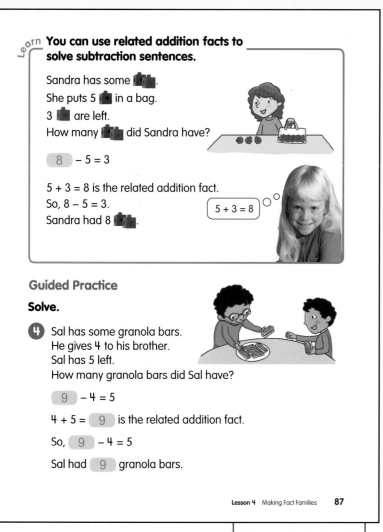

Learn You can use related addition facts to solve subtraction sentences.

Sandra has some ▮.
She puts 5 ▮ in a bag.
3 ▮ are left.
How many ▮ did Sandra have?

8 − 5 = 3

5 + 3 = 8 is the related addition fact.
So, 8 − 5 = 3.
Sandra had 8 ▮.

5 + 3 = 8

Guided Practice

Solve.

4 Sal has some granola bars.
He gives 4 to his brother.
Sal has 5 left.
How many granola bars did Sal have?

9 − 4 = 5

4 + 5 = 9 is the related addition fact.

So, 9 − 4 = 5

Sal had 9 granola bars.

Student Book A p. 87

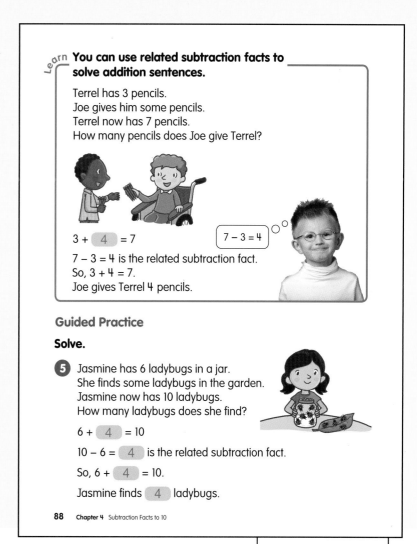

Learn You can use related subtraction facts to solve addition sentences.

Terrel has 3 pencils.
Joe gives him some pencils.
Terrel now has 7 pencils.
How many pencils does Joe give Terrel?

3 + 4 = 7

7 − 3 = 4 is the related subtraction fact.
So, 3 + 4 = 7.
Joe gives Terrel 4 pencils.

7 − 3 = 4

Guided Practice

Solve.

5 Jasmine has 6 ladybugs in a jar.
She finds some ladybugs in the garden.
Jasmine now has 10 ladybugs.
How many ladybugs does she find?

6 + 4 = 10

10 − 6 = 4 is the related subtraction fact.

So, 6 + 4 = 10.

Jasmine finds 4 ladybugs.

Student Book A p. 88

Learn

Use Related Addition Facts to Solve Subtraction Sentences (page 87) 🎲

This example shows how related addition facts within the same fact family can be used to solve subtraction sentences.

- Show children 5 blue and 3 green **connecting cubes** placed on a table.

- Put the 5 blue cubes into a **clear plastic container**. *Ask*: How many cubes have I put into the container? (5) How many cubes are left on the table? (3)

- Write on the board this subtraction sentence: __ − 5 = 3 and the number bond ◯—5-3, and ask children what the missing number is. Ask them how they found the answer.

- Explain that they can find the answer by adding 5 and 3. Write the addition sentence 5 + 3 = 8 on the board.

- Explain how addition was used to solve a subtraction sentence.

✓ Guided Practice (page 87) 🎲

4 Have children act out the story in this exercise using **connecting cubes**. Guide children in completing the number sentences in this fact family.

Learn

Use Related Subtraction Facts to Solve Addition Sentences (page 88) 🎲

This example shows how related subtraction facts within the same fact family can be used to solve addition sentences.

- Show children 3 blue **connecting cubes** arranged in a group on the table. Have a volunteer add from 1 to 6 green cubes to the group. *Ask*: How many cubes are on the table now? (*n*)

- Write 3 + __ = ? on the board.

- Ask children to say how many green cubes were added.

- Explain that they can find the answer by subtracting 3 from *n*. Write the subtraction sentence on the board.

- Explain how subtraction was used to solve an addition sentence.

✓ Guided Practice (page 88) 🎲

5 Have children act out the story in this exercise using **connecting cubes**. Guide children in completing the number sentences in this fact family.

Let's Practice

Use the pictures to write a fact family.

1

3 + 4 = 7
4 + 3 = 7
7 – 3 = 4
7 – 4 = 3

Use the numbers to write a fact family.

2 10   2   8

2 + 8 = 10
8 + 2 = 10
10 – 2 = 8
10 – 8 = 2

Find the missing number.
Use related facts to help you.

3 2 + 5 = 7

4 6 + 3 = 9

5 7 – 4 = 3

6 10 – 6 = 4

7 2 + 3 = 5

8 3 + 5 = 8

9 8 – 4 = 4

10 9 – 6 = 3

ON YOUR OWN
Go to Workbook A:
Practice 5, pages 81–82

Lesson 4   Making Fact Families   **89**

Student Book A p. 89

Practice and Apply
Workbook pages for Chapter 4, Lesson 4

Name: _____   Date: _____

Practice 5   Making Fact Families
Write a fact family for each picture.

— Example —

big dolphin

small dolphins

1 + 2 = 3
2 + 1 = 3
3 – 1 = 2
3 – 2 = 1

1.

4 + 3 = 7
3 + 4 = 7
7 – 3 = 4
7 – 4 = 3

2.

6 + 3 = 9
3 + 6 = 9
9 – 3 = 6
9 – 6 = 3

Lesson 4   Making Fact Families   **81**

Workbook A p. 81

Solve.
Use related facts to help you.

3. Simone has some tomatoes.
She throws away 5 rotten tomatoes.
She has 4 tomatoes left.
How many tomatoes did she have at first?

$\boxed{9}$ – 5 = 4

5 + 4 = $\boxed{9}$ is the related addition fact.

She had _____9_____ tomatoes at first.

4. Marcus has 6 magnets.
Susan gives him some magnets.
Marcus now has 9 magnets.
How many magnets did Susan give Marcus?

6 + $\boxed{3}$ = 9

9 – 6 = $\boxed{3}$ is the related subtraction fact.

Susan gave Marcus _____3_____ magnets.

Find the missing number.
Use related facts to help you.

5. $\boxed{5}$ + 5 = 10   **6.** 2 + $\boxed{5}$ = 7

7. $\boxed{10}$ – 8 = 2   **8.** 9 – $\boxed{6}$ = 3

82   Chapter 4   Subtraction Facts to 10

Workbook A p. 82

Let's Practice (page 89)

These exercises let children practice writing number sentences within a fact family. Exercises **1** and **2** require children to identify part-whole relationships and write a fact family first from pictures then from given numbers. Exercises **3** to **10** require children to use related facts to solve the number sentences.

Common Error Children may incorrectly arrange the given numbers to try to make a fact family. Have them first find the total objects or the greatest number given. Explain that this is the whole, so it is the last number in both addition sentences and the first number in both subtraction sentences.

ON YOUR OWN

Children practice using related addition and subtraction facts to solve problems in Practice 5, pp. 81–82 of **Workbook 1A**. These pages (with the answers) are shown at the right.

Differentiation Options Depending on children's success with the Workbook pages, use these materials as needed.
Struggling: Reteach 1A, pp. 61–66
On Level: Extra Practice 1A, pp. 59–60

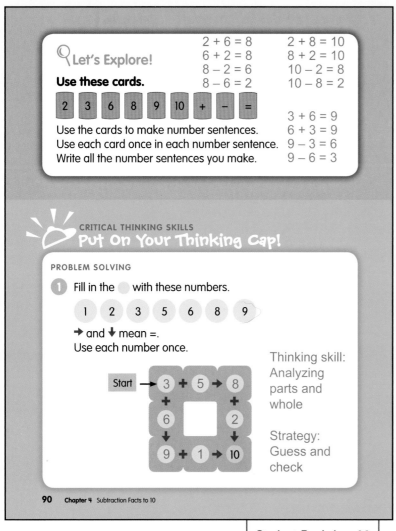

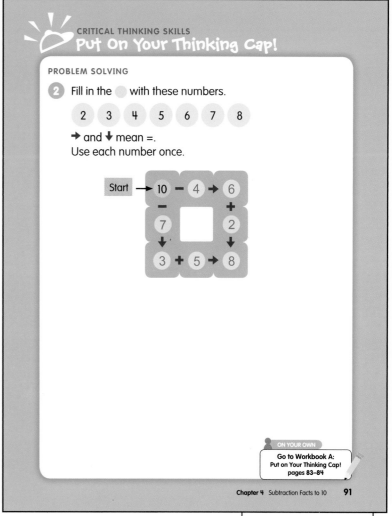

Let's Explore!
Use Cards to Make Number Sentences
(page 90)

This exploration helps children identify all the number bonds that exist in a small set of numbers. Help children see that for each number bond, they can then write four number sentences that belong to that fact family. The possible number bonds are 2-6–8, 2-8–10, and 3-6–9. A total of 12 number sentences are possible. Children may work in small groups. Use **Number/Symbol cards** TR04.

CRITICAL THINKING AND PROBLEM SOLVING
Put on Your Thinking Cap!
(pages 90 and 91)

Exercise ① uses children's abilities to connect numbers that form addition facts and to use logical reasoning. A copy of the **Problem-Solving Grids** shown here and on page 91 can be found in TR05.

• Have children look for two pairs of numbers that total 10. The two pairs among the numbers given are 8-2 and 9-1. Then 8 and 9 belong in the two corner circles, because no two numbers total 1 or 2. There are two possible solutions since the 8 and 9 can go in either corner.

• Place the remaining three numbers by looking for combinations of these numbers that total 8 or 9.

Exercise ② uses children's abilities to connect numbers that form addition and subtraction facts and to use logical reasoning.

• Have children look for pairs of numbers that total 10 to find the numbers that belong in the top row and the left column.

• After that use Guess and Check to place the numbers correctly.

Thinking Skill

• Analyzing parts and whole

Problem Solving Strategy

• Guess and check

Practice and Apply

Workbook pages for Put on Your Thinking Cap!

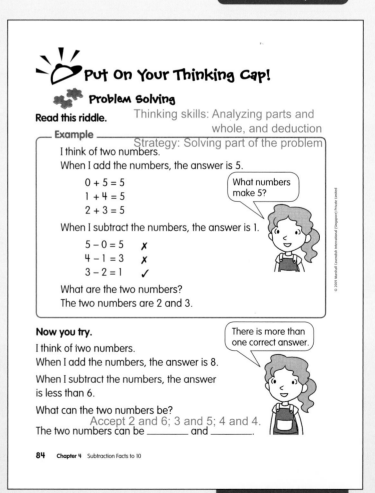

Best Practices Children will require much practice with addition and subtraction facts in order to achieve fluency. You may want to end the chapter by having them write all of the fact families for sums to 10. Suggest that children save the fact families to use as a review and reference for future work with addition and subtraction facts to 20.

ON YOUR OWN

Because all children should be challenged, have all children try the Challenging Practice and Problem-Solving pages in **Workbook 1A**, pp. 83–84. These pages (with the answers) are shown at the right.

Differentiation Options Depending on children's success with the Workbook pages, use these materials as needed.

On Level: Extra Practice 1A, pp. 61–62
Advanced: Enrichment 1A, pp. 26–32

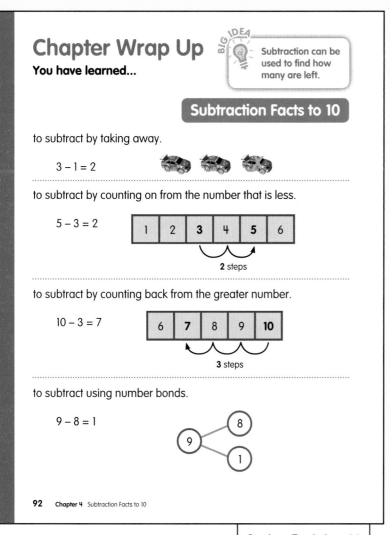

Chapter Wrap Up

You have learned...

BIG IDEA Subtraction can be used to find how many are left.

Subtraction Facts to 10

to subtract by taking away.

$3 - 1 = 2$

to subtract by counting on from the number that is less.

$5 - 3 = 2$

| 1 | 2 | **3** | 4 | **5** | 6 |

2 steps

to subtract by counting back from the greater number.

$10 - 3 = 7$

| 6 | **7** | 8 | 9 | **10** |

3 steps

to subtract using number bonds.

$9 - 8 = 1$

9 — 8, 1

92   Chapter 4 Subtraction Facts to 10

Student Book A p. 92

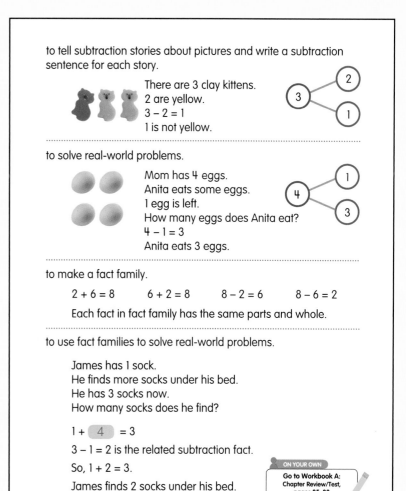

to tell subtraction stories about pictures and write a subtraction sentence for each story.

There are 3 clay kittens.
2 are yellow.
$3 - 2 = 1$
1 is not yellow.

3 — 2, 1

to solve real-world problems.

Mom has 4 eggs.
Anita eats some eggs.
1 egg is left.
How many eggs does Anita eat?
$4 - 1 = 3$
Anita eats 3 eggs.

4 — 1, 3

to make a fact family.

$2 + 6 = 8$ $6 + 2 = 8$ $8 - 2 = 6$ $8 - 6 = 2$

Each fact in fact family has the same parts and whole.

to use fact families to solve real-world problems.

James has 1 sock.
He finds more socks under his bed.
He has 3 socks now.
How many socks does he find?

$1 + \boxed{4} = 3$

$3 - 1 = 2$ is the related subtraction fact.
So, $1 + 2 = 3$.
James finds 2 socks under his bed.

ON YOUR OWN
Go to Workbook A:
Chapter Review/Test,
pages 85–88

Chapter 4 Subtraction Facts to 10   93

Student Book A p. 93

Chapter Wrap Up (pages 92 and 93)

Use the examples on page 92 to review the subtraction strategies. Use the examples on page 93 to review fact families and subtraction stories. Encourage children to use the chapter vocabulary:

- take away
- subtraction sentence
- minus (–)
- less than
- subtract
- subtraction story

ON YOUR OWN

Have children review the vocabulary, concepts, and skills from Chapter 4 with the Chapter Review/Test in **Workbook 1A**, pp. 85–88. These pages (with the answers) are shown on page 93A.

You may also wish to use the Cumulative Review for Chapters 3 and 4 from **Workbook 1A**, pp. 89–92. These pages (with the answers) are shown on page 93C.

Assessment

Use the Chapter 4 Test Prep on pages 23–27 of **Assessments 1** to assess how well children have learned the material of this chapter.

This assessment is appropriate for reporting results to adults at home and administrators. This test is shown on page 93B.

You may also wish to use the Benchmark Assessment 1 for Chapters 1 to 4 on pages 28–37 of **Assessments 1**.

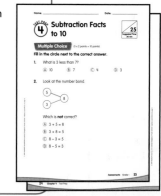

Assessments 1 pp. 23–27

Workbook pages for Chapter Review/Test

Name: _____ Date: _____

Chapter Review/Test
Vocabulary
Choose the correct word.

1. + is plus, – is __minus__.

2. 3 is __less than__ 7.

3. 8 – 2 means to __take away__ 2 from 8.

4. 4 – 3 = 1 is a __subtraction sentence__.

| subtraction sentence |
| take away |
| minus |
| less than |

Concepts and Skills
Complete each subtraction sentence.

5.

8 – __3__ = __5__

6. What is 4 less than 6?

6 – __4__ = __2__

Workbook A p. 85

---

7. What is 3 less than 9?

9 – __3__ = __6__

Count on from the number which is less.

8. 6 – 3 = __3__

9. 9 – 7 = __2__

Count back from the greater number.

10. 10 – 5 = __5__

11. 7 – 6 = __1__

Complete the number bond.
Then complete the subtraction sentence.

12. 7 – 2 = ?

7 – 2 = __5__

13. ? – 2 = 8

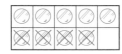

__10__ – 2 = 8

Subtract.
Use related facts.

14. 8 – 4 = __4__

15. 7 – 3 = __4__

16. 10 – __3__ = 7

17. 5 – __0__ = 5

Workbook A p. 86

Name: _____ Date: _____

Write a subtraction story.

Answers vary.

18.

There are 9 children.

5 children are jumping.

_____

__9__ – __5__ = __4__

4 children are not jumping.

Write a fact family.

19.

__6__ + __4__ = __10__

__4__ + __6__ = __10__

__10__ – __4__ = __6__

__10__ – __6__ = __4__

Workbook A p. 87

Problem Solving
Draw .
Cross them out to solve.
Then write a number sentence.

20. James has 9 fish in his fish tank.
He gives his friend 4 fish.
How many fish does he have left?

__9__ – __4__ = __5__

James has __5__ fish left.

Solve.
Use related facts to help you.

21. Mr. Peterson bakes 10 pies.
He eats some of them.
He now has 8 pies.
How many pies did he eat?

10 – __2__ = 8

Mr. Peterson ate __2__ pies.

Workbook A p. 88

Assessments Book pages for Chapter 4 Test Prep
Answer key appears in Assessments Book.

Name: _____ Date: _____

TEST PREP 4 Subtraction Facts to 10

25
Suggested Time: 30 min

Multiple Choice (5 x 2 points = 10 points)

Fill in the circle next to the correct answer.

1. What is 3 less than 7?

   Ⓐ 10   Ⓑ 7   Ⓒ 4   Ⓓ 3

2. Look at the number bond.

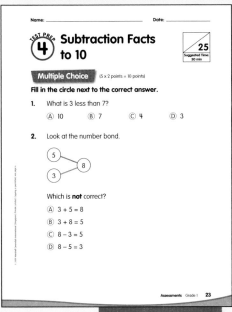

   Which is **not** correct?

   Ⓐ 3 + 5 = 8
   Ⓑ 3 + 8 = 5
   Ⓒ 8 − 3 = 5
   Ⓓ 8 − 5 = 3

Assessments Grade 1 **23**

Assessments p. 23

Name: _____ Date: _____

Extended Response (Question 11: 2 points, Question 12: 3 points)

Solve.
Show your work.

11. Peter buys 9 fish.
    He gives 3 fish away.
    How many fish does Peter have left?

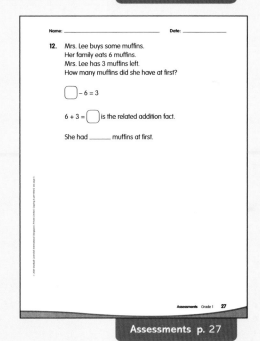

    ◯ ◯ ◯ = ◯

    Peter has _____ fish left.

26 Chapter 4 Test Prep

Assessments p. 26

Name: _____ Date: _____

3. Nick has 8 apples.
   He gives 5 apples away.
   How many apples does Nick have left?

   Ⓐ 13   Ⓑ 8   Ⓒ 5   Ⓓ 3

4. Bob has 7 buttons.
   Pam has 2 fewer buttons than Bob.
   How many buttons does Pam have?

   Bob   Pam

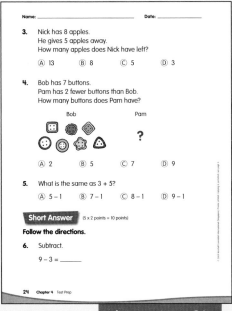

   ?

   Ⓐ 2   Ⓑ 5   Ⓒ 7   Ⓓ 9

5. What is the same as 3 + 5?

   Ⓐ 5 − 1   Ⓑ 7 − 1   Ⓒ 8 − 1   Ⓓ 9 − 1

Short Answer (5 x 2 points = 10 points)

Follow the directions.

6. Subtract.

   9 − 3 = _____

24 Chapter 4 Test Prep

Assessments p. 24

Name: _____ Date: _____

12. Mrs. Lee buys some muffins.
    Her family eats 6 muffins.
    Mrs. Lee has 3 muffins left.
    How many muffins did she have at first?

    ◯ − 6 = 3

    6 + 3 = ◯ is the related addition fact.

    She had _____ muffins at first.

Assessments Grade 1 **27**

Assessments p. 27

Name: _____ Date: _____

7. Look at the picture.
   Write a subtraction sentence.

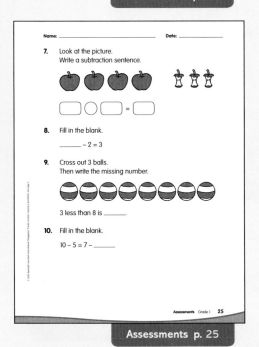

   ◯ ◯ ◯ = ◯

8. Fill in the blank.

   _____ − 2 = 3

9. Cross out 3 balls.
   Then write the missing number.

   3 less than 8 is _____.

10. Fill in the blank.

    10 − 5 = 7 − _____

Assessments Grade 1 **25**

Assessments p. 25

Cumulative Review for Chapters 3 and 4

Name: _____ Date: _____

Cumulative Review
for Chapters 3 and 4

Concepts and Skills

Look at the pictures.
Complete the number sentences.

1.

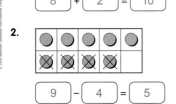

$$\boxed{8} + \boxed{2} = \boxed{10}$$

2.

$$\boxed{9} - \boxed{4} = \boxed{5}$$

Complete the number bonds.
Fill in the blanks.

3. $\underline{5} + 5 = 10$

```
      5
10 <
      5
```

4. $8 - 3 = \underline{5}$

```
     3
8 <
     5
```

Workbook A p. 89

Name: _____ Date: _____

Problem Solving
Look at the pictures.
Write an addition or subtraction story.

12.

There are _____5_____ ⬤.

There are _____4_____ ⬤.

$$\boxed{5} \; \boxed{+} \; \boxed{4} \; \boxed{=} \; \boxed{9}$$

There are _____9_____ ⬤⬤ in all.

13.

There are _____9_____ 🎈.

Jamal lets go of _____3_____ 🎈.

$$\boxed{9} \; \boxed{-} \; \boxed{3} \; \boxed{=} \; \boxed{6}$$

_____6_____ 🎈 are left.

Workbook A p. 91

Fill in the blanks.

5. 2 more than 8 is _____10_____.

6. 3 less than 7 is _____4_____.

7. _____7_____ is 2 more than 5.

8. _____5_____ is 5 less than 10.

Find the missing number.
Use related facts to help you.

9. $2 + \underline{6} = 8$

10. $\underline{6} - 6 = 0$

Pick three numbers and make a fact family.

11.

```
4  +  1  =  5
1  +  4  =  5
5  -  1  =  4
5  -  4  =  1
```

Workbook A p. 90

Solve.
Write addition or subtraction sentences.

14. Ellen has 3 spoons.
Her sister gives her 5 spoons.
How many spoons does Ellen have now?

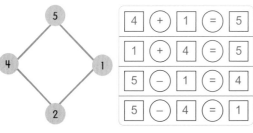

$$3 + 5 = 8$$

Ellen has _____8_____ spoons now.

15. There are 8 fish in a fish tank.
6 are angelfish and the rest are goldfish.
How many goldfish are there?

$$8 - 6 = 2$$

There are _____2_____ goldfish.

Workbook A p. 92

Shapes and Patterns

Math Background

Children have learned in Kindergarten to identify, name, and describe a variety of plane shapes such as circles, squares, triangles, and rectangles as well as recognize solid shapes such as spheres, cubes, and pyramids. In this chapter, children will extend that knowledge to compare shapes, and determine how they are alike and different, by describing their geometric attributes and properties. In learning about solid shapes, with the addition of rectangular prisms and pyramids, children are taught to recognize them from different perspectives and orientations.

The mathematical concepts in geometry can be related to objects in the real world, so children are encouraged to use basic shapes and spatial reasoning to model objects in their environment.

Children will get to compose and decompose plane and solid shapes, and make patterns with plane and solid shapes. As they combine figures, they will develop a better understanding of part-whole relationships as well as the properties of the original and composite shapes. This will also build a background for learning about measurement and properties of geometry such as congruence and symmetry at higher grades.

Cross-Curricular Connections

Reading/Language Arts Discuss with children some of the common meanings of the word *shape*.
• **n.** form or figure; *has the shape of a rectangle*
• **n.** condition; *a car in good shape*
• **v.** form into a shape; *to shape dough in a ball*
Encourage children to name shapes they see in the classroom.

Physical Education Clear an area of the classroom or move to an open area. Assign a leader, and ask children to jog along a route that has the shape of a rectangle. Continue by assigning new leaders each time and asking children to jog along routes that have the shape of a square, triangle, circle, and any combination of these four shapes.

Grade K	Identify and name the four basic plane shapes. (Chap. 7)
Grade 1	Explore, identify, and compare plane and solid shapes in patterns and in the real world. (Chap. 5)
Grade 2	Describe, extend and create two- and three- dimensional shape patterns. (Chap. 19)

EVERY DAY COUNTS® Calendar Math

The November activities provide...

Review of comparing and ordering numbers (Chapter 1)

Preview of measuring length (Chapter 9)

Practice of attributes of triangles (Lesson 1 in this chapter) and finding patterns (Lessons 5 and 6 in this chapter)

Differentiation Resources

Differentiation for Special Populations

	English Language Learners	Struggling Reteach 1A	On Level Extra Practice 1A	Advanced Enrichment 1A
Lesson 1	p. 99	pp. 67-76	pp. 71-76	
Lesson 2	p. 111	pp. 77-80	pp. 77-78	Enrichment pages can be used to challenge advanced children.
Lesson 3	p. 117	pp. 81-84	pp. 79-84	
Lesson 4	p. 124	pp. 85-86	pp. 85-86	
Lesson 5	p. 130	pp. 87-88	pp. 87-88	
Lesson 6	p. 133	pp. 89-90	p. 89	

Additional Support

For English Language Learners

Select activities that reinforce the chapter vocabulary and the connections among these words, such as having children

- create and display a list of terms to define and give examples throughout this chapter
- make flash cards for terms, then have children choose two at a time and create a sentence using the terms
- match models of plane and solid shapes to flash cards
- discuss the Chapter Wrap Up, encouraging children to use the chapter vocabulary

For Struggling Learners

Select activities that go back to the appropriate stage of the Concrete-Pictorial-Abstract spectrum, such as having children

- use models of plane shapes and solids to sort in various ways, such as size, color, and shape.
- use models of shapes to create and describe patterns
- create and solve riddles about various shapes and solids
- describe and make pictures and models by combining shapes and solids

See also page 124A

If necessary, review:

- Chapter 3 (Addition Facts to 10)
- Chapter 4 (Subtraction Facts to 10)

For Advanced Learners

See suggestions on pages 100–101 and 118.

Assessment and Remediation

Chapter 5 Assessment

Prior Knowledge

	Resource	Page numbers
Quick Check	Student Book 1A	p. 97
Pre-Test	Assessments 1	pp. 38–39

Ongoing Diagnostic

Guided Practice	Student Book 1A	pp. 99, 100, 102, 103, 107, 112, 117, 123, 124, 125, 130, 133
Common Error	Teacher's Edition 1A	pp. 104, 114–115, 120, 127–128, 131, 134
Best Practices	Teacher's Edition 1A	p. 124A

Formal Evaluation

Chapter Review/Test	Workbook 1A	pp. 133–136
Chapter 5 Test Prep	Assessments 1	pp. 40–44

Remediation Options

Problems with these items...   Can be remediated with...

Objective	Review/Test Items Workbook 1A pp. 25–28	Chapter Assessment Items Assessments 1 pp. 40–44	Reteach Reteach 1A	Student Book Student Book 1A
Use chapter vocabulary correctly.	1–5	Not assessed	pp. 68–90	pp. 98, 110, 129
Identify, classify, and describe plane shapes.	1, 6–8	2, 5–6, 12–14	pp. 68–74	Lesson 1
Make same and different shapes.	15	4	pp. 75–76	Lesson 1
Identify, classify, and sort solid shapes.	4, 9–10	11	pp. 77–80	Lesson 2
Combine and separate plane and solid shapes.	11–12	7	pp. 81–84	Lesson 3
Identify plane and solid shapes in real life.	12	1, 3, 8	pp. 85–86	Lesson 4
Use plane shapes to identify, extend, and create patterns.	13	9	pp. 87–88	Lesson 5
Use solid shapes to identify, extend, and create patterns.	14	10	pp. 89–90	Lesson 6

Chapter Planning Guide

CHAPTER 5 Shapes and Patterns

Lesson	Pacing	Instructional Objectives	Vocabulary
Chapter Opener pp. 94–97 Recall Prior Knowledge Quick Check	*1 day	🔆**Big Idea** Explore, identify, and compare plane and solid shapes in patterns and in the real world.	
Lesson 1, pp. 98–109 Exploring Plane Shapes	3 days	• Identify, classify, and describe plane shapes • Make same and different shapes	• circle • triangle • square • rectangle • side • corner • sort • color • alike • shape • size • different
Lesson 2, pp. 110–115 Exploring Solid Shapes	1 day	• Identify, classify, and sort solid shapes	• rectangular prism • cube • sphere • cone • cylinder • pyramid • stack • slide • roll
Lesson 3, pp. 116–123 Making Pictures and Models with Shapes	2 days	• Combine and separate plane and solid shapes	

* Assume that 1 day is a 45–55 minute period

Resources	Materials	NCTM Focal Points	NCTM Process Standards
Student Book 1A, pp. 94–97 **Assessments 1,** pp. 38–39			
Student Book 1A, pp. 98–109 **Workbook 1A,** pp. 93–100 **Extra Practice 1A,** pp. 71–76 **Reteach 1A,** pp. 67–76	• attribute blocks • 2 Squares to Fold per pair (TR06) • 1 set of Shapes to Fold per pair (TR07) • rectangular piece of paper for the teacher	*Geometry* Describe geometric attributes and properties Determine how figures are alike and different Develop initial understanding of such properties as congruence and symmetry	Reasoning/Proof Communication Connections
Student Book 1A, pp. 110–115 **Workbook 1A,** pp. 101–104 **Extra Practice 1A,** pp. 77–78 **Reteach 1A,** pp. 77–80	• 1 set of geometric solids per group • Table of Shapes (TR08)	*Geometry* Describe geometric attributes and properties	Reasoning/Proof Communication
Student Book 1A, pp. 116–123 **Workbook 1A,** pp. 105–112 **Extra Practice 1A,** pp. 79–84 **Reteach 1A,** pp. 81–84	• attribute blocks • geometric solids • Shapes to Combine for the teacher (TR09) • Shapes to Cut Out (TR10) • Table of Solids (TR11) • scissors • markers • Blu-Tack® • blank transparency (optional)	*Geometry* Compose and break down plane and solid figures	Reasoning/Proof Communication Connections

Chapter Planning Guide

Lesson	Pacing	Instructional Objectives	Vocabulary
Lesson 4, pp. 124–128 Seeing Shapes Around Us	1 day 43	• Identify plane and solid shapes in real life	
Lesson 5, pp. 129–131 Making Patterns with Plane Shapes	2 days 44 45	• Use plane shapes to identify, extend, and create patterns	Repeating pattern
Lesson 6, pp. 132–134 Making Patterns with Solid Shapes	1 day 46	• Use solid shapes to identify, extend, and create patterns	
Problem Solving p. 135 Put on Your Thinking Cap!	2 days 47 48	Thinking Skills • Induction, Analyzing patterns and relationships Problem Solving Strategies • Guess and Check, Solving part of the problem	
Chapter Wrap Up pp. 136–137	1 day 49	• Reinforce and consolidate chapter skills and concepts	
Chapter Assessment	1 day 5		

Resources	Materials	NCTM Focal Points	NCTM Process Standards
Student Book 1A, pp. 124–128 **Workbook 1A,** pp. 113–116 **Extra Practice 1A,** pp. 85–86 **Reteach 1A,** pp. 85–86	• 1 set of geometric solids per group • a colored pipe-cleaner for the teacher • common objects, e.g. CD, book, tumbler for the teacher	***Geometry*** Determine how figures are alike and different. Combine figures and recognize them from different perspectives.	Communication Connections
Student Book 1A, pp. 129–131 **Workbook 1A,** pp. 117–122 **Extra Practice 1A,** pp. 87–88 **Reteach 1A,** pp. 87–88	• attribute blocks • markers	***Geometry*** Describe geometric attributes and properties.	Problem Solving Reasoning/Proof Connections
Student Book 1A, pp. 132–134 **Workbook 1A,** pp. 123–124 **Extra Practice 1A,** p. 89 **Reteach 1A,** pp. 89–90	• 1 set of geometric solids per group	***Geometry*** Describe geometric attributes and properties.	Problem Solving Reasoning/Proof Communication Connections
Student Book 1A, p. 135 **Workbook 1A,** pp. 127–132 **Extra Practice 1A,** p. 90 **Enrichment 1A,** pp. 33–41			
Student Book 1A, pp. 136–137 **Workbook 1A,** pp. 133–136		***Geometry*** Determine how figures are alike and different.	Problem Solving Reasoning/Proof Connections
Assessments 1, pp. 40–44			

Technology Resources for easy classroom management
• *Math in Focus* eBook
• *Math in Focus* Teaching Resources CD
• *Math in Focus* Virtual Manipulatives
• On-Line Web Resources

Shapes and Patterns

Chapter 5
Vocabulary

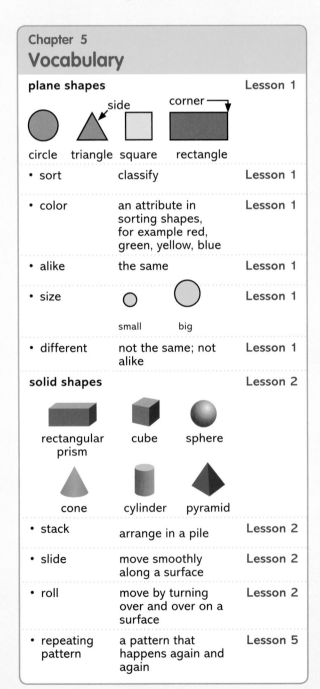

plane shapes		Lesson 1
circle	triangle · square · rectangle (side, corner)	
• sort	classify	Lesson 1
• color	an attribute in sorting shapes, for example red, green, yellow, blue	Lesson 1
• alike	the same	Lesson 1
• size	small · big	Lesson 1
• different	not the same; not alike	Lesson 1
solid shapes	rectangular prism · cube · sphere · cone · cylinder · pyramid	Lesson 2
• stack	arrange in a pile	Lesson 2
• slide	move smoothly along a surface	Lesson 2
• roll	move by turning over and over on a surface	Lesson 2
• repeating pattern	a pattern that happens again and again	Lesson 5

Shapes and Patterns

Once upon a time, there was a place called the Land of Shapes. Many shapes lived there. They worked, played, and ate together.

One day, a strange visitor came. The visitor wanted to live in the Land of Shapes. The shapes looked at the visitor. One shape said, "You are not like us. How can you live here?"

94

Student Book A p. 94

Big Idea (page 95)

Plane and solid shapes in patterns and the real world are the focus of this chapter.

• Children classify and compare plane and solid shapes based on their geometric properties, using the appropriate vocabulary for describing shapes.

• Children make composite shapes, models, and patterns with these shapes.

Chapter Opener (pages 94 and 95)

The pictures and story in this section illustrate how the real world may be interpreted in terms of geometric shapes in a variety of sizes and colors. Children have learned to identify different shapes and relate them to geometric ideas in the real world. In this chapter, they will learn to make new shapes, pictures, models, and patterns with familiar shapes.

• Have children look at the first picture as you read aloud the first paragraph.

• *Ask*: What are some of the shapes you see in the picture? (Buildings: triangle, square, rectangle, circles; Shape characters: circle, triangle, square, rectangle)

The visitor smiled.
He said, "I am not only one shape, I can be any shape!"
He then turned himself into the different shapes.

The shapes thought this was great!
They decided to let the visitor stay.
So the visitor stayed and they all lived happily ever after.

BIG IDEA
Explore, identify, and compare plane and solid shapes in patterns and in the real world.

95

Student Book A p. 95

Differentiated Instruction

English Language Learners

As you introduce the vocabulary in the chapter, create a graphic organizer on a large sheet of paper or poster board. English language learners can use this as a visual reference for geometry concepts. Expand the table below to include other shapes.

Shape	Sides	Corners	Properties
square	4	4	4 equal sides 4 corners

- Encourage children to describe the shapes using color or size.

- Read the second paragraph with children.

- *Ask*: How is the visitor not like the other shapes? (star shaped)

- Read on to page 95 and the end of the story.

- *Ask*: Why did the shapes let the visitor stay? (He was like them after all.)

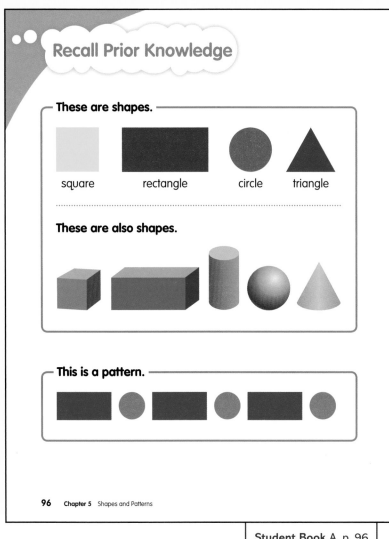

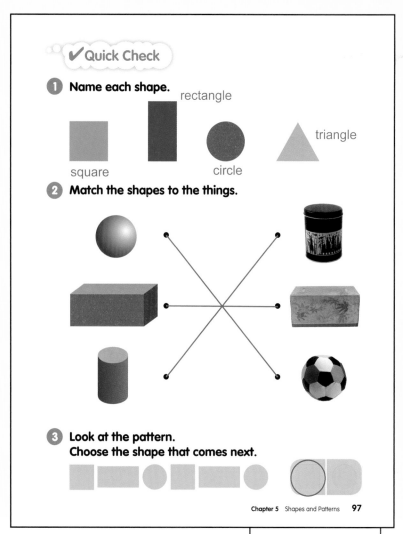

Recall Prior Knowledge (page 96)

Shapes

Children learned in Kindergarten to identify plane shapes and are exposed to solid shapes.

- Have children name the plane shapes on the page.

- Ask children if they can name the solid shapes as well. (cube, rectangular prism, cylinder, sphere, cone) Accept terms that they use to relate to their own experience, for example, *box* and *ball* instead of *rectangular prism* and *sphere*.

Patterns

Children learned to recognize repeating patterns with shapes in Kindergarten.

- Have children name the shapes in the pattern as they occur: rectangle, circle, rectangle, circle, rectangle, circle.

- *Ask*: What shape comes next in this pattern? (rectangle)

✔Quick Check (page 97)

Use this section as a diagnostic tool to assess children's level of prerequisite knowledge before they progress to this chapter. Exercise ① checks that children can identify plane shapes as taught in Kindergarten. Exercise ② checks children's ability to match solid shapes to real-world objects. Exercise ③ checks that children can continue a repeating pattern, a skill taught in Kindergarten.

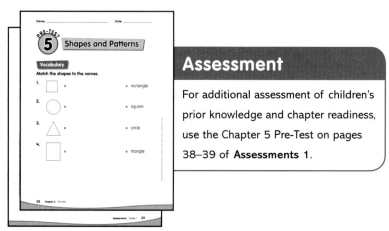

Assessment

For additional assessment of children's prior knowledge and chapter readiness, use the Chapter 5 Pre-Test on pages 38–39 of **Assessments 1**.

Assessments 1 pp. 38–39

Chapter 5

Exploring Plane Shapes

LESSON OBJECTIVES
- Identify, classify, and describe plane shapes.
- Make same and different shapes.

TECHNOLOGY RESOURCES
- *Math in Focus* eBook
- *Math in Focus* Teaching Resources CD
- *Math in Focus* Virtual Manipulatives

Vocabulary

circle	triangle	square	rectangle
side	corner	sort	color
alike	shape	size	different

DAY 1 Student Book 1A, pp. 98–102

MATERIALS
- attribute blocks (as shown on pages 98, 99, and 101 for the teacher)
- attribute blocks (1 set per group as shown)
- 2 Squares to Fold per pair (TR06)
- 1 set of Shapes to Fold (TR07) per pair
- a rectangular piece of paper for the teacher

DAY 2 Student Book 1A, pp. 102–105
Workbook 1A, pp. 93–98

DIFFERENTIATION RESOURCES
- Reteach 1A, pp. 67–74
- Extra Practice 1A, pp. 71–74

DAY 3 Student Book 1A, pp. 106–109
Workbook 1A, pp. 99–100

DIFFERENTIATION RESOURCES
- Reteach 1A, pp. 75–76
- Extra Practice 1A, pp. 75–76

5-minute Warm Up

- Pick out the following shapes from the attribute blocks: rectangle, square, triangle, and circle, in 3 different colors.

- When you hold up a shape (for example, a green square), have half the class say the color (green) and the other half say the shape (square).

- Repeat with a different colored shape. This prepares children to classify shapes in the lesson.

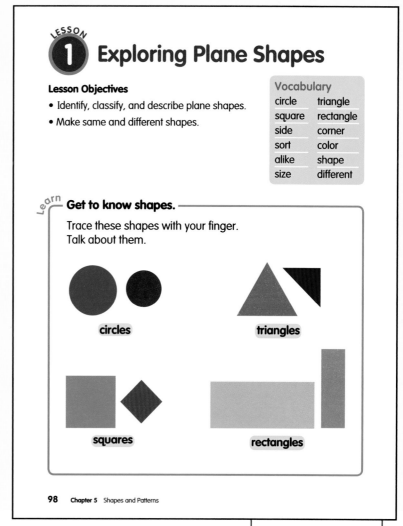

LESSON **1**

Exploring Plane Shapes

Lesson Objectives
- Identify, classify, and describe plane shapes.
- Make same and different shapes.

Vocabulary

circle	triangle
square	rectangle
side	corner
sort	color
alike	shape
size	different

Learn Get to know shapes.

Trace these shapes with your finger.
Talk about them.

circles   triangles

squares   rectangles

98   **Chapter 5** Shapes and Patterns

Student Book A p. 98

DAY 1 **Teach**

Get to Know Shapes (page 98)

Children review the names of the four shapes and learn to identify them in different orientations.

- Hold up a circle and ask children to name the shape.

- Draw a circle on the board. Trace it on the board with your finger, and have children trace the circle in their Student Book.

- Turn the circle in your hand, and trace it in the air to show children that it looks the same from any orientation.

- Hold up the square and ask children to name it.

- Draw a square on the board. Trace it on the board with your finger, and have children trace the square in their Student Book. Show children they can start tracing it from any corner of the square, in either direction.

- Turn the square in your hand to show the other orientation in the Student Book. Draw it on the board and trace it with your finger. Have children trace the other square in their book. Explain that they are both squares.

- Repeat this activity using the triangle and rectangle.

Guided Practice

Find the shapes that are <u>not</u> squares.

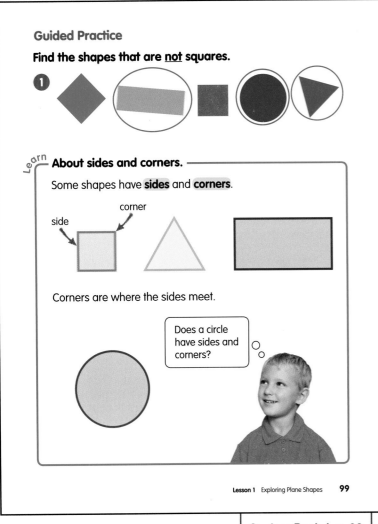

① About sides and corners.

Some shapes have **sides** and **corners**.

Corners are where the sides meet.

Does a circle have sides and corners?

Lesson 1 Exploring Plane Shapes **99**

Student Book A p. 99

Problem of the Lesson

Look at these shapes. List all the letters of any shapes that are:

1. the same shape.
2. the same size.
3. the same color.

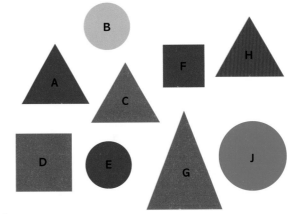

Answers:

1. A, C, G and H or B, E and J or D and F are the same shape.
2. A, C and H or F, B and E are the same size.
3. A, E and F.

Best Practices You may want to create a shapes bulletin board display while working on this chapter. Pin up the names of the plane shapes and solid shapes that are introduced in Lessons 1 and 2. Invite children to add to the display by bringing in pictures they find from magazines and newspapers or shapes that they cut out.

Check for Understanding

✓ **Guided Practice** (page 99)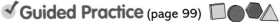

① Have children name each shape from left to right.
• *Ask*: Which shapes are squares? (the light blue and red shapes) Which shapes are not squares? (all the others)

Sides and Corners (page 99)

Shapes can be described based on their geometrical properties of sides and corners.

• Give each child one set of **attribute blocks**.

• Hold up a square, model feeling the sides of the square. Have children do the same and *ask*: How many sides does a square have? (4)

• Show children the corners and have them feel and count the corners of a square. Explain that corners are where the sides meet. *Ask*: How many corners does a square have? (4)

• Repeat this with a triangle and a rectangle.

• Hold up a rectangle and *ask*: What shape is this? (rectangle)

• *Ask*: How do you tell it is not a square? Lead them to see that a square has 4 equal sides but a rectangle only has equal opposite sides.

• Now hold up a circle and *ask*: How many sides does a circle have? (0) *Ask*: How many corners does a circle have? (0)

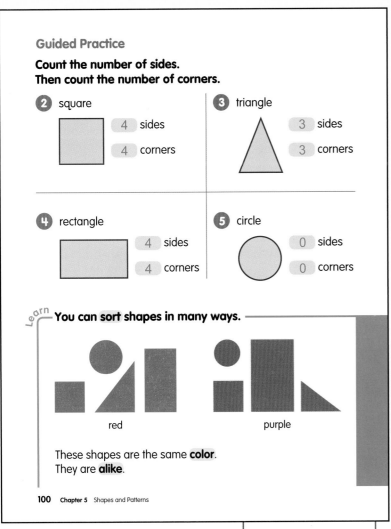

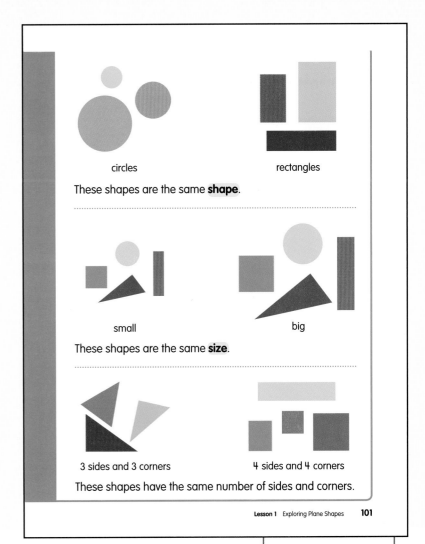

For Advanced Learners Have children work in pairs. One child hides a shape and the other child guesses the shape by asking only two questions. The name of the shape cannot be mentioned. For example, "How many corners does the shape have? How many sides are there ?" Partners switch roles and repeat.

✓ Guided Practice (page 100)

2 to **5** Have children count the number of sides and corners for each shape. Remind children that circles are special shapes that have neither sides nor corners.

Sort Shapes in Many Ways
(pages 100 and 101)

Children learn to compare and sort shapes. Besides counting the number of sides and corners, shapes can also be sorted by color and size. (These pages may be taught by showing certain parts of the Student Book pages to children one at a time, or by using attribute blocks to match those on the pages.)

- Ask children to name the red shapes on page 100. Then *ask*: How are they alike? (They are red./They are the same color.) *Say*: They are alike because they are the same color. They are all red.

- Do the same for the purple shapes, and for the other groups of shapes on page 101.

- Ask children to name each group of shapes. Have them identify the property that makes the shapes in each group the same, for example, shape, size or number of sides and corners.

- For the last group of shapes, be careful to note that while only triangles have 3 sides and 3 corners, both squares and rectangles have 4 sides and 4 corners. Help children recall from the previous section that squares have 4 equal sides.

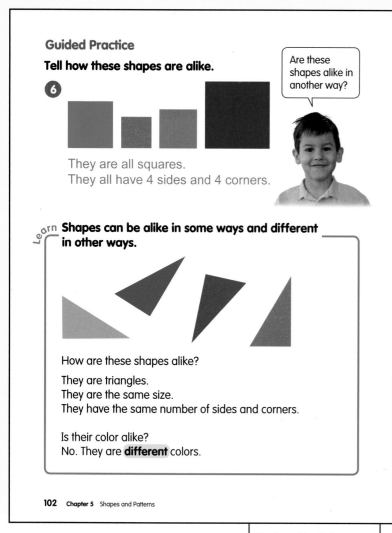

Guided Practice

Tell how these shapes are alike.

6

> Are these shapes alike in another way?

They are all squares.
They all have 4 sides and 4 corners.

Learn **Shapes can be alike in some ways and different in other ways.**

How are these shapes alike?

They are triangles.
They are the same size.
They have the same number of sides and corners.

Is their color alike?
No. They are **different** colors.

102   **Chapter 5** Shapes and Patterns

Student Book A p. 102

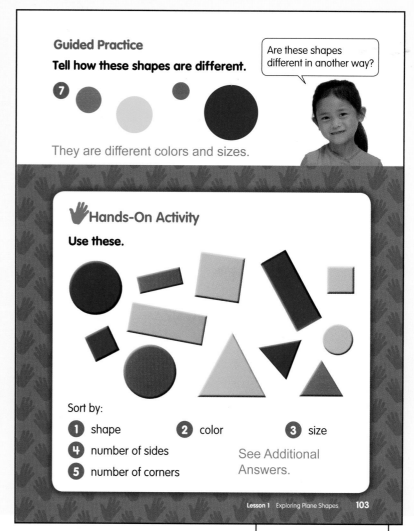

Guided Practice

Tell how these shapes are different.

7

> Are these shapes different in another way?

They are different colors and sizes.

✋ Hands-On Activity

Use these.

Sort by:

1 shape   2 color   3 size

4 number of sides   See Additional Answers.

5 number of corners

Lesson 1 Exploring Plane Shapes   103

Student Book A p. 103

✔Guided Practice (page 102)

6 **Ask**: How are these shapes alike? Lead children to give all the possible ways in which they are alike, and not just that they are squares – they have 4 equal sides and 4 corners.

DAY 2 Teach

See the Lesson Organizer on page 98 for Day 2 resources.

Learn

Shapes Can be Alike and Different (page 102)

Children use appropriate vocabulary for describing and classifying shapes based on observable similarities and differences.

- Have children look at the shapes on the Student Book and **ask**: How are these shapes alike? Encourage them to say they are all triangles, they are all the same size, and they all have 3 sides and corners.

- Then **ask**: Is their color alike? (No. They are different colors.)

✔Guided Practice (page 103)

7 **Ask**: How are these shapes alike? (They are circles. They have no sides and no corners.) **Ask**: How are these shapes different? Encourage children to say the shapes have different sizes and colors, and to name the colors.

✋ Hands-On Activity: ▢●⬡△

Sort Shapes (page 103)

This activity provides practice sorting shapes based on the observable attributes taught in the previous pages: shape, color, size, number of sides and corners.

- Arrange children in groups of 5. Give each group a set of **attribute blocks** that match the set of shapes shown in the Student Book.

- Have children sort the shapes according to shape (Exercise 1), color (Exercise 2), size (Exercise 3), number of sides (Exercise 4) and number of corners (Exercise 5).

- You may want to introduce the fact that a square is a special type of rectangle before children begin to sort by shape in Exercise 1. All rectangles and squares have four sides. The opposite sides of rectangles and squares are of equal length. In addition, all sides of a square are of equal length. So a square is a rectangle. A rectangle can be a square when all the sides are of equal length.

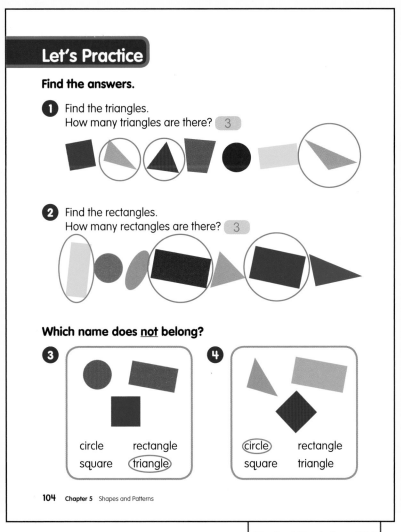

Let's Practice

Find the answers.

1 Find the triangles.
How many triangles are there? 3

2 Find the rectangles.
How many rectangles are there? 3

Which name does not belong?

3
circle   rectangle
square   ~~triangle~~

4
~~circle~~   rectangle
square   triangle

104 Chapter 5 Shapes and Patterns

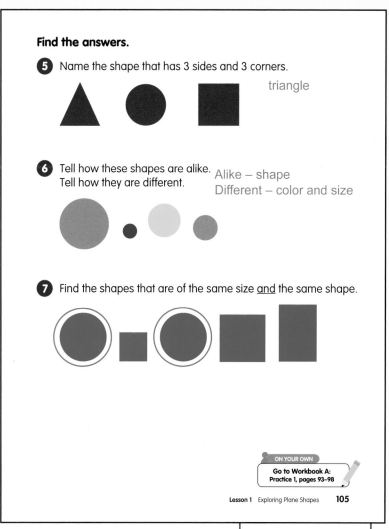

Find the answers.

5 Name the shape that has 3 sides and 3 corners.

triangle

6 Tell how these shapes are alike.
Tell how they are different.   Alike – shape
Different – color and size

7 Find the shapes that are of the same size and the same shape.

ON YOUR OWN
Go to Workbook A:
Practice 1, pages 93–98

Lesson 1 Exploring Plane Shapes **105**

• You may wish to make this a race among the groups. Call out the words *shape, color, size, sides* or *corners* at random and see which group can sort the shapes the fastest according to what you call out.

Additional Answers (page 103)

1 circles : 3   rectangles : 3
squares : 3   triangles : 3

2 red : circle, rectangle, and triangle
blue : circle, square, rectangle, and triangle
yellow : rectangle, triangle, circle and two squares

3 big : two circles, triangle, square and two rectangles
small : two squares, two triangles, rectangle and circle

4 and **5** one side and no corners : circles
three sides and corners : triangles
four sides and corners : squares and rectangles

Let's Practice (pages 104 and 105)

This practice reinforces identifying and sorting shapes. Exercises **1** and **2** require children to identify and count specified shapes. Exercises **3** and **4** require children to match the names of shapes to the pictures and single out the name that does not belong. Exercise **5** requires children to identify and name a shape based on its attributes. Exercises **6** and **7** require children to sort shapes to show their understanding of *same, alike* and *different*.

Common Error Some children may not understand the difference between a square and a rectangle. Use the **attribute blocks** of squares and rectangles. Show children that all four sides of the squares are the same length. The rectangles have two sides that are longer than the other two sides.

ON YOUR OWN

Children practice identifying and comparing shapes in Practice 1, pp. 93–98 of **Workbook 1A**. These pages (with the answers) are shown on pages 105A-106.

Differentiation Options Depending on children's success with the Workbook pages, use these materials as needed.
Struggling: Reteach 1A, pp. 67–74
On Level: Extra Practice 1A, pp. 71–74

Practice and Apply

Workbook pages for Chapter 5, Lesson 1

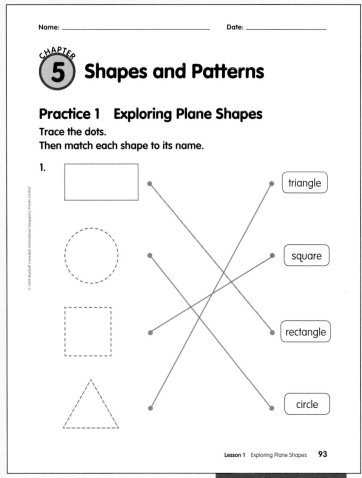

Name: _____ Date: _____

CHAPTER 5 Shapes and Patterns

Practice 1 Exploring Plane Shapes

Trace the dots.
Then match each shape to its name.

1.

- triangle
- square
- rectangle
- circle

Lesson 1 Exploring Plane Shapes **93**

Workbook A p. 93

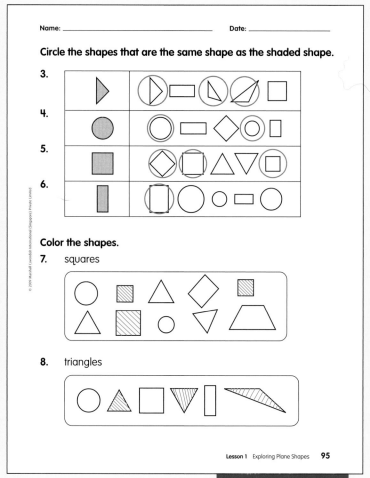

Name: _____ Date: _____

Circle the shapes that are the same shape as the shaded shape.

3.

4.

5.

6.

Color the shapes.

7. squares

8. triangles

Lesson 1 Exploring Plane Shapes **95**

Workbook A p. 95

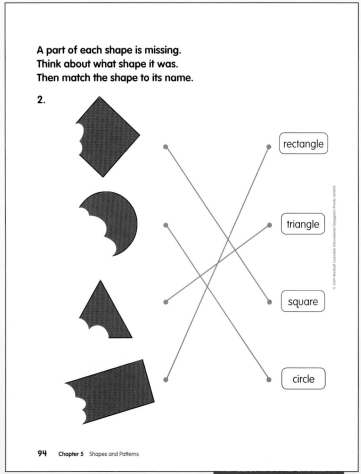

A part of each shape is missing.
Think about what shape it was.
Then match the shape to its name.

2.

- rectangle
- triangle
- square
- circle

94 **Chapter 5** Shapes and Patterns

Workbook A p. 94

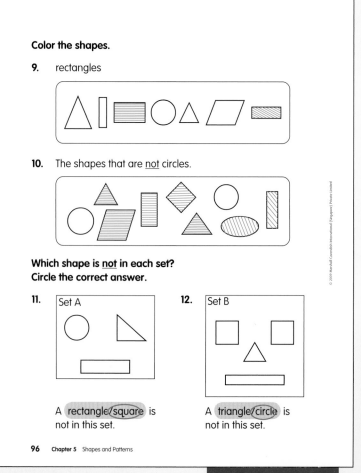

Color the shapes.

9. rectangles

10. The shapes that are <u>not</u> circles.

Which shape is <u>not</u> in each set?
Circle the correct answer.

11. Set A

A rectangle/square is
not in this set.

12. Set B

A triangle/circle is
not in this set.

96 **Chapter 5** Shapes and Patterns

Workbook A p. 96

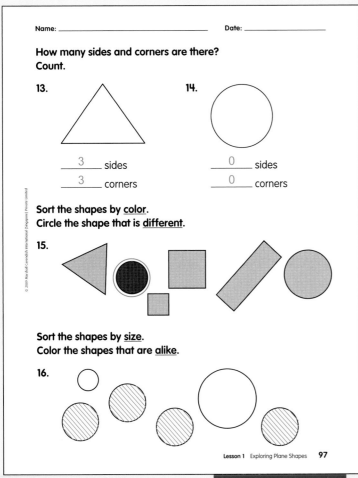

Name: _____ Date: _____

How many sides and corners are there?
Count.

13.

_3_ sides
_3_ corners

14.

_0_ sides
_0_ corners

Sort the shapes by color.
Circle the shape that is different.

15.

Sort the shapes by size.
Color the shapes that are alike.

16.

Lesson 1 Exploring Plane Shapes **97**

Workbook A p. 97

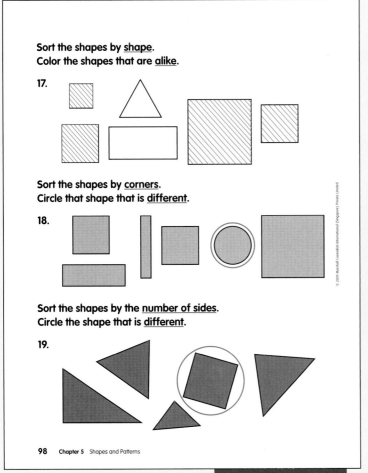

Sort the shapes by shape.
Color the shapes that are alike.

17.

Sort the shapes by corners.
Circle that shape that is different.

18.

Sort the shapes by the number of sides.
Circle the shape that is different.

19.

98 Chapter 5 Shapes and Patterns

Workbook A p. 98

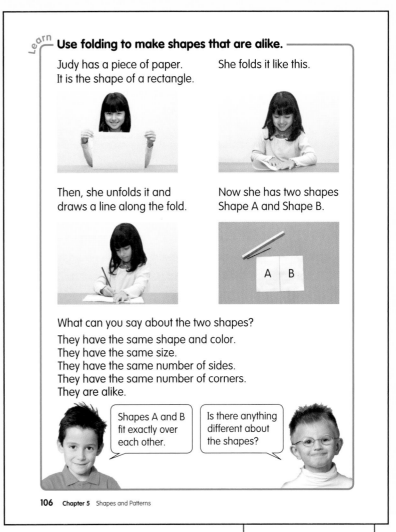

Learn

Use folding to make shapes that are alike.

Judy has a piece of paper. It is the shape of a rectangle.

She folds it like this.

Then, she unfolds it and draws a line along the fold.

Now she has two shapes Shape A and Shape B.

What can you say about the two shapes?
They have the same shape and color.
They have the same size.
They have the same number of sides.
They have the same number of corners.
They are alike.

Shapes A and B fit exactly over each other.

Is there anything different about the shapes?

106 Chapter 5 Shapes and Patterns

Student Book A p. 106

DAY 3 | **Teach** | See the Lesson Organizer on page 98 for Day 3 resources.

Learn

Use Folding to Make Shapes That Are Alike (page 106)

Children learn to construct shapes that are alike by folding paper. This prepares them for learning about congruence and symmetry in later grades.

- Read with children the steps in the Student Book. Explain that the steps read from top left to right and then bottom left to right.

- As you read, model the steps with a piece of paper. Write A and B on the shapes you have made.

- *Ask*: What can you say about the shapes A and B?

- Guide children to see that the shapes are identical in shape, size and number of sides and corners.
  Say: Shapes A and B are exactly alike.

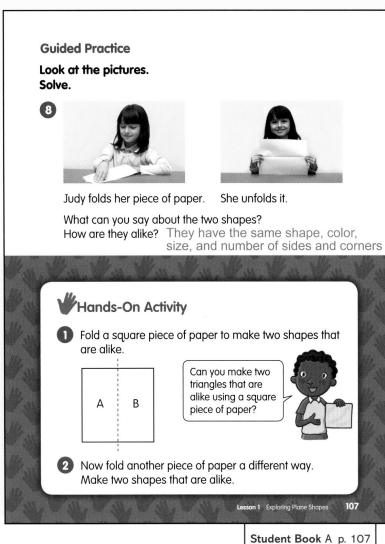

Guided Practice

Look at the pictures.
Solve.

8

Judy folds her piece of paper.   She unfolds it.

What can you say about the two shapes?
How are they alike? They have the same shape, color,
size, and number of sides and corners

**Hands-On Activity**

1 Fold a square piece of paper to make two shapes that
are alike.

A   B

Can you make two
triangles that are
alike using a square
piece of paper?

2 Now fold another piece of paper a different way.
Make two shapes that are alike.

Lesson 1 Exploring Plane Shapes **107**

Student Book A p. 107

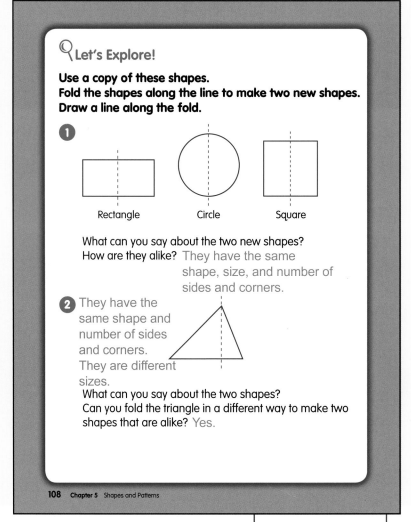

Let's Explore!

Use a copy of these shapes.
Fold the shapes along the line to make two new shapes.
Draw a line along the fold.

1

Rectangle   Circle   Square

What can you say about the two new shapes?
How are they alike? They have the same
shape, size, and number of
sides and corners.

2 They have the
same shape and
number of sides
and corners.
They are different
sizes.
What can you say about the two shapes?
Can you fold the triangle in a different way to make two
shapes that are alike? Yes.

108 Chapter 5 Shapes and Patterns

Student Book A p. 108

✓ Guided Practice (page 107)

8 *Ask*: How are the shapes alike? Guide children to see that
the shapes are identical in shape, size, and number of sides
and corners. *Say*: The two shapes are exactly alike.

✋ Hands-On Activity:
Fold Paper to Make Shapes
That are Alike (page 107)

This activity lets children explore making a pair of identical
shapes by folding a square piece of paper.

- Have children do this activity in pairs, and give each pair
  Squares to Fold (TR06).

- Have each pair work on one square together first to make
  2 rectangles, as shown in the Student Book.

- *Ask*: Are the shapes alike? How are they alike? Discuss the
  possible ways they are alike.

- Then *ask*: Can you make 2 triangles that are alike using the
  other piece of paper?

- Guide children to fold the paper along the diagonal to form 2
  identical triangles. Discuss the ways the 2 triangles are alike.

🔍 Let's Explore!
Fold Paper to Make Two New Shapes
(page 108)

In this exploration, children learn whether one can always
make two alike shapes just by folding a piece of paper. Have
children do this activity in pairs, and give each pair a set of
Shapes to Fold (TR07).

- For Exercise **1**, have children fold the given shapes as
  shown on the page in the Student Book. For each fold,
  ask: How are the two new shapes alike? (same shape and
  size, same number of sides and corners)

- For Exercise **2**, have children fold the triangle as shown on
  the page, and *ask*: Are these two shapes alike? (Same
  shape, number of sides and corners) Are these two shapes
  different? (size)

- Guide them to turn the shape clockwise so that they can
  fold it along the line of symmetry to make two triangles that
  are exactly alike:

Practice and Apply
Workbook pages for Chapter 5, Lesson 1

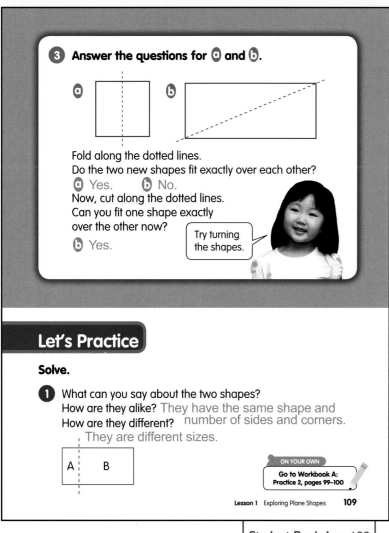

3 Answer the questions for **a** and **b**.

Fold along the dotted lines.
Do the two new shapes fit exactly over each other?
a Yes. **b** No.
Now, cut along the dotted lines.
Can you fit one shape exactly over the other now?
b Yes.

Try turning the shapes.

Let's Practice

Solve.

1 What can you say about the two shapes?
How are they alike? They have the same shape and
How are they different? number of sides and corners.
They are different sizes.

ON YOUR OWN
Go to Workbook A:
Practice 2, pages 99–100

Lesson 1 Exploring Plane Shapes **109**

Student Book A p. 109

• For Exercise **3**, have children fold the shapes in **a** and
b as shown on the page and *ask*: Do the new shapes
fit exactly over each other? (**a** yes, **b** no)

• Have children cut **b** along the dotted line and try to fit one
on top of the other until they fit exactly. *Say*: The two new
shapes are exactly alike.

Let's Practice (page 109)

This practice reinforces children's learning about comparing
shapes that are alike and different. From Exercise **1**, children
will observe that only certain folds will produce two identical
shapes.

ON YOUR OWN

Children practice comparing shapes in Practice 2, pp. 99–100
of **Workbook 1A**. These pages (with the answers) are shown
at the right.

Differentiation Options Depending on children's success
with the Workbook pages, use these materials as needed.
Struggling: Reteach 1A, pp. 75–76
On Level: Extra Practice 1A, pp. 75–76

Name: _____   Date: _____

Practice 2   Exploring Plane Shapes
Read.
Then answer the questions.

1. Josh has a square piece of paper.
He folds it and unfolds it.
Then he draws a line along the fold.
Now he has two new shapes, A and B.

Write *yes* or *no*.

   a. Are Shape A and Shape B the same shape? __yes__

   b. Are Shape A and Shape B the same size? __yes__

Count.

   c. How many sides are there?

   Shape A __4__   Shape B __4__

   d. How many corners are there?

   Shape A __4__   Shape B __4__

Lesson 1 Exploring Plane Shapes **99**

Workbook A p. 99

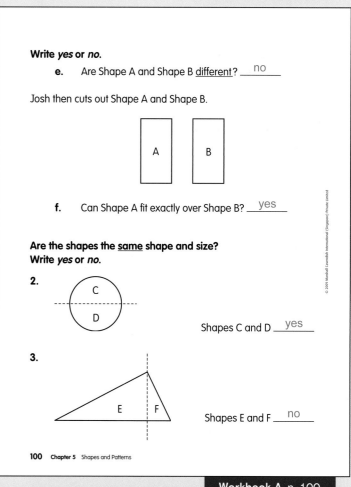

Write *yes* or *no*.

   e. Are Shape A and Shape B <u>different</u>? __no__

Josh then cuts out Shape A and Shape B.

   f. Can Shape A fit exactly over Shape B? __yes__

Are the shapes the <u>same</u> shape and size?
Write *yes* or *no*.

2.

Shapes C and D __yes__

3.

Shapes E and F __no__

100 Chapter 5 Shapes and Patterns

Workbook A p. 100

LESSON 2 Exploring Solid Shapes

LESSON OBJECTIVE
• Identify, classify, and sort solid shapes.

TECHNOLOGY RESOURCES
• *Math in Focus* eBook
• *Math in Focus* Teaching Resources CD
• *Math in Focus* Virtual Manipulatives

Vocabulary

rectangular prism	cube
sphere	cone
cylinder	pyramid
stack	slide
roll	

DAY 1 Student Book 1A, pp. 110–115
Workbook 1A, pp. 101–104

MATERIALS
• geometric solids (1 set of 12 solids per group)
• Table of Shapes (TRO8)

DIFFERENTIATION RESOURCES
• Reteach 1A, pp. 77–80
• Extra Practice 1A, pp. 77–78

 5-minute Warm Up

• Ask children to think of real-world objects that come in the shape of a square, rectangle, circle or triangle. As you draw a shape on the board, children take turns calling out the names of objects that are of that shape or contain parts that are of that shape.

• For example, if you call out circle, some possible objects are a clock face, coin, CD, etc. This prepares children to relate the plane shapes to solid shapes of objects around them.

• You can limit the activity to things in the classroom.

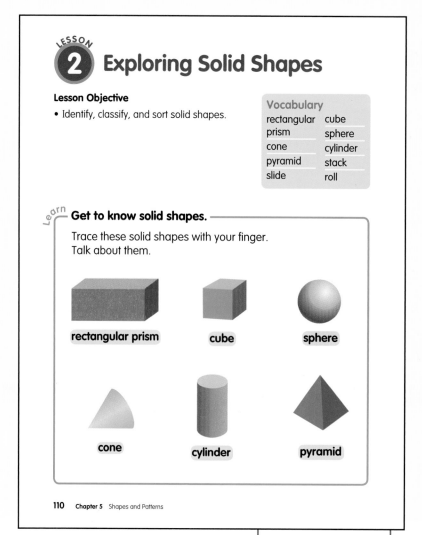

LESSON 2 Exploring Solid Shapes

Lesson Objective
• Identify, classify, and sort solid shapes.

Vocabulary

rectangular prism	cube
cone	sphere
pyramid	cylinder
slide	stack
	roll

Learn **Get to know solid shapes.**
Trace these solid shapes with your finger.
Talk about them.

rectangular prism   cube   sphere

cone   cylinder   pyramid

110 Chapter 5 Shapes and Patterns

Student Book A p. 110

DAY 1 # Teach

Learn
Get to Know Solid Shapes

Children have learned about plane shapes. Solid shapes are the three-dimensional forms of plane shapes. Help children relate plane shapes to the corresponding solid shapes.

• Hold up a rectangular prism. Trace the bottom face with your finger. *Ask*: Which shape did I trace? (rectangle)

• Draw a rectangle on the board. Explain that while a rectangle is flat, a rectangular prism is solid. Turn the prism around and have children see that it has 3 other rectangles and 2 squares, or small rectangles.

• Repeat this by holding each solid up in turn and asking children to trace the shape after you have drawn it on the board.

• Explain that while a square is flat, a cube is solid. Turn the cube around and have children see that it has 6 squares. You may wish to point out that cubes are special types of rectangular prisms.

• Explain that while a circle is flat, a sphere is solid. Turn the sphere around and have children see a circle regardless of how you hold it.

Name and compare solid shapes.

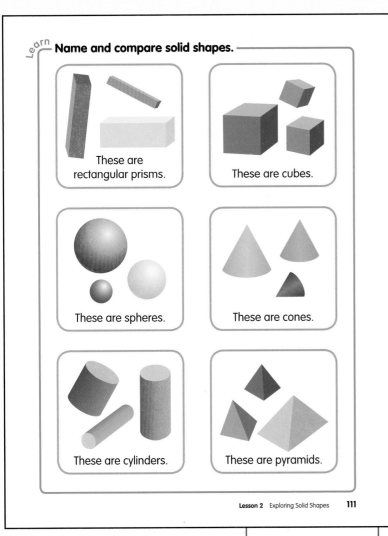

These are rectangular prisms.

These are cubes.

These are spheres.

These are cones.

These are cylinders.

These are pyramids.

Lesson 2 Exploring Solid Shapes **111**

Student Book A p. 111

- Explain that while a triangle is flat, a cone is solid. Turn the cone around horizontally and have children see the triangle from all directions.

- For the cylinder, have children see the circles at the top and bottom, as well as the rectangle from all sides.

- Explain that a pyramid is solid. Turn the pyramid around and have children see the square at the bottom and the triangle on all sides.

Problem of the Lesson

Which solid shape can you not slide and stack?

Answer:

sphere

Differentiated Instruction

English Language Learners

English language learners may benefit from a physical demonstration of the solid shapes and the ways that they can move. Use geometric solids (or other real-world containers) and demonstrate movement. Demonstrate while you **say**: This is a rectangular prism. It can stack. It can slide. Continue with the other solid shapes and show each movement it can make.

Name and Compare Solid Shapes

(page 111)

Children become aware of the variety of solid shapes within each shape that was shown on the previous page of the Teacher's Edition.

- Hold up any **geometric solid** shape and **ask**: What solid shape is this?

- Then have children look at the corresponding group of shapes on the page.

- Encourage children to talk about each group of shapes by asking them questions, for example, **ask**: How are these shapes the same? (same shape, same plane shapes) How are they different? (size, color)

Best Practices Many children will gain a better understanding of the attributes and properties of solid figures if they are able to see and manipulate real-world examples. Set up a solid center in the classroom. Display a variety of containers each labeled with the name of a solid. As children complete the lesson, allow them to visit the center as needed.

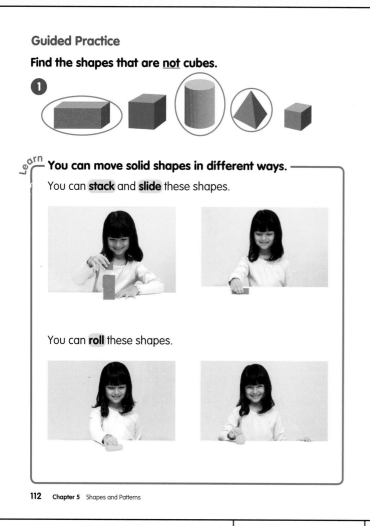

Guided Practice

Find the shapes that are <u>not</u> cubes.

1

^{Learn} **You can move solid shapes in different ways.**

You can **stack** and **slide** these shapes.

You can **roll** these shapes.

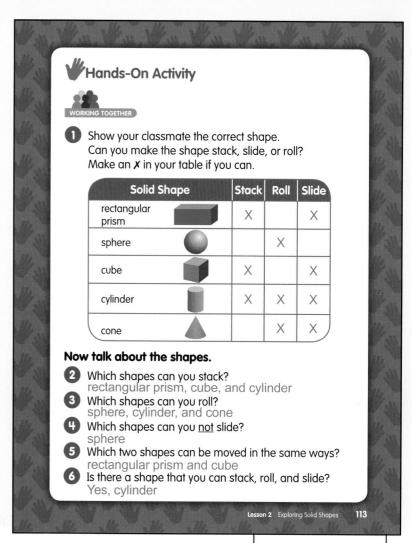

✋Hands-On Activity

WORKING TOGETHER

1 Show your classmate the correct shape.
Can you make the shape stack, slide, or roll?
Make an ✗ in your table if you can.

Solid Shape		Stack	Roll	Slide
rectangular prism		X		X
sphere			X	
cube		X		X
cylinder		X	X	X
cone			X	X

Now talk about the shapes.

2 Which shapes can you stack?
rectangular prism, cube, and cylinder
3 Which shapes can you roll?
sphere, cylinder, and cone
4 Which shapes can you <u>not</u> slide?
sphere
5 Which two shapes can be moved in the same ways?
rectangular prism and cube
6 Is there a shape that you can stack, roll, and slide?
Yes, cylinder

Check for Understanding

✔Guided Practice (page 112)

1 Have children name each solid shape from left to right.
Ask: Which of these shapes are not cubes? Explain that a cube has a square on every side.

^{Learn}
Move Solid Shapes in Different Ways

(page 112)

Knowing how solid shapes can be moved can help children relate the shapes to real-world objects.

• Show children that cubes can be stacked one on top of another. *Say*: I can stack the cubes. *Ask*: Which other shape can I stack in this way? Try it with any answer that you hear from the children to show them whether or not the shape can be stacked. Do this with different shapes. Each time, *say*: I can (or cannot) stack the (shape).

• Now place a rectangle prism on a flat surface and slide it gently along the surface. *Say*: I can slide the rectangular prism. Which other shape can I slide? Try sliding other shapes, based on children's responses. Each time, *say*: I can (or cannot) slide the (shape).

• Repeat the above steps as you roll a cylinder.

WORKING TOGETHER

✋Hands-On Activity:

Find How to Move Solid Shapes (page 113)

1 This activity lets children find out for themselves how each solid shape can be moved.

• Arrange children in groups of four or five, so that each group gets a set of geometric solids.

• Have them do what you did in the previous Learn element for each shape and record their findings with a ✗ on the **Table of Shapes** (TRO8). If necessary, model by stacking the rectangular prism.

2 to **6** Discuss their findings using the completed **Table of Shapes** (TRO8).

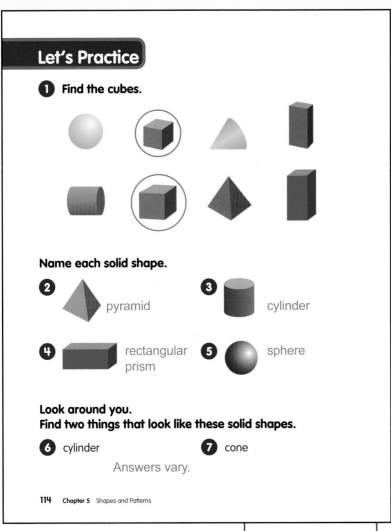

Let's Practice

1 Find the cubes.

Name each solid shape.

2 pyramid

3 cylinder

4 rectangular prism

5 sphere

Look around you.
Find two things that look like these solid shapes.

6 cylinder

7 cone

Answers vary.

114 **Chapter 5** *Shapes and Patterns*

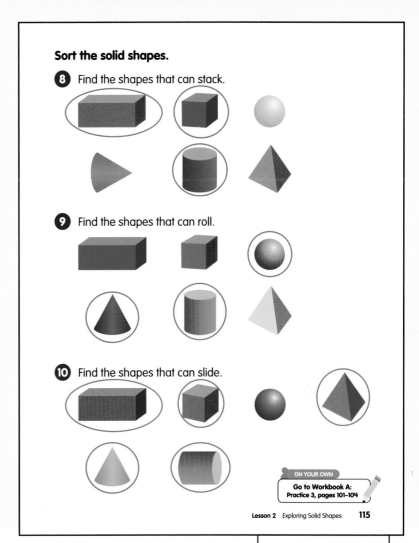

Sort the solid shapes.

8 Find the shapes that can stack.

9 Find the shapes that can roll.

10 Find the shapes that can slide.

ON YOUR OWN
Go to Workbook A:
Practice 3, pages 101–104

Lesson 2 Exploring Solid Shapes **115**

Let's Practice (pages 114 and 115)

This activity lets children practice identifying and describing the way solid shapes can be moved. Exercise **1** requires children to identify the cubes. Exercises **2** to **5** require children to name the shapes, and Exercises **6** and **7** require children to identify the solid shapes in the real world. Exercises **8** to **10** require children to identify the way(s) different solid shapes can be moved.

Common Error Some children may not understand the difference between *slide* and *roll*. Demonstrate sliding with a rectangular prism. Point out that when the shape slides, it stays on the same flat surface. Now roll a ball, and point out that the shape moves all around its curved surface.

ON YOUR OWN

Children practice identifying and comparing shapes in Practice 3, pp. 101–104 of **Workbook 1A**. These pages (with the answers) are shown on page 115A.

Differentiation Options Depending on children's success with the Workbook pages, use these materials as needed.
Struggling: Reteach 1A, pp. 77–80
On Level: Extra Practice 1A, pp. 77–78

Practice and Apply
Workbook pages for Chapter 5, Lesson 2

Name: _____ Date: _____

Practice 3 Exploring Solid Shapes
Match each shape to its name.

1.

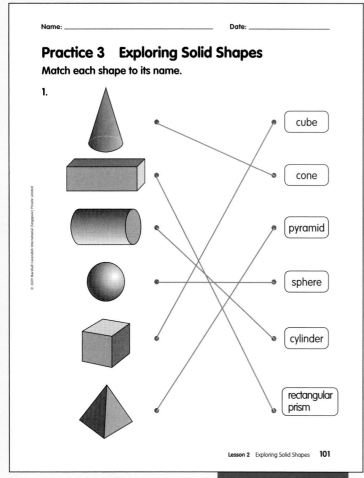

- cube
- cone
- pyramid
- sphere
- cylinder
- rectangular prism

Workbook A p. 101

Name: _____ Date: _____

Answer the questions.
Circle the shapes.

4. Which shapes can you stack?

5. Which shapes can you slide?

6. Which shapes can you roll?

Workbook A p. 103

Answer the questions.
Circle the shapes.

2. Which shapes are <u>not</u> cylinders?

3. Which shapes are <u>not</u> pyramids?

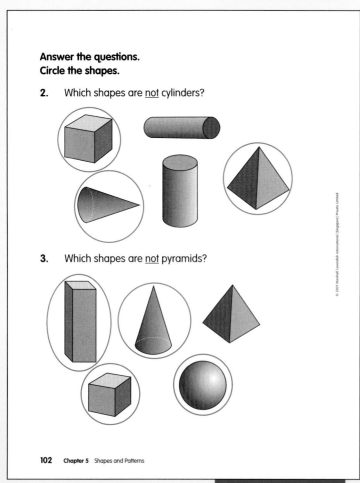

Workbook A p. 102

---

7. Which shape can you <u>only</u> slide?

8. Which shape can you <u>only</u> roll?

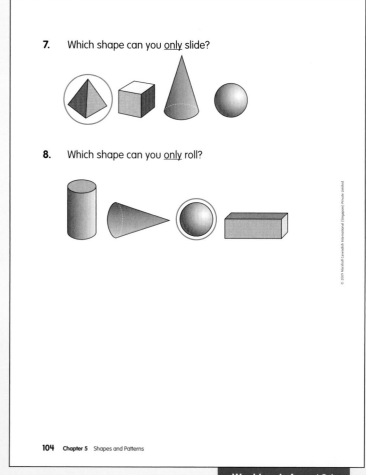

Workbook A p. 104

3 Making Pictures and Models with Shapes

LESSON OBJECTIVE
- Combine and separate plane and solid shapes.

TECHNOLOGY RESOURCES
- *Math In Focus* eBook
- *Math In Focus* Teaching Resources CD
- *Math In Focus* Virtual Manipulatives

DAY 1 Student Book 1A, pp. 116–120
Workbook 1A, pp. 105–110

MATERIALS
- attribute blocks for the teacher
- geometric solids (1 set of 12 solids per group)
- attribute blocks (1 set per group as shown on page 118)
- Shapes to Combine (TR09) for the teacher
- Shapes to Cut Out (TR10) – one set per pair
- Table of Solids (TR11)
- scissors
- markers
- Blu-Tack®
- blank transparency (optional)

DIFFERENTIATION RESOURCES
- Reteach 1A, pp. 81–82
- Extra Practice 1A, pp. 79–82

DAY 2 Student Book 1A, pp. 121–123
Workbook 1A, pp. 111–112

DIFFERENTIATION RESOURCES
- Reteach 1A, pp. 83–84
- Extra Practice 1A, pp. 83–84

 5-minute Warm Up

- Have children draw a picture of a house using only squares, triangles, and rectangles. Ask volunteers to share their pictures and name the shapes in their drawings.

Problem of the Lesson

How many squares are in this picture? (Encourage children to trace the shapes as they count them.)

Answer:
5 (4 small and 1 large)

---

3 Making Pictures and Models with Shapes

Lesson Objective
- Combine and separate plane and solid shapes.

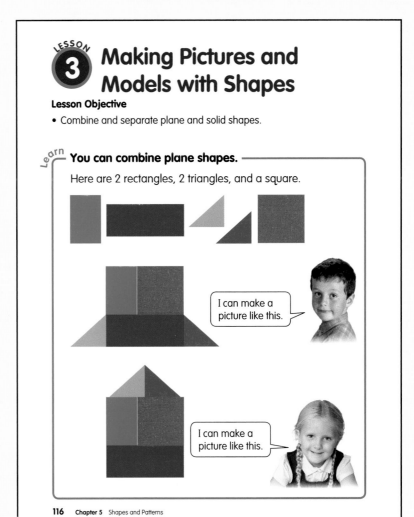

Learn You can combine plane shapes.

Here are 2 rectangles, 2 triangles, and a square.

I can make a picture like this.

I can make a picture like this.

116 **Chapter 5** Shapes and Patterns

Student Book A p. 116

DAY 1 Teach

Learn Combine Plane Shapes (page 116)

Children have learned about plane shapes. In this lesson, children will combine different plane shapes to make new composite shapes.

- Use **Shapes to Combine** (TR09) and colored markers to make a copy of the shapes at the top of page 116. You may also copy the shapes to a blank transparency. Cut out the shapes.

- Hold up each shape and have children name the shape and color, for example, blue rectangle, red square.

- Have children give you instructions for putting the picture at the top together. You may do this on the board (with pieces of Blu-Tack® on the back of each shape) or by using an overhead projector.

- Repeat this with the picture at the bottom of the page. You may ask volunteers to try this while other children give instructions.

Best Practices This lesson requires the use of cut-out shapes or pattern blocks. Look through the lesson ahead of time to see how many copies of what shapes you need. Prepare the copies, cut-outs, and pattern blocks that you need for the entire class prior to starting the lesson.

Guided Practice

Solve.

1 Name the shapes that make this picture.

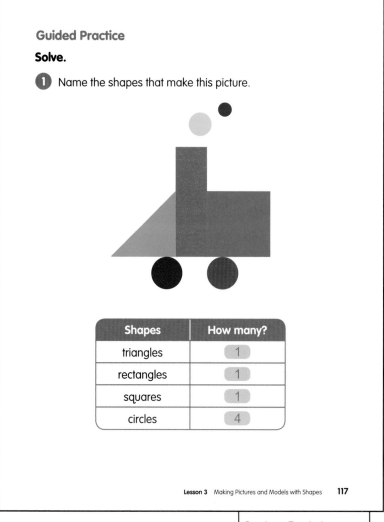

Shapes	How many?
triangles	1
rectangles	1
squares	1
circles	4

Student Book A p. 117

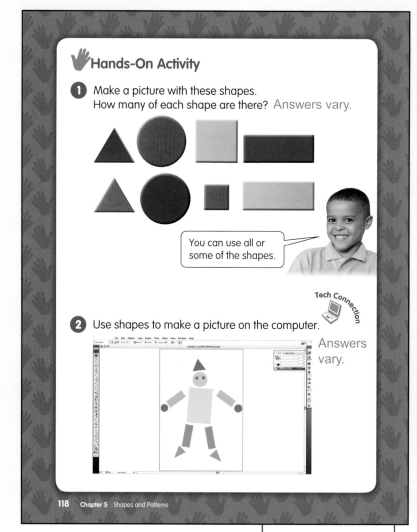

Student Book A p. 118

Check for Understanding

✓ Guided Practice (page 117)

1 Have children count the shapes that make the picture, beginning with the triangles, then the rectangles, squares, and circles. If possible, display the picture and have children count with you.

Common Error Ensure that children do not include squares when counting the rectangles.

🖐 Hands-On Activity:

Combine Shapes to Make a Picture, Make a Picture with Shapes on a Computer

(page 118)

1 This activity lets children make different pictures with the given shapes.

• Have children work in groups of 4 or 5 so that each group gets a set of **attribute blocks** as shown on the Student Book page.

• Encourage children to make different pictures with the shapes and give each picture a title. If necessary, model to show them how it is done.

For Advanced Learners After some practice, challenge children to make a picture using all the given shapes.

2 This activity develops children's creativity on the computer.

• Model how to draw shapes on the computer and fill them with different colors. Show how to drag and rotate the shapes.

• Encourage children to explore making different pictures on their own.

117-118 CHAPTER 5: LESSON 3

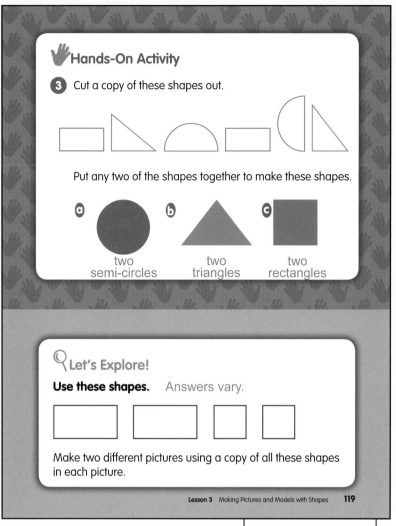

Hands-On Activity

3 Cut a copy of these shapes out.

Put any two of the shapes together to make these shapes.

a two semi-circles

b two triangles

c two rectangles

Let's Explore!

Use these shapes. Answers vary.

Make two different pictures using a copy of all these shapes in each picture.

Lesson 3 Making Pictures and Models with Shapes **119**

Student Book A p. 119

Hands-On Activity:
Combine Shapes to Make a New Shape

3 This activity helps develop children's spatial skills and part-whole relationships. They manipulate shapes to make new shapes.

- Have children work in pairs or small groups; distribute a copy of **Shapes to Cut Out** (TR10) to each group or pair.

- Have children cut out the shapes.

- Children will combine any two of the shapes to make the colored shape on the page of their Student Book.

- Explain that two semi-circles make a circle, two triangles make a larger triangle, and two rectangles make a square.

- You may also encourage children to discover that they can make a rectangle from two triangles, and a longer rectangle from two rectangles.

Let's Explore!
Make a Picture Using Cut-out Shapes
(page 119)

This exploration lets children practice making pictures by combining given shapes.

- Have children do this activity in pairs. Give each pair a copy of **Shapes to Cut Out** (TR10).

- Tell children that it is possible to overlap the shapes. If necessary, model to show them how it is done.

- Have children cut out the shapes and make different shapes using all the given shapes.

- Invite volunteers to share their pictures with the class.

Let's Practice

Count.
Look at the picture.

1 This picture is made of many shapes.

How many of these shapes can you find?

Shapes	How many?
triangles	8
rectangles	10
squares	2
circles	10

ON YOUR OWN
Go to Workbook A:
Practice 4, pages 105–110

120   **Chapter 5** Shapes and Patterns

Student Book A p. 120

Let's Practice (page 120)

This practice lets children identify and count plane shapes from a composite picture. It helps children develop geometric ideas of orientation and spatial relations. Exercise **1** requires children to identify and count the number of triangles, rectangles, squares, and circles of different sizes, colors, and orientations in the given picture.

Common Error Children can easily lose track of the shapes that they have already counted as they complete the chart. Provide children with small objects, such as beans or grains of rice that they can place on top of each shape as they count it.

ON YOUR OWN

Children practice identifying plane shapes in pictures, composing plane shapes and making pictures with plane shapes in Practice 4, pp. 105–110 of **Workbook 1A**. These pages (with the answers) are shown at the right and on page 120A.

Differentiation Options Depending on children's success with the Workbook pages, use these materials as needed.
Struggling: Reteach 1A, pp. 81–82
On Level: Extra Practice 1A, pp. 79–82

120   **CHAPTER 5: LESSON 3**

Practice and Apply
Workbook pages for Chapter 5, Lesson 3

Name: _____   Date: _____

Practice 4   Making Pictures and Models with Shapes

Find the shapes in the pictures.
Count how many of each shape there are.
Write the number.

1.

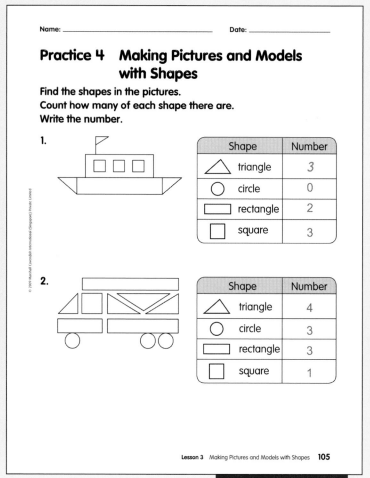

Shape		Number
△	triangle	3
○	circle	0
▭	rectangle	2
□	square	3

2.

Shape		Number
△	triangle	4
○	circle	3
▭	rectangle	3
□	square	1

Lesson 3 Making Pictures and Models with Shapes **105**

Workbook A p. 105

Match the pieces to make a shape.
Name the shapes.
Use the words in the box.

| circle |
| square |
| triangle |
| rectangle |

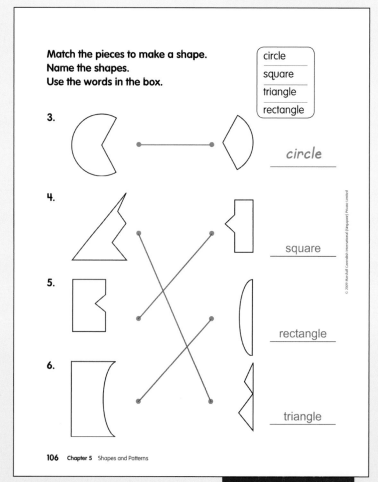

3.   _circle_

4.   square

5.   rectangle

6.   triangle

106   **Chapter 5** Shapes and Patterns

Workbook A p. 106

Name: _____ **Date:** _____

Cut out the shapes below and make a picture.
Paste the picture here or use your own paper.
You do not need to use all the shapes.

7.

Answers vary.

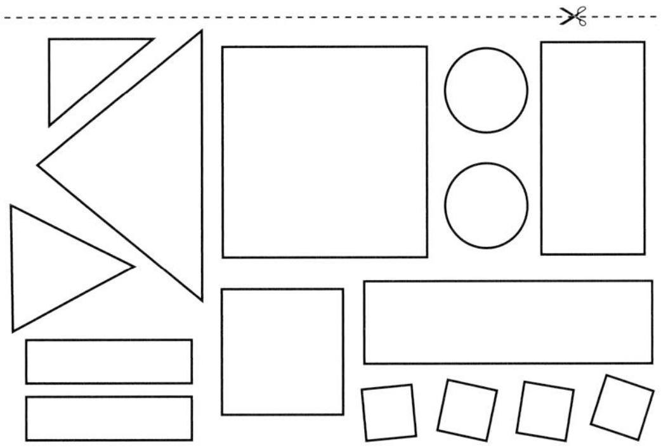

✂- -

Workbook A p. 107

Name: _____ **Date:** _____

Look at the pictures.
Then fill in the blanks.

8. How many triangles can you see?

I can see ___0___ triangles.

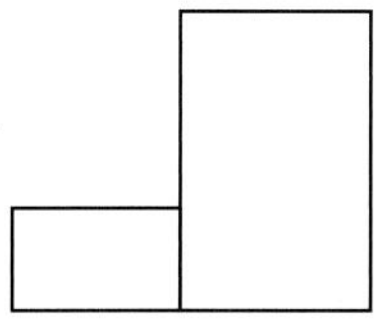

9. A star can be made of triangles.

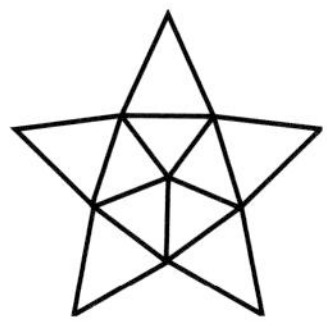

This star is made of ___10___ triangles.

Draw triangles another way to make up this star.

Answers vary.

This star is made
of ___8___ triangles.

Workbook A p. 109

BLANK

Workbook A p. 108

---

10. **Draw a picture with shapes.**
Count how many of each shape there are.
Write the number.

Answers vary.

Shape		Number
△	triangle	
○	circle	
▭	rectangle	
□	square	

Workbook A p. 110

Learn **You can build models with solid shapes.**

Here is 1 sphere, 2 pyramids, 4 cylinders, 2 cubes, 1 cone, and 1 rectangular prism.

I can make a model like this.

I can make a model like this.

Lesson 3 *Making Pictures and Models with Shapes* **121**

👋 **Hands-On Activity**

👥 WORKING TOGETHER

Use 🧊.

Make your own model. **Answers vary.**
Find the number of each solid shape in your model.

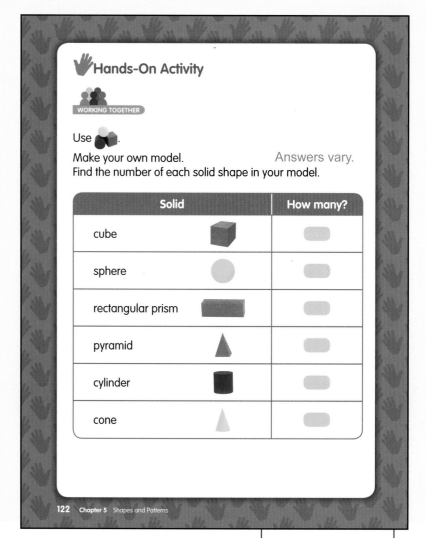

Solid		How many?
cube	🟦	⬭
sphere	⚪	⬭
rectangular prism	▬	⬭
pyramid	🔺	⬭
cylinder	⬛	⬭
cone	🔺	⬭

122 **Chapter 5** *Shapes and Patterns*

DAY 2 | **Teach**

See the Lesson Organizer on page 116 for Day 2 resources.

Learn

Build Models with Solid Shapes (page 121)

Children have learned about solid shapes. In this lesson, children will combine different **geometric solids** to build new complex models.

- Have children name the solid shapes and colors in the picture, for example, red pyramids, blue and yellow cylinders, yellow cone, yellow sphere, red cubes, and rectangular prisms.

- Have children give you instructions for putting the model together.

- Repeat with the second picture at the bottom of the page. Ask volunteers to try putting the model together while children take turns giving instructions.

👥 WORKING TOGETHER

👋 Hands-On Activity:

Make a Model with Solid Shapes (page 122)

This activity lets children build different models with the given solid shapes.

- Have children work individually or in groups of 4 or 5, so that each group gets a set of **geometric solids** as shown on the Student Book page.

- Encourage children to make different models with the shapes.

- Have them count the number of each solid shape in their model and complete the **Table of Solids** (TR11) on page 122 of the Student Book.

- You may model the completion of the table using one of the models on page 121 of the Student Book.

Guided Practice

Look at the model.
Find the number of each solid shape in the model.

2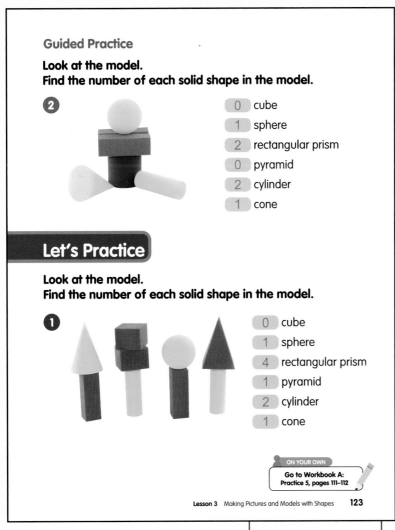

0	cube
1	sphere
2	rectangular prism
0	pyramid
2	cylinder
1	cone

Let's Practice

Look at the model.
Find the number of each solid shape in the model.

1

0	cube
1	sphere
4	rectangular prism
1	pyramid
2	cylinder
1	cone

ON YOUR OWN
Go to Workbook A:
Practice 5, pages 111–112

Lesson 3   Making Pictures and Models with Shapes   **123**

Student Book A p. 123

✓ Guided Practice (page 123)

2 Have children name the solid shapes in the model, for example, sphere. *Ask:* How many spheres are in the model? (1) Continue with the other shapes and have children count the solid shapes that make the model.

Let's Practice (page 123)

This practice reinforces the skills of identifying and naming the solid shapes in the model. Exercise **1** requires children to find and count each named solid shape in the model.

ON YOUR OWN

Children practice identifying solid shapes in models in Practice 5, pp. 111–112 of **Workbook 1A**. These pages (with the answers) are shown at the right.

Differentiation Options Depending on children's success with the Workbook pages, use these materials as needed.
Struggling: Reteach 1A, pp. 83–84
On Level: Extra Practice 1A, pp. 83–84

Name: _____   Date: _____

Practice 5   Making Pictures and Models with Shapes

Look at the pictures.
Count how many of each solid shape there are.
Write the number.

1.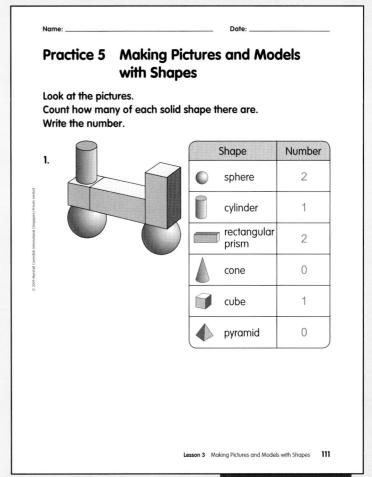

Shape		Number
●	sphere	2
▮	cylinder	1
▭	rectangular prism	2
▲	cone	0
◻	cube	1
◭	pyramid	0

Lesson 3   Making Pictures and Models with Shapes   **111**

Workbook A p. 111

2.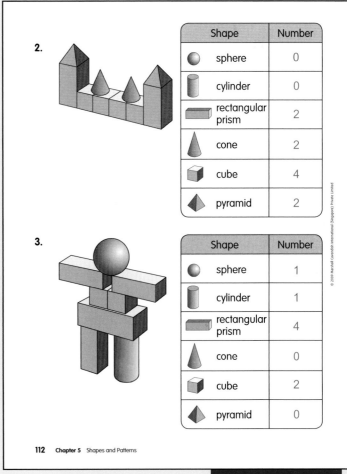

Shape		Number
●	sphere	0
▮	cylinder	0
▭	rectangular prism	2
▲	cone	2
◻	cube	4
◭	pyramid	2

3.

Shape		Number
●	sphere	1
▮	cylinder	1
▭	rectangular prism	4
▲	cone	0
◻	cube	2
◭	pyramid	0

112   Chapter 5   Shapes and Patterns

Workbook A p. 112

Seeing Shapes Around Us

LESSON OBJECTIVE
• Identify plane and solid shapes in real life.

TECHNOLOGY RESOURCES
• *Math in Focus* eBook
• *Math in Focus* Teaching Resources CD
• *Math in Focus* Virtual Manipulatives

DAY 1 Student Book 1A, pp. 124–128
Workbook 1A, pp. 113–116

MATERIALS
• geometric solids (1 set per group)
• a colored pipe-cleaner for the teacher
• common objects as examples of plane and solid shapes, for example, CD, book, tumbler for the teacher

DIFFERENTIATION RESOURCES
• Reteach 1A, pp. 85–86
• Extra Practice 1A, pp. 85–86

 5-minute Warm Up

• Show children a pipe-cleaner and demonstrate how to twist it to form plane shapes.

• Ask volunteers to take turns making different shapes from the pipe-cleaner and let other children say what shape it is. This requires children to twist the pipe-cleaner to change from one shape to another.

• Encourage children to try more complex shapes such as two circles, or two triangles.

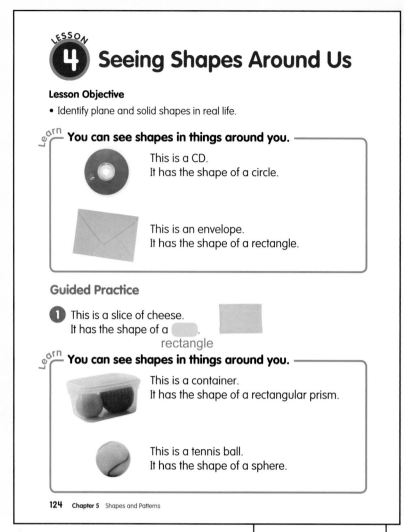

Student Book A p. 124

DAY 1 # Teach

See Shapes in Things Around You (page 124)

Children have learned about plane and solid shapes. In this lesson, children will relate these shapes to real-life objects. Begin with plane shapes.

• Hold up a thin book. *Ask*: What shape is this book? (rectangle) *Say*: It has the shape of a rectangle.

• Repeat with a CD (circle) and an envelope (rectangle).

• Encourage children to name other objects in the classroom in which they see plane shapes. *Ask*: Can you see shapes in the things around you? Tell us what shapes you see.

Check for Understanding
✓ **Guided Practice** (page 124)

❶ Have children look at the picture of the cheese slice on their Student Book page. Ask them to trace the shape with their fingers and say what shape it is.

Problem of the Lesson

This shape is a solid figure called a triangular prism.

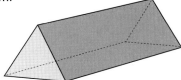

Solution:

1. What plane shapes do you see?
2. How many of each are there?

Answer:

1. triangles and rectangles
2. 2 triangles and 3 rectangles

Differentiated Instruction

English Language Learners

Give children additional practice identifying shapes and using geometric language in a game setting. In small groups, children take turns describing an object in the classroom in terms of its shape, color, size, and so on. Group members guess what the object is. The child with the correct guess gives clues for a different object.

For Struggling Learners Discuss the attributes of the real-world objects in Exercises ❶ and ❷ to help children match the object to a plane shape or solid figure. For example, the cheese slice has 4 sides and 4 corners like a rectangle; the popcorn tin has a top and bottom that are circles and a curved surface like a cylinder.

See Shapes in Things Around You (page 124)

In this Learn, children will relate solid shapes to real-life objects.

- Hold up a rectangular container, like the one shown on the page in the Student Book. *Ask*: What shape is this container? (rectangular prism)
- Repeat with a tennis ball or any other ball. (sphere)

Best Practices In this lesson, children need to see the difference between flat figures, and those that have three dimensions. Gather and display pairs of similar objects, such as a sheet of paper, a box, a CD, and a ball. Allow children to handle the objects and determine which are flat and which are three-dimensional.

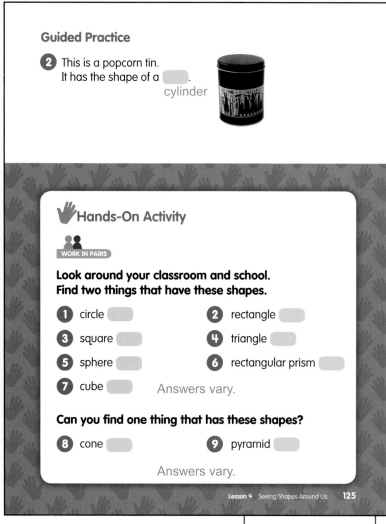

Guided Practice

2 This is a popcorn tin.
It has the shape of a ▭.
cylinder

✋**Hands-On Activity**

WORK IN PAIRS

**Look around your classroom and school.
Find two things that have these shapes.**

1 circle ▭   **2** rectangle ▭

3 square ▭   **4** triangle ▭

5 sphere ▭   **6** rectangular prism ▭

7 cube ▭   Answers vary.

Can you find one thing that has these shapes?

8 cone ▭   **9** pyramid ▭

Answers vary.

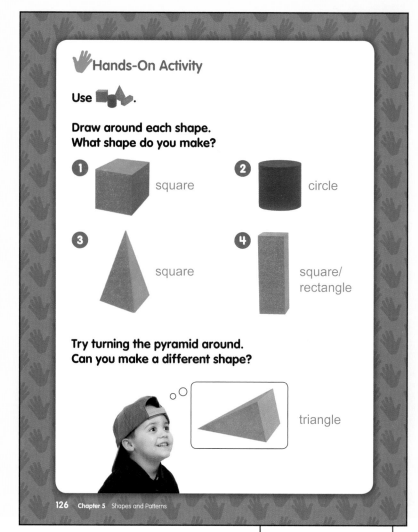

✋**Hands-On Activity**

Use ▭▲.

**Draw around each shape.
What shape do you make?**

1 square

2 circle

3 square

4 square/rectangle

**Try turning the pyramid around.
Can you make a different shape?**

triangle

✔**Guided Practice** (page 125)

2 Have children look at the picture of the tin on their Student Book page. Ask them to name the solid shape. If possible, encourage them to name other objects around them that have the same shape.
(Examples: tumbler, sharpener)

✋**Hands-On Activity:**
Find Plane and Solid Shapes Around You (page 125)

This activity builds observation skills and lets children relate their learning about shapes to objects around them.

- Show children a can. Trace the base of the can on the board to show the shape. **Ask**: What shape do you see? (circle)

- **Ask** children if the can has more than one shape, and if they say 'yes', turn it on its side to trace the rectangle. **Ask**: What shape do you see now?

- Recall for children that these are solid shapes and have them recognize the different plane shapes when the objects are viewed from different directions.

- Have children work in pairs. Give children about 10 minutes to walk outside their classroom around a specified part of the school.

- Encourage them to look for things that have the shapes listed in Exercises **1** to **9** on the Student Book page.

- Have them share their findings with the class.

✋**Hands-On Activity:**
Draw Around Solid Shapes to Find Plane Shapes (page 126)

This activity shows children that solid shapes may have different plane shapes on different surfaces. This helps develop their spatial awareness. Have children work in groups of 4 or 5, so that each group gets a set of **geometric solids**.

- Have children place each solid flat on their books as shown in the Student Book, and draw around the base of it. **Ask**: What shape do you make?

- Encourage them to turn each solid around, and draw again, to get more shapes.

- For Exercises **3** and **4** explain that different surfaces of a solid shape may have different plane shapes.

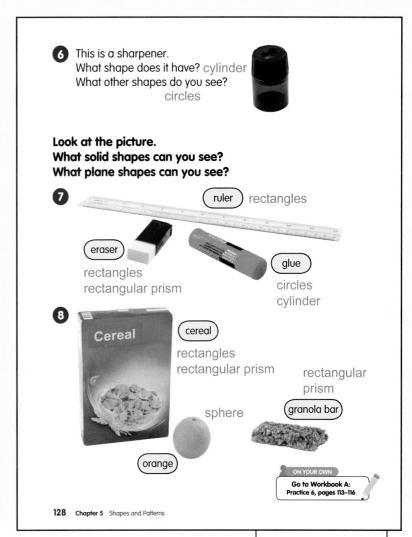

Let's Practice (pages 127 and 128)

Exercises **1** to **8** reinforce the skills of identifying and naming plane and solid shapes in the objects children see around them.

Common Error Some children may have trouble visualizing the flat surfaces of solid shapes. Use geometric solids or cut out nets of the different solids. Have children fold and unfold the nets to view the solid and the shapes of the surfaces or examine the geometric solids from different sides.

ON YOUR OWN

Children practice identifying plane and solid shapes in things they see around them in Practice 6, pp. 113–116 of **Workbook 1A**. These pages (with the answers) are shown on page 128A.

Differentiation Options Depending on children's success with the Workbook pages, use these materials as needed.
Struggling: Reteach 1A, pp. 85–86
On Level: Extra Practice 1A, pp. 85–86

Practice and Apply
Workbook pages for Chapter 5, Lesson 4

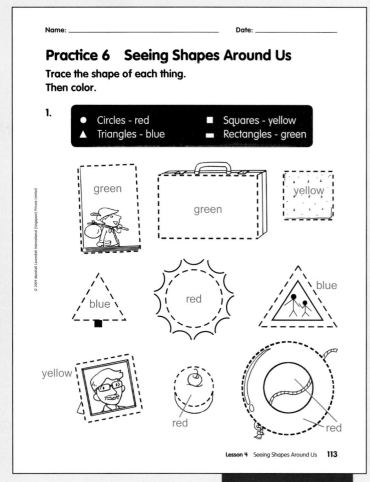

Name: _____   Date: _____

Practice 6   Seeing Shapes Around Us
Trace the shape of each thing.
Then color.

1.

| ● Circles - red | ■ Squares - yellow |
| ▲ Triangles - blue | ▬ Rectangles - green |

green

green

yellow

blue

red

blue

yellow

red

red

Workbook A p. 113

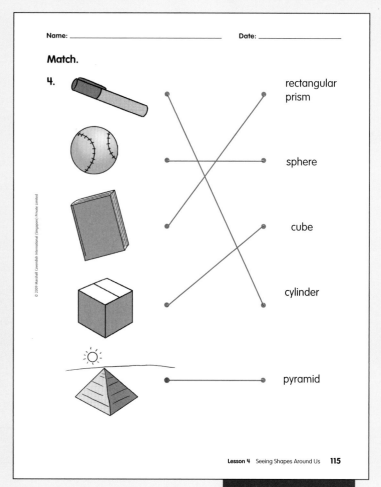

Name: _____   Date: _____

Match.

4.

rectangular prism

sphere

cube

cylinder

pyramid

Workbook A p. 115

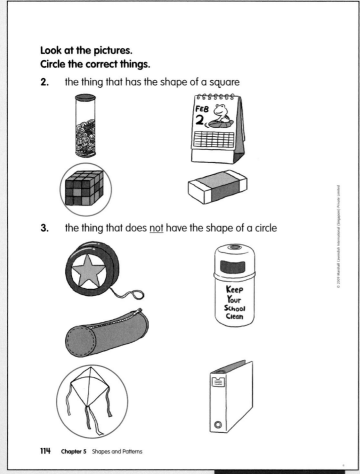

Look at the pictures.
Circle the correct things.

2.   the thing that has the shape of a square

3.   the thing that does <u>not</u> have the shape of a circle

Keep Your School Clean

Workbook A p. 114

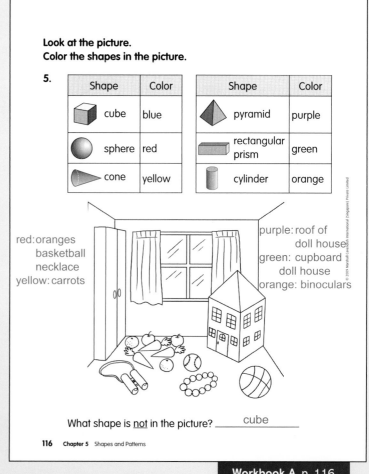

Look at the picture.
Color the shapes in the picture.

5.

Shape	Color
cube	blue
sphere	red
cone	yellow

Shape	Color
pyramid	purple
rectangular prism	green
cylinder	orange

red: oranges basketball necklace
yellow: carrots

purple: roof of doll house
green: cupboard doll house
orange: binoculars

What shape is <u>not</u> in the picture? _____ cube

Workbook A p. 116

Making Patterns with Plane Shapes

LESSON OBJECTIVE

• Use plane shapes to identify, extend, and create patterns.

TECHNOLOGY RESOURCES

• *Math in Focus* eBook
• *Math in Focus* Teaching Resources CD
• *Math in Focus* Virtual Manipulatives

Vocabulary

repeating patterns

 DAY 1 Student Book 1A, pp. 129–131
Workbook 1A, pp. 117–122

MATERIALS

• attribute blocks
• markers

DIFFERENTIATION RESOURCES

• Reteach 1A, pp. 87–88
• Extra Practice 1A, pp. 87–88

 5-minute Warm Up

Use blue and red markers to draw dots on the board in an alternate repeating pattern, as shown below:

Then ask children to continue the pattern.

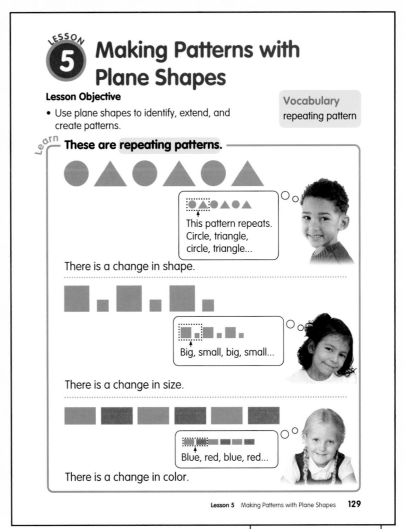

DAY 1 **Teach**

Repeating Patterns (page 129)

Children learned to identify and extend number patterns in Chapter 1. They now learn to identify and extend repeating patterns made up of plane shapes.

• Have 8 children hold 4 circles and 4 triangles that are the same size and color. Ask them to stand according to the pattern shown: circle, triangle, circle, triangle, …

• *Ask*: What do you notice about the way the shapes are arranged? Tell children that the repeating shapes of circle and triangle follow a pattern.

• Provide a non-example to help pupils discriminate a pattern and a non-pattern. Have the 8 children stay in a row, take the shapes from them, mix them up and give them back to the children at random. Have children see that there is no pattern.

• Encourage children to show other ways of forming other patterns. For example, circle, circle, triangle, triangle, circle, circle, triangle, triangle.

• Repeat patterns that change in size only and color only.

Guided Practice
Complete the patterns.

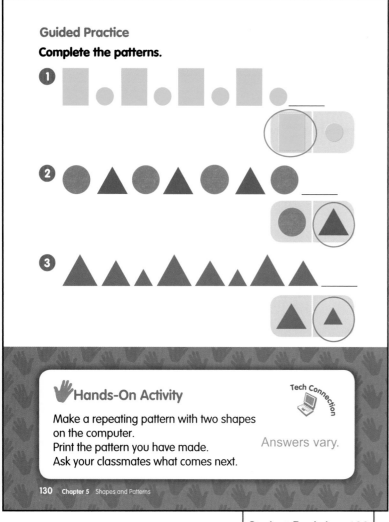

①

②

③

Hands-On Activity

Tech Connection

Make a repeating pattern with two shapes on the computer.
Print the pattern you have made.
Ask your classmates what comes next.

Answers vary.

130   **Chapter 5** *Shapes and Patterns*

Student Book A p. 130

Problem of the Lesson

Look at this pattern of shapes and colors.
Draw and color the next shape.

Solution:
(Note: the different colors are included to make children aware of color being an observable attribute to look out for in forming and extending patterns, but in this problem, it is not a changing attribute as all the circles are red, the triangles are blue, and the squares are yellow.)

Answer:

Differentiated Instruction

English Language Learners

Many of the patterns in this lesson include different colors. Review color names with children. Hold up pieces of construction paper, and invite children to say the color in their native language. Say and write the color name in English, and have children repeat after you. You may want to keep the colored paper on display with the color words written below each piece.

Best Practices You may want to begin the lesson with an exercise on translating a pattern in different ways to accommodate auditory and kinesthetic learners. For auditory learners, describe the pattern aloud. For kinesthetic learners, provide pattern blocks. Other children may find it helpful to use letters to describe the pattern.

Check for Understanding
✔ **Guided Practice** (page 130)

① to ③ Have children complete the patterns. Ask children why they chose the particular shape, size, or color for their answers. Have them say how they identified the required shape and its color or size. Guide them to use the attributes of shape, size, and color to establish the pattern.

✋**Hands-On Activity:** Tech Connection
Make a Repeating Pattern on a Computer
(page 130)

This activity lets children combine their computer skills in drawing shapes and moving them around with their creative skills of repeating patterns.

• Encourage children to make different repeating patterns, for example ABABAB, AABBAABB, or ABBABBABB. Have them print their patterns.

• Have children take turns sharing their patterns, and asking what comes next in each pattern.

Let's Practice

Complete the patterns.

ON YOUR OWN
Go to Workbook A:
Practice 7, pages 117–122

Lesson 5 Making Patterns with Plane Shapes **131**

Student Book A p. 131

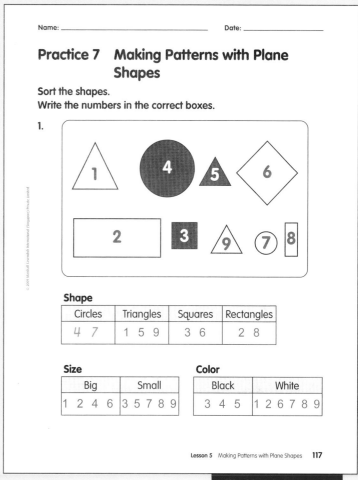

Name: _____ Date: _____

Practice 7   Making Patterns with Plane Shapes

Sort the shapes.
Write the numbers in the correct boxes.

1.

Shape

Circles	Triangles	Squares	Rectangles
4 7	1 5 9	3 6	2 8

Size

Big	Small
1 2 4 6	3 5 7 8 9

Color

Black	White
3 4 5	1 2 6 7 8 9

Lesson 5 Making Patterns with Plane Shapes **117**

Workbook A p. 117

Complete the patterns.
Draw the missing shape.

┌── Example ──────────────────────────┐
│   │
└──────────────────────────────────────┘

2.

3.

4.

5.

6.

7.

118 Chapter 5 Shapes and Patterns

Workbook A p. 118

Let's Practice (page 131)

This practice reinforces the skills of identifying and extending repeating patterns with plane shapes. In Exercise ❶, only the color changes in the pattern, and in Exercise ❷, only the shape changes. In Exercise ❸, both the shape and size change, and in Exercise ❹, there are changes in the shape and color.

Common Error Children may have difficulty identifying the pattern unit. Have them examine the shapes in the pattern and describe each element in detail. Tell children to look for similarities and differences to find the parts that repeat. Have children place counters on the shapes to show the pattern unit.

ON YOUR OWN

Children practice identifying and extending repeating patterns with plane shapes in Practice 7, pp. 117–122 of **Workbook 1A**. These pages (with the answers) are shown at the right and on page 131A.

Differentiation Options Depending on children's success with the Workbook pages, use these materials as needed.
Struggling: Reteach 1A, pp. 87–88
On Level: Extra Practice 1A, pp. 87–88

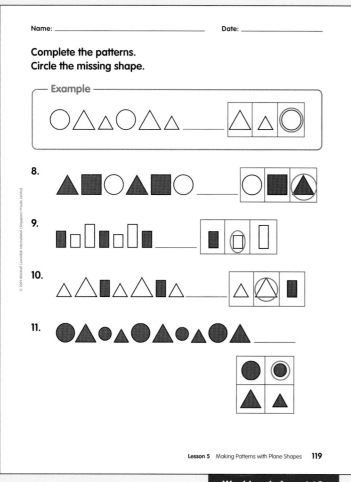

Workbook A p. 119

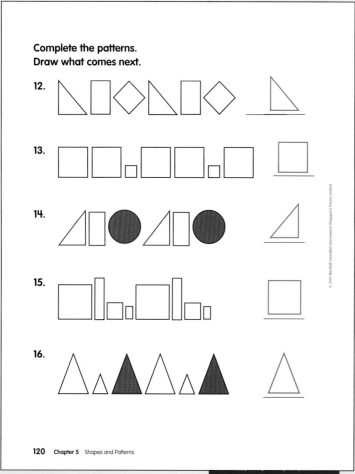

Workbook A p. 120

Page 119 content

Name: _____ Date: _____

Complete the patterns.
Circle the missing shape.

Example

8.

9.

10.

11.

Page 120 content

Complete the patterns.
Draw what comes next.

12.

13.

14.

15.

16.

Page 121 content

Name: _____ Date: _____

Cut out the shapes below.
Make two patterns.
You do not need to use all the shapes.

17. Paste your first pattern here.

Answers vary.

Workbook A p. 121

Page 122 content

18. Paste your second pattern here.

Answers vary.

Workbook A p. 122

Chapter 5

6 Making Patterns with Solid Shapes

LESSON OBJECTIVE
• Use solid shapes to identify, extend, and create patterns.

TECHNOLOGY RESOURCES
• *Math in Focus* eBook
• *Math in Focus* Teaching Resources CD
• *Math in Focus* Virtual Manipulatives

| DAY 1 | Student Book 1A, pp. 132–134
Workbook 1A, pp. 123–124 |

MATERIALS
• geometric solids (1 set per group)

DIFFERENTIATION RESOURCES
• Reteach 1A, pp. 89–90
• Extra Practice 1A, p. 89

 5-minute Warm Up

• Using objects that are easily available in the classroom, (e.g., erasers and pencils) make a repeating AB pattern with 3 sets of repeating units.

• Ask volunteers to continue the pattern.

• Repeat with another pattern, for example, with AAB as the repeating unit.

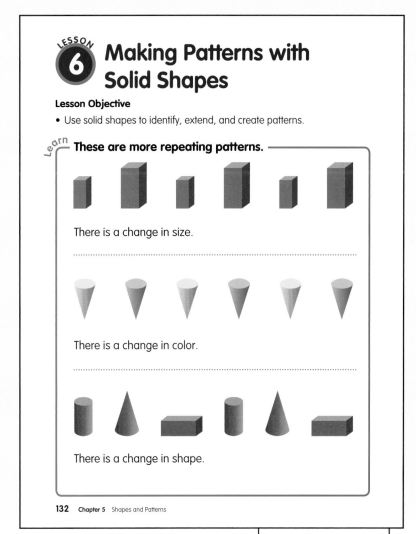

6 Making Patterns with Solid Shapes

Lesson Objective
• Use solid shapes to identify, extend, and create patterns.

Learn **These are more repeating patterns.**

There is a change in size.

There is a change in color.

There is a change in shape.

132 Chapter 5 Shapes and Patterns

Student Book A p. 132

DAY 1 Teach

Learn

Repeating Patterns (page 132)

Children learned to identify and extend repeating shape patterns made up of plane shapes in Lesson 5. They now look for changes in the attributes of shape, size, and color to identify, extend, and create repeating patterns made up of **geometric solids**.

• Form a pattern with rectangular prisms of two different sizes. *Ask*: What are these shapes? (rectangular prisms) *Say*: Look at the pattern. How is it made? (by repeating solids of different sizes) Guide children to see that the shape and color remain the same.

• Form a pattern with cones that are of the same size but different colors. *Ask*: What are these shapes? (cones) *Say*: Look at the pattern. How is it made? (by repeating solids of different colors) Guide children to see that the shape and size remain the same.

• Form a pattern with cylinders, cones, and prisms. *Ask*: What are these shapes? (cylinders, cones, and rectangular prisms) *Say*: Look at the pattern. How is it made? (by repeating solids of different shapes) Guide children to see that the color and size remain the same.

Guided Practice
Complete the patterns.

❶ ___

❷ ___

❸ ___

✋Hands-On Activity

WORK IN PAIRS

Use  .

Make your own pattern.
Ask your classmate to show what comes next.

Example Answers vary.

Lesson 6 *Making Patterns with Solid Shapes* **133**

Student Book A p. 133

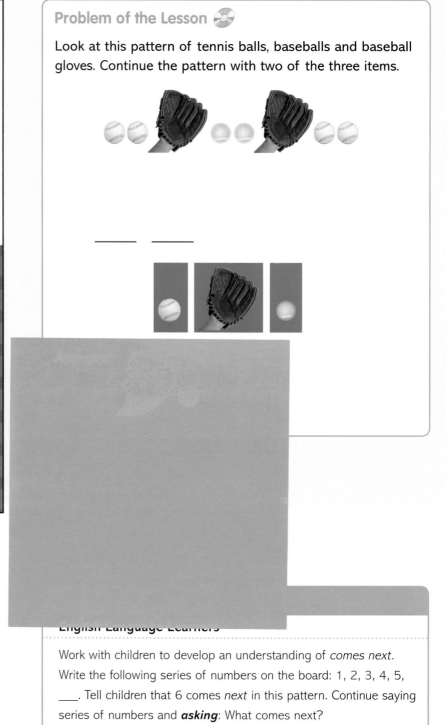

Problem of the Lesson 💿

Look at this pattern of tennis balls, baseballs and baseball gloves. Continue the pattern with two of the three items.

___ ___

English Language Learners

Work with children to develop an understanding of *comes next*.
Write the following series of numbers on the board: 1, 2, 3, 4, 5,
___. Tell children that 6 comes *next* in this pattern. Continue saying
series of numbers and ***asking***: What comes next?

Check for Understanding
✔ **Guided Practice** (page 133)

❶ to ❸ Have children complete the patterns. Ask why they chose a particular shape, size or color. Have children explain how they identified the required shape and its color or size. Guide them to use the attributes of shape, size, and color to establish the pattern.

✋Hands-On Activity:
Make a Repeating Pattern with Solid Shapes (page 133)

This activity lets children try making different patterns with the given shapes.

- Have children work in pairs and give each pair a set of **geometric solids**.

- Have children make different repeating patterns with the given solid shapes.

- Children take turns sharing their pattern, and asking what comes next in each pattern.

Best Practices The Hands-On Activity calls for children to work in pairs. You may want to keep the pairs together to complete the lesson. They can take turns asking each other questions about the elements in the pattern with the goal of finding the pattern unit. Partners can complete the patterns on their own and then compare answers.

Practice and Apply
Workbook pages for Chapter 5, Lesson 6

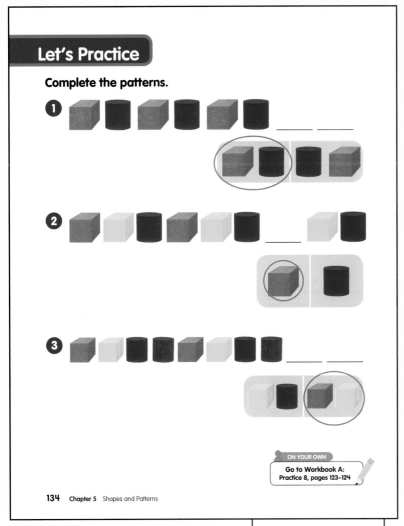

Student Book A p. 134

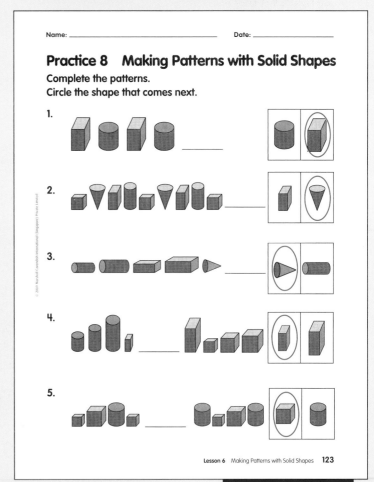

Workbook A p. 123

Let's Practice (page 134)

This practice reinforces the skills of identifying and extending repeating patterns with solid shapes. Exercise ❶ requires children to identify the shape changes in the pattern. In Exercises ❷ and ❸, both the shape and color change.

Common Error Children may be distracted by all of the colors and shapes on the page. It may be difficult to visualize the pattern unit on the page with the elements in the correct order. Suggest that they study each pattern and talk about the pattern unit with their classmate.

ON YOUR OWN

Children practice identifying and extending repeating patterns with solid shapes in Practice 8, pp. 123–124 of **Workbook 1A.** These pages (with the answers) are shown at the right. The Math Journal on pp. 125–126 of **Workbook 1A,** consolidates Lessons 2, 4, and 6. These pages (with the answers) are shown on page 135.

Differentiation Options Depending on children's success with the Workbook pages, use these materials as needed.
Struggling: Reteach 1A, pp. 89–90
On Level: Extra Practice 1A, p. 89

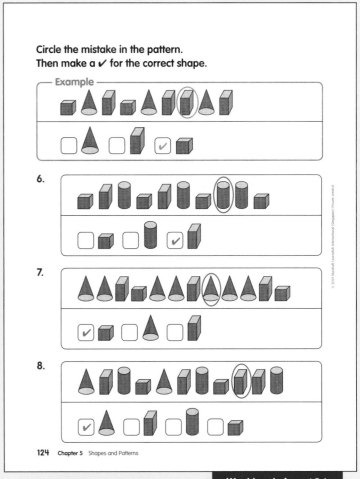

Workbook A p. 124

Workbook A p. 125

Name: _____ Date: _____

📓 Math Journal

Choose two things.
Circle them.

1.

jar [Peanut Butter]   sharpener   brick   ice-cream cone

Answers vary.

Now write about them.
Use the words in the box to help you.

| cylinder sphere cube cone pyramid rectangular prism |
| stacking sliding rolling size shape |

2. The _____ has the shape of a _____.
3. The _____ has the shape of a _____.
4. I can move the _____ by _____.
5. I can move the _____ by _____.

Continued on next page ➡️

Chapter 5 Shapes and Patterns **125**

Workbook A p. 125

Workbook A p. 126

6. My things are alike because they _____
_____

7. My things are different because they _____
_____

Make a pattern with plane shapes.
Read and draw.

8. The shapes in this pattern are alike.
The sizes of the shapes are different.

Answers vary.

126 Chapter 5 Shapes and Patterns

Workbook A p. 126

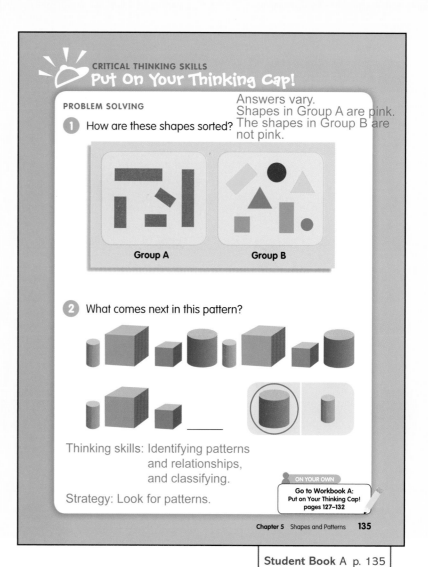

CRITICAL THINKING SKILLS
Put On Your Thinking Cap!

PROBLEM SOLVING

1. How are these shapes sorted?

Answers vary.
Shapes in Group A are pink.
The shapes in Group B are not pink.

Group A   Group B

2. What comes next in this pattern?

Thinking skills: Identifying patterns and relationships, and classifying.

Strategy: Look for patterns.

ON YOUR OWN
Go to Workbook A:
Put on Your Thinking Cap!
pages 127–132

Chapter 5 Shapes and Patterns **135**

Student Book A p. 135

CRITICAL THINKING AND PROBLEM SOLVING
Put on Your Thinking Cap! (page 135)

1. This activity requires children to use their classifying skills.

- Have children look at the shapes in Group A and Group B. *Ask*: How are the groups different?

- Elicit as many varied responses as possible. If children are not able to give the differences, lead them by *asking*: What do you notice about the color of the shapes?

- Accept all possible answers. For example: All the shapes in Group A are rectangles but not in Group B; All the shapes in Group A are pink but none in Group B are pink.; Group A contains only rectangle and Group B has 4 shapes.

2. This activity helps children develop skills in identifying patterns and relationships.

- Have children look at the given pattern. Guide children to identify the repeating unit of four solids: orange cylinder, big cube, small cube, purple cylinder.

- Have children choose the object that completes the pattern and explain why they chose the object.

135 **CHAPTER 5: LESSON 6**

Practice and Apply
Workbook pages for Put on Your Thinking Cap!

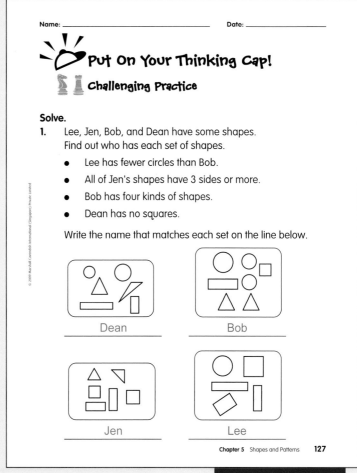

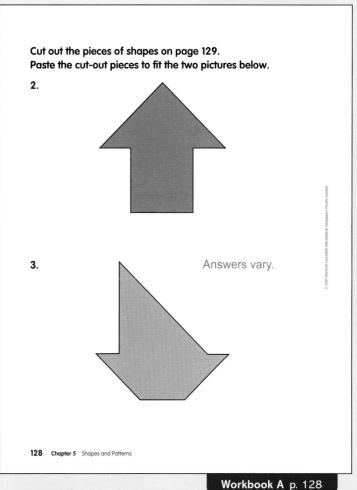

Thinking Skills

• Identifying patterns and relationships
• Classifying

Problem Solving Strategy

• Look for patterns

👤 ✏️ **ON YOUR OWN**

Because all children should be challenged, have all children try the Challenging Practice and Problem-Solving pages in **Workbook 1A**, pages 127–132. These pages (with the answers) are shown on the right and on page 135B.

Differentiation Options Depending on children' success with the Workbook pages, use these materials as needed.
On level: Extra Practice 1A, p. 90
Advance: Enrichment 1A, pp. 33–41

Name: _____   Date: _____

2.

3.

Workbook A p. 129

BLANK

Workbook A p. 130

Put On Your Thinking Cap!
Problem Solving

Draw and complete the pattern.
Each row (↔) and column (↕) must have these four
shapes, ○ △ □ ▭.   Answers vary.

1.

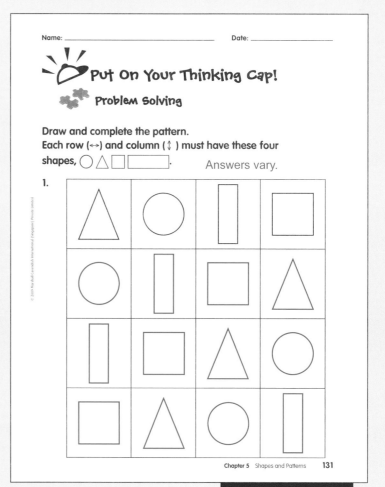

Workbook A p. 131

Draw and complete the pattern.
Each row (↔) and column must have these four shapes,
○ □ □ △.

2.

○	□	□	△
□	□	△	○
□	△	○	□
△	○	□	□

Workbook A p. 132

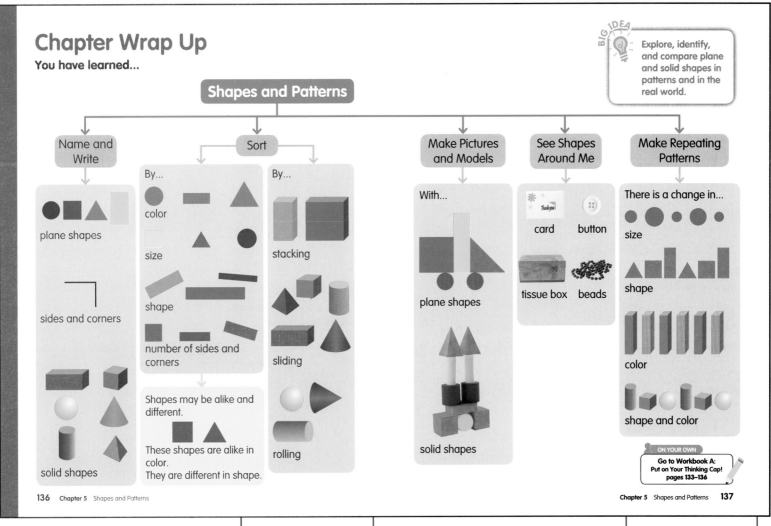

Chapter Wrap Up

You have learned...

Shapes and Patterns

Student Book A p. 136

BIG IDEA Explore, identify, and compare plane and solid shapes in patterns and in the real world.

Name and Write
- plane shapes
- sides and corners
- solid shapes

Sort
By...
- color
- size
- shape
- number of sides and corners

Shapes may be alike and different.

These shapes are alike in color.
They are different in shape.

By...
- stacking
- sliding
- rolling

Make Pictures and Models
With...
- plane shapes
- solid shapes

See Shapes Around Me
- card
- button
- tissue box
- beads

Make Repeating Patterns
There is a change in...
- size
- shape
- color
- shape and color

ON YOUR OWN
Go to Workbook A:
Put on Your Thinking Cap!
pages 133–136

136 Chapter 5 Shapes and Patterns

Chapter 5 Shapes and Patterns **137**

Student Book A p. 137

Chapter Wrap Up (pages 136 and 137)

Review shapes and patterns by going through the chart and examples given on the Student Book pages. Have children recall the names of plane and solid shapes. Have them describe these shapes by their attributes of color, size, number of sides and corners, and for solid shapes, how they can be moved. Review how shapes can be used to make pictures and models. Have children give examples of objects in school and outside of school that have shapes. Then discuss how repeating patterns can be formed with shapes by changing the shape, size or color. As you work through the examples, encourage children to use the chapter vocabulary:

- circle
- square
- side
- sort
- alike
- size
- rectangular
- sphere
- cylinder
- stack
- roll

- triangle
- rectangle
- corner
- color
- shape
- different
- cube
- cone
- pyramid
- slide
- repeating pattern

ON YOUR OWN

Have children review the vocabulary, concepts and skills from Chapter 5 with the Chapter Review/Test in Workbook 1A pp. 133–136. These pages (with the answers) are shown on page 137A.

Assessment

Use the Chapter 5 Test Prep on pages 40–44 of **Assessments 1** to assess how well children have learned the material of this chapter. This assessment is appropriate for reporting results to adults at home and administrators. This test is shown on page 137B.

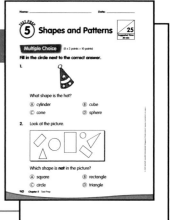

Assessments 1 pp. 40–44

Workbook pages for Chapter Review/Test

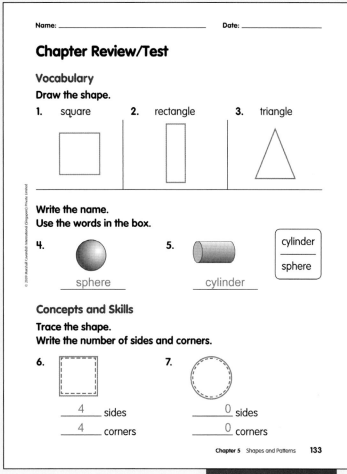

Name: _____   Date: _____

Chapter Review/Test

Vocabulary
Draw the shape.

1. square   **2.** rectangle   **3.** triangle

Write the name.
Use the words in the box.

4. sphere   **5.** cylinder

cylinder
sphere

Concepts and Skills
Trace the shape.
Write the number of sides and corners.

6. ___4___ sides   ___4___ corners

7. ___0___ sides   ___0___ corners

Chapter 5   Shapes and Patterns   **133**

Workbook A p. 133

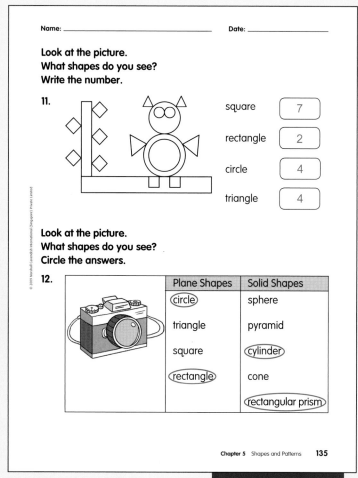

Name: _____   Date: _____

Look at the picture.
What shapes do you see?
Write the number.

11.

square   7
rectangle   2
circle   4
triangle   4

Look at the picture.
What shapes do you see?
Circle the answers.

12.

Plane Shapes	Solid Shapes
(circle)	sphere
triangle	pyramid
square	(cylinder)
(rectangle)	cone
	(rectangular prism)

Chapter 5   Shapes and Patterns   **135**

Workbook A p. 135

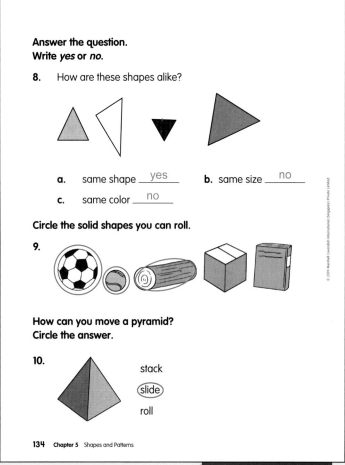

Answer the question.
Write *yes* or *no*.

8. How are these shapes alike?

a. same shape ___yes___   **b.** same size ___no___

c. same color ___no___

Circle the solid shapes you can roll.

9.

How can you move a pyramid?
Circle the answer.

10.

stack
(slide)
roll

134   Chapter 5   Shapes and Patterns

Workbook A p. 134

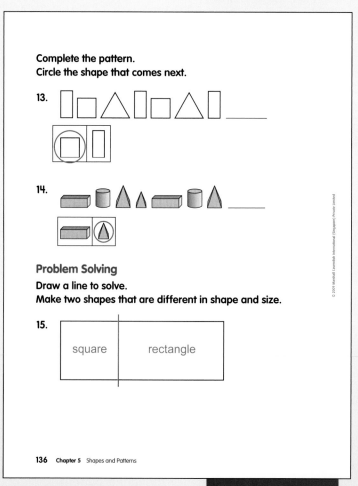

Complete the pattern.
Circle the shape that comes next.

13.

14.

Problem Solving
Draw a line to solve.
Make two shapes that are different in shape and size.

15.

square	rectangle

136   Chapter 5   Shapes and Patterns

Workbook A p. 136

Assessments Book pages for Chapter 5 Test Prep

Answer key appears in Assessments Book.

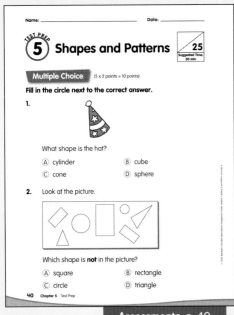

Name: _____ Date: _____

TEST PREP
5 Shapes and Patterns

Suggested Time: 30 min | 25

Multiple Choice (5 x 2 points = 10 points)

Fill in the circle next to the correct answer.

1.

What shape is the hat?

Ⓐ cylinder   Ⓑ cube

Ⓒ cone   Ⓓ sphere

2. Look at the picture.

Which shape is **not** in the picture?

Ⓐ square   Ⓑ rectangle

Ⓒ circle   Ⓓ triangle

40 Chapter 5 Test Prep

Assessments p. 40

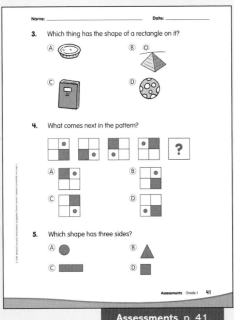

Name: _____ Date: _____

3. Which thing has the shape of a rectangle on it?

Ⓐ   Ⓑ

Ⓒ   Ⓓ

4. What comes next in the pattern?

Ⓐ   Ⓑ

Ⓒ   Ⓓ

5. Which shape has three sides?

Ⓐ   Ⓑ

Ⓒ   Ⓓ

Assessments Grade 1   41

Assessments p. 41

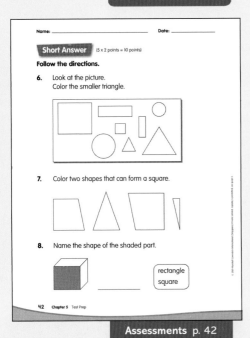

Name: _____ Date: _____

Short Answer (5 x 2 points = 10 points)

Follow the directions.

6. Look at the picture.
   Color the smaller triangle.

7. Color two shapes that can form a square.

8. Name the shape of the shaded part.

   rectangle
   square

   _____

42 Chapter 5 Test Prep

Assessments p. 42

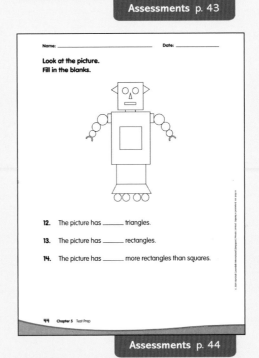

Name: _____ Date: _____

9. What comes next?
   Draw the next shape in the box.

10. What comes next?
    Color the correct shape.

Extended Response (Question 11: 2 points, Questions 12 to 14: 3 x 1 point = 3 points)

Solve.
Show your work.

11. Circle the shapes that can roll.

Assessments Grade 1   43

Assessments p. 43

Name: _____ Date: _____

Look at the picture.
Fill in the blanks.

12. The picture has _____ triangles.

13. The picture has _____ rectangles.

14. The picture has _____ more rectangles than squares.

44 Chapter 5 Test Prep

Assessments p. 44

Notes

Chapter Overview

Ordinal Numbers and Position

Math Background

As children continue to build their knowledge of number relationships, ordering numbers is an important skill. Ordering numbers and number positions with ordinal numbers are key number concepts. Children have learned in Kindergarten to order cardinal numbers. Numbers such as 1, 2, 3, and 4 are cardinal or counting numbers. Numbers such as *first*, *second*, *third*, and *fourth* are ordinal or positional numbers.

Children need practice in identifying ordinal positions as well as the words (written and oral) associated with the positions. They learn to use ordinal numbers in their full (first, second, … tenth) and abbreviated forms (1st, 2nd, …10th) to describe the positions of specific objects or persons in a row. Children also integrate their understanding of spatial relationships in the real world, and the concept of order and position. Relevant vocabulary that is essential for understanding relative positions in a row includes *left*, *right*, *in front of*, and *behind*. These establish the starting point for determining ordinal positions. Children also use position words such as *just before*, *just after* or *between* to indicate the position of something relative to another.

Cross-Curricular Connections

Reading/Language Arts Read aloud ***Let's Find Rain Forest Animals: Up, Down, Around*** by Janice Behrens (Children's Press, © 2007) which includes simple questions using positional words, along with photos that answer the questions. Have children choose a position word from the story, create a drawing to illustrate the word, and write a sentence to accompany the drawing.

Science Display in a flow chart this summary of the scientific method:

1) Ask a question.
2) Do research.
3) Make a hypothesis.
4) Plan and do a fair test.
5) Collect and record data.
6) Study the results.
7) Make and share your conclusion.

Tell children that this is one way to describe the scientific method. Ask children to read the information in the flow chart using ordinal words to introduce each step.

Skills Trace

Grade K	Know ordinal numbers first to third and some position words. (Chaps. 3, 5, and 10)
Grade 1	Describe order and position using numbers and words. (Chap. 6)
Grade 2	Describe terms in patterns and steps in games and algorithms. (Chaps. 1, 2, and 3)

EVERY DAY COUNTS®
Calendar Math

The November activities provide...

Preview of place-value concepts (Chapter 7)

Review of patterns (Chapter 5)

Practice of ordinal numbers
(Lesson 1 in this chapter)

Differentiation Resources

Differentiation for Special Populations

	English Language Learners	Struggling Reteach 1A	On Level Extra Practice 1A	Advanced Enrichment 1A
Lesson 1	p. 141	pp. 91–94	pp. 91–94	Enrichment pages can be used to challenge advanced children.
Lesson 2	p. 146	pp. 95–102	pp. 95–99	

Additional Support

For English Language Learners

Select activities that reinforce the chapter vocabulary and the connections among these words, such as having children

- add terms, definitions, and examples to the Word Wall
- create and practice with flash cards that show ordinal numbers on one side and ordinal words on the other
- draw and label pictures with examples and terms they represent
- discuss the Chapter Wrap Up, encouraging children to use the chapter vocabulary

For Struggling Learners

Select activities that go back to the appropriate stage of the Concrete-Pictorial-Abstract spectrum, such as having children

- act out ordinal words and position terms
- use manipulatives to model terms
- describe classroom objects using ordinal terms and position words
- tell and draw pictures of stories using ordinal terms and position words

See also pages 151–152 and 157–158.

If necessary, review:
- Chapter 1 (Numbers to 10)

For Advanced Learners

See suggestions on pages 142–143.

Assessment and Remediation

Chapter 6 Assessment

Prior Knowledge		
	Resource	**Page numbers**
Quick Check	Student Book 1A	p. 139
Pre-Test	Assessments 1	pp. 45–47
Ongoing Diagnostic		
Guided Practice	Student Book 1A	pp. 142–143, 147, 152, 153
Common Error	Teacher's Edition 1A	pp. 144, 149–150
Best Practices	Teacher's Edition 1A	p. 146
Formal Evaluation		
Chapter Review/Test	Workbook 1A	pp. 151–154
Chapter 6 Test Prep	Assessments 1	pp. 48–52
Cumulative Review for Chapters 5 and 6	Workbook 1A	pp. 155–160

Remediation Options

Problems with these items...   Can be remediated with...

Objective	Review/Test Items Workbook 1A pp. 151–154	Chapter Assessment Items Assessments 1 pp. 48–52	Reteach Reteach 1A	Student Book Student Book 1A
Use chapter vocabulary correctly.	1	Not assessed	pp. 92–102	pp. 141, 145
Use ordinal numbers.	17	1, 3, 5, 6–8, 11–15	pp. 91–94	Lesson 1
Use position words to name relative positions.	2–5, 6–11, 12–16, 17	1–7, 9–10	pp. 95–102	Lesson 2

Chapter Planning Guide

CHAPTER
6 Ordinal Numbers and Position

Lesson	Pacing	Instructional Objectives	Vocabulary	
Chapter Opener pp. 138–139 Recall Prior Knowledge Quick Check	*1 day	💡 **Big Idea** Numbers and words can be used to describe order and position.		
Lesson 1, pp. 140–144 Ordinal Numbers	1 day	• Use ordinal numbers	• first • third • fifth • seventh • ninth • last	• second • fourth • sixth • eighth • tenth
Lesson 2, pp. 145–157 Position Words	2 days	• Use position words to name relative positions	• before • between • right • under • below • in front of • down • far	• after • left • next to • above • behind • up • near
Problem Solving pp. 157–159 👉 Put on Your Thinking Cap!	1 day	Thinking Skills • Deduction, Sequencing, and Identifying relationships Problem Solving Strategies • Use a diagram/model • Act it out		
Chapter Wrap Up pp. 160–161	1 day	• Reinforce and consolidate chapter skills and concepts		
Chapter Assessment	1 day			
Review				

*Assume that 1 day is a 45–55 minute period.

Resources	Materials	NCTM Focal Points	NCTM Process Standards
Student Book 1A, pp. 138–139 **Assessments 1,** pp. 45–47			
Student Book 1A, pp. 140–144 **Workbook 1A,** pp. 137–140 **Extra Practice 1A,** pp. 91–94 **Reteach 1A,** pp. 91–94	• 10 connecting cubes (optional)	***Number and Operations*** Understand the sequential order of the counting numbers.	Communication Connections
Student Book 1A, pp. 145–157 **Workbook 1A,** pp. 141–146 **Extra Practice 1A,** pp. 95–99 **Reteach 1A,** pp. 95–102	• 20 connecting cubes (10 of each color) per group • Ordinal Position Table (TR12) • 1 blank transparency	***Number and Operations*** Review of Kindergarten: Interpret the physical world with geometric ideas.	Reasoning/Proof Communication Connections
Student Book 1A, pp. 157–159 **Workbook 1A,** pp. 147–150 **Extra Practice 1A,** p. 100 **Enrichment 1A,** pp. 42–50		***Number and Operations*** and ***Algebra*** Solve both routine and non-routine problems.	Problem Solving Reasoning/Proof
Student Book 1A, pp. 160–161 **Workbook 1A,** pp. 151–154			
Assessments 1, pp. 48–52			
Workbook 1A, pp. 155–160			

Technology Resources for easy classroom management
• *Math in Focus* eBook
• *Math in Focus* Teaching Resources CD
• *Math in Focus* Virtual Manipulatives
• On-Line Web Resources

CHAPTER 6 Ordinal Numbers and Position

Lesson 1 Ordinal Numbers

Lesson 2 Position Words

Chapter 6 Vocabulary

Lesson 1

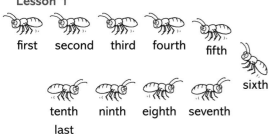

first   second   third   fourth   fifth

sixth

tenth   ninth   eighth   seventh

last

Lesson 2

before — the dog is before the cat

after — the bunny is after the cat

between — the cat is between the dog and the bunny

Lesson 2

above

under

below

Lesson 2

behind

up

left ⬅️➡️ right

down

next to   in front of

Lesson 2

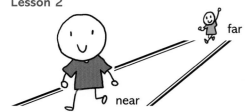

far

near

CHAPTER 6 Ordinal Numbers and Position

Lesson 1 Ordinal Numbers
Lesson 2 Position Words

Stand In Line

BIG IDEA Numbers and words can be used to describe order and position.

138

Student Book A p. 138

💡 Big Idea (page 138)

Describing order and position using ordinal numbers and words is the main focus of this chapter.

• Children use ordinal numbers from first to tenth to describe order and position of objects or persons.

• Children enhance their vocabulary with position words including *in front of*, *before*, and *after* to describe the position of something relative to another.

Chapter Opener (page 138)

The picture illustrates how ordinal numbers can be used to describe the positions of children in a line. In this chapter, they will use ordinal numbers and the corresponding words to describe positions.

• Have children look at the picture.

• *Ask*: What are the children in the picture doing? (standing in line to get on a school bus)

• *Ask*: Where else do you stand in line? (Examples: when buying food or tickets, waiting to go on a ride)

• Explain that by standing in line to board the bus, we show care and concern for the safety of others.

• *Ask*: How many children are standing in line? (3)

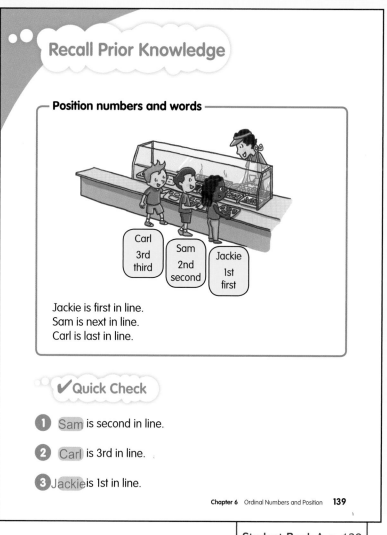

Recall Prior Knowledge

Position numbers and words

Carl 3rd third
Sam 2nd second
Jackie 1st first

Jackie is first in line.
Sam is next in line.
Carl is last in line.

✔ Quick Check

1 **Sam** is second in line.

2 **Carl** is 3rd in line.

3 **Jackie** is 1st in line.

Chapter 6 Ordinal Numbers and Position **139**

Student Book A p. 139

- Encourage children to talk about the children in the line. Here are some suggested prompt questions:

- *Ask*: Who is first in line? (the boy in glasses)

- *Ask*: Who is next? (the girl in blue) *Say*: Yes, the girl in blue is next in line, or second.

- *Ask*: Who comes after the girl in blue? (the girl with a ponytail.) *Say*: Yes, the girl with a ponytail is third in line.

Recall Prior Knowledge (page 139)

Position numbers and words

Children learned in Kindergarten to order numbers and ordinal numbers from first to third.

- Have children look at the picture and *ask*: Who is first in line? (Jackie, or the girl) How do you know? (She has food on her tray while the others do not.)

- Write *1st* and *first* on the board. Explain that the –*st* on *1st* comes from the last two letters of *first*.

- *Ask*: Who is next in line? (Sam). *Ask*: What comes next after first? (second). *Say*: Sam is second in line.
Write *2nd* and *second* on the board on the left of *first*.
Explain how *second* is shortened to *2nd*.

- Do the same for the third in line. Then *say*: Carl is last in line. There is no one else after Carl.

✔ Quick Check (page 139)

Use this section as a diagnostic tool to assess children's level of prerequisite knowledge before they progress to this chapter. Exercises 1 to 3 assess if children can read and use ordinal numbers and words to describe the order of people in a line.

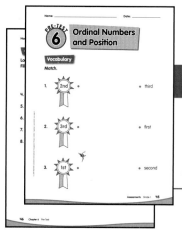

Assessment

For additional assessment of children's prior knowledge and chapter readiness, use the Chapter 6 Pre-Test on pages 45–47 of **Assessments 1**.

Assessments 1 pp. 45–47

1 Ordinal Numbers

LESSON OBJECTIVE
• Use ordinal numbers.

TECHNOLOGY RESOURCES
• *Math in Focus* eBook
• *Math in Focus* Teaching Resources CD
• *Math in Focus* Virtual Manipulatives

Vocabulary

first (1st)	second (2nd)
third (3rd)	fourth (4th)
fifth (5th)	sixth (6th)
seventh (7th)	eighth (8th)
ninth (9th)	tenth (10th)
last	

DAY 1
Student Book 1A, pp. 140–144
Workbook 1A, pp. 137–140

MATERIALS
• 10 connecting cubes
(optional for Let's Practice, page 144)

DIFFERENTIATION RESOURCES
• Reteach 1A, pp. 91–94
• Extra Practice 1A, pp. 91–94

 5-minute Warm Up

1. Invite three volunteers to stand in front of the class at one side of the room.

2. Instruct one to take 5 large steps, another to hop (on one foot) 5 steps, and the last one to jump (feet together) 5 steps. Have them stay at the spot where they stop.

3. *Ask*: Who moved the farthest? (Child A) *Say*: (Child A) is first!

4. Ask who is second and third.

---

1 Ordinal Numbers

Lesson Objective
• Use ordinal numbers.

Learn **You can use ordinal numbers to tell order.**

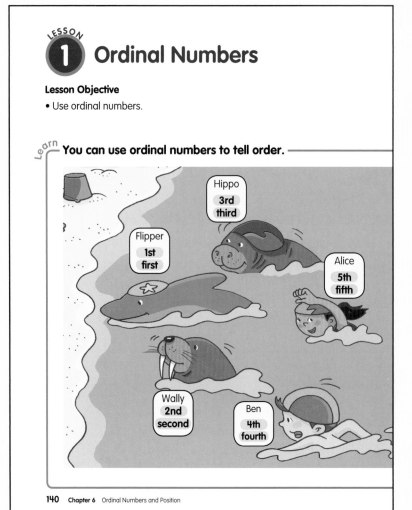

140 Chapter 6 Ordinal Numbers and Position

Student Book A p. 140

DAY 1 ## Teach

Learn

Use Ordinals to Tell Order (pages 140 and 141)

Children use ordinal numbers (both words and numerals) to describe order.

• Invite five volunteers to form a line in front of the class, facing the left.

• Use ordinal numbers *1st* to *5th* to describe their positions. Write the ordinal numbers on the board above each volunteer.

• Guide children to see the difference between ordinal numbers (1st, 2nd, ...) and counting numbers (1, 2, ...). Tell them that the last child in the line is the fifth child, since there are only 5 children in the line.

• Write the word form of ordinal numbers *first* to *fifth* on the board.

• Have each of the 5 children step to the left or right so that they are no longer in a straight line. Show that their positions (1st, 2nd, 3rd,…) remain the same. Explain that you can tell order even if the objects or people are not in a straight line.

• Look at the picture on page 140 of the Student Book with the children and talk about the individuals in positions *first* to *fifth*.

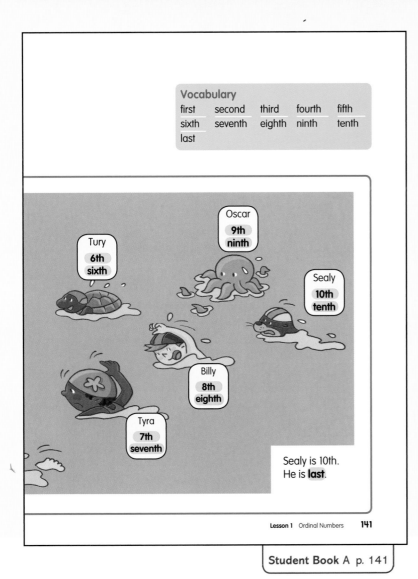

Vocabulary

first   second   third   fourth   fifth
sixth   seventh   eighth   ninth   tenth
last

Tury
6th
sixth

Oscar
9th
ninth

Sealy
10th
tenth

Billy
8th
eighth

Tyra
7th
seventh

Sealy is 10th.
He is **last**.

Lesson 1   Ordinal Numbers   **141**

Student Book A p. 141

Problem of the Lesson 💿

Kate is in line to buy a movie ticket.
There are five people in the line.
If she is the last in line, which position is
she in the line?

Solution

Start   Kate (last)

◯   ◯   ◯   ◯   ⬤

first   second   third   fourth   fifth
1st   2nd   3rd   4th   5th

Answer: 5th or fifth

Differentiated Instruction

English Language Learners

In the Let's Practice on page 144, children may have trouble
reading the questions and understanding the vocabulary words.
Pair English language learners with fluent English speakers, who
will read each question aloud. The English language learner
points to the floor of the building that answers the question. If
a child is struggling with vocabulary, the partner points to the
correct floor and describes what is there using the vocabulary in
the question.

- Add five more volunteers to the line to teach *6th (sixth)* to
  10th (tenth).

- Say that the last child in the line is now the tenth child, since
  there are 10 children in the line.

- Look at the picture on page 141 of the Student Book with
  the children and talk about the individuals in positions *sixth*
  to *tenth*. Explain that Sealy is *last* because there is no one
  else behind him.

Best Practices   Most children will understand ordinals written
with numbers (2nd), but they may not easily recognize the
word form of ordinals. On each of ten sheets of paper write a
numeral, the number form of the ordinal, and the word form of
the ordinal (1, 1st, first). Display the sheets in the front of the
classroom in order from left to right.

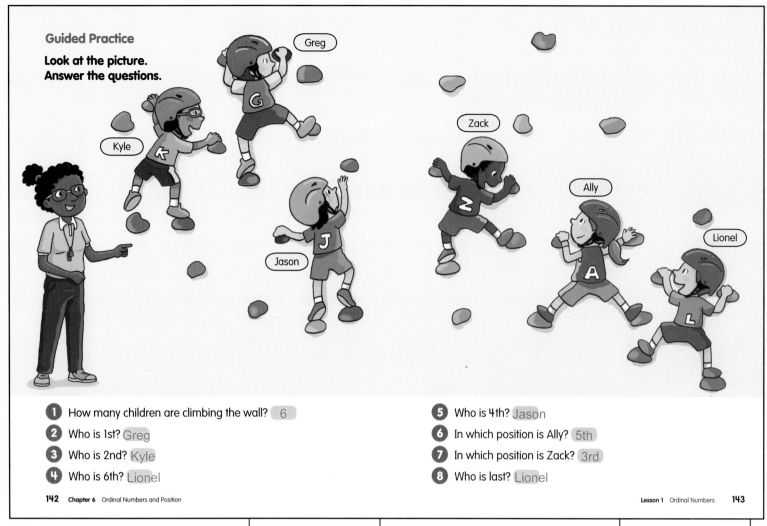

Guided Practice

**Look at the picture.
Answer the questions.**

Greg

Kyle

Zack

Ally

Jason

Lionel

1 How many children are climbing the wall? 6

2 Who is 1st? Greg

3 Who is 2nd? Kyle

4 Who is 6th? Lionel

5 Who is 4th? Jason

6 In which position is Ally? 5th

7 In which position is Zack? 3rd

8 Who is last? Lionel

Student Book A p. 142

Student Book A p. 143

Check for Understanding

✓ **Guided Practice** (pages 142 and 143)

1 to **8** Have children study the picture shown on these two pages.

- Explain that in this section, the positions are from top to bottom, with the first being the highest and the last being the lowest. Ensure children do not include the teacher in their counting or ordering.

- Have children say the position using an ordinal number for each child on the wall before they answer each question.

For Advanced Learners Have children use the picture to answer other kinds of questions.

- Lionel is in the sixth position. How many children are in front of him? (5)

- What place is the child that is two places above Jason? (second)

Encourage children to make up their own ordinal number clues.

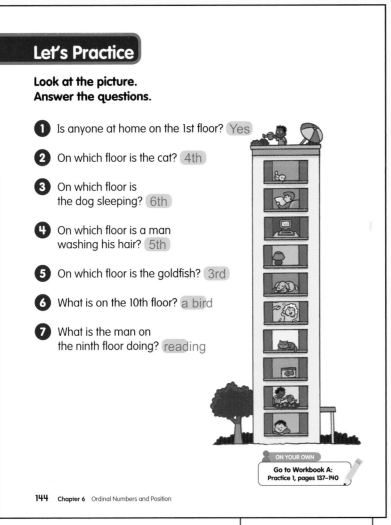

Let's Practice

Look at the picture.
Answer the questions.

1. Is anyone at home on the 1st floor? Yes

2. On which floor is the cat? 4th

3. On which floor is the dog sleeping? 6th

4. On which floor is a man washing his hair? 5th

5. On which floor is the goldfish? 3rd

6. What is on the 10th floor? a bird

7. What is the man on the ninth floor doing? reading

ON YOUR OWN
Go to Workbook A:
Practice 1, pages 137–140

144 Chapter 6 Ordinal Numbers and Position

Student Book A p. 144

Let's Practice (page 144)

This practice reinforces telling order using ordinal numbers. In this exercise, unlike the previous ones in this chapter, the ordering occurs from the bottom to the top. Have children say what they see on each floor in the picture.

For Struggling Learners Before having children complete the exercise set, you may want to build a tower using 10 **connecting cubes** and use it to model the bottom (first) to top (tenth) order.

Common Error Children may think that the first floor is at the top of the building, especially since in the previous activity, the highest climber was in first place. Explain that the floors of a building are numbered from bottom to top, so the first floor is on the bottom of the building.

ON YOUR OWN

Children practice using ordinal numbers to tell order in Practice 1, pp. 137–140 of **Workbook 1A**. These pages (with the answers) are shown on page 144A.

Differentiation Options Depending on children's success with the Workbook pages, use these materials as needed.
Struggling: Reteach 1A, pp. 91–94
On Level: Extra Practice 1A, pp. 91–94

Practice and Apply
Workbook pages for Chapter 6, Lesson 1

Name: _____ Date: _____

CHAPTER 6 Ordinal Numbers and Position

Practice 1   Ordinal Numbers

Circle.

Example

the 2nd corn

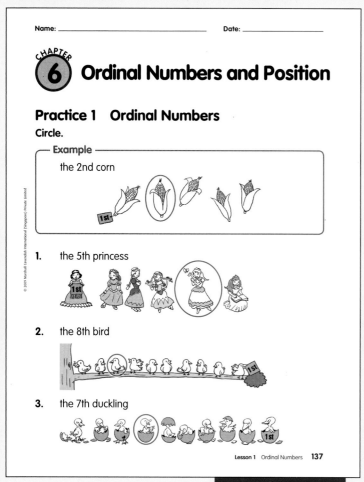

1. the 5th princess

2. the 8th bird

3. the 7th duckling

Workbook A p. 137

Name: _____ Date: _____

Match.

6.

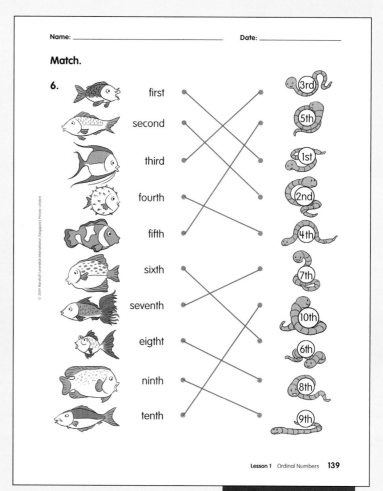

first — second — third — fourth — fifth — sixth — seventh — eigtth — ninth — tenth

Workbook A p. 139

Color.

4. 3 frogs

Answers vary.

the 3rd frog

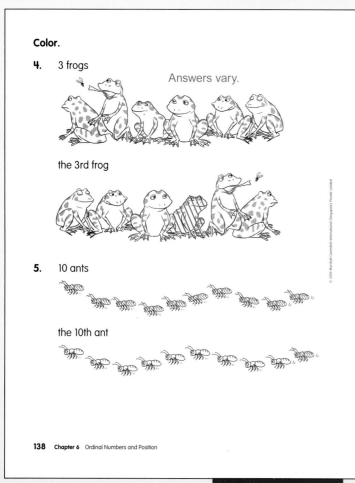

5. 10 ants

the 10th ant

Workbook A p. 138

Look at the picture.
Answer the questions.

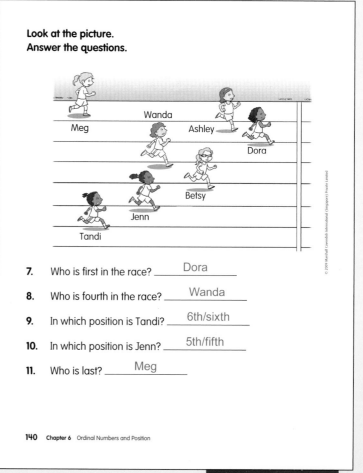

Meg   Wanda   Ashley   Dora   Betsy   Jenn   Tandi

7. Who is first in the race? _____Dora_____

8. Who is fourth in the race? _____Wanda_____

9. In which position is Tandi? _____6th/sixth_____

10. In which position is Jenn? _____5th/fifth_____

11. Who is last? _____Meg_____

Workbook A p. 140

Chapter 6

LESSON
2 Position Words

LESSON OBJECTIVE
- Use position words to name relative positions.

TECHNOLOGY RESOURCES
- *Math in Focus* eBook
- *Math in Focus* Teaching Resources CD
- *Math in Focus* Virtual Manipulatives

Vocabulary

before	after
between	left
right	next to
under	above
below	behind
in front of	up
down	near
far	

DAY 1
Student Book 1A, pp. 145–150
Workbook 1A, pp. 141–144

MATERIALS
- 20 connecting cubes
  (10 of each color; 1 set per group)
- Ordinal Position Table (TR12)
- 1 blank transparency

DIFFERENTIATION RESOURCES
- Reteach 1A, pp. 95–98
- Extra Practice 1A, pp. 95–98

DAY 2
Student Book 1A, pp. 151–157
Workbook 1A, pp. 145–146

DIFFERENTIATION RESOURCES
- Reteach 1A, pp. 99–102
- Extra Practice 1A, p. 99

 5-minute Warm Up

Have ten children form a line and tell what their ordinal position is.

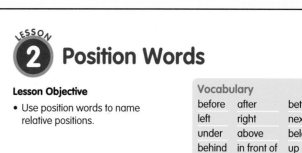

LESSON
2 Position Words

Lesson Objective
- Use position words to name relative positions.

Vocabulary

before	after	between
left	right	next to
under	above	below
behind	in front of	up
down	near	far

Learn You can use position words to tell order and position.

Alan is **before** Ben.
Chris is **after** Ben.
Ben is **between** Alan and Chris.

Guided Practice

Name the positions of Demi and Evan using these words.

1. before   between   after

Demi is before Evan.
Demi is between Chris and Evan.
Demi is after Chris.
Evan is after Demi.

Lesson 2 Position Words **145**

Student Book A p. 145

DAY 1 # Teach

Use Position Words to Tell Order and Position
(page 145)

Children have learned to use ordinal numbers to tell order. In this lesson, children will name relative positions using position words.

- Invite five volunteers to form a line in front of the board, facing the left.
- Have children use ordinal numbers to describe their positions from left to right. Write the ordinal numbers on the board.
- Introduce *before*, *after* and *between* by describing the position of the children.
- Have children look at the picture in the Student Book and read out the sentences.

Check for Understanding
✓**Guided Practice** (page 145)

1. Have children describe the positions of Demi and Evan using *before*, *after* and *between*, making as many sentences as possible.

You can use left, right, and next to to tell where things are in relation to each other.

The T-shirt is first on the **left**.
The pants are second from the left.

The T-shirt is fifth from the **right**.
It is also last from the right.

The towel is third from the left.
It is also third from the right.

The dress is **next to** the towel.
The dress is also next to the skirt.

The pants are between the T-shirt and the towel.

146 **Chapter 6** Ordinal Numbers and Position

Student Book A p. 146

Problem of the Lesson

Ellie is standing in line to board the bus.
There are two people in front of her.
There are three people behind her.
How many people are in the line?

Solution:
Front

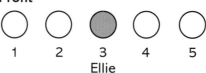

Answer: There are 6 people in the line.

Differentiated Instruction

English Language Learners

Children may need additional practice with the many position words included in the lesson. Play "Simon Says" with the children using commands and position words. For example, Put your left hand under your right hand. Put one hand above your head. Stand between two desks. Point a finger up toward the ceiling. Correct any mistakes as they play.

Learn

Use *Left, Right,* and *Next to* to Tell Relative Position (page 146)

The terms *left*, *right*, and *next to* are commonly used, and can be used with ordinal numbers to describe the relative positions of things.

• Have children show you their left hand and their right hand. Have them point to and name the objects on the clothesline from left to right. Draw on the board a horizontal arrow from left to right and write *left* and *right* at opposite ends of the arrow.

• *Ask*: What is first on the left? (T-shirt) What is second/third, fourth/fifth/last from the left? (pants, towel, dress, skirt, skirt)

• Draw another horizontal arrow from right to left on the board, and then *ask*: What is first on the right? (skirt) What is second/third/fourth/fifth/last from the right? (dress, towel, pants, T-shirt, T-shirt)

• *Ask*: What is next to the towel? (dress, skirt). Explain that there can be more than one answer or just one answer.
  Ask: What is next to the T-shirt? (pants)

Best Practices This lesson includes many vocabulary words and concepts. To help keep track of what words children do and do not understand, use the Let's Practice activities as an assessment. Provide extra vocabulary practice for those children who get more than one incorrect.

Guided Practice
Answer the questions.

LEFT   RIGHT

2. Who is first on the right? Jorge
3. Who is second from the left? Megan
4. Who is last from the left? Jorge
5. Who is next to Mr. Smith? Dylan and Jorge

Who is between Dylan and Jorge?

Lesson 2 Position Words **147**

✋Hands-On Activity

WORKING TOGETHER

Carry out these activities.

1. Your teacher will choose ten children. They should stand in a row facing the class.

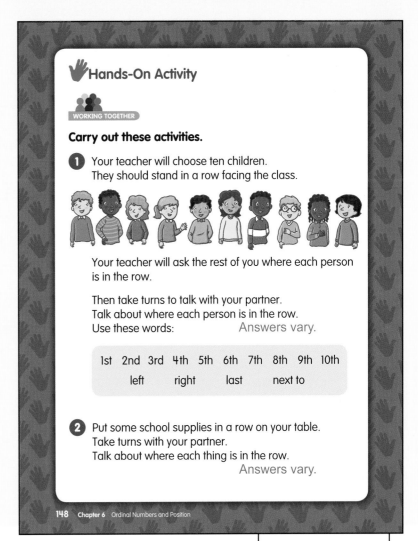

Your teacher will ask the rest of you where each person is in the row.

Then take turns to talk with your partner. Talk about where each person is in the row. Use these words: Answers vary.

1st	2nd	3rd	4th	5th	6th	7th	8th	9th	10th
left		right		last		next to			

2. Put some school supplies in a row on your table. Take turns with your partner. Talk about where each thing is in the row.

Answers vary.

148 Chapter 6 Ordinal Numbers and Position

✔Guided Practice (page 147)

2 to 5 Remind children to read each question carefully to find out if it asks for ordering from the right or left.

WORKING TOGETHER

✋Hands-On Activity:
Talk about Where Children are in a Row
(page 148)

1 This activity lets children practice using the ordinal numbers and position words to describe positions and relative positions of children in a row.

- Have ten children stand in a row facing the class.

- Have other children work in pairs.

- Model the activity for children by asking them questions about anyone in the row. **Ask**: Who is second from the right? Who is next to Child B? and so on.

- Have children take turns stating where each person is in the row. Encourage them to use the terms given on the Student Book page.

Talk about Where Things are on Your Desk
(page 148)

2 This activity lets children work in groups to practice using ordinal numbers and position words to describe positions and relative positions of things in a row.

- Model the activity by placing some school supplies in a row on your table, and say a statement about where one thing is in the row. For example, *say*: The pen is next to the book, or the stapler is third from the right.

WORKING TOGETHER Game

Find it First!

Players: 3
You need:
• 10 ▮
• 10 ▮

How to play: Use only 1, 2, or 3 fingers to count.

STEP 1 Players 1 and 2 put their ▮ in a row.

STEP 2 Player 3 calls out an ordinal position.

9th from the left!

STEP 3 The first player to grab the correct ▮ from the other player's row scores 1 point.

STEP 4 Put the ▮ back. Player 3 then calls out another ordinal position. The first player to score 5 points wins.

STEP 5 Take turns calling out and playing.

Lesson 2 Position Words **149**

Student Book A p. 149

Let's Practice

**Look at the picture.
Complete the sentences.**

1 The black mouse is before the brown mouse. The white mouse is after the brown mouse.

2 The brown mouse is ▢ the black mouse and the white mouse. between

3 The peanut butter is second from the left.

4 The cheese is first on the right.

5 The apple is next to the peanut butter.

6 The potato is third from the left and the right.

ON YOUR OWN
Go to Workbook A:
Practice 2, pages 141–144

150 Chapter 6 Ordinal Numbers and Position

Student Book A p. 150

 **Game:**

Find It First! (page 149)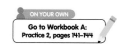

This game lets children practice using ordinal numbers to tell position. It also develops children's awareness of spatial relationships.

• Have children play in groups of three and give Player 1 10 red **connecting cubes** and Player 2 10 blue **connecting cubes**.

• Have Players 1 and 2 put their **connecting cubes** in a row in front of them.

• Player 3 calls out an ordinal position, for example, 9th from the left.

• Each player takes the correct cube from the other player's row of cubes. The first player to take the correct cube scores a point.

• Replace the cubes and Player 3 calls out another ordinal position.

• The first player to score 5 points wins. Players switch roles.

Let's Practice (page 150)

In Exercises **1** to **6**, children practice using ordinal number words and relative position words to describe the position of objects in a row.

Common Error In Exercise **1** of Let's Practice, children might answer that the white mouse is behind the brown mouse. Explain that this is true, but point out that the first sentence uses the word *before*, so the better answer is *after*. You may want to point out the opposites in the vocabulary.

ON YOUR OWN

Children practice using ordinal number words and relative position words to describe the position of objects or persons in a row in Practice 2, pp. 141–144 of **Workbook 1A**. These pages (with the answers) are shown on page 150A.

Differentiation Options Depending on children's success with the Workbook pages, use these materials as needed.
Struggling: Reteach 1A, pp. 95–98
On Level: Extra Practice 1A, pp. 95–98

Practice and Apply
Workbook pages for Chapter 6, Lesson 2

Name: _____ **Date:** _____

Practice 2 Position Words
Look at the picture.
Circle the correct name.

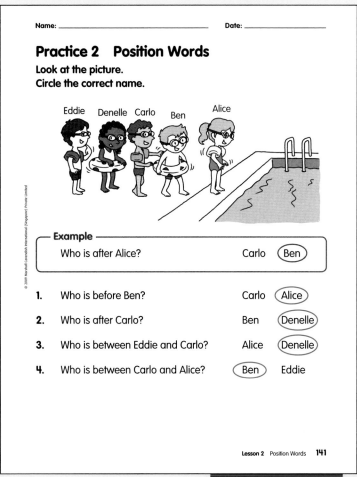

Eddie   Denelle   Carlo   Ben   Alice

Example
| Who is after Alice? | Carlo | (Ben) |

1. Who is before Ben? — Carlo (Alice)
2. Who is after Carlo? — Ben (Denelle)
3. Who is between Eddie and Carlo? — Alice (Denelle)
4. Who is between Carlo and Alice? — (Ben) Eddie

Name: _____ **Date:** _____

Look at the picture.
Fill in the blanks with the words in the box.

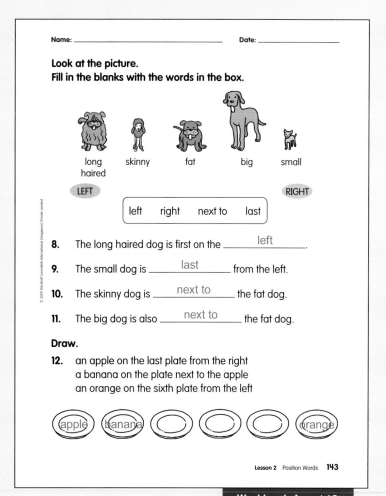

long haired   skinny   fat   big   small

LEFT   RIGHT

| left | right | next to | last |

8. The long haired dog is first on the ___left___.
9. The small dog is ___last___ from the left.
10. The skinny dog is ___next to___ the fat dog.
11. The big dog is also ___next to___ the fat dog.

Draw.

12. an apple on the last plate from the right
a banana on the plate next to the apple
an orange on the sixth plate from the left

(apple) (banana) ( ) ( ) ( ) (orange)

Color.

Example
the fourth bird from the left

Left   Right

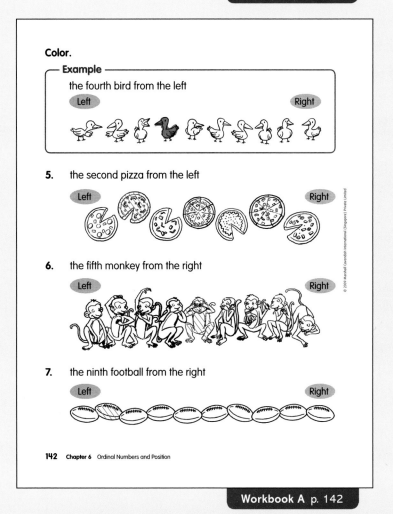

5. the second pizza from the left

Left   Right

6. the fifth monkey from the right

Left   Right

7. the ninth football from the right

Left   Right

Read the clues to answer the question.
Then write the letters in the correct ☐.

13. What is the capital of the United States of America?

| W | A | S | H | I | N | G | T | O | N | D.C. |

a   b   c   d   e   f   g   h   i   j

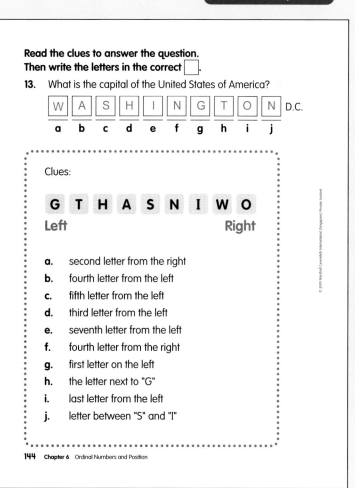

Clues:

G T H A S N I W O
Left   Right

a. second letter from the right
b. fourth letter from the left
c. fifth letter from the left
d. third letter from the left
e. seventh letter from the left
f. fourth letter from the right
g. first letter on the left
h. the letter next to "G"
i. last letter from the left
j. letter between "S" and "I"

Learn **You can use the picture to learn more position words.**

Jasmine is **under** the table.

Shenice is **above** Pedro.
Pedro is **below** Shenice.

Danny is **behind** the curtains.
Jacob is **in front of** the curtains.

Guided Practice

Look at the picture.
Find the missing position words.

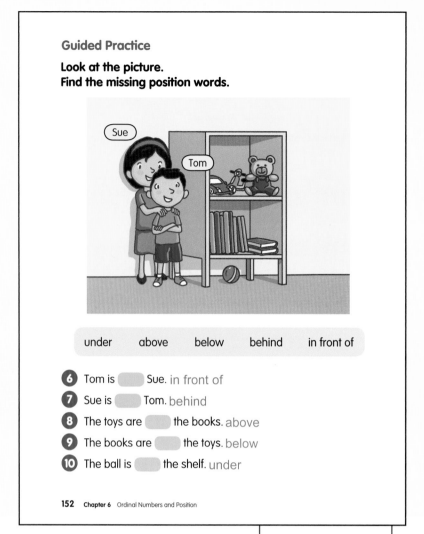

under	above	below	behind	in front of

6 Tom is ⬭ Sue. in front of
7 Sue is ⬭ Tom. behind
8 The toys are ⬭ the books. above
9 The books are ⬭ the toys. below
10 The ball is ⬭ the shelf. under

DAY 2 **Teach** See the Lesson Organizer on page 145 for Day 2 resources.

Learn
More Position Words (page 151)

Children have learned to use ordinal numbers and some position words. In this lesson, children acquire more position words to describe the position of children in a picture.

- Have children look at the picture. You may want to display it using the Interactive eBook or an opaque projector.

- *Ask*: Where is Jasmine? (under the table) Where is Shenice? (above Pedro) Where is Pedro? (below Shenice) Where is Danny? (behind the curtains) Where is Jacob? (in front of the curtains/in front of Danny)

- Guide children to use the appropriate vocabulary to express relative positions. For example, if a child says, "Shenice is on top," help the child to recast that as a position relative to another child, that is, *above Pedro*.

✔ **Guided Practice** (page 152)

6 to **10** Have children use the correct position words to describe the position of each person or object in the picture.

[For Struggling Learners] Before children begin, you may want to review the position words using a pencil and a piece of paper. For example, tell the child to hold up the paper. Then ask the child to put the pencil *behind* or *in front of* the paper.

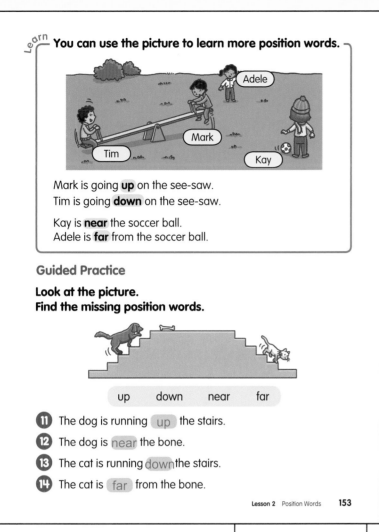

Learn You can use the picture to learn more position words.

Mark is going **up** on the see-saw.
Tim is going **down** on the see-saw.

Kay is **near** the soccer ball.
Adele is **far** from the soccer ball.

Guided Practice

Look at the picture.
Find the missing position words.

| up | down | near | far |

11 The dog is running (up) the stairs.

12 The dog is (near) the bone.

13 The cat is running down the stairs.

14 The cat is (far) from the bone.

Lesson 2   Position Words   **153**

Student Book A p. 153

Learn

More Position Words (page 153)

Besides position words such as *near* and *far*, children can use *up* and *down* to describe directional movement in a picture.

• Have children look at the picture.

• *Ask*: What can you say about the children on the see-saw? Guide children to use the words *up* and *down*, then highlight those words as vocabulary. As these are words in common usage, there is probably no need to teach them formally, but it is useful to make children aware of their use in math concepts.

• Talk about *near* and *far* using the children in the picture. Use other examples in the classroom to illustrate the use of *near* and *far*. Have children make statements about the position of things and children in the classroom using *near* and *far*.

✓ Guided Practice (page 153)

11 to 14 Have children use the correct position words to describe the position and movement of the dog and cat in the picture.

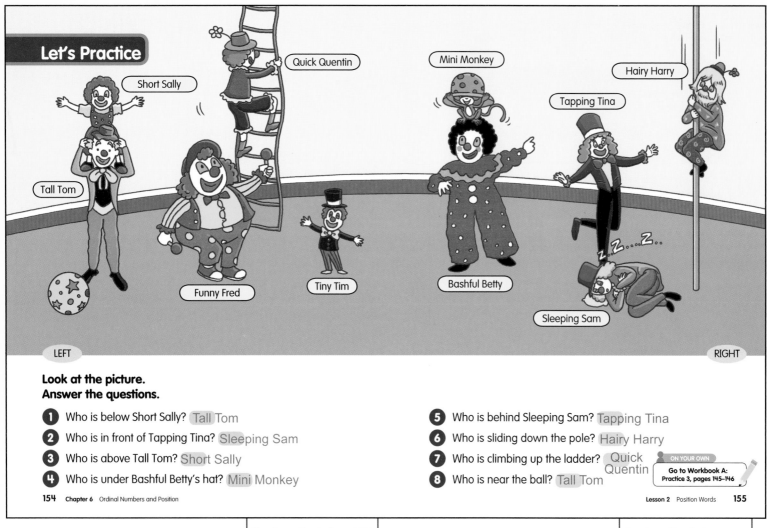

Let's Practice

Look at the picture.
Answer the questions.

1. Who is below Short Sally? Tall Tom
2. Who is in front of Tapping Tina? Sleeping Sam
3. Who is above Tall Tom? Short Sally
4. Who is under Bashful Betty's hat? Mini Monkey

5. Who is behind Sleeping Sam? Tapping Tina
6. Who is sliding down the pole? Hairy Harry
7. Who is climbing up the ladder? Quick Quentin
8. Who is near the ball? Tall Tom

ON YOUR OWN
Go to Workbook A:
Practice 3, pages 145–146

Student Book A p. 154

Student Book A p. 155

Let's Practice (pages 154 and 155)

In Exercises 1 to 8, have children practice using other
position words to describe the positions of people in a
picture. Ensure that children look at the two pages together as
they practice today's position words and answer the exercises.

ON YOUR OWN

Children practice using position words to describe the
positions of people and animals in a picture in Practice 3,
pp. 145–146 of **Workbook 1A**. These pages (with the
answers) are shown on page 156.

Differentiation Options Depending on children's success
with the Workbook pages, use these materials as needed.
Struggling: Reteach 1A, pp. 99–102
On Level: Extra Practice 1A, p. 99

Practice and Apply

Workbook pages for Chapter 6, Lesson 2

Name: _____   Date: _____

Practice 3   Position Words

Color.

1. the rabbit below the black rabbit pink
   the rabbit above the black rabbit gray
   the rabbit under the paper brown
   the hair of the boy behind the shelf yellow
   the hair of the boy in front of the shelf red

yellow

gray

red

pink   brown

Lesson 2   Position Words   **145**

Workbook A p. 145

Look at the picture.
Fill in the blanks with the words in the box.

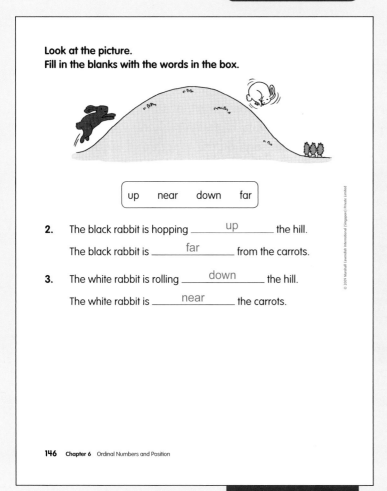

up	near	down	far

2. The black rabbit is hopping _____ **up** _____ the hill.
   The black rabbit is _____ **far** _____ from the carrots.

3. The white rabbit is rolling _____ **down** _____ the hill.
   The white rabbit is _____ **near** _____ the carrots.

146   Chapter 6   Ordinal Numbers and Position

Workbook A p. 146

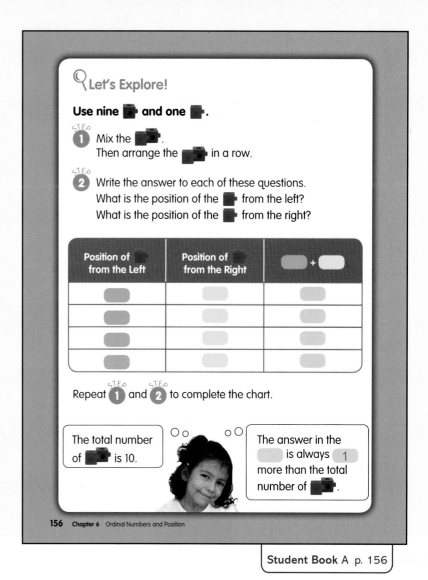

Let's Explore!

Use nine ■ and one ■.

STEP **1** Mix the ■.
Then arrange the ■ in a row.

STEP **2** Write the answer to each of these questions.
What is the position of the ■ from the left?
What is the position of the ■ from the right?

Position of ■ from the Left	Position of ■ from the Right	▭ + ▭

Repeat STEP **1** and STEP **2** to complete the chart.

The total number of ■ is 10.

The answer in the ▭ is always **1** more than the total number of ■.

156   **Chapter 6**   Ordinal Numbers and Position

Student Book A p. 156

WORKING TOGETHER

Let's Explore! (page 156) 🎲

Use Connecting Cubes to Describe a Pattern Involving the Sum of Number Positions

This exploration helps children to develop critical inquiry skills as they compare the ordinal positions of an object in a row, ordering from opposite directions.

- Have children work in pairs and give each pair nine **blue connecting cubes** and one **red connecting cube**.

- Have children follow Steps **1** and **2**.

- Using the **Ordinal Position Table** (TR12), and an example row from one of the pairs of children, model how this is done.

- Add the positions. Lead children to see that the number is always 11. Make children aware that this is 1 more than the total number of cubes.

- *Ask*: Why do you think this is so? Guide them to see that it is so because the red cube is counted twice when you add the positions together.

CHAPTER 6: LESSON 2   **156**

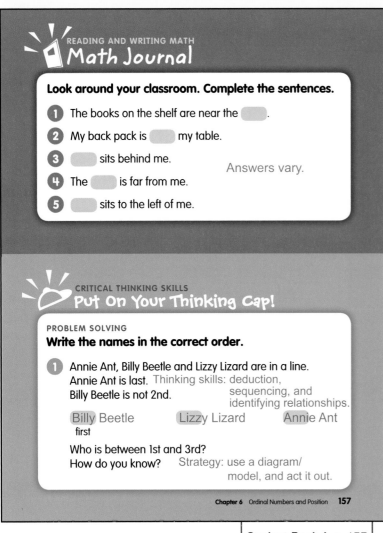

READING AND WRITING MATH
Math Journal

Look around your classroom. Complete the sentences.

1. The books on the shelf are near the [____].
2. My back pack is [____] my table.
3. [____] sits behind me.
4. The [____] is far from me.
5. [____] sits to the left of me.

Answers vary.

CRITICAL THINKING SKILLS
Put On Your Thinking Cap!

PROBLEM SOLVING
Write the names in the correct order.

1. Annie Ant, Billy Beetle and Lizzy Lizard are in a line.
   Annie Ant is last. *Thinking skills: deduction, sequencing, and identifying relationships.*
   Billy Beetle is not 2nd.

   Billy Beetle   Lizzy Lizard   Annie Ant
   first

   Who is between 1st and 3rd?
   How do you know? *Strategy: use a diagram/ model, and act it out.*

Chapter 6 Ordinal Numbers and Position **157**

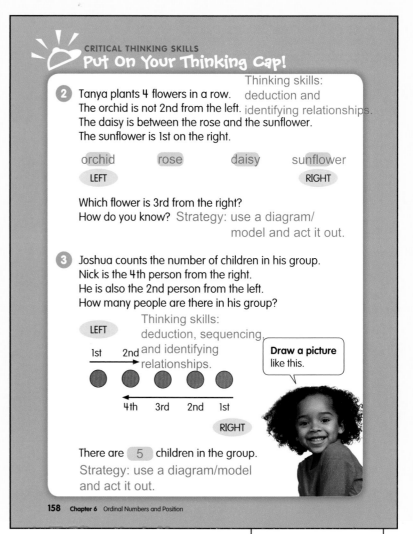

CRITICAL THINKING SKILLS
Put On Your Thinking Cap!

2. Tanya plants 4 flowers in a row. *Thinking skills: deduction and identifying relationships.*
   The orchid is not 2nd from the left.
   The daisy is between the rose and the sunflower.
   The sunflower is 1st on the right.

   orchid   rose   daisy   sunflower
   LEFT   RIGHT

   Which flower is 3rd from the right?
   How do you know? *Strategy: use a diagram/ model and act it out.*

3. Joshua counts the number of children in his group.
   Nick is the 4th person from the right.
   He is also the 2nd person from the left.
   How many people are there in his group?

   LEFT   *Thinking skills: deduction, sequencing, and identifying relationships.*

   1st   2nd
   ● ● ● ● ●
   4th   3rd   2nd   1st
   RIGHT

   Draw a picture like this.

   There are [5] children in the group.
   Strategy: use a diagram/model and act it out.

158 Chapter 6 Ordinal Numbers and Position

READING AND WRITING MATH
Math Journal (page 157)

The journal exercises help children to be more aware of their immediate physical environment, and enable them to describe the positions of objects and people around them in the real world using the newly learned vocabulary. Guide individual children to complete the sentences as answers may vary from child to child.

CRITICAL THINKING AND PROBLEM SOLVING
Put on Your Thinking Cap!
(pages 157 to 159)

1 This activity requires children to exercise their deductive skills. The exercise may be completed in pairs.

• Read the question with children. As you read the second line: Annie Ant is last, write *Annie Ant* on one side of the board, and write *last* below that. Explain that as there are three of them, Annie Ant is also 3rd in line. Write *1st* and *2nd* on the left of Annie Ant, leaving the names blank for now.

• Read the third line of the question: Billie Beetle is not 2nd. Guide children to reason that since Billie Beetle is not 2nd and not 3rd, he must be 1st in line. *Write Billie Beetle* in the 1st place.

• Now read: Who is between 1st and 3rd? Have children answer that Lizzy Lizard is between them.

2 to 4 These exercises are similar to Exercise 1 but are more complex because they involve ordering from opposite directions. Lead children to draw arrows and write ordinal numbers in both directions on the diagram or model.

For Struggling Learners These problems can be solved by having children take the places of the three characters in the problem and going through the same deductive process.

Thinking Skills

• Deduction
• Sequencing
• Identifying relationships

Problem Solving Strategies

• Use a diagram/model
• Act it out

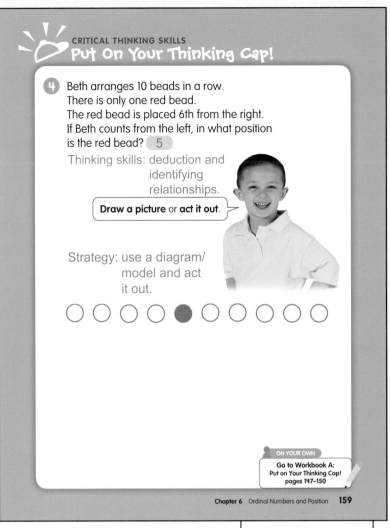

CRITICAL THINKING SKILLS
Put On Your Thinking Cap!

4 Beth arranges 10 beads in a row.
There is only one red bead.
The red bead is placed 6th from the right.
If Beth counts from the left, in what position
is the red bead? 5

Thinking skills: deduction and
identifying
relationships.

Draw a picture or act it out.

Strategy: use a diagram/
model and act
it out.

○ ○ ○ ○ ● ○ ○ ○ ○ ○

ON YOUR OWN
Go to Workbook A:
Put on Your Thinking Cap!
pages 147–150

Chapter 6 Ordinal Numbers and Position **159**

Student Book A p. 159

ON YOUR OWN

Because all children should be challenged, have all children
try the Challenging Practice and Problem-Solving pages in
Workbook 1A, pp. 147–150. These pages (with the answers)
are shown on page 159A.

Differentiation Options Depending on children's success
with the Workbook pages, use these materials as needed.

On Level: Extra Practice 1A, p. 100
Advanced: Enrichment 1A, pp. 42–50

Practice and Apply

Workbook pages for Put on Your Thinking Cap!

Name: _____ **Date:** _____

☀ Put On Your Thinking Cap!
♟ Challenging Practice

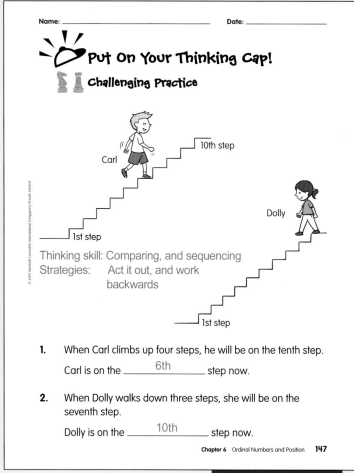

Thinking skill: Comparing, and sequencing
Strategies: Act it out, and work
          backwards

1. When Carl climbs up four steps, he will be on the tenth step.

   Carl is on the ____6th____ step now.

2. When Dolly walks down three steps, she will be on the
   seventh step.

   Dolly is on the ____10th____ step now.

Chapter 6 Ordinal Numbers and Position **147**

Workbook A p. 147

Name: _____ **Date:** _____

2. Look at the pictures.
   Put them in order.
   Write the ordinal number that belongs with each picture.

7th	4th	6th	2nd	1st
8th	3rd	9th	5th	10th

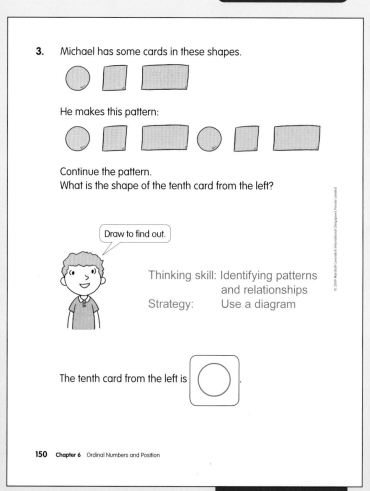

Thinking skills: Sequencing, and deduction
Strategy: Make suppositions

Chapter 6 Ordinal Numbers and Position **149**

Workbook A p. 149

☀ Put On Your Thinking Cap!
🧩 Problem Solving

1. There are four rabbits A, B, C and D.
   Read the clues.
   Fill in the circles with the correct letters.

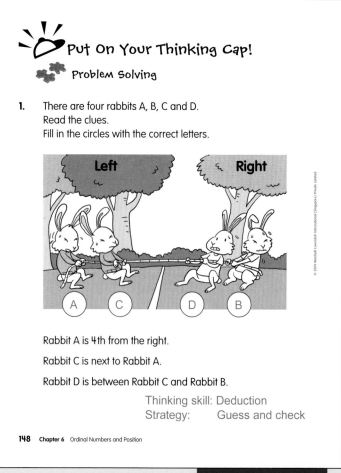

Rabbit A is 4th from the right.

Rabbit C is next to Rabbit A.

Rabbit D is between Rabbit C and Rabbit B.

Thinking skill: Deduction
Strategy: Guess and check

148 **Chapter 6** Ordinal Numbers and Position

Workbook A p. 148

---

3. Michael has some cards in these shapes.

   ⬤ ▢ ▭

   He makes this pattern:

   ⬤ ▢ ▭ ⬤ ▢ ▭

   Continue the pattern.
   What is the shape of the tenth card from the left?

   Draw to find out.

   Thinking skill: Identifying patterns
             and relationships
   Strategy: Use a diagram

   The tenth card from the left is ▢.

150 **Chapter 6** Ordinal Numbers and Position

Workbook A p. 150

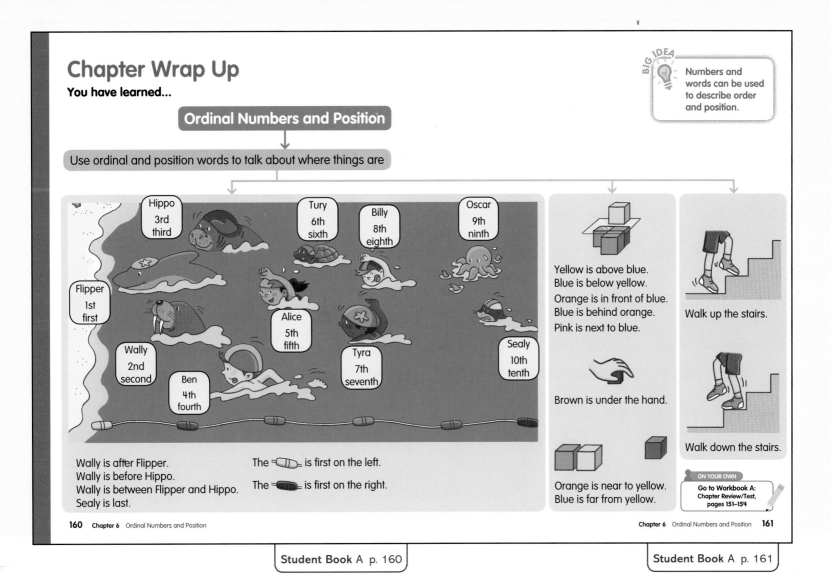

Chapter Wrap Up

You have learned...

Ordinal Numbers and Position

Use ordinal and position words to talk about where things are

Hippo
3rd
third

Tury
6th
sixth

Billy
8th
eighth

Oscar
9th
ninth

Flipper
1st
first

Wally
2nd
second

Alice
5th
fifth

Tyra
7th
seventh

Sealy
10th
tenth

Ben
4th
fourth

Wally is after Flipper.
Wally is before Hippo.
Wally is between Flipper and Hippo.
Sealy is last.

The ⬤▬ is first on the left.
The ▬⬤ is first on the right.

Yellow is above blue.
Blue is below yellow.
Orange is in front of blue.
Blue is behind orange.
Pink is next to blue.

Brown is under the hand.

Orange is near to yellow.
Blue is far from yellow.

Walk up the stairs.

Walk down the stairs.

ON YOUR OWN
Go to Workbook A:
Chapter Review/Test,
pages 151–154

BIG IDEA
Numbers and
words can be used
to describe order
and position.

Student Book A p. 160

Student Book A p. 161

Chapter Wrap Up (pages 160 and 161)

Review ordinal numbers and position by talking about the pictures using ordinal numbers and position words. As you work through the examples, encourage children to use the chapter vocabulary:

• first	• second
• third	• fourth
• fifth	• sixth
• seventh	• eighth
• ninth	• tenth
• last	• before
• after	• between
• left	• right
• next to	• under
• above	• below
• behind	• in front of
• up	• down
• near	• far

Assessment

Use the Chapter 6 Test Prep on pages 48–52 of **Assessments 1** to assess how well children have learned the material of this chapter. This assessment is appropriate for reporting results to adults at home and administrators. This test is shown on page 161B.

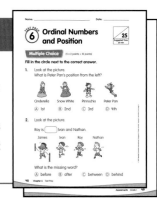

Assessments 1 pp. 48–52

ON YOUR OWN

Have children review the vocabulary, concepts and skills from Chapter 6 with the Chapter Review/Test in **Workbook 1A**, pp. 151–154. These pages (with the answers) are shown on page 161A.

You may also wish to use the Cumulative Review for Chapters 5 and 6 from **Workbook 1A**, pp. 155–160. These pages (with the answers) are shown on pages 161C and 161D.

Workbook pages for Chapter Review/Test

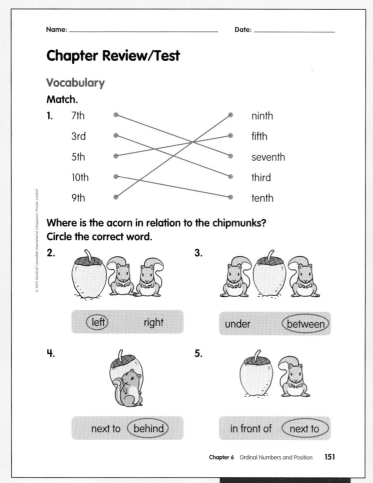

Name: _____ Date: _____

Chapter Review/Test

Vocabulary

Match.

1.
7th   ninth
3rd   fifth
5th   seventh
10th   third
9th   tenth

Where is the acorn in relation to the chipmunks?
Circle the correct word.

2.   (left)   right

3.   under   (between)

4.   next to   (behind)

5.   in front of   (next to)

Chapter 6 Ordinal Numbers and Position **151**

Workbook A p. 151

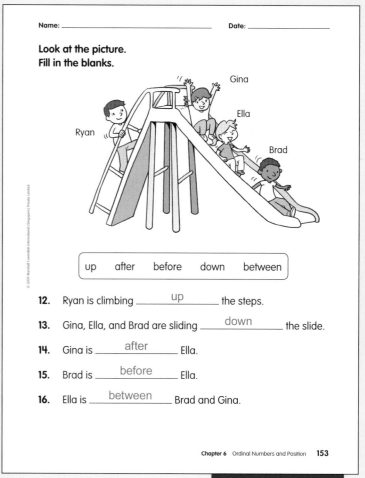

Name: _____ Date: _____

Look at the picture.
Fill in the blanks.

| up | after | before | down | between |

12. Ryan is climbing ____up____ the steps.

13. Gina, Ella, and Brad are sliding ____down____ the slide.

14. Gina is ____after____ Ella.

15. Brad is ____before____ Ella.

16. Ella is ____between____ Brad and Gina.

Chapter 6 Ordinal Numbers and Position **153**

Workbook A p. 153

Concepts and Skills

Read and draw.

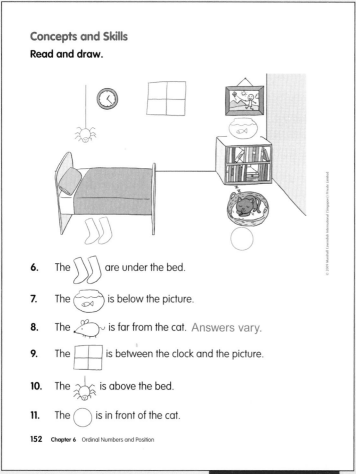

6. The 🧦 are under the bed.

7. The 🐟 is below the picture.

8. The 🐭 is far from the cat. Answers vary.

9. The ▦ is between the clock and the picture.

10. The 🕷 is above the bed.

11. The ◯ is in front of the cat.

152 Chapter 6 Ordinal Numbers and Position

Workbook A p. 152

Problem Solving

Color.

17.

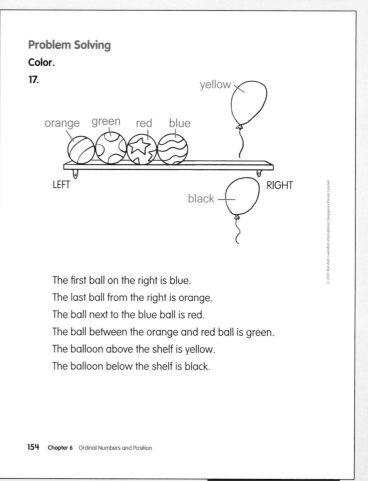

The first ball on the right is blue.
The last ball from the right is orange.
The ball next to the blue ball is red.
The ball between the orange and red ball is green.
The balloon above the shelf is yellow.
The balloon below the shelf is black.

154 Chapter 6 Ordinal Numbers and Position

Workbook A p. 154

Assessments Book pages for Chapter 6 Test Prep
Answer key appears in Assessments Book.

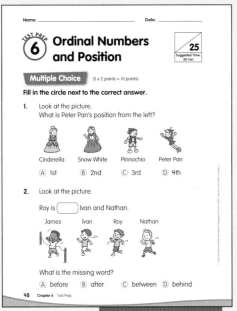

Assessments p. 48

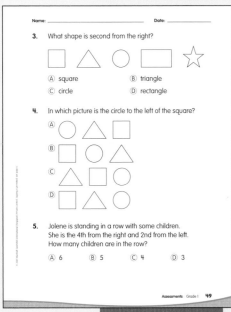

Assessments p. 49

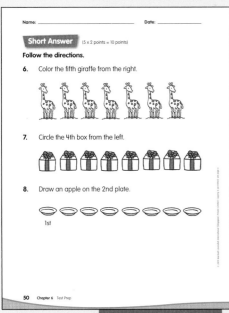

Assessments p. 50

Assessments p. 51

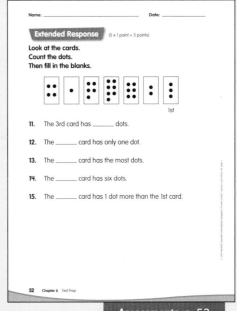

Assessments p. 52

Cumulative Review for Chapters 5 and 6

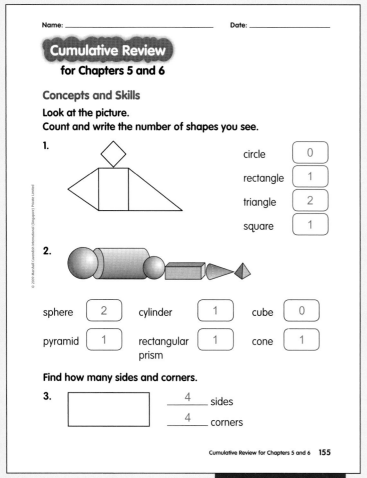

Name: _____ **Date:** _____

Cumulative Review
for Chapters 5 and 6

Concepts and Skills

Look at the picture.
Count and write the number of shapes you see.

1.

circle	0
rectangle	1
triangle	2
square	1

2.

| sphere | 2 | cylinder | 1 | cube | 0 |
| pyramid | 1 | rectangular prism | 1 | cone | 1 |

Find how many sides and corners.

3.

___4___ sides
___4___ corners

Cumulative Review for Chapters 5 and 6   **155**

Workbook A p. 155

Name: _____ **Date:** _____

Look at the picture.
Circle the correct shape.

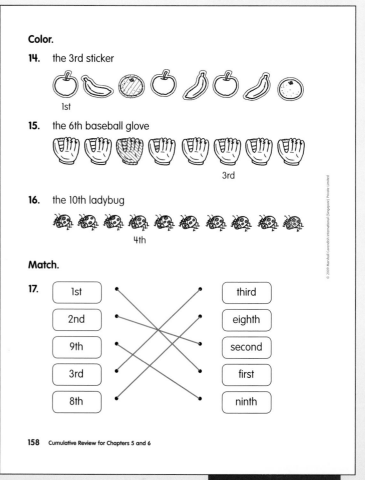

8. The soup can is the shape of a cone (cylinder).

9. The cereal box is the shape of a (rectangular prism) rectangle.

10. The roll of paper towel is the shape of a sphere (cylinder).

11. The pizza box is the shape of a cube (square).

Complete the pattern.
Circle the missing shape.

12.

13.

Cumulative Review for Chapters 5 and 6   **157**

Workbook A p. 157

Sort the shapes by size.
Color the shapes that are different.

4.

Sort the shapes by the number of sides.
Color the shapes that are alike.

5.

Circle the shapes that roll.

6.

Circle the shapes that stack and slide.

7.

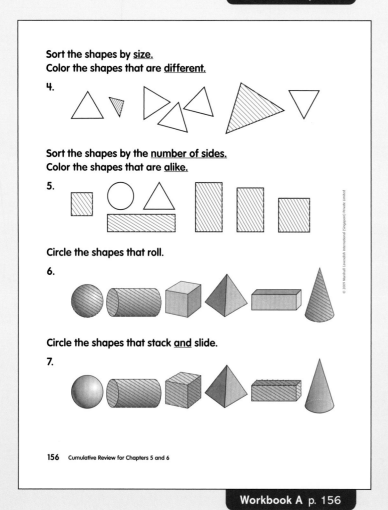

156   Cumulative Review for Chapters 5 and 6

Workbook A p. 156

Color.

14. the 3rd sticker

1st

15. the 6th baseball glove

3rd

16. the 10th ladybug

4th

Match.

17.

1st		third
2nd		eighth
9th		second
3rd		first
8th		ninth

158   Cumulative Review for Chapters 5 and 6

Workbook A p. 158

Name: _____ Date: _____

Look at each picture.
Circle the correct word.

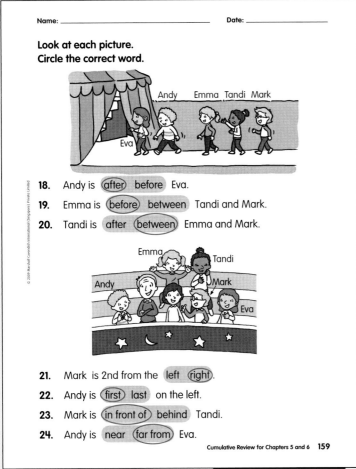

18. Andy is (after) before Eva.
19. Emma is (before) between Tandi and Mark.
20. Tandi is after (between) Emma and Mark.

21. Mark is 2nd from the left (right).
22. Andy is (first) last on the left.
23. Mark is (in front of) behind Tandi.
24. Andy is near (far from) Eva.

Cumulative Review for Chapters 5 and 6 **159**

Workbook A p. 159

Problem Solving

Solve.

25. Shantel draws a rectangle.
    Then she draws a line to make two new shapes.
    The two new shapes are alike.
    Each new shape is the same shape and size.
    Each new shape has 3 corners and 3 sides.

    Draw a line to make the two shapes.

Complete.

26. This is a shape pattern.

    □ △ ◎ □ △ ○ □ △ ○

    a. Color the 3rd shape.

    b. Draw the next three shapes in the pattern.

    c. Draw the 9th shape.
       ○

    d. The 1st shape is a square.
       The 4th shape is a square.

       The __7th__ shape is also a square.

160 Cumulative Review for Chapters 5 and 6

Workbook A p. 160

Notes

CHAPTER 7

Chapter Overview

Numbers to 20

Math Background

In this chapter, children will learn how to count, read and write numbers within 20. This involves counting on from 10, an extension of what children learned in Chapter 1. Number words and numerals are connected to the quantities they represent using various physical models and representations. Children will learn to recognize the numbers 11 to 20 as 1 group of ten and particular numbers of ones, as an introduction to the concept of place value. This is a key stage and sets the foundation for developing the idea of tens and ones and being able to make sense of two-digit numbers. Children need to be confident in their understanding of place value in order to handle the arithmetic operations of addition and subtraction, which will require children to recognize two-digit numbers as groups of tens and ones.

Children's understanding of the number concepts in this chapter will be applied to comparing numbers to build number relationships. At this stage, they compare more than two numbers, using the concepts of *greatest* and *least*, and order a set of numbers according to their relative magnitude. Children also learn to recognize and make increasing and decreasing number patterns which involve a difference of 1 or 2 between consecutive steps in the pattern.

Cross-Curricular Connections

Reading/Language Arts Review with children that adding a word ending (suffix), such as -er and -est changes the meaning of the word. Provide examples, such as *bigger* and *biggest*. Tell children that some vocabulary words in this chapter include the word ending -teen, which means *ten more than*. Use this information to discuss the meanings of the number words thirteen through nineteen.

Art Remind children that numbers can be shown in terms of *place value*, for example, 15 is 1 ten and 5 ones. Explain that the word *value* is also used in art. Every color has value, and the value of a color can be changed by making it darker or lighter. When white is mixed with a color, it gets lighter. When black is mixed with a color it becomes darker. If possible, have children mix different paint colors with black and white paint.

Skills Trace

Grade K	Count and write numbers 0 to 20. (Chaps. 1, 2, 4 and 6)
Grade 1	Count, and compare numbers to 100. (Chaps. 1, 7, 12, and 16)
Grade 2	Count and compare numbers to 1,000. (Chap. 1)

EVERY DAY COUNTS®
Calendar Math

The December activities provide...

Review the attributes of solid shapes (Chapter 5)

Preview comparing numbers to 31 (Chapter 12)

Practice finding patterns (Lesson 4 in this chapter)

Differentiation Resources

Differentiation for Special Populations

	English Language Learners	Struggling Reteach 1A	On Level Extra Practice 1A	Advanced Enrichment 1A
Lesson 1	pp. 166–167	pp. 103–108	pp. 101–106	
Lesson 2	pp. 172	pp. 109–112	pp. 107–108	Enrichment pages can be used to challenge advanced children.
Lesson 3	pp. 176	pp. 113–120	pp. 109–110	
Lesson 4	pp. 184	pp. 121–126	pp. 111–114	

Additional Support

For English Language Learners

Select activities that reinforce the chapter vocabulary and the connections among these words, such as having children

- add terms, definitions, and examples to the Word Wall
- create and order flash cards with number words on one side and the number on the other
- use manipulatives to give and follow directions using number words and comparison and order terms
- discuss the Chapter Wrap Up, encouraging children to use the chapter vocabulary

For Struggling Learners

Select activities that go back to the appropriate stage of the Concrete-Pictorial-Abstract spectrum, such as having children

- act out number words and comparison terms
- use manipulatives to model patterns
- identify and describe sets of classroom objects using number words, place value, and comparison terms
- draw pictures to illustrate number words and patterns

See also pages 177–178, and 189.

If necessary, review:

- Chapter 2 (Number Bonds)
- Chapter 3 (Addition Facts to 10).

For Advanced Learners

See suggestions on pages 179–180.

Assessment and Remediation

Chapter 7 Assessment

Prior Knowledge		
Quick Check	Student Book 1A	p. 164
Pre-Test	Assessments 1	pp. 53–54
Ongoing Diagnostic		
Guided Practice	Student Book 1A	pp. 168, 170, 171, 172, 173, 176, 178, 179, 184, 185, 186
Common Error	Teacher's Edition 1A	pp. 170, 173–174, 181, 187–188
Formal Evaluation		
Chapter Review/Test	Workbook 1A	pp. 187–190
Chapter 7 Test Prep	Assessments 1	pp. 55–57

Remediation Options

	Problems with these items...		Can be remediated with...	
	Review/Test Items	Chapter Assessment Items	Reteach	Student Book
Objective	Workbook 1A pp. 187–190	Assessments 1 pp. 55–57	Reteach 1A	Student Book 1A
Use chapter vocabulary correctly.	1–4, 5–6	Not assessed	pp. 104–126	pp. 165, 171, 175, 183
Count on from 10 to 20.	7–8	4	pp. 104–106, 108	Lesson 1
Read and write 11 to 20 in numbers and words.	1–4	6	pp. 104, 106–108	Lesson 1
Use a place-value chart to show numbers up to 20.	15	3, 7	pp. 109–112	Lesson 2
Compare numbers to 20.	9, 14–15	1, 4–5, 8, 11–15	pp. 113–120	Lesson 3
Order numbers and make number patterns.	10–13	2, 9,10	pp. 121–126	Lesson 4

Chapter Planning Guide

CHAPTER 7 Number to 20

Lesson	Pacing	Instructional Objectives	Vocabulary
Chapter Opener pp. 162–164 Recall Prior Knowledge *59* Quick Check	*1 day	💡**Big Idea** Count, compare, and order numbers to 20	
Lesson 1, pp. 165–170 *60* Counting to 20	1 day	• Count on from 10 to 20 • Read and write 11 to 20 in numbers and words	• eleven • twelve • thirteen • fourteen • fifteen • sixteen • seventeen • eighteen • nineteen • twenty
Lesson 2, pp. 171–174 *61* Place Value	1 day	• Use a place-value chart to show numbers up to 20 • Show objects up to 20 as tens and ones	• place-value chart
Lesson 3, pp. 175–182 *62 63* Comparing Numbers	2 days	• Compare numbers to 20	• greatest • least
Lesson 4, pp. 183–188 *64* Making Patterns and Ordering Numbers	1 day	• Order numbers by making number patterns	• order
Problem Solving p. 189 *65* 👏 Put on Your Thinking Cap!	1 day	Thinking Skill: • Analyzing patterns and relationships Problem Solving Strategy: • Look for patterns	
Chapter Wrap Up pp. 190–191 *66*	1 day	• Reinforce and consolidate chapter skills and concepts	
Chapter Assessment *67*	1 day		

•Assume that 1 day is a 45–55 minute period.

Resources	Materials	NCTM Focal Points	NCTM Process Standards
Student Book 1A, pp. 162–164 **Assessments 1,** pp. 53–54			
Student Book 1A, pp. 165–170 **Workbook 1A,** pp. 161–166 **Extra Practice 1A,** pp. 101–106 **Reteach 1A,** pp. 103–108	• 10 connecting cubes for the teacher • 20 counters for the teacher • 1 number cube per group • 80 unit cubes per group • 8 tens rods per group • Ten Frames (TR01) for the teacher	**_Number and Operations_** Understand the sequential order of the counting numbers.	Communication Connections Representation
Student Book 1A, pp. 171–174 **Workbook 1A,** pp. 167–170 **Extra Practice 1A,** pp. 107–108 **Reteach 1A,** pp. 109–112	• 20 unit cubes for the teacher • 20 connecting cubes (10 of each color) per group • 20 craft sticks • 1 Place-Value Chart (TR13) per child • 2 clear containers • paper bag • a rubber band or string	**_Number and Operations_** Think of whole numbers between 10 and 100 in terms of groups of tens and ones.	Problem Solving Connections Representation
Student Book 1A, pp. 175–182 **Workbook 1A,** pp. 171–178 **Extra Practice 1A,** pp. 109–110 **Reteach 1A,** pp. 113–120	• 30 connecting cubes for the teacher • 20 unit cubes and 2 tens rods for the teacher • 40 connecting cubes, 20 of each color per group • 1 copy of Place-Value Chart (TR13) for the teacher • 2 copies of Place-Value Chart (TR13) for each child • 20 counters • 2 bags	**_Number and Operations_** Compare and order whole numbers.	Problem Solving Reasoning/Proof Representation
Student Book 1A, pp. 183–188 **Workbook 1A,** pp. 179–182 **Extra Practice 1A,** pp. 111–114 **Reteach 1A,** pp. 121–126	• 22 connecting cubes (10 each of two colors, 2 of another color) for the teacher • Place-Value Chart (TR13) for the teacher	**_Number and Operations_** Compare and order whole numbers.	Problem Solving Reasoning/Proof Representation
Student Book 1A, p. 189 **Workbook 1A,** pp. 183–186 **Extra Practice 1A,** pp. 115–116 **Enrichment 1A,** pp. 51–58		**_Number and Operations_** and **_Algebra_** Solve both routine and non-routine problems.	Problem Solving Reasoning/Proof
Student Book 1A, pp. 190–191 **Workbook 1A,** pp. 187–190			
Assessments 1, pp. 55–57			

Technology Resources for easy classroom management
• *Math in Focus* eBook
• *Math in Focus* Teaching Resources CD
• *Math in Focus* Virtual Manipulatives
• On-Line Web Resources

Chapter Introduction

CHAPTER 7 Numbers to 20

Lesson 1   Counting to 20
Lesson 2   Place Value
Lesson 3   Comparing Numbers
Lesson 4   Making Patterns and
              Ordering Numbers

Chapter 2
Vocabulary

eleven	11	Lesson 1
twelve	12	Lesson 1
thirteen	13	Lesson 1
fourteen	14	Lesson 1
fifteen	15	Lesson 1
sixteen	16	Lesson 1
seventeen	17	Lesson 1
eighteen	18	Lesson 1
nineteen	19	Lesson 1
twenty	20	Lesson 1
place-value chart	A chart that shows how many tens and ones are in a number	Lesson 2
greatest	Highest in value or magnitude	Lesson 3
least	Lowest in value or magnitude	Lesson 3
order	Arrange in sequence from least to greatest or greatest to least	Lesson 4

Student Book A p. 162

Big Idea (page 162)

Counting, comparing, and ordering numbers to 20 is the main focus of this chapter.

- Children count to 20 using pictorial representations of concrete objects.

- Children recognize numbers 10–20 as 1 group of ten and a particular number of ones.

- Children compare numbers and establish number relationships such as *greater than* and *less than*.

- Children identify number patterns from these number relationships and extend the patterns.

Chapter Opener (page 162)

The picture illustrates how counting can be carried out in real-life situations. Children have learned to count, compare, and order numbers to 10. In this chapter, children will learn to count on from 10 and work with numbers to 20.

- Have children look at the picture. *Ask:* How old is the boy in the blue hat? (10) How old is the other birthday girl? (3) *Say:* Count the candles on her cake. *Ask:* Who is older? (the boy)

- Encourage children to count the people and objects in the picture, for example, the candles, balloons, gifts, party hats, boys and girls.

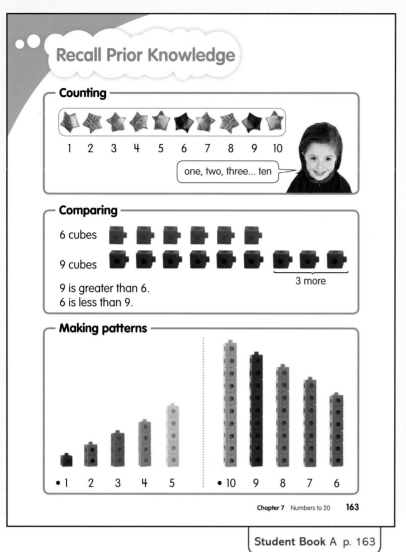

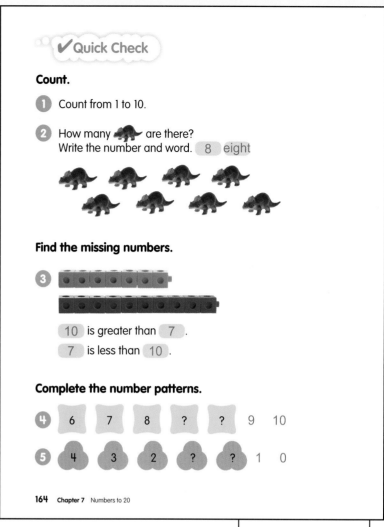

Recall Prior Knowledge (pages 163 and 164)

Counting
Children learned in Chapter 1 to count to 10.

- Have children count the stars in the picture. Write the words and numerals on the board to help children recall numbers to 10.

Comparing
Children learned in Chapter 1 to compare numbers within 10, using the terms *more than*, *less than*, *greater than* and *less than*.

- Have children count the cubes in each row. *Ask*: Which row has more cubes? (the row of purple cubes) *Say*: 9 cubes is more than 6 cubes. 9 is greater than 6.

- Also *say*: 6 cubes is fewer than 9 cubes. 6 is less than 9.

- *Ask*: How many more purple cubes are there? Count with them to see that there are 3 more.

Making Patterns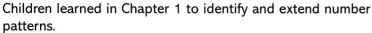
Children learned in Chapter 1 to identify and extend number patterns.

- Make number towers to form an increasing and decreasing pattern using **connecting cubes** as shown in the Student Book.

- Invite volunteers to count the number of cubes in each tower, and then show that the towers are arranged in an increasing or decreasing pattern, by adding 1 more or taking away 1 for each tower.

- Arrange the towers to show an increasing pattern of 1 to 10 and a decreasing pattern of 10 to 1.

✔Quick Check (page 164)

Use this section as a diagnostic tool to assess children's level of prerequisite knowledge before they progress to this chapter. Exercises 1 and 2 assess if children can count and write numbers and number words. Exercise 3 assesses if children can compare numbers using *greater than* and *less than* and Exercises 4 and 5 assess if children can complete increasing and decreasing number patterns, all taught in Chapter 1.

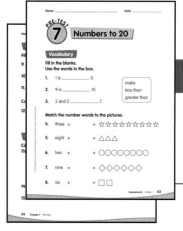

Assessment

For additional assessment of children's prior knowledge and chapter readiness, use the Chapter 7 Pre-Test on pages 53–54 of **Assessments 1**.

Assessments 1 pp. 53–54

1 Counting to 20

LESSON OBJECTIVES
- Count on from 10 to 20.
- Read and write 11 to 20 in numbers and words.

TECHNOLOGY RESOURCES
- *Math in Focus* eBook
- *Math in Focus* Teaching Resources CD
- *Math in Focus* Virtual Manipulatives

Vocabulary

eleven	twelve
thirteen	fourteen
fifteen	sixteen
seventeen	eighteen
nineteen	twenty

DAY 1 Student Book 1A, pp. 165–170
Workbook 1A, pp. 161–166

MATERIALS
- 10 connecting cubes for the teacher
- 20 counters for the teacher
- 1 number cube per group
- 80 unit cubes per group
- 8 tens rods per group
- Ten Frames (TR01) for the teacher

DIFFERENTIATION RESOURCES
- Reteach 1A, pp. 103–108
- Extra Practice 1A, pp. 101–106

 5-minute Warm Up

- Use connecting cubes to make a number train of any number from 1 to 10.
- Have children count the cubes in the number train and show the number using their fingers.
- Make this a race and reward children who are faster.

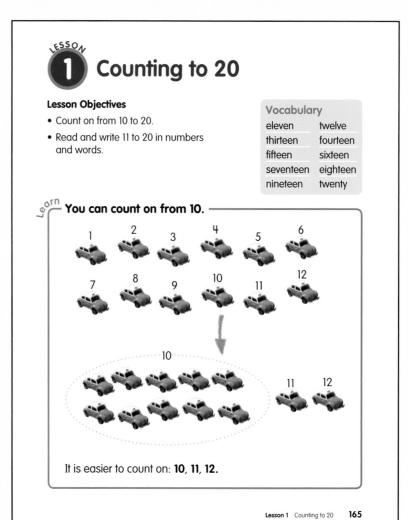

Student Book A p. 165

DAY 1 # Teach

Count On from 10 (pages 165 to 167)

Children learn to count a set of between 10 and 20 objects by counting on from 10.

- Use 12 **counters** to show two different ways of counting them.
- First way: Count all the counters starting from 1: 1, 2, 3, 4, ... 12.
- Second way: Count on from 10. First make a group of 10 counters, then count on from 10 to get 12: 10, 11, 12.
- Explain that you can count on to 20 by adding 1 each time to the group of 10.
- Show children the group of 10 counters again, then add one and *say:* 11. Point to the number and word on page 166. Have children repeat after you.
- Add one counter at a time and say the number, pointing to the number and word on pages 166 and 167, and have children say the number.
- When you reach 20, take away the counters and start over from 10.

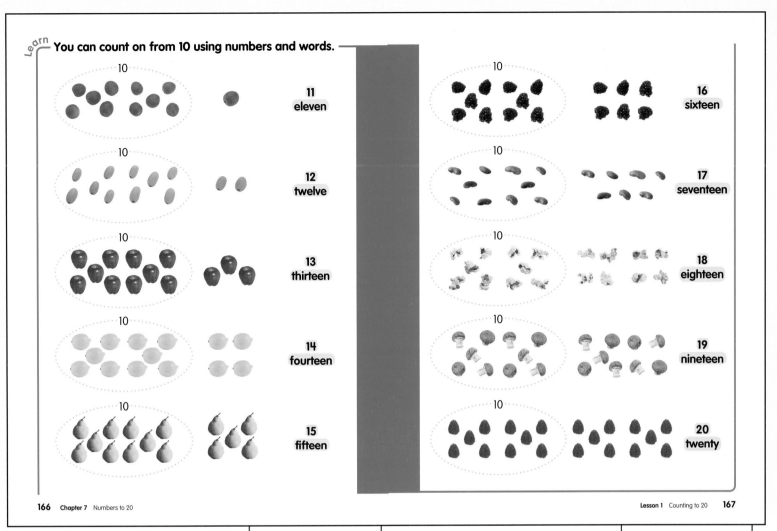

Learn You can count on from 10 using numbers and words.

Student Book A p. 166

Student Book A p. 167

Problem of the Lesson

May has 20 grapes.

Make a 10 and count on by ones to show the grapes.

Solution:

Answer: 10, 11, 12, 13, 14, 15, 16, 17, 18, 19, 20

Differentiated Instruction

English Language Learners

Children may need extra practice time with the number words for eleven through twenty. Have them make flash cards on index cards. On one side they write the numeral and on the back side they write the number word. They can practice at home by reading the numeral, spelling the number word, and then flipping the card over to check.

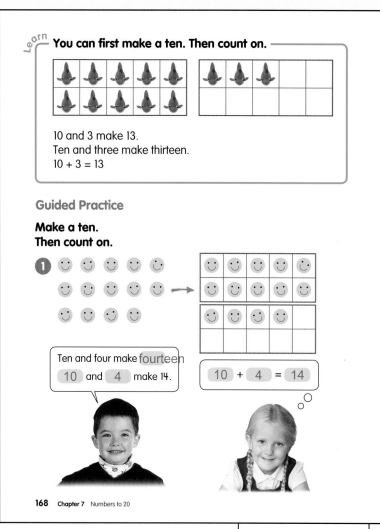

Learn

You can first make a ten. Then count on.

10 and 3 make 13.
Ten and three make thirteen.
10 + 3 = 13

Guided Practice

Make a ten.
Then count on.

1

Ten and four make fourteen
10 and 4 make 14.

10 + 4 = 14

168 Chapter 7 Numbers to 20

Student Book A p. 168

WORKING TOGETHER Game

Players: 4
You need:
• one number cube
• base ten blocks

Roll the Number Cube!

STEP 1 Roll the number cube.
Then take this number of ⬡.

6!

STEP 2 Each player take turns to roll the number cube and take ⬡.

STEP 3 On your next turn, roll the number cube again.
Then take this number of ⬡.
If you have 10 ⬡, trade them for one ▭.

6 + 4 = 10!

The first player to get 2 ▭ wins!

Lesson 1 Counting to 20 169

Student Book A p. 169

Learn

Make a Ten, Then Count On (page 168)

Children learn to make a set of 10 using a ten frame and count on from there.

• Make a copy of **Ten Frames** (TR01). Take 13 **counters** and make a set of 10 on one ten frame. Then put 3 more counters on another ten frame.

• Have children count the counters by counting on from 10: 10, 11, 12, 13. *Say:* 10 and 3 make 13. Write 10 + 3 = 13 (thirteen) on the board.

• Now place any number of counters on the second ten frame and ask volunteers to count the counters by counting on from 10. Say and write the addition sentence on the board each time, until you have modeled each number from 11 to 20.

Check for Understanding
✓ **Guided Practice** (page 168)

1 Guide children to count on from 10: 10, 11, 12, 13, 14.

• Check that children can write the number word as well as the number.

WORKING TOGETHER Game:

Roll the Number Cube! (page 169)

This game helps children learn to see numbers between 11 and 20 as one group of 10 and a particular number of ones.

• Have children play the game in groups of 4. Give each group one **number cube**, 80 **unit cubes** and 8 **tens rods**.

• In each group, have Player 1 roll the number cube and take that number (1–6) of ⬡.

• In turn, have each of the other players do the same.

• On the next round, after each player's turn, the player should trade 10 ⬡ for one ▭.

• The first player to get 2 ▭ wins.

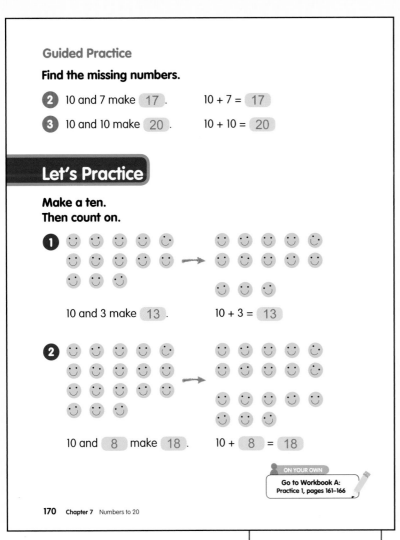

Guided Practice

Find the missing numbers.

2 10 and 7 make 17 .   10 + 7 = 17

3 10 and 10 make 20 .   10 + 10 = 20

Let's Practice

Make a ten.
Then count on.

1

10 and 3 make 13 .   10 + 3 = 13

2

10 and 8 make 18 .   10 + 8 = 18

ON YOUR OWN
Go to Workbook A:
Practice 1, pages 161–166

170   Chapter 7   Numbers to 20

Student Book A p. 170

Best Practices The game on page 169 requires an understanding of base-ten blocks. You may want to precede the game with a mini-lesson on regrouping ones cubes for a ten rod. Demonstrate with several numbers from 11 through 20. Show how ten cubes is equal to one ten rod.

✓**Guided Practice** (page 170)

2 Guide children to count on from 10 to make the required number.

3 Help children see that 10 and 10 make 2 tens or 20.

Let's Practice (page 170)

This practice reinforces adding by making a ten first, then counting on from 10. Exercises **1** and **2** show children how to make a ten first and then count on.

Common Error Children may miscount the number of objects when they look for tens and ones. Suggest that they cover groups of tens with strips of paper as they count. Children can count the strips of paper by tens and then add the leftover objects.

ON YOUR OWN

Children practice adding by making a ten first, then count on in Practice 1, pp. 161–166 of **Workbook 1A**. These pages (with the answers) are shown on pages 170A and 170B.

Differentiation Options Depending on children's success with the Workbook pages, use these materials as needed.
Struggling: Reteach 1A, pp. 103–108
On Level: Extra Practice 1A, pp. 101–106

Practice and Apply
Workbook pages for Chapter 7, Lesson 1

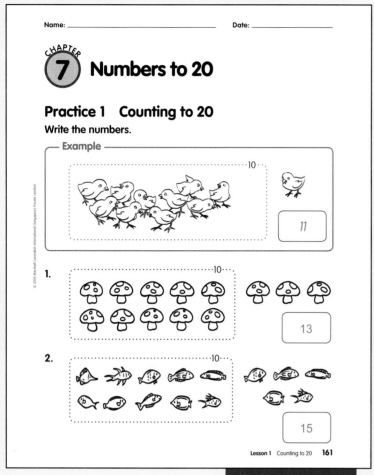

Name: _____ **Date:** _____

7 Numbers to 20

Practice 1   Counting to 20
Write the numbers.

Example

·10·

`11`

1.

·10·

`13`

2.

·10·

`15`

Lesson 1   Counting to 20   **161**

Workbook A p. 161

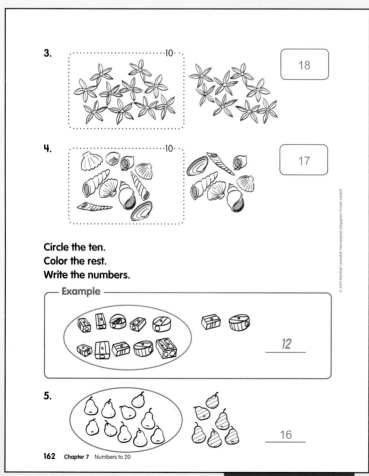

3.

·10·

`18`

4.

·10·

`17`

Circle the ten.
Color the rest.
Write the numbers.

Example

_12_

5.

_16_

162   Chapter 7   Numbers to 20

Workbook A p. 162

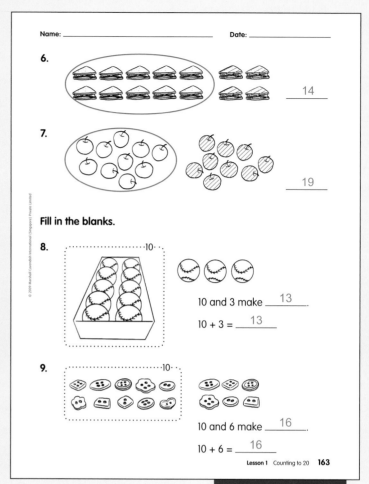

Name: _____ **Date:** _____

6.

_14_

7.

_19_

Fill in the blanks.

8.

·10·

10 and 3 make _13_.

10 + 3 = _13_

9.

·10·

10 and 6 make _16_.

10 + 6 = _16_

Lesson 1   Counting to 20   **163**

Workbook A p. 163

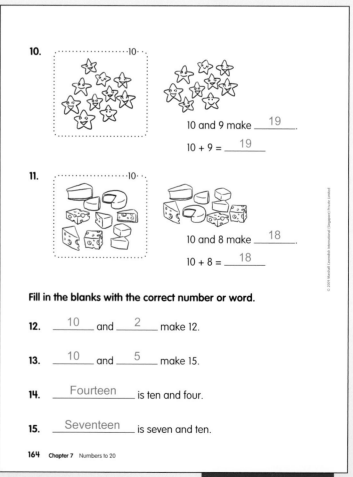

10.

·10·

10 and 9 make _19_.

10 + 9 = _19_

11.

·10·

10 and 8 make _18_.

10 + 8 = _18_

Fill in the blanks with the correct number or word.

12. _10_ and _2_ make 12.

13. _10_ and _5_ make 15.

14. _Fourteen_ is ten and four.

15. _Seventeen_ is seven and ten.

164   Chapter 7   Numbers to 20

Workbook A p. 164

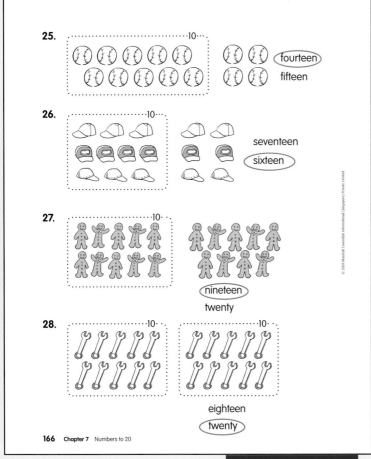

Name: _____ **Date:** _____

Fill in the blanks.

16. $10 + 3 = \underline{\quad13\quad}$ **17.** $10 + 4 = \underline{\quad14\quad}$

18. $10 + 5 = \underline{\quad15\quad}$ **19.** $10 + 6 = \underline{\quad16\quad}$

20. $10 + 9 = \underline{\quad19\quad}$ **21.** $10 + 10 = \underline{\quad20\quad}$

22. $2 + 10 = \underline{\quad12\quad}$ **23.** $8 + 10 = \underline{\quad18\quad}$

Count.
Circle the correct word.

— Example —

·····10·····

seven

(eleven)

24.

·····10·····

twelve

two

Lesson 1 Counting to 20   **165**

Workbook A p. 165

25.

·····10·····

(fourteen)

fifteen

26.

·····10·····

seventeen

(sixteen)

27.

·····10·····

(nineteen)

twenty

28.

·····10·····   ·····10·····

eighteen

(twenty)

166   Chapter 7 Numbers to 20

Workbook A p. 166

Notes

LESSON 2 Place Value

LESSON OBJECTIVES
- Use a place-value chart to show numbers up to 20.
- Show objects up to 20 as tens and ones.

TECHNOLOGY RESOURCES
- *Math in Focus* eBook
- *Math in Focus* Teaching Resources CD
- *Math in Focus* Virtual Manipulatives

Vocabulary
place-value chart

DAY 1	Student Book 1A, pp. 171–174
	Workbook 1A, pp. 167–170

MATERIALS
- 20 unit cubes for the teacher
- 20 connecting cubes, 10 of each color (1 set per group)
- 20 craft sticks
- 1 Place-Value Chart (TR13) per child
- 2 clear containers
- paper bag
- a rubber band or string

DIFFERENTIATION RESOURCES
- Reteach 1A, pp. 109–112
- Extra Practice 1A, pp. 107–108

5-minute Warm Up

- Put two clear containers on a table and 20 unit cubes in a bag. Label one container Tens and the other container Ones.

- Ask a volunteer to remove a few cubes from the bag and put them aside.

- Start to count the cubes in the bag by placing them into the Tens container one at a time, counting aloud, until you reach 10. Then place the remaining cubes into the Ones container, counting on from 10. Write the number on the board.

- Now count the cubes in the Ones container. Guide children to see that the number of cubes in the Ones container corresponds to the ones digit in the number on the board.

- Repeat with other volunteers and different numbers.

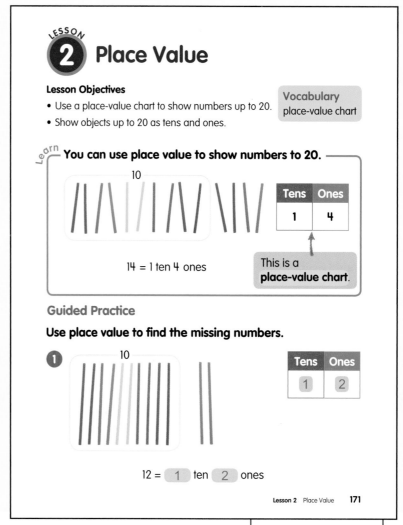

Student Book A p. 171

DAY 1 Teach

Use Place Value to Show Numbers to 20

(page 171)

Children have learned to count on from 10 after making one group of 10. In this lesson, they will connect this with place value so they can apply the concept of making sets of 10 to numbers greater than 20 in the future.

- Show 14 **craft sticks**. Put 10 craft sticks in a group apart from the others, using a rubber band or string.

- Introduce children to the concept of 1 ten and 4 ones with the help of a place-value chart. Connect it to the idea of "10 and 4 make 14."

Check for Understanding
✔ **Guided Practice** (pages 171 and 172)

❶ and ❷ Check children's understanding by asking volunteers to group the **craft sticks** into 1 ten and the number of ones, and then fill in the place-value chart.

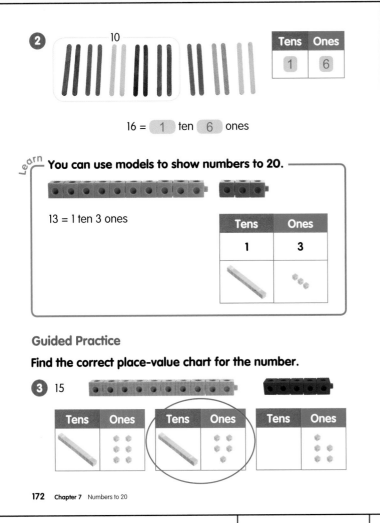

② 10

Tens | Ones
1 | 6

16 = 1 ten 6 ones

^{Learn} **You can use models to show numbers to 20.**

13 = 1 ten 3 ones

Tens	Ones
1	**3**

Guided Practice

Find the correct place-value chart for the number.

③ 15

Tens	Ones		Tens	Ones		Tens	Ones

172 Chapter 7 Numbers to 20

Student Book A p. 172

^{Learn}

Use Models to Show Numbers to 20

(page 172)

Children have learned to count on from 10 after making one group of 10.

• Show 13 **connecting cubes**. Connect 10 cubes of the same color to make 1 ten.

• Show 13 as 1 ten and 3 ones.

• Show the number 13 on the place-value chart. Guide children to relate the digits of the number 13 to 1 ten and 3 ones.

Best Practices This Learn requires the use of connecting cubes. Children may also want to use the cubes with the rest of the lesson to help model tens and ones. At the beginning of the lesson, prepare several sets of 20 connecting cubes. Allow children to take a set and use it as needed throughout the lesson.

Problem of the Lesson

Tom has these unit cubes.

Tom wants to use the unit cubes to show the number 16.

He wants to use 16 but he has only 10 .

How can he show the number 16 using the blocks?

Solution:

Answer: Tom can use one ⬛⬛⬛⬛ and six 🔲 to show 16.

Differentiated Instruction

English Language Learners

Use the models on Student Book page 172 to develop the meaning of place value. Point to each digit in the number 16. **Say:** One is a digit and six is a digit. The value of a digit depends upon its place in a number. The one is in the tens place. It stands for one ten. The six is in the ones place. It stands for six ones. Name other numbers (11–20) and ask children to express them as tens and ones.

✓**Guided Practice** (pages 172 and 173)

③ and ④ Model forming the ten and ones number trains using **connecting cubes**. Count the cubes together with children and write the number on the board before having children find the matching place-value chart in their books.

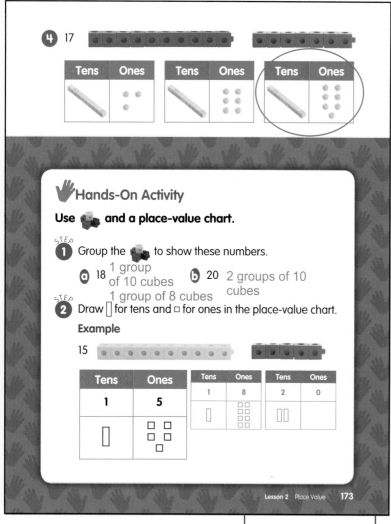

Student Book A p. 173

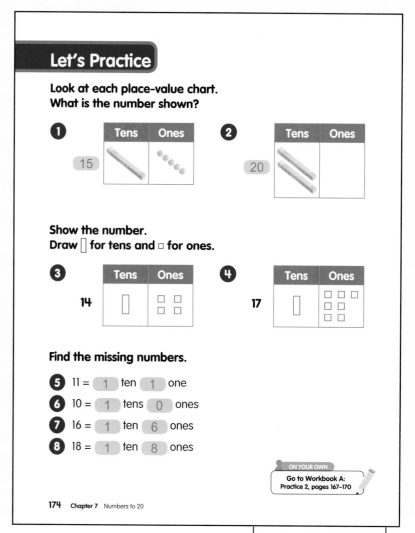

Student Book A p. 174

 Hands-On Activity:

Show Numbers by Grouping Connecting Cubes into a Ten and Ones and Drawing Place-Value Charts (page 173)

This activity lets children practice using connecting cubes to make tens and ones from a given number, and then to complete the corresponding place-value chart.

- Have children work in groups of four. Give each group 20 **connecting cubes**, with 10 of each color and a copy of a **Place-Value Chart** (TR13).

- Have children form the groups of tens and ones with connecting cubes to show the given number. Check that children can do this with any other given number.

- Model and guide children to complete the place-value charts using pictorial representations.

Let's Practice (page 174)

In this activity, children practice interpreting and completing place-value charts for given numbers. Exercises **1** and **2** require children to write the numbers given the charts, Exercises **3** and **4** require children to complete the chart using pictorial representations, and Exercises **5** and **7** provide further practice in analyzing 2-digit numbers up to 20 in terms of place value, without the use of the chart.

Common Error Children may reverse the digits as they write numbers. Tell them to look at the place-value chart. Write the tens digit first on the left. Then write the ones digits to the right of the tens digit.

ON YOUR OWN

Children practice interpreting and completing place-value charts for given numbers in Practice 2, pp. 167–170 of **Workbook 1A**. These pages (with the answers) are shown on page 174A.

Differentiation Options Depending on children's success with the Workbook pages, use these materials as needed.

Struggling: Reteach 1A, pp. 109–112

On Level: Extra Practice 1A, pp. 107–108

Practice and Apply
Workbook pages for Chapter 7, Lesson 2

Name: _____ Date: _____

Practice 2   Place Value

Look at the pictures.
Fill in the blanks.

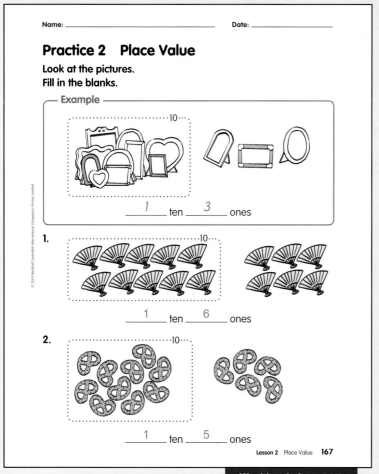

Example

_1_ ten _3_ ones

1.

_1_ ten _6_ ones

2.

_1_ ten _5_ ones

Workbook A p. 167

Name: _____ Date: _____

Show the number.
Draw ▯ for tens and □ for ones.

Example

Tens	Ones
▯	□ □ □

13

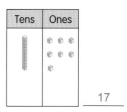

8.

Tens	Ones
▯	□ □

12

9.

Tens	Ones
▯	□ □ □ / □ □ □

16

10.

Tens	Ones
▯	□ □ □ / □ □ □ / □ □

18

11.

Tens	Ones
▯	□ □ □ / □ □ □ / □ □ □

19

Workbook A p. 169

3.

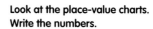

_2_ tens _0_ ones

Fill in the place-value charts.

Example

	Tens	Ones
19	1	9

4.

	Tens	Ones
11	1	1

5.

	Tens	Ones
12	1	2

6.

	Tens	Ones
15	1	5

7.

	Tens	Ones
20	2	0

Workbook A p. 168

Look at the place-value charts.
Write the numbers.

12.

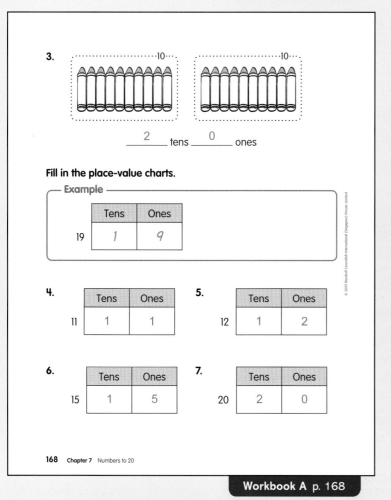

Tens	Ones

13

13.

Tens	Ones

17

14.

Tens	Ones

14

15.

Tens	Ones

11

Fill in the blanks.

16. 13 = 1 ten _3_ ones

17. 17 = _1_ ten 7 ones

18. 15 = 1 ten _5_ ones

19. 12 = _1_ ten 2 ones

20. 19 = 1 ten _9_ ones

Workbook A p. 170

3 Comparing Numbers

LESSON OBJECTIVE
• Compare numbers to 20.

TECHNOLOGY RESOURCES
• *Math in Focus* eBook
• *Math in Focus* Teaching Resources CD
• *Math in Focus* Virtual Manipulatives

Vocabulary	
greatest	least

DAY 1 Student Book 1A, pp. 175–178

MATERIALS
• 30 connecting cubes for the teacher
• 20 unit cubes and 2 tens rods for the teacher
• 40 connecting cubes, 10 of each color (1 set per group of 4 children)
• 1 copy of Place-Value Chart (TR13) for the teacher
• 2 copies of Place-Value Chart (TR13) for each child
• 20 counters
• 2 bags

DAY 2 Student Book 1A, pp. 179–182
Workbook 1A, pp. 171–178

DIFFERENTIATION RESOURCES
• Reteach 1A, pp. 113–120
• Extra Practice 1A, pp. 109–110

 5-minute Warm Up

• Give two volunteers each a bag of small countable objects such as coins or **counters**. Ask each to grab a handful of objects from the bag and place them on a table. Encourage them to take as many objects as possible in one handful.

• Have each child count the objects.

• *Ask:* Who has more? How many more?

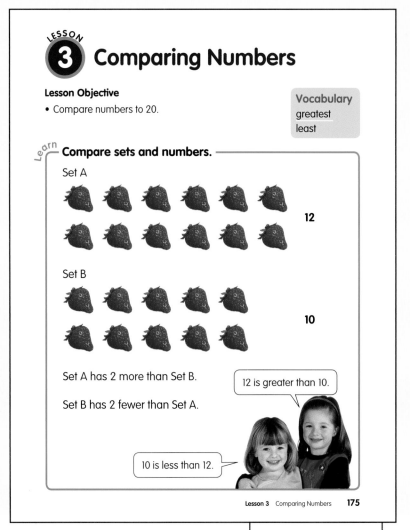

Student Book A p. 175

DAY 1 # Teach

Compare Sets and Numbers (page 175)

Children have learned to compare numbers less than 10 in Chapter 1. They extend that knowledge in this chapter by comparing numbers to 20.

• Join **connecting cubes** to make two number trains, one of 10 and the other of 12. *Ask:* Which set has more cubes? How many more? *Say:* This set has 2 more than the other set. Then *say:* 12 is 2 greater than 10. Help children recall the difference between *more than* (for countable objects) and *greater than* (for comparing magnitude of numbers).

• Go through the example in the Student Book with children.

• Using the connecting cubes, make different number trains and review the terms *more than, fewer than, how many more than, how many fewer than, greater than,* and *less than.*

Best Practices Before beginning this lesson, you may want to review counting numbers to 20. To do this, have children create a counting tape from 0 to 20. Children can use their counting tape as a visual tool for comparing two and three numbers throughout the lesson.

Guided Practice

Count.
Then answer the questions.

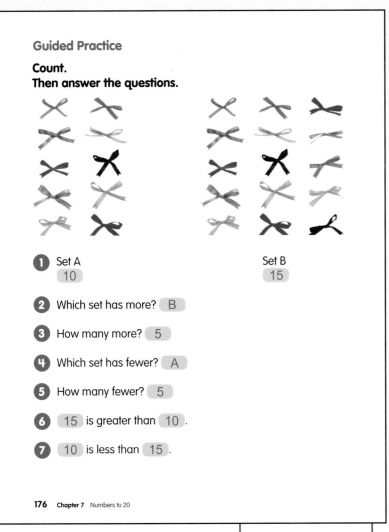

1. Set A
   10

   Set B
   15

2. Which set has more? **B**

3. How many more? **5**

4. Which set has fewer? **A**

5. How many fewer? **5**

6. **15** is greater than **10** .

7. **10** is less than **15** .

176 Chapter 7 Numbers to 20

Student Book A p. 176

Check for Understanding

✓ **Guided Practice** (page 176)

1. Have children count the ribbons in the Student Book.

2. to 5. Guide children to compare the sets and say how many more or fewer ribbons each set has.

6. and 7. Lead children to complete statements on comparing numbers using *greater than* and *less than*.

Problem of the Lesson

Note: This problem of the lesson should be administered after the completion of Student Book page 182.

Michael has 10 marbles. His brother, Darryl, has 12 marbles.

(a) How many more marbles does Darryl have than Michael?

(b) Mom says Darryl has to give Michael some marbles. Now they both have the same number of marbles.

How many marbles did Darryl give to Michael?

Solution:

Michael ○ ○ ○ ○ ○
         ○ ○ ○ ○ ○ 10

Darryl ● ● ● ● ● ●
        ● ● ● ● ● ● 12

12 is 2 greater than 10. So, Darryl has 2 more marbles than Michael.

(b) Michael ○ ○ ○ ○ ○
            ○ ○ ○ ○ ● 11

Darryl ● ● ● ● ●
        ● ● ● ● ● ● 11

Darryl gives 1 marble to Michael.

Answer: (a) 2 marbles

(b) 1 marble

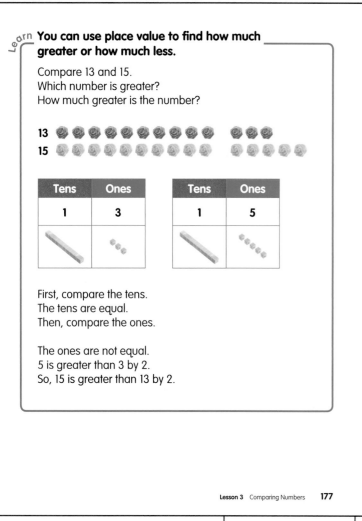

You can use place value to find how much greater or how much less.

Compare 13 and 15.
Which number is greater?
How much greater is the number?

13
15

Tens	Ones
1	3

Tens	Ones
1	5

First, compare the tens.
The tens are equal.
Then, compare the ones.

The ones are not equal.
5 is greater than 3 by 2.
So, 15 is greater than 13 by 2.

Lesson 3 Comparing Numbers **177**

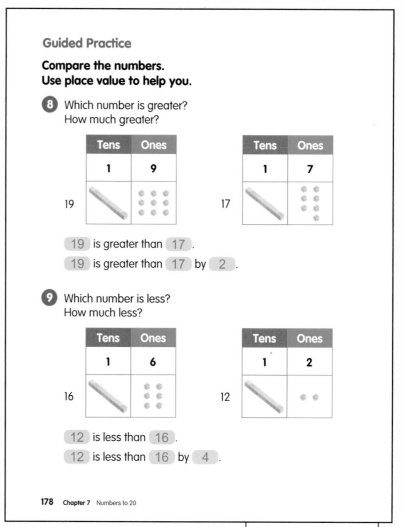

Guided Practice

Compare the numbers.
Use place value to help you.

8 Which number is greater?
How much greater?

Tens	Ones
1	9

19

Tens	Ones
1	7

17

19 is greater than 17 .
19 is greater than 17 by 2 .

9 Which number is less?
How much less?

Tens	Ones
1	6

16

Tens	Ones
1	2

12

12 is less than 16 .
12 is less than 16 by 4 .

178 Chapter 7 Numbers to 20

Use Place Value to Find Out How Much Greater or How Much Less

(page 177)

Children use place-value concepts learned in the previous lesson to compare numbers.

• Use **connecting cubes** to make number trains to show children the numbers 13 and 15. Make each set consist of a 10-train and additional cubes.

• *Ask:* Which set has more? How many more?

• Then show 13 and 15 under each other on a **Place-Value Chart** (TR13).

• Explain the procedure for comparing which number is greater or smaller.

Step 1: Compare the tens.

Step 2: Compare the ones.

• Relate the concrete representation to the numbers to show which is greater.

Guided Practice (page 178)

8 and 9 Guide children to align the two numbers one below the other for comparing which is greater or less.

Example:

19

17

Say: The tens are equal. 9 is greater than 7.
So, 19 is greater.
9 is greater than 7 by 2.
So 19 is greater than 17 by 2.

For Struggling Learners You may want to have children use connecting cubes to make the number trains for the numbers 19 and 17 also. By placing the trains above each other, they can use one-to-one comparison to determine the set with more cubes.

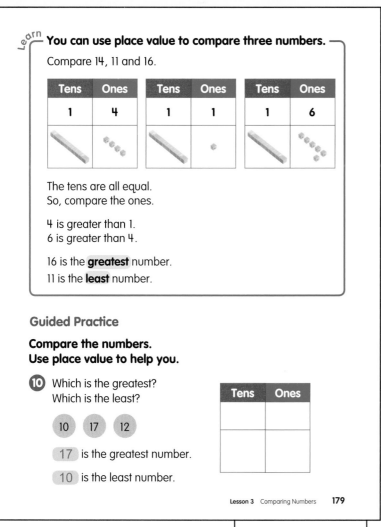

Learn You can use place value to compare three numbers.

Compare 14, 11 and 16.

Tens	Ones	Tens	Ones	Tens	Ones
1	4	1	1	1	6

The tens are all equal.
So, compare the ones.

4 is greater than 1.
6 is greater than 4.

16 is the **greatest** number.
11 is the **least** number.

Guided Practice

Compare the numbers.
Use place value to help you.

10 Which is the greatest?
Which is the least?

10 17 12

Tens	Ones

17 is the greatest number.

10 is the least number.

Lesson 3 Comparing Numbers **179**

Student Book A p. 179

Let's Practice

Count and compare.

1 Which set has more?

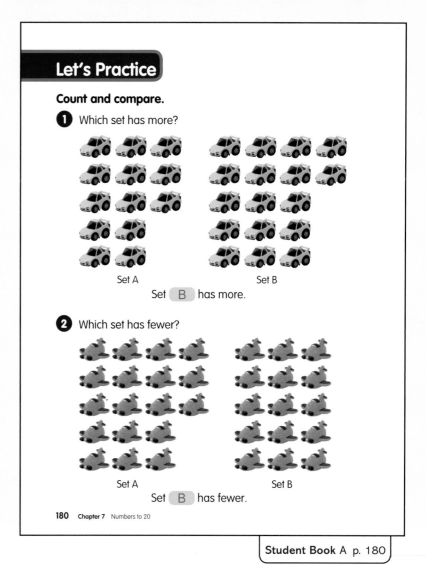

Set A   Set B

Set B has more.

2 Which set has fewer?

Set A   Set B

Set B has fewer.

180 Chapter 7 Numbers to 20

Student Book A p. 180

DAY 2 **Teach**   See the Lesson Organizer on page 175 for Day 2 Resources.

Learn

Use Place Value to Compare Three Numbers

(page 179)

Children use place value to compare three numbers.

- Use a **Place-Value Chart** (TR13) to show 14, 11, and 16. Align the numbers one below the other.

- Help children recall the procedures for comparing which number is the greatest or least.

    Step 1: Compare the tens.

    Step 2: Compare the ones.

✔ Guided Practice (page 179)

10 Guide children to align the three numbers one below the other on a **Place-Value Chart** (TR13) to compare which is greatest and which is least.

For Advanced Learners Have children who are able to cope work together to put pieces of construction paper together to make a large counting tape to 20 that can be displayed in front of the class.

Let's Practice (page 180)

In these exercises, children practice comparing numbers. Exercises **1** and **2** require children to count and compare concrete representations.

Left panel (Student Book A p. 181)

Which number is greater?
How much greater?

3 ⑨ or ⑤

⑨ is greater.

It is greater by ④.

Which number is less?
How much less?

4 ⑲ or ⑩

⑩ is less.

It is less by ⑨.

Compare these numbers.

5 12 18 14

Which is the least? 12

Which is the greatest? 18

6 11 20 10

Which is the least? 10

Which is the greatest? 20

ON YOUR OWN
Go to Workbook A:
Practice 3, pages 171–178

Lesson 3 Comparing Numbers **181**

Student Book A p. 181

Let's Practice (page 181)

Exercises **3** and **4** require children to compare the magnitude of two numbers without the help of concrete representations. Exercises **5** and **6** give children practice comparing three numbers.

Common Error In Exercises **3** and **4** on page 181, children may incorrectly add to determine how much more or less one number is than another. Use concrete visuals such as connecting cubes to help them count how much greater or less a number is.

ON YOUR OWN

Children practice counting, and comparing numbers in Practice 3, pp. 171–178 of **Workbook 1A**. These pages (with the answers) are shown at the right and on pages 181A and 182.

Differentiation Options Depending on children's success with the Workbook pages, use these materials as needed.
Struggling: Reteach 1A, pp. 113–120
On Level: Extra Practice 1A, pp. 109–110

Right panel

Practice and Apply
Workbook pages for Chapter 7, Lesson 3

Name: _____ Date: _____

Practice 3   Comparing Numbers
Write the number in each set.
Then fill in the blanks.

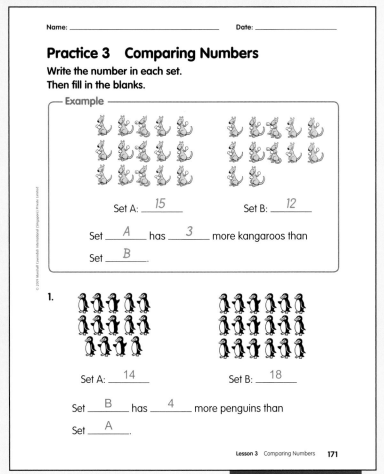

Example

Set A: *15*   Set B: *12*

Set ___*A*___ has ___*3*___ more kangaroos than Set ___*B*___.

1.

Set A: ___14___   Set B: ___18___

Set ___*B*___ has ___*4*___ more penguins than Set ___*A*___.

Lesson 3 Comparing Numbers **171**

Workbook A p. 171

Write the number in each set.
Then fill in the blanks.

2.

Set A: ___19___   Set B: ___11___

Set ___*A*___ has ___*8*___ more crocodiles than Set ___*B*___.

3.

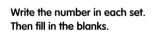

Set A: ___11___   Set B: ___13___

Set ___*A*___ has ___*2*___ fewer fish than Set ___*B*___.

172 Chapter 7 Numbers to 20

Workbook A p. 172

Name: _____   **Date:** _____

4.

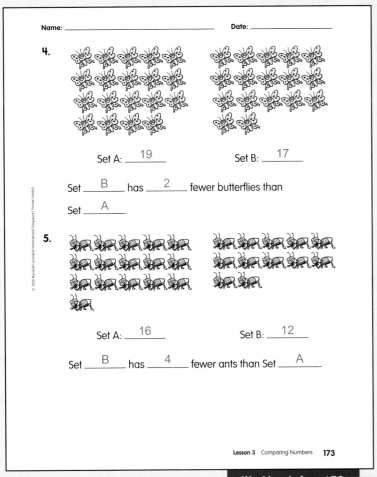

Set A: __19__   Set B: __17__

Set __B__ has __2__ fewer butterflies than

Set __A__.

5.

Set A: __16__   Set B: __12__

Set __B__ has __4__ fewer ants than Set __A__.

Workbook A p. 173

Color the animal with the number that is less red.
Color the animal with the number that is greater blue.

8.

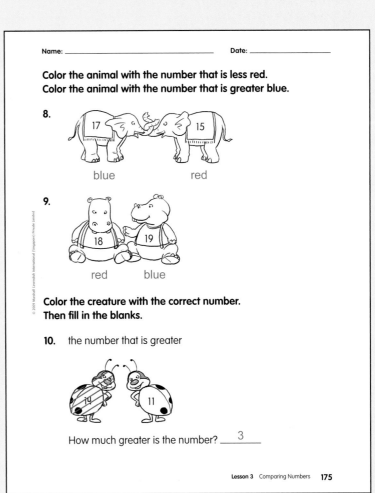

blue   red

9.

red   blue

Color the creature with the correct number.
Then fill in the blanks.

10. the number that is greater

How much greater is the number? __3__

Workbook A p. 175

Color the house with the number that is less.
Then fill in the blanks.

— **Example** —

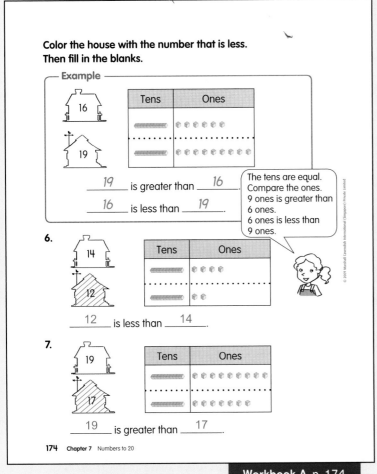

Tens	Ones

__19__ is greater than __16__
__16__ is less than __19__.

> The tens are equal.
> Compare the ones.
> 9 ones is greater than 6 ones.
> 6 ones is less than 9 ones.

6.

Tens	Ones

__12__ is less than __14__

7.

Tens	Ones

__19__ is greater than __17__.

Workbook A p. 174

---

11. the number that is less

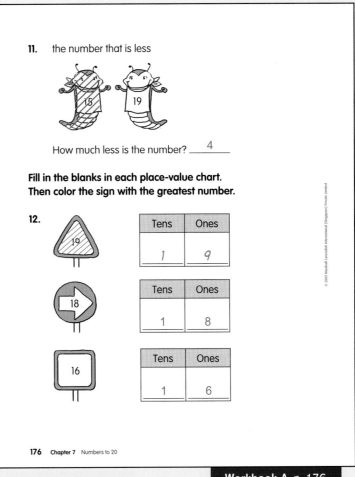

How much less is the number? __4__

Fill in the blanks in each place-value chart.
Then color the sign with the greatest number.

12.

19

Tens	Ones
1	9

18

Tens	Ones
1	8

16

Tens	Ones
1	6

Workbook A p. 176

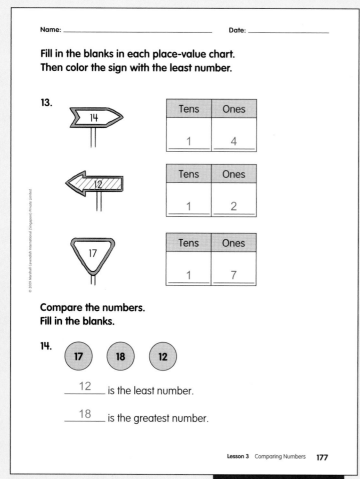

Name: _____ Date: _____

Fill in the blanks in each place-value chart.
Then color the sign with the least number.

13.

Tens	Ones
1	4

Tens	Ones
1	2

Tens	Ones
1	7

Compare the numbers.
Fill in the blanks.

14. 17   18   12

__12__ is the least number.

__18__ is the greatest number.

Workbook A p. 177

Compare the numbers.
Fill in the blanks.

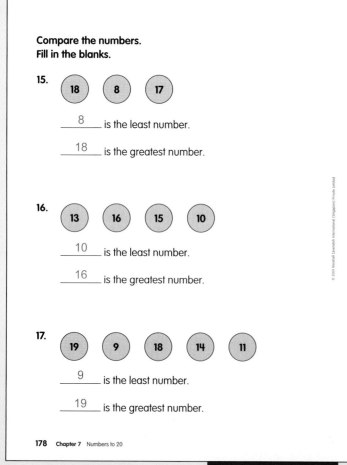

15. 18   8   17

__8__ is the least number.

__18__ is the greatest number.

16. 13   16   15   10

__10__ is the least number.

__16__ is the greatest number.

17. 19   9   18   14   11

__9__ is the least number.

__19__ is the greatest number.

Workbook A p. 178

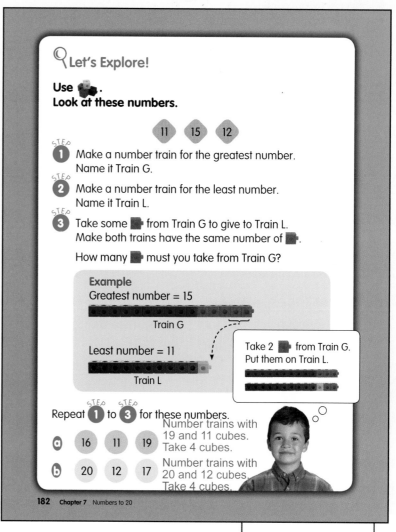

Let's Explore!

Use cubes.
Look at these numbers.

11   15   12

STEP **1** Make a number train for the greatest number.
Name it Train G.

STEP **2** Make a number train for the least number.
Name it Train L.

STEP **3** Take some cubes from Train G to give to Train L.
Make both trains have the same number of cubes.

How many cubes must you take from Train G?

Example
Greatest number = 15

Train G

Least number = 11

Train L

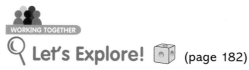
Take 2 cubes from Train G.
Put them on Train L.

Repeat STEP **1** to STEP **3** for these numbers.

a 16   11   19   Number trains with 19 and 11 cubes. Take 4 cubes.

b 20   12   17   Number trains with 20 and 12 cubes. Take 4 cubes.

Student Book A p. 182

WORKING TOGETHER

Let's Explore! (page 182)

Understand Greatest and Least Using Number Trains

This exploration helps children develop problem-solving skills as they use **connecting cubes** to compare numbers.

- Have children work in groups of four and give each group one set of 40 connecting cubes; 10 of each color.

- Lead children through STEP **1** to STEP **3** in the Student Book by modelling.

- Have children repeat STEP **1** to STEP **3** to explore different numbers in **a** and **b** as well.

- Ask children to explain how they found their answers and encourage them to articulate their thinking.

- *Note:* Some children may arrive at the answer by trial and error, and that is completely acceptable at this stage. Others may determine that the number of cubes to move from one train to another is half the difference of the number of cubes between the two trains. For example, if Train G has 15 cubes and Train L has 11 cubes, their difference is $15 - 11 = 4$. Half of 4 is 2. So 2 cubes should be moved from Train G to Train L to make both trains have the same number.

LESSON 4 Making Patterns and Ordering Numbers

LESSON OBJECTIVE
• Order numbers by making number patterns.

TECHNOLOGY RESOURCES
• *Math in Focus* eBook
• *Math in Focus* Teaching Resources CD
• *Math in Focus* Virtual Manipulatives

Vocabulary
order

DAY 1	Student Book 1A, pp. 183–188 Workbook 1A, pp. 179–182

MATERIALS
• 22 connecting cubes (10 each of two colors, 2 of another color) for the teacher
• Place-Value Chart (TR13) for the teacher

DIFFERENTIATION RESOURCES
• Reteach 1A, pp. 121–126
• Extra Practice 1A, pp. 111–114

 5-minute Warm Up

• Use connecting cubes to make number trains of 1, 2, 3, 4, and 5, and place them next to one another.

• Have children look at the number trains and *say:* These number trains form a pattern.

• Ask for volunteers to say what comes next.

• Have children continue the pattern one at a time until they reach 10.

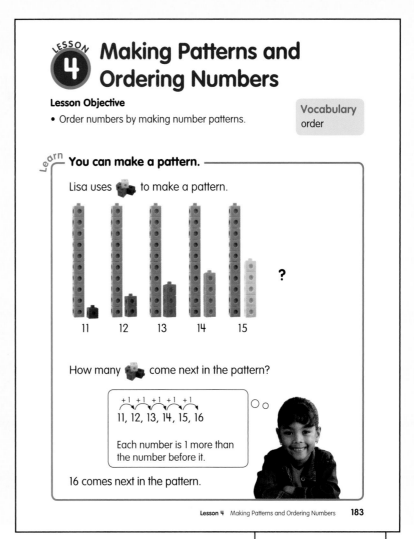

Student Book A p. 183

DAY 1 Teach

Make Patterns with Connecting Cubes (page 183)

Children have learned how to make repeating shape patterns and increasing number patterns up to 10 in Chapters 5 and 1 respectively. In this chapter, children continue making number patterns with numbers to 20, and use these patterns to order numbers.

• Use **connecting cubes** to make a pattern as shown in the Student Book.

• Guide children to find the relationship between the consecutive numbers: each number is 1 more than the number before it.

• If necessary, remove one connecting cube from the next number to show the similarity and difference between two consecutive numbers.

• Have volunteers make additional number trains to continue the pattern.

Best Practices This lesson begins with a model of counting by ones, or adding one. As you introduce the lesson to children, you may also want to model adding two. This will help prepare them for Exercises later in the Let's Practice section.

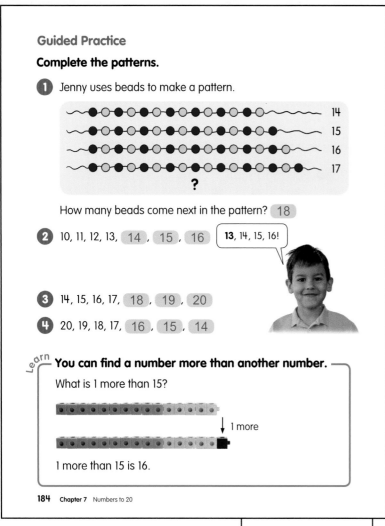

Guided Practice

Complete the patterns.

1. Jenny uses beads to make a pattern.

14
15
16
17
?

How many beads come next in the pattern? 18

2. 10, 11, 12, 13, 14 , 15 , 16   *13, 14, 15, 16!*

3. 14, 15, 16, 17, 18 , 19 , 20

4. 20, 19, 18, 17, 16 , 15 , 14

You can find a number more than another number.

What is 1 more than 15?

↓ 1 more

1 more than 15 is 16.

Student Book A p. 184

Check for Understanding
✓ **Guided Practice** (page 184)

1 Have children decide how the strings of beads are arranged in a pattern. Have children say how many beads come next in the pattern.

2 and 3 Lead children to observe an increasing pattern from the numbers, increasing by 1 more each time. Have them continue the patterns.

4 *Ask:* How is this pattern different from the others in this practice? (Each number in the pattern is 1 fewer than, instead of 1 more than, the number before it.)

Guide children to continue the decreasing pattern.

Find a Number More Than the Number Given (page 184)

Children use **connecting cubes** to find relationships between numbers. This helps children identify and extend number patterns.

• Make two number trains each with 15 connecting cubes (10 of one color and 5 of another).

Problem of the Lesson

Andy, José, Kim, and Dave are in a bean-bag tossing contest.
Andy gets 8 points.
José gets 19 points.
Kim gets 12 points.
Dave gets 10 points.
Who wins the contest?
Solution: Arrange the children from first to fourth position.

Andy	José	Kim	Dave
8	19	12	10
4th	1st	2nd	3rd

Answer: José wins the contest. The positions in first to fourth order are José, Kim, Dave, Andy.

Differentiated Instruction

English Language Learners

Use the beads model at the top of the page to introduce language related to patterns. Say: Each group has one more bead than the one above it. Add one to each group of beads to make the next group. Each number is one more than the number before it. Add one to each number to find the next number.
Have children practice using this language with a partner.

• Add one cube of a third color to one of the trains.

• Lead children to see that 16 is 1 more than 15. *Say:* 1 more than 15 is 16.

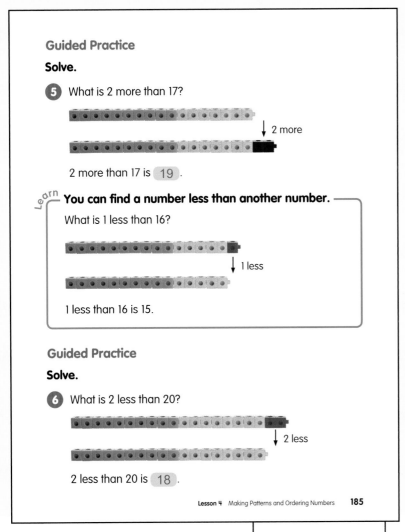

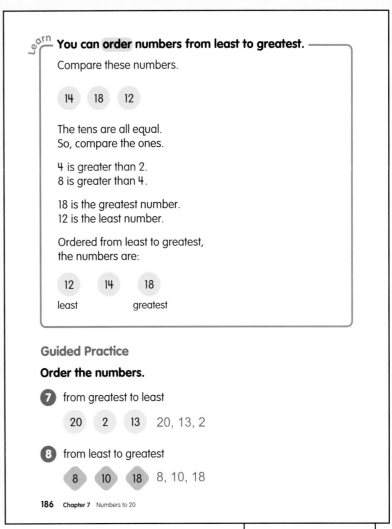

✔ Guided Practice (page 185)

5 Model the 15- and 16-number trains from the Learn box on page 184. Remind children that 1 more than 15 is 16. Add another color cube to the 16-number train. *Ask:* What is 2 more than 15? *Say:* 2 more than 15 is 17. Have children complete Exercise **5**.

Learn
Find a Number Less Than the Number Given
(page 185)

Children use **connecting cubes** to find relationships between numbers. This helps children identify and extend number patterns.

- Make two number trains each with 16 connecting cubes (10 of one color and 6 of another).
- Remove one cube from one of the trains.
- Lead children to compare the trains and see that 1 fewer than 16 is 15.
- Repeat by removing a different number of cubes from the shorter train, and have children give the answer each time you ask: What is … fewer than 16?

✔ Guided Practice (page 185)

6 Have children complete the Exercise. Model the question using connecting cubes if necessary.

Learn
Order Numbers from Least to Greatest
(page 186)

Children compare and order numbers up to 20.

- Make number trains for 13, 11, and 16, using **connecting cubes** (each containing 10 of one color and the remaining cubes of another color).
- Lead children to compare the trains and order them from fewest to most: 11, 13, 16.
- Write the numbers on the board one below the other to align the place values. Have children compare the numbers by tens and then by ones. Lead children to see that ordered from least to greatest, the order is 11, 13, 16. This helps children to relate concrete representations to the numbers.
- Lead children through the example in the Student Book without using connecting cubes. Write the numbers on the board and guide them to compare by using place value.

✔ Guided Practice (page 186)

7 and **8** Write the numbers on the board. Align them one below the other. Guide children to compare the tens, followed by the ones, and order the numbers according to the questions.

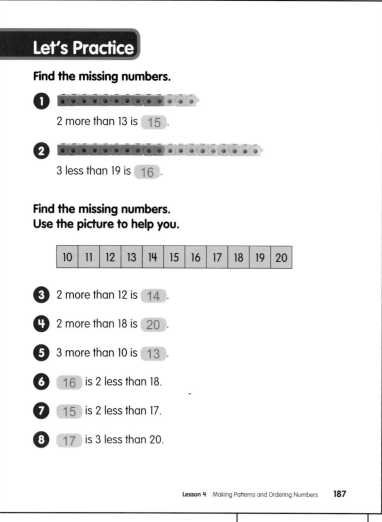

Let's Practice

Find the missing numbers.

1 2 more than 13 is 15 .

2 3 less than 19 is 16 .

**Find the missing numbers.
Use the picture to help you.**

| 10 | 11 | 12 | 13 | 14 | 15 | 16 | 17 | 18 | 19 | 20 |

3 2 more than 12 is 14 .

4 2 more than 18 is 20 .

5 3 more than 10 is 13 .

6 16 is 2 less than 18.

7 15 is 2 less than 17.

8 17 is 3 less than 20.

Student Book A p. 187

Complete the patterns.

9 11, 12, 13, 14 , 15, 16

10 17, 16, 15, 14 , 13 , 12, 11

11 7, 9, 11 , 13, 15, 17 , 19

12 20 , 18, 16, 14 , 12 , 10, 8

Order the numbers from greatest to least.

13 11 9 18 15   18, 15, 11, 9

Order the numbers from least to greatest.

14 20 6 12 16   6, 12, 16, 20

ON YOUR OWN
Go to Workbook A:
Practice 4, pages 179–181

Student Book A p. 188

Let's Practice (pages 187 and 188)

These exercises let children practice making number patterns and ordering numbers. Exercises **1** to **8** require children to find a number more or less than another. Exercises **9** and **10** require children to identify and continue number patterns involving adding or removing 1 to continue the sequence. Exercises **11** and **12** require children to identify and continue number patterns involving adding or removing 2 to continue the sequence. Exercises **13** and **14** require children to order numbers from both greatest-to-least and least-to-greatest.

Common Error Children may get incorrect answers because they confuse the terms *more* and *less*. Tell them to first answer all the problems with *more*. With these problems, children will find the number in the picture and count to the right. Next, they do the *less* problems by counting to the left.

ON YOUR OWN

Children practice making number patterns and ordering numbers in Practice 4, pp. 179–182 of **Workbook 1A**. These pages (with the answers) are shown on page 188A.

Differentiation Options Depending on children's success with the Workbook pages, use these materials as needed.
Struggling: Reteach 1A, pp. 121–126
On Level: Extra Practice 1A, pp. 111–114

Practice and Apply
Workbook pages for Chapter 7, Lesson 4

Name: _____ Date: _____

Practice 4   Making Patterns and Ordering Numbers

Solve.

1. Alex uses circles to make a pattern.
   How many circles come next in the pattern?
   Draw the circles in the empty box.
   Write the number of circles below this box.

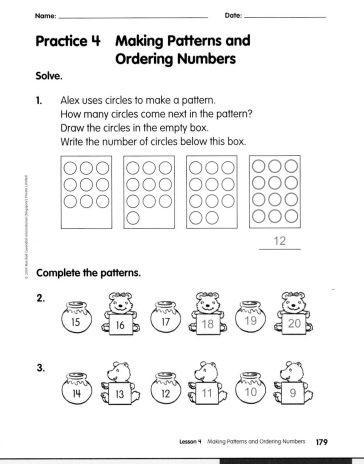

   _12_

Complete the patterns.

2. 15 16 17 18 19 20

3. 14 13 12 11 10 9

Workbook A p. 179

Name: _____ Date: _____

Help Rosa order the bowling pins and balls.

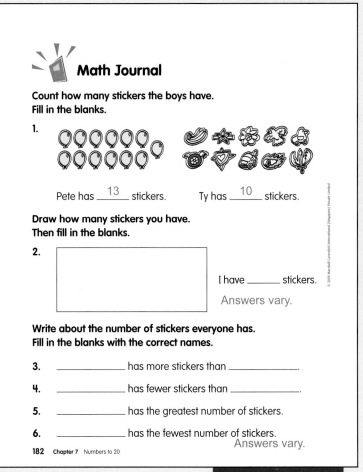

13. Write the numbers on the 🎳 in order from least to greatest.

    _12_ 13 15 18 20

    least

14. Write the numbers on the ⚫ in order from greatest to least.

    17 16 14 11 8

    greatest

Workbook A p. 181

Look at the numbers.
Fill in the blanks.

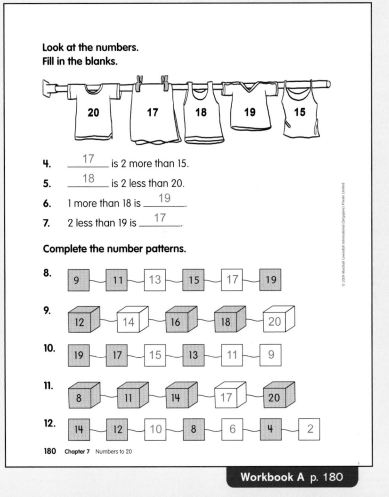

20   17   18   19   15

4. _17_ is 2 more than 15.
5. _18_ is 2 less than 20.
6. 1 more than 18 is _19_.
7. 2 less than 19 is _17_.

Complete the number patterns.

8. 9 11 13 15 17 19

9. 12 14 16 18 20

10. 19 17 15 13 11 9

11. 8 11 14 17 20

12. 14 12 10 8 6 4 2

Workbook A p. 180

Math Journal

Count how many stickers the boys have.
Fill in the blanks.

1.

   Pete has _13_ stickers.   Ty has _10_ stickers.

Draw how many stickers you have.
Then fill in the blanks.

2.

   I have _____ stickers.

   Answers vary.

Write about the number of stickers everyone has.
Fill in the blanks with the correct names.

3. _____ has more stickers than _____.
4. _____ has fewer stickers than _____.
5. _____ has the greatest number of stickers.
6. _____ has the fewest number of stickers.

   Answers vary.

Workbook A p. 182

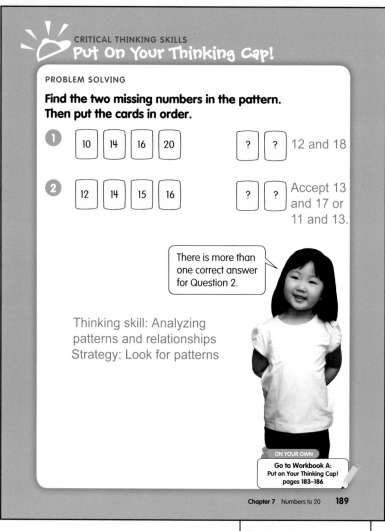

CRITICAL THINKING SKILLS
Put On Your Thinking Cap!

PROBLEM SOLVING

**Find the two missing numbers in the pattern.
Then put the cards in order.**

❶ | 10 | 14 | 16 | 20 | | ? | ? | 12 and 18

❷ | 12 | 14 | 15 | 16 | | ? | ? | Accept 13 and 17 or 11 and 13.

There is more than one correct answer for Question 2.

Thinking skill: Analyzing patterns and relationships
Strategy: Look for patterns

ON YOUR OWN
Go to Workbook A:
Put on Your Thinking Cap!
pages 183–186

Chapter 7 Numbers to 20 **189**

Student Book A p. 189

CRITICAL THINKING AND PROBLEM SOLVING
Put on Your Thinking Cap! (page 189)

This activity requires children to apply their analytical skills. Children can work in pairs.

- Read the direction lines with children. Be sure that they understand that the cards make up part of a number pattern.

- Explain that they are finding the two missing numbers that may go anywhere in the pattern and not necessarily at the end.

- Have them attempt to solve the problem with their partners. Ask them to explain their solution to the class.

- In Exercise ❷, one of the missing numbers can be used to begin the pattern for one of two possible solutions.

For Struggling Learners If children need help, write the numbers on the board and show the relationships between consecutive numbers. Then lead children to say what the missing numbers are.

Thinking Skill

- Analyzing patterns and relationships

Problem Solving Strategy

- Look for patterns

ON YOUR OWN

Because all children should be challenged, have all children try the Challenging Practice and Problem-Solving pages in **Workbook 1A**, pp. 183–186. These pages (with the answers) are shown on page 189A.

Differentiation Options Depending on children's success with the Workbook pages, use these materials as needed.
On Level: Extra Practice, pp. 115–116
Advanced: Enrichment 1A, pp. 51–58

Practice and Apply

Workbook pages for Put on Your Thinking Cap!

Name: _____   Date: _____

Put On Your Thinking Cap!

Challenging Practice

1. Class 1A of Greenfield School holds a basketball contest.
   Find out who won.

   CLUES

   Rita scores the fewest number of baskets.
   John scores 3 more baskets than Rita.
   Dion scores more baskets than Rachel but less than Frank.

   Write the names next to the number of baskets scored.

   Baskets Scored

   Rachel   🏀🏀🏀🏀🏀🏀

   Dion   🏀🏀🏀🏀🏀🏀🏀

   Frank   🏀🏀🏀🏀🏀🏀🏀🏀
   🏀🏀

   Thinking skills: Comparing, and deduction

   Rita   🏀🏀

   John   🏀🏀🏀🏀🏀

   Strategies: Use a diagram, and make suppositions

   Who won the contest? ____Frank____

   Chapter 7 Numbers to 20 **183**

Workbook A p. 183

Fill in the blanks.

2. $10 + \underline{5} = 15$ Thinking skill: Analyzing parts and whole.

3. $10 + \underline{1} = 11$

4. $10 + \underline{8} = 18$

5. $\underline{4} + 10 = 14$

6. $\underline{7} + 10 = 17$

Write the correct names.

7. These are the numbers of 12 players on a team.

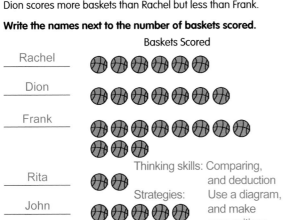

Roy 19   Bess 5   Shanon 14   Anita 1   Brad 8   Ally 3   Sally 11

Rafer 16   Anuya 0   Robin 20   Ben 7   Seth 10

Thinking skills: Comparing, and deduction
Strategies: Act it out
Whose names have the following numbers?

Numbers less than 5	Numbers from 5 to 9	Numbers from 10 to 14	Numbers from 15 to 20
Anuya	Bess	Seth	Rafer
Anita	Ben	Sally	Roy
Ally	Brad	Shanon	Robin

184 Chapter 7 Numbers to 20

Workbook A p. 184

Name: _____   Date: _____

Put On Your Thinking Cap!

Problem Solving

Use the clues on the next page.
Help Tony find which numbers his counters covered.
Thinking skills: Deduction, and comparing
Strategy: Guess and check

Chapter 7 Numbers to 20 **185**

Workbook A p. 185

Read what Tony's friends said.
Circle the numbers that were covered on Tony's card.

First, cover the greatest number.

Next, cover the number that is 2 less than the greatest number.

Then, cover the number that is the least.

There are two more numbers. I remember that one of these numbers is 3 less than the other.

Tony's card.

①	9	13	⑱
5	3	7	17
⑯	11	⑮	⑫

Accept 9 and 12

186 Chapter 7 Numbers to 20

Workbook A p. 186

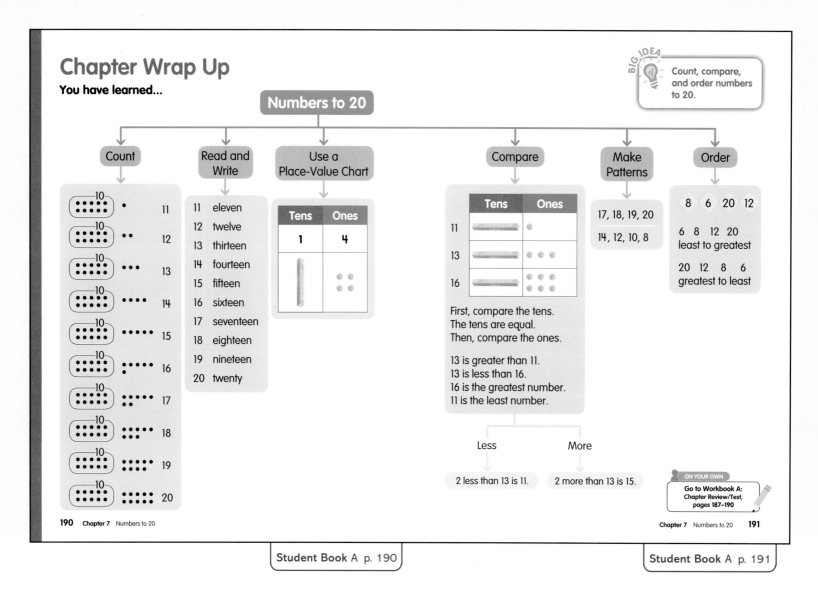

Student Book A p. 190

Student Book A p. 191

Chapter Wrap Up (pages 190 and 191)

Review numbers from 10 to 20 as one set of 10 and a particular number of ones, as shown on the chart in the Student Book. Help children recall counting on from 10. Review reading and writing the numbers and number words. Review the use of a place-value chart to show and compare numbers by aligning the tens and ones. Help children recall that making patterns may involve finding 1 or 2 less than or more than a previous number. As you work through the examples with the children, encourage them to use the chapter vocabulary:

- eleven
- twelve
- thirteen
- fourteen
- fifteen
- sixteen
- seventeen
- eighteen
- nineteen
- twenty
- place-value chart
- greatest
- least
- order

ON YOUR OWN

Have children review the vocabulary, concepts and skills from Chapter 7 with the Chapter Review/Test in **Workbook 1A,** pp. 187–190. These pages (with the answers) are shown on page 191A.

Assessment

Use the Chapter 7 Test Prep on pages 55–57 of **Assessments 1** to assess how well children have learned the material of this chapter. This assessment is appropriate for reporting results to adults at home and administrators. This test is shown on page 191B.

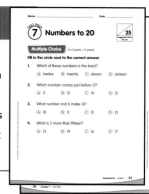

Assessments 1 pp. 55–57

Practice and Apply
Workbook pages for Chapter Review/Test

Name: _____ Date: _____

Chapter Review/Test
Vocabulary
Unscramble the letters to spell each number.

1. 15 f i e e t f n
fifteen

2. 11 e v l e e n
eleven

3. 18 e g e e t h n i
eighteen

4. 20 t w y n e t
twenty

Fill in the blank with the correct word.

| place-value chart   compare |

5. You can show numbers as tens and ones in
a __place-value chart__.

6. When you __compare__ 12 and 15, 12 is the number that is less.

Concepts and Skills
Count. Write the number.

7.

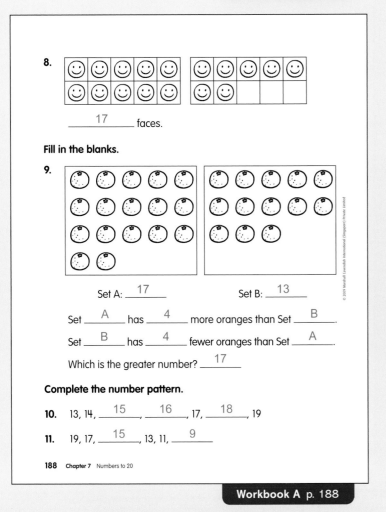

___13___ puppets

Workbook A p. 187

Name: _____ Date: _____

Write the numbers in order from least to greatest.

12.

| 17 | 3 | 0 | 10 | 15 |

_0_, _3_, _10_, _15_, _17_

Write the numbers in order from greatest to least.

13.

| 11 | 19 | 8 | 9 | 14 |

_19_, _14_, _11_, _9_, _8_

Problem Solving
Read the clues.
Then cross out the numbers to solve.

┌─ Example ──────────────────────────┐
| |
| 10 11 12 13 14 15 16 17 18 19 20 |
| |
| I am greater than 13. |
| I am less than 17. |
| Of the numbers that are left: |
| I am not the least. |
| I am not the greatest. |
| What number am I? ___15___ |
└────────────────────────────────────┘

Workbook A p. 189

8.

| ☺ ☺ ☺ ☺ ☺ ☺ ☺ ☺ ☺ ☺ |
| ☺ ☺ ☺ ☺ ☺ ☺ ☺ |

___17___ faces.

Fill in the blanks.

9.

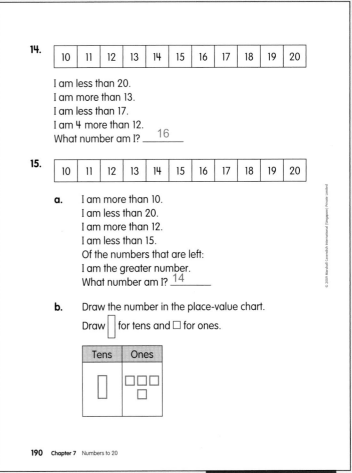

Set A: ___17___   Set B: ___13___

Set __A__ has __4__ more oranges than Set __B__.

Set __B__ has __4__ fewer oranges than Set __A__.

Which is the greater number? ___17___

Complete the number pattern.

10. 13, 14, _15_, _16_, 17, _18_, 19

11. 19, 17, _15_, 13, 11, _9_

Workbook A p. 188

14.

| 10 | 11 | 12 | 13 | 14 | 15 | 16 | 17 | 18 | 19 | 20 |

I am less than 20.
I am more than 13.
I am less than 17.
I am 4 more than 12.
What number am I? ___16___

15.

| 10 | 11 | 12 | 13 | 14 | 15 | 16 | 17 | 18 | 19 | 20 |

a. I am more than 10.
I am less than 20.
I am more than 12.
I am less than 15.
Of the numbers that are left:
I am the greater number.
What number am I? _14_

b. Draw the number in the place-value chart.
Draw ▯ for tens and ☐ for ones.

Tens	Ones
▯	☐☐☐ ☐

Workbook A p. 190

Assessments Book pages for Chapter 7 Test Prep
Answer key appears in Assessments Book.

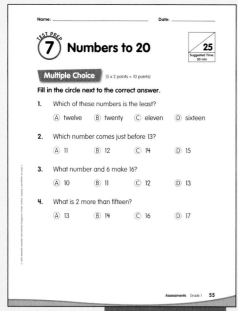

Assessments p. 55

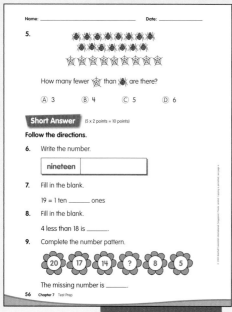

Assessments p. 56

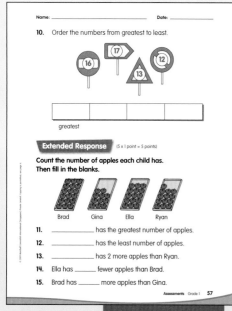

Assessments p. 57

Chapter Overview

Addition and Subtraction Facts to 20

Math Background

Children have learned the concepts of part-whole and number bonds. They have applied these concepts in addition and subtraction of numbers to 10. In this chapter, children will learn more strategies for addition and subtraction as they solve problems that include numbers between 10 and 20. They have learned the concept of place value in 2-digit numbers, which will be built on in this chapter when they add or subtract by grouping the two-digit number as a 10 and ones. The concept of number bonds, with 10 as one part, too, is built on to help develop these new strategies of addition and subtraction.

The strategy of using doubles facts is introduced at this stage, and leads to a related strategy, doubles plus one facts. Number bonds have the added benefit of displaying fact families. Since addition and subtraction are inverse operations, there are families of facts that relate addition and subtraction facts around two parts and a whole. Such strategies are a foundation for adding and subtracting larger numbers. Children also apply the strategies to solve real-world problems.

Cross-Curricular Connections

Reading/Language Arts In this chapter, children use doubles and doubles plus one facts to add. Tell children that the word double can be used as a noun, verb, and adjective. Present several examples to demonstrate the multiple meanings of the word. *Say:* A doubles fact is 5 + 5 = 10. The entrance to the school has double doors. The baseball player hit a double. She doubled the cookie recipe.

Drama Put children in small groups. Have them write either an addition or subtraction story that they can act out. Groups should write the problem and also create a script for their act. Invite groups to present their acts. As a class, discuss each act. Ask children to describe the problem. Write the problem on the board and find the solution with the class.

Skills Trace

Grade K	Represent addition stories with small whole numbers. (Chap. 17)
Grade 1	Add 2-digit to 2-digit numbers up to 100. (Chaps. 3, 8, 13, and 17)
Grade 2	Add 3-digit to 3-digit numbers up to 1,000. (Chaps. 2 and 10)

EVERY DAY COUNTS® Calendar Math

The December activities provide...

Review comparing and ordering numbers (Chapter 7)

Preview telling time (Chapter 15)

Practice addition and subtraction stories (Lesson 3 in this chapter)

Differentiation Resources

Differentiation for Special Populations

	English Language Learners	Struggling Reteach 1A	On Level Extra Practice 1A	Advanced Enrichment 1A
Lesson 1	p. 196	pp. 127–136	pp. 117–124	Enrichment pages can be used to challenge advanced children.
Lesson 2	p. 204	pp. 137–142	pp. 125–130	
Lesson 3	p. 210	pp. 143–146	pp. 131–132	

Additional Support

For English Language Learners

Select activities that reinforce the chapter vocabulary and the connections among these words, such as having children

- add terms, definitions, and examples to the Word Wall

- use manipulatives to act out the meaning of each term

- draw pictures to illustrate each term

- discuss the Chapter Wrap Up, encouraging children to use the chapter vocabulary

For Struggling Learners

Select activities that go back to the appropriate stage of the Concrete-Pictorial-Abstract spectrum, such as having children

- act out addition and subtraction stories in the chapter

- use manipulatives to act out different ways to add and subtract

- draw pictures of addition and subtraction stories.

- create addition and subtraction stories for given addition and subtraction sentences

See also page 196.

If necessary, review:
- Chapter 3 (Addition Facts to 10), or
- Chapter 4 (Subtraction Facts to 10)

For Advanced Learners

See suggestions on pages 204 and 211–212.

Assessment and Remediation

Chapter 8 Assessment

Prior Knowledge		
	Resource	**Page numbers**
Quick Check	Student Book 1A	p. 194
Pre-Test	Assessments 1	pp. 58–59
Ongoing Diagnostic		
Guided Practice	Student Book 1A	pp. 197, 199, 200, 202, 204, 206, 209, 210
Common Error	Teacher's Edition 1A	pp. 202, 207-208, 211-212
Formal Evaluation		
Chapter Review/Test	Workbook 1A	pp. 217–218
Chapter 8 Test Prep	Assessments 1	pp. 60–63

Problems with these items...   Can be remediated with...

Remediation Options

Objective	Review/Test Items Workbook 1A pp. 217–218	Chapter Assessment Items Assessments 1 pp. 60–63	Reteach Reteach 1A	Student Book Student Book 1A
Use chapter vocabulary correctly.	1–3	Not assessed	pp. 130–146	p. 195
Use different strategies to add 1- and 2-digit numbers.	4–5, 6–7, 10, 12, 14	1, 5–6	pp. 130–136	Lesson 1
Subtract a 1-digit from a 2-digit number with and without regrouping.	8–9, 11, 13	2–3, 5, 7–10	pp. 137–142	Lesson 2
Solve real-world problems.	12–13	4, 11–12	pp. 143–146	Lesson 3

Chapter Planning Guide

8 Addition and Subtraction Facts to 20

Lesson	Pacing	Instructional Objectives	Vocabulary
Chapter Opener pp. 192–194 Recall Prior Knowledge Quick Check	*1 day	💡 **Big Idea** Different strategies can be used to add and subtract.	
Lesson 1, pp. 195–202 Ways to Add	3 days	• Use different strategies to add 1- and 2-digit numbers	• group • doubles fact • same • doubles plus one
Lesson 2, pp. 203–208 Ways to Subtract	2 day	• Subtract a 1–digit from a 2–digit number with and without regrouping	
Lesson 3, pp. 209–213 Real-World Problems: Addition and Subtraction Facts	1 day	• Solve real-world problems	
Problem Solving pp. 214–215 👏 Put on Your Thinking Cap!	1 day	Thinking Skills: • Analyzing parts and whole Problem Solving Strategies: • Guess and check • Solve part of the problem	
Chapter Wrap Up pp. 216–217	1 day	• Reinforce and consolidate chapter skills and concepts	
Chapter Assessment	1 day		

*Assume that 1 day is a 45–55 minute period.

Resources	Materials	NCTM Focal Points	NCTM Process Standards
Student Book 1A, pp. 192–194 **Assessments 1,** pp. 58–59			
Student Book 1A, pp. 195–202 **Workbook 1A,** pp. 191–202 **Extra Practice 1A,** pp. 117–124 **Reteach 1A,** pp. 127–136	• 20 connecting cubes, 10 of each color for the teacher • 20 counters (10 of each color) per pair • Ten Frames (TR01)	*Number and Operations* Develop strategies for adding and subtracting whole numbers	Problem Solving Reasoning/Proof Connections Representation
Student Book 1A, pp. 203–208 **Workbook 1A,** pp. 203–210 **Extra Practice 1A,** pp. 125–130 **Reteach 1A,** pp. 137–142	• 20 connecting cubes (10 of each color) for the teacher • 2 spinner bases for each group (TR14)	*Number and Operations* Develop strategies for adding and subtracting whole numbers Relate addition and subtraction as inverse operations	Problem Solving Reasoning/Proof Connections Representation
Student Book 1A, pp. 209–213 **Workbook 1A,** pp. 211–212 **Extra Practice 1A,** pp. 131–132 **Reteach 1A,** pp. 143–146	• 20 connecting cubes (10 of each color) for the teacher	*Number and Operations* Create and use strategies to solve addition and subtraction problems involving basic facts	Problem Solving Reasoning/Proof Communication Representation
Student Book 1A, pp. 214–215 **Workbook 1A,** pp. 213–216 **Extra Practice 1A,** pp. 133–134 **Enrichment 1A,** pp. 59–65	• A copy of Puzzle Grids (TR15) for each child	*Number and Operations and Algebra* Solve both routine and non-routine problems	Problem Solving Reasoning/Proof
Student Book 1A, pp. 216–217 **Workbook 1A,** pp. 217–218 **Assessments 1,** pp. 60–63			

Technology Resources for easy classroom management
• *Math in Focus* eBook
• *Math in Focus* Teaching Resources CD
• *Math in Focus* Virtual Manipulatives
• On-Line Web Resources

Chapter Introduction

Chapter 8
Vocabulary

group	a set of objects or people	Lesson 1
same	alike or equal	Lesson 1
doubles fact	the numbers that are added together are the same: 3 + 3 = 6	Lesson 1
doubles plus one	4 + 5 is 4 + 4 plus 1 more: 4 + 5 = 9	Lesson 1

BIG IDEA Different strategies can be used to add and subtract.

192

Student Book A p. 192

Big Idea (page 192)

Adding and subtracting within 20 using different strategies is the main focus of this chapter.

• Children apply strategies, such as grouping into a ten and ones, number bonds, and using doubles facts to add and subtract.

• They use addition and subtraction sentences to solve real-world problems.

Chapter Opener (page 192)

The picture provides a familiar context for children to make up their own addition and subtraction stories that reflect their understanding of the concepts of addition and subtraction. The ability to make up stories is a higher order skill compared to writing number sentences.

• Lead children to make addition and subtraction stories based on the picture, and write the corresponding addition or subtraction sentences on the board.

• Encourage children to make as many sentences as possible.

- *Ask:* How many birds do you see above the water (7) and over the sand? (2) How many birds are there in all? (7 + 2 = 9)

- How many starfish are there? (6)

- How many children are there in all? (12) How many are swimming in the ocean? (2) How many are on the sand? (12 − 2 = 10)

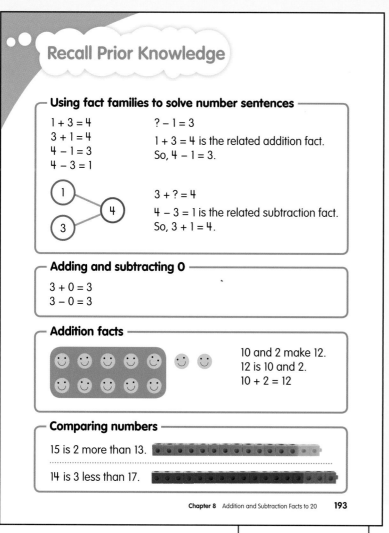

Recall Prior Knowledge

Using fact families to solve number sentences

$$1 + 3 = 4$$
$$3 + 1 = 4$$
$$4 - 1 = 3$$
$$4 - 3 = 1$$

$$? - 1 = 3$$
$1 + 3 = 4$ is the related addition fact.
So, $4 - 1 = 3$.

$$3 + ? = 4$$
$4 - 3 = 1$ is the related subtraction fact.
So, $3 + 1 = 4$.

Adding and subtracting 0

$$3 + 0 = 3$$
$$3 - 0 = 3$$

Addition facts

10 and 2 make 12.
12 is 10 and 2.
$10 + 2 = 12$

Comparing numbers

15 is 2 more than 13.

14 is 3 less than 17.

Chapter 8 Addition and Subtraction Facts to 20 **193**

Student Book A p. 193

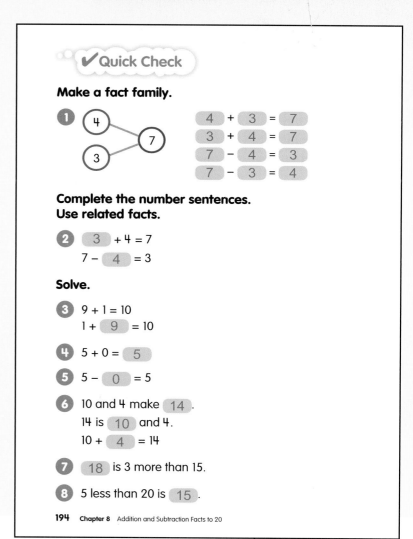

✔ Quick Check

Make a fact family.

1.

$$4 + 3 = 7$$
$$3 + 4 = 7$$
$$7 - 4 = 3$$
$$7 - 3 = 4$$

**Complete the number sentences.
Use related facts.**

2. $3 + 4 = 7$
$7 - 4 = 3$

Solve.

3. $9 + 1 = 10$
$1 + 9 = 10$

4. $5 + 0 = 5$

5. $5 - 0 = 5$

6. 10 and 4 make 14.
14 is 10 and 4.
$10 + 4 = 14$

7. 18 is 3 more than 15.

8. 5 less than 20 is 15.

194 Chapter 8 Addition and Subtraction Facts to 20

Student Book A p. 194

Recall Prior Knowledge (page 193)

Using fact families to solve number sentences
Children learned to make fact families in Chapter 4.

- Write the number bond 1-3—4 on the board and help children recall the related addition and subtraction facts.

Adding and subtracting 0
Children learned the zero concept in Chapter 4.

- Help children recall that $3 + 0 = 3$, and $0 + 3 = 3$, and 0 can be seen as a *part*. The order of the two parts is not important in addition.

- Make children aware that although $3 - 0 = 3$, $0 - 3$ is not 3. The order in subtraction is important.

Addition facts
Children learned basic addition facts to 10 in Chapter 3 and to count on from 10 in Chapter 7. Help children recall counting on from 10 to add.

Comparing numbers
Children learned to compare and order numbers in Chapters 1 and 7. Help children recall the concepts of *more than* and *less than*.

✔ Quick Check (page 194)

Use this section as a diagnostic tool to assess children's level of prerequisite knowledge before they progress to this chapter. Exercises ❶ to ❸ assess the skill of using fact families to solve number sentences, taught in Chapter 4. Exercises ❹ and ❺ assess the zero concept taught in Chapter 4. Exercise ❻ assesses basic addition skills taught in Chapters 1 and 7, and Exercises ❼ and ❽ assess skills of counting on and counting back to compare numbers taught in Chapters 1 and 7.

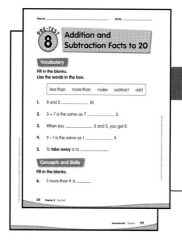

Assessments 1 pp. 58–59

Assessment

For additional assessment of children's prior knowledge and chapter readiness, use the Chapter 8 Pre-Test on pages 58–59 of **Assessments 1**.

1 Ways to Add

LESSON OBJECTIVE
• Use different strategies to add 1- and 2-digit numbers.

TECHNOLOGY RESOURCES
• *Math in Focus* eBook
• *Math in Focus* Teaching Resources CD
• *Math in Focus* Virtual Manipulatives

Vocabulary

group	doubles fact
same	doubles plus one

DAY 1 Student Book 1A, pp. 195–197
Workbook 1A, pp. 191–196

MATERIALS
• 20 connecting cubes, 10 of each color for the teacher
• 20 counters (10 of each color) per pair
• Ten Frames (TR01)

DIFFERENTIATION RESOURCES
• Reteach 1A, pp. 127–132
• Extra Practice 1A, pp. 117–120

DAY 2 Student Book 1A pp. 198–199
Workbook 1A pp. 197–198

DIFFERENTIATION RESOURCES
• Reteach 1A, pp. 133–134
• Extra Practice 1A, pp. 121–122

DAY 3 Student Book 1A, pp. 200–202
Workbook 1A, pp. 199–202

DIFFERENTIATION RESOURCES
• Reteach 1A, pp. 135–136
• Extra Practice 1A, pp. 123–124

 5-minute Warm Up

Have children work with a partner. Ask each child to hold up fingers on two hands to show a number between 5 and 10, and say the number. Have each child join the hand showing 5 with the partner's hand showing 5, with palms touching. Explain that that makes a 10. Then ask children to count on with the fingers on the other hand to find the sum.

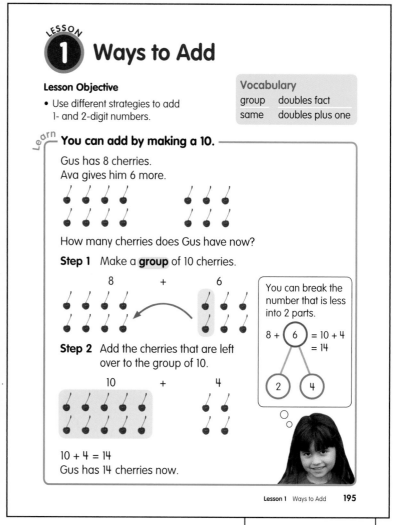

Student Book A p. 195

DAY 1 # Teach

 ## Add by Making a 10 (page 195)

Children learn to add by making a 10 first, using the strategy of number bonds.

• Show a group of 8 red **connecting cubes** and a group of 6 yellow **connecting cubes**. Tell children you are going to add all the cubes.

• Take 2 cubes from the yellow group and put them in the red group to make 10 cubes. Ask children to count the number of tens and ones.

• Write the following number bond 6—2-4 on the board. Also write the addition sentence $8 + 6 = 10 + 4 = 14$, showing how 2 is added to 8 to make 10.

• (Note the position of 2 and 4 in the 6—2-4 number bond in the Student Book. Ensure that the 2 is closest to the addend 8 so that children can see you are adding these numbers to make a 10.)

• Emphasize that children should make 10 first when adding.

• Revise the number bonds for 10, if necessary.

• Using the connecting cubes, demonstrate the addition of other 1-digit numbers, whose sum is from 11 to 20, using the same strategy.

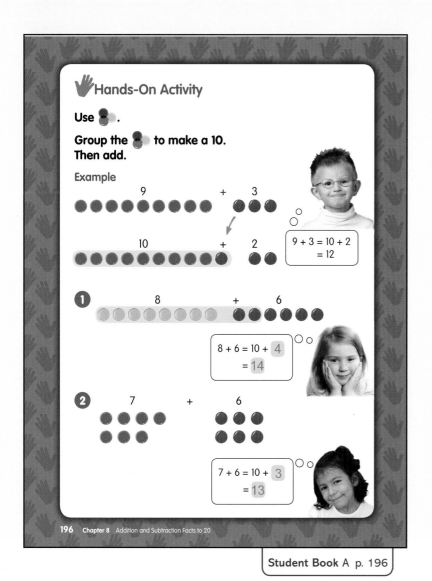

Problem of the Lesson

Susan has 9 star stickers and then finds 3 more stickers.
Draw and make a 10 to show how many stickers Susan has in all.

Solution

9 + 3

✭✭✭✭
✭✭✭✭✭   ✭✭✭

= 10 + 2

Answer: 12 stickers

Differentiated Instruction

English Language Learners

In this lesson, *group* is used as both a noun and a verb. Demonstrate this idea for children. Display a group of 15 objects. **Say:** This is a group of 15 (name of object). Now separate the objects into a group of 10 and 5. **Say:** I am grouping the (name of objects) to make a 10. Give children counters and encourage them to imitate your actions and statements.

Best Practices After children have completed all of this lesson, discuss when a particular strategy might be more appropriate than another. Allow children to tell which strategies they prefer and explain why.

✋Hands-On Activity:
Add Using Counters by First Making a 10 (page 196)

This activity lets children practice how to make 10 with concrete representation.

• Have children work individually or in pairs.

• Model the activity for children by doing the example 9 + 3 = 12 on the Student Book page.

• Show children that they remove **counters** from the smaller group to make 10. Take 1 counter from the red group of 3 to make 10, before adding the 2. Write the addition sentences and the 3—1-2 number bond on the board.

• As children work through Exercises ❶ and ❷, encourage them to write number bonds for the number which is less in each case.

For Struggling Learners Before children can copy the making-ten strategy, it might help to remind children of the names for 10. Start with the doubles fact first. Then use counters and count on to find the other names for 10.

$$5 + 5 = 10 \qquad 6 + 4 = 10 \qquad 7 + 3 = 10$$
$$8 + 2 = 10 \qquad 9 + 1 = 10$$

These names for 10 will help children know how many counters from the smaller group they need to move to make 10.

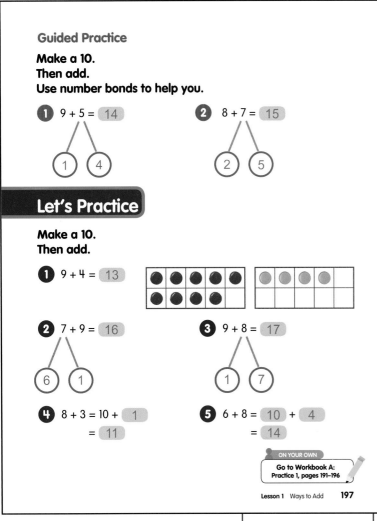

Guided Practice

Make a 10.
Then add.
Use number bonds to help you.

1 9 + 5 = 14

2 8 + 7 = 15

Let's Practice

Make a 10.
Then add.

1 9 + 4 = 13

2 7 + 9 = 16

3 9 + 8 = 17

4 8 + 3 = 10 + 1
 = 11

5 6 + 8 = 10 + 4
 = 14

ON YOUR OWN
Go to Workbook A:
Practice 1, pages 191–196

Lesson 1 Ways to Add **197**

Student Book A p. 197

Check for Understanding

✔ **Guided Practice** (page 197)

1 and **2** Help children see what number they need to make 10. Then guide children to make the suitable number bond with the number which is less.

Let's Practice (page 197)

This practice reinforces adding by making a 10 first. Children may use **counters** and a **ten frame** (TR01) to complete Exercise **1**. Exercises **2** and **3** require children to use number bonds. Exercises **4** and **5** require them to add without the help of the ten frame or number bond, so as to develop mental math dexterity.

ON YOUR OWN

Children practice adding by making a 10 first, with and without number bonds in Practice 1, pp. 191–196 of **Workbook 1A**. These pages (with the answers) are shown at the right and on page 197A.

Differentiation Options Depending on children's success with the Workbook pages, use these materials as needed.
Struggling: Reteach 1A, pp. 127–132
On Level: Extra Practice 1A, pp. 117–120

Practice and Apply
Workbook pages for Chapter 8, Lesson 1

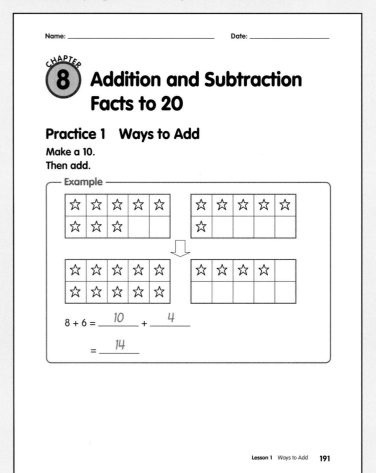

Name: _____ Date: _____

CHAPTER 8 Addition and Subtraction Facts to 20

Practice 1 Ways to Add

Make a 10.
Then add.

Example

8 + 6 = 10 + 4
 = 14

Lesson 1 Ways to Add **191**

Workbook A p. 191

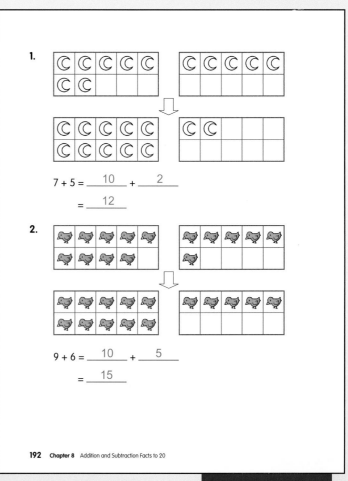

1.

7 + 5 = 10 + 2
 = 12

2.

9 + 6 = 10 + 5
 = 15

192 Chapter 8 Addition and Subtraction Facts to 20

Workbook A p. 192

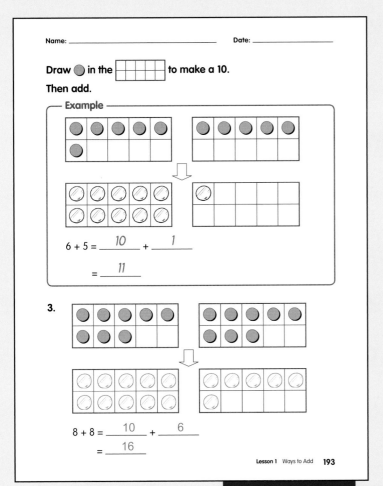

Draw ⬤ in the [ ] to make a 10.
Then add.

Example

$6 + 5 = \underline{\quad 10 \quad} + \underline{\quad 1 \quad}$
$ = \underline{\quad 11 \quad}$

3.

$8 + 8 = \underline{\quad 10 \quad} + \underline{\quad 6 \quad}$
$ = \underline{\quad 16 \quad}$

Workbook A p. 193

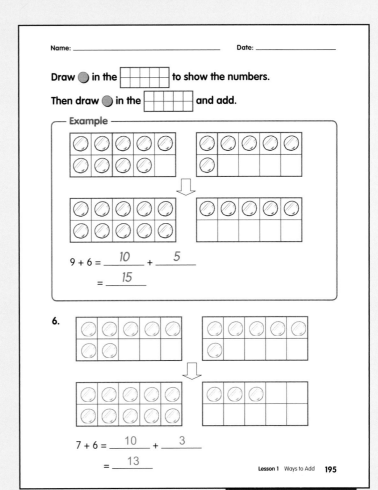

Draw ⬤ in the [ ] to show the numbers.
Then draw ⬤ in the [ ] and add.

Example

$9 + 6 = \underline{\quad 10 \quad} + \underline{\quad 5 \quad}$
$ = \underline{\quad 15 \quad}$

6.

$7 + 6 = \underline{\quad 10 \quad} + \underline{\quad 3 \quad}$
$ = \underline{\quad 13 \quad}$

Workbook A p. 195

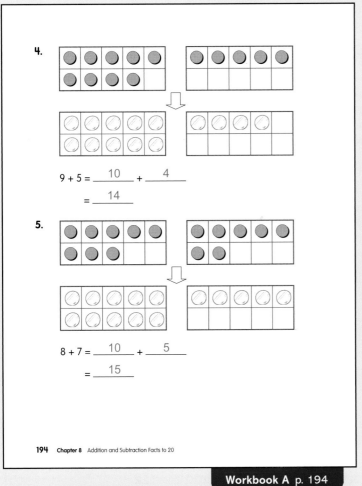

4.

$9 + 5 = \underline{\quad 10 \quad} + \underline{\quad 4 \quad}$
$ = \underline{\quad 14 \quad}$

5.

$8 + 7 = \underline{\quad 10 \quad} + \underline{\quad 5 \quad}$
$ = \underline{\quad 15 \quad}$

Workbook A p. 194

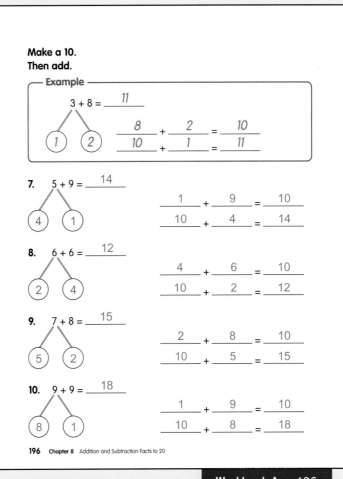

Make a 10.
Then add.

Example

$3 + 8 = \underline{\quad 11 \quad}$

① ②

$\underline{\quad 8 \quad} + \underline{\quad 2 \quad} = \underline{\quad 10 \quad}$
$\underline{\quad 10 \quad} + \underline{\quad 1 \quad} = \underline{\quad 11 \quad}$

7. $5 + 9 = \underline{\quad 14 \quad}$

④ ①

$\underline{\quad 1 \quad} + \underline{\quad 9 \quad} = \underline{\quad 10 \quad}$
$\underline{\quad 10 \quad} + \underline{\quad 4 \quad} = \underline{\quad 14 \quad}$

8. $6 + 6 = \underline{\quad 12 \quad}$

② ④

$\underline{\quad 4 \quad} + \underline{\quad 6 \quad} = \underline{\quad 10 \quad}$
$\underline{\quad 10 \quad} + \underline{\quad 2 \quad} = \underline{\quad 12 \quad}$

9. $7 + 8 = \underline{\quad 15 \quad}$

⑤ ②

$\underline{\quad 2 \quad} + \underline{\quad 8 \quad} = \underline{\quad 10 \quad}$
$\underline{\quad 10 \quad} + \underline{\quad 5 \quad} = \underline{\quad 15 \quad}$

10. $9 + 9 = \underline{\quad 18 \quad}$

⑧ ①

$\underline{\quad 1 \quad} + \underline{\quad 9 \quad} = \underline{\quad 10 \quad}$
$\underline{\quad 10 \quad} + \underline{\quad 8 \quad} = \underline{\quad 18 \quad}$

Workbook A p. 196

Learn You can add by grouping into a 10 and ones.

Paul has 16 dinosaurs.
His sister gives him 3 more dinosaurs.
How many dinosaurs does Paul have now?

Step 1 Group 16 into a 10 and ones.
16 = 10 + 6

$$(16) + 3 = ?$$

(10) (6)

16 + 3 = ?

Step 2 Add the ones.
6 + 3 = 9

Step 3 Add the 10 and ones.
10 + 9 = 19

So, 16 + 3 = 19.

Paul has 19 dinosaurs now.

198 Chapter 8 Addition and Subtraction Facts to 20

Guided Practice

**Group into a 10 and ones.
Then add.**

3 13 + 3 = 16

(10) (3)

4 12 + 7 = 19

(10) (2)

Let's Practice

**Group into a 10 and ones.
Then add.**

1 11 + 7 = 18

(10) (1)

2 4 + 13 = 17

(3) (10)

3 14 + 5 = 19

(10) (4)

4 2 + 17 = 19

(7) (10)

ON YOUR OWN
Go to Workbook A:
Practice 2, pages 197–198

Lesson 1 Ways to Add **199**

DAY 2 **Teach** See the Lesson Organizer on page 195 for Day 2 resources.

Learn

Add by Grouping into 10 and Ones

(page 198)

Children learn to add a two-digit number and a one-digit number by grouping the two-digit number into a 10 and ones using place value.

- Show children two different problems:

    4 + 5 and 16 + 3

- Ask children if they can see the difference between the two problems and what the difference is. (The second involves a 2-digit number.)

- Help children recall the place value of 16 and show the number bond for 16: 16—10-6. *Say*: 16 is 1 ten and 6 ones.

- Using **connecting cubes**, follow Steps 1 to 3 in the Student Book.

- Repeat the steps by writing the number bond and addition sentence on the board.

✓**Guided Practice** (page 199)

3 and **4** Help children practice grouping 2-digit numbers into a 10 and ones before adding. Ask volunteers to show grouping into tens and ones using **connecting cubes** for the exercises.

Let's Practice (page 199)

This practice reinforces adding by grouping into a 10 and ones before adding the ones.

Common Error Children may try to break the lesser addend into two parts, as they did in the previous Practice. Remind them that they need to break the greater addend into a 10 and ones now.

ON YOUR OWN

Children practice adding by making a 10 first, with and without number bonds in Practice 2, pp. 197–198 of **Workbook 1A**. These pages (with the answers) are shown on page 199A.

Differentiation Options Depending on children's success with the Workbook pages, use these materials as needed.
Struggling: Reteach 1A, pp. 133–134
On Level: Extra Practice 1A, pp. 121–122

Practice and Apply

Workbook pages for Chapter 8, Lesson 1

Name: _____ Date: _____

Practice 2 Ways to Add

Group the numbers into a 10 and ones.
Then add.

Example

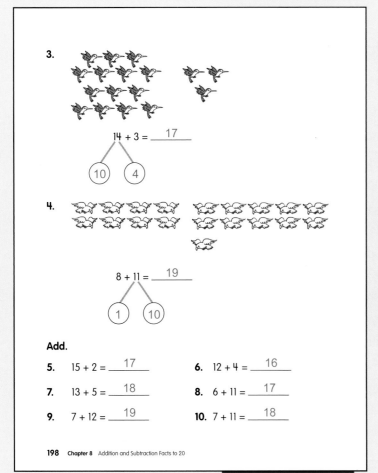

$12 + 5 =$ ___17___

10   2

1.

$12 + 3 =$ ___15___

10   2

2.

$11 + 5 =$ ___16___

10   1

Workbook A p. 197

3.

$14 + 3 =$ ___17___

10   4

4.

$8 + 11 =$ ___19___

1   10

Add.

5. $15 + 2 =$ ___17___   **6.** $12 + 4 =$ ___16___

7. $13 + 5 =$ ___18___   **8.** $6 + 11 =$ ___17___

9. $7 + 12 =$ ___19___   **10.** $7 + 11 =$ ___18___

Workbook A p. 198

Notes

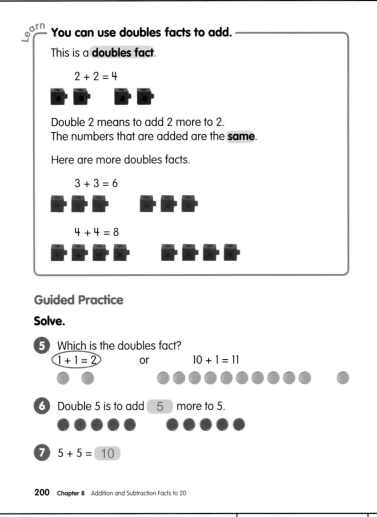

You can use doubles facts to add.

This is a **doubles fact**.

$$2 + 2 = 4$$

Double 2 means to add 2 more to 2. The numbers that are added are the **same**.

Here are more doubles facts.

$$3 + 3 = 6$$

$$4 + 4 = 8$$

Guided Practice

Solve.

5. Which is the doubles fact?

   $\boxed{1 + 1 = 2}$ or $10 + 1 = 11$

6. Double 5 is to add $\boxed{5}$ more to 5.

7. $5 + 5 = \boxed{10}$

200   **Chapter 8**   Addition and Subtraction Facts to 20

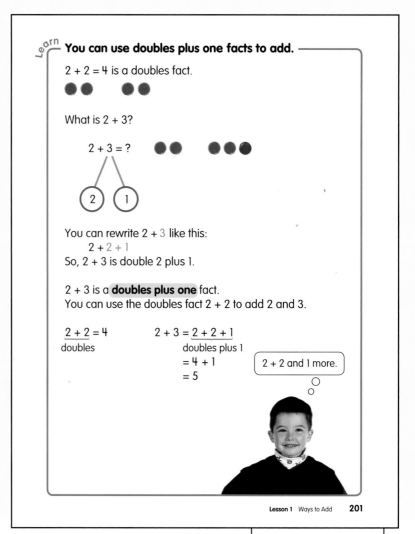

You can use doubles plus one facts to add.

$2 + 2 = 4$ is a doubles fact.

What is $2 + 3$?

$$2 + 3 = ?$$

You can rewrite $2 + 3$ like this:
$$2 + 2 + 1$$
So, $2 + 3$ is double 2 plus 1.

$2 + 3$ is a **doubles plus one** fact.
You can use the doubles fact $2 + 2$ to add 2 and 3.

$2 + 2 = 4$
doubles

$2 + 3 = \underline{2 + 2 + 1}$
doubles plus 1
$= 4 + 1$
$= 5$

2 + 2 and 1 more.

Lesson 1   Ways to Add   **201**

Add Using Doubles Facts (page 200)

Children learn to add by doubling a number.

- Show children two **connecting cubes**.

- Ask a volunteer to make another group with the same number.

- *Ask*: How many cubes are there now?

- Write the number sentence: $2 + 2 = 4$ on the board. Have children see that the number 2 is doubled. *Say:* Double 2 means adding two of the same number 2, or adding 2 more to 2. That gives 4.

- Repeat this activity to model double 3 and double 4.

- Encourage children to memorize doubles facts up to $9 + 9$.

✓ Guided Practice (page 200)

5 to 7 Help children recognize that doubling a number is adding two of the same number. Use **connecting cubes** to show the doubles, if necessary.

200–201   **CHAPTER 8: LESSON 1**

Add Using Doubles Plus One Facts

(page 201)

Children learn to add by adding 1 to a double.

- Show children two **connecting cubes**.

- Ask a volunteer to make another group with the same number.

- *Ask:* How many cubes are there now? Write the doubles fact $2 + 2 = 4$ on the board.

- Add a connecting cube of another color to one of the groups of 2, and *ask*: How many cubes are in this group? (3) How many cubes are there in all? (5)

- Write $2 + 3$, showing the number bond 3—2-1, and explain that $2 + 3$ is the same as $2 + 2 + 1 = 5$. *Say:* $2 + 3$ is double 2 plus 1.

- Repeat as needed with a different doubles plus one fact.

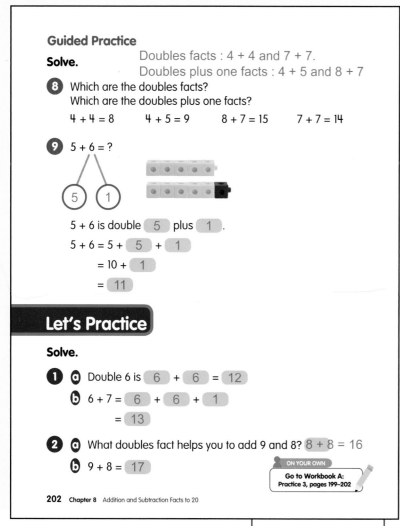

Guided Practice

Solve.

Doubles facts : 4 + 4 and 7 + 7.
Doubles plus one facts : 4 + 5 and 8 + 7

8 Which are the doubles facts?
Which are the doubles plus one facts?

4 + 4 = 8　　　4 + 5 = 9　　　8 + 7 = 15　　　7 + 7 = 14

9 5 + 6 = ?

⑤　①

5 + 6 is double ⑤ plus ①.

5 + 6 = 5 + ⑤ + ①

= 10 + ①

= ⑪

Let's Practice

Solve.

1 ⓐ Double 6 is ⑥ + ⑥ = ⑫

ⓑ 6 + 7 = ⑥ + ⑥ + ①

= ⑬

2 ⓐ What doubles fact helps you to add 9 and 8? ⑧ + 8 = 16

ⓑ 9 + 8 = ⑰

ON YOUR OWN
Go to Workbook A:
Practice 3, pages 199–202

202 **Chapter 8** Addition and Subtraction Facts to 20

Student Book A p. 202

✓ **Guided Practice** (page 202) 🎲

8 Guide children to recognize doubles in the addition sentences and explain that those are doubles facts. Have children identify the doubles plus one facts and ask them to say what the doubles facts are in these addition sentences.

9 Ask children whether this sentence forms a doubles fact or a doubles plus one fact (doubles plus one). Have children complete the number bond for 6—5-1, and complete the answers in this exercise.

Let's Practice (page 202)

This practice reinforces adding using doubles facts and doubles plus one facts. Exercise 1 requires children to apply the doubles fact for 6 and 6 plus one in adding two numbers, while Exercise 2 guides children to recognize which doubles facts and doubles plus one fact can be used.

Common Error Children may select the wrong addend to write a doubles plus one fact. Write on the board 6 + 7 = __. Tell children that they need to write a doubles fact with the addend that is (one) less than the other. The doubles plus one fact is 6 + 6 + 1.

ON YOUR OWN

Children practice adding using doubles facts and doubles plus one facts in Practice 3, pp. 199–202 of **Workbook 1A**. These pages (with the answers) are shown on page 202A.

Differentiation Options Depending on children's success with the Workbook pages, use these materials as needed.
Struggling: Reteach 1A, pp. 135–136
On Level: Extra Practice 1A, pp. 123–124

Practice and Apply
Workbook pages for Chapter 8, Lesson 1

Name: _____ Date: _____

Practice 3 Ways to Add
Complete each addition sentence.

Example

What is double 1?

Double 1 means to add ___1___ more to 1.

1 + ___1___ = ___2___

---

1. What is double 2?

Double 2 means to add ___2___ more to 2.

___2___ + ___2___ = ___4___

2. What is double 3?

Double 3 means to add ___3___ more to 3.

___3___ + ___3___ = ___6___

3. 4 + 4 = ___8___

4. 5 + 5 = ___10___

Workbook A p. 199

Name: _____ Date: _____

Use doubles facts to complete the addition sentences.

Example

[2] + [2] = 4

8. [0] + [0] = 0

9. [6] + [6] = 12

10. [5] + [5] = 10

11. [8] + [8] = 16

12. [9] + [9] = 18

13. [10] + [10] = 20

Workbook A p. 201

Complete each addition sentence.

5. a.   3 + 3 = ___6___

   3 + 4 = ___7___

   b.   3 + 3 is double ___3___.

   3 + 4 is double ___3___ plus ___1___.

Complete the number bonds.
Then fill in the blanks.

Example

6 + 7 = ?

6 + 7 is double 6 plus ___1___.

6 + 6 + ___1___

= 12 + ___1___

= 13

(6) (1)

6. 7 + 8 = ?

(7) (1)

   7 + 8 is double ___7___ plus 1.

   7 + ___7___ + 1

   = ___14___ + 1

   = 15

7. 5 + 4 = ?

(1) (4)

   5 + 4 is double ___4___ plus 1.

   ___4___ + ___4___ + ___1___

   = ___9___

Workbook A p. 200

Add the doubles-plus one numbers.
Use doubles facts to help you.
Then write the doubles fact you used.

Example

5 + 6 = ___11___

Doubles fact: ___5___ + ___5___ = ___10___

14. 7 + 6 = ___13___

   Doubles fact: ___6___ + ___6___ = ___12___

15. 7 + 8 = ___15___

   Doubles fact: ___7___ + ___7___ = ___14___

16. 9 + 10 = ___19___

   Doubles fact: ___9___ + ___9___ = ___18___

17. 8 + 9 = ___17___

   Doubles fact: ___8___ + ___8___ = ___16___

Workbook A p. 202

LESSON 2 Ways to Subtract

LESSON OBJECTIVE
- Subtract a 1-digit number from a 2-digit number with and without grouping.

TECHNOLOGY RESOURCES
- *Math in Focus* eBook
- *Math in Focus* Teaching Resources CD
- *Math in Focus* Virtual Manipulatives

DAY 1 Student Book 1A, pp. 203–206

MATERIALS
- 20 connecting cubes (10 of each color) for the teacher
- 2 spinner bases for each group of 3 children (TR14)

DAY 2 Student Book 1A, pp. 207–208
Workbook 1A, pp. 203–210

DIFFERENTIATION RESOURCES
- Reteach 1A, pp. 137–142
- Extra Practice 1A, pp. 125–130

5-minute Warm Up

- Ask for 3 volunteers. Have Child 1 and Child 2 each say a number less than 10. Child 3 has to subtract the number which is less from the greater number to find the difference between the numbers. Write the number sentence on the board.

- When children understand the steps, repeat this with the other children, having each child say a number in turn in this sequence: 1st number, 2nd number, difference, after which you write the number sentence on the board.

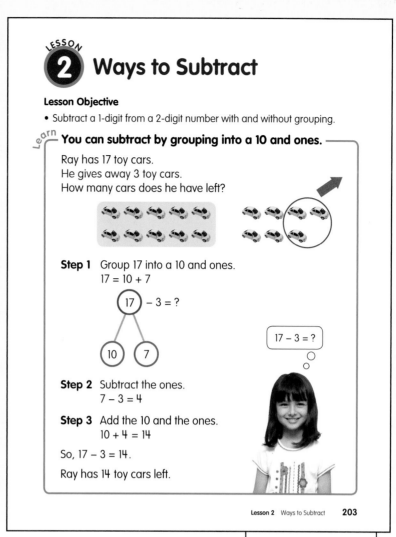

Student Book A p. 203

DAY 1 Teach

Subtract by Grouping into a 10 and Ones
(page 203)

Children will learn how to subtract a 1-digit number from a 2-digit number by grouping the 2-digit number into a 10 and some first and then subtracting the ones.

- Help children recall the *taking away* concept of subtraction and relate this concept to the word problem in the Student Book. Check that children understand that *giving away or taking away* is the same as subtracting. *Say:* Taking 3 away from 17 is the same as 17 − 3.

- Help children recall place value of the number 17 and show the number bond for 17: 17—10-7. *Say:* 17 is 1 ten and 7 ones.

- Write the subtraction sentence on the board with 17 as a number bond, as shown in the Student Book. Bring children's attention to the positions of 10 and 7, and explain that 7 is placed on the right, nearest to 3 because the next step involves subtracting 3 from 7.

- Show children the subsequent steps in solving the problem.

Guided Practice

**Group the numbers into a 10 and ones.
Then subtract.**

1 17 – 5 = 12

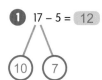

(10) (7)

2 18 – 3 = 15

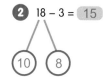

(10) (8)

**Solve the riddle.
Subtract, then write the letter on the correct line.**

3 13 – 3 = (10) **T**   17 – 6 = (11) **S**

15 – 3 = (12) **H**   18 – 5 = (13) **W**

16 – 1 = (15) **E**   19 – 3 = (16) **I**

17 – 0 = (17) **U**   18 – 4 = (14) **O**

Where does the President of the United States live?

THE <u>W</u> <u>H</u> <u>I</u> <u>T</u> <u>E</u>
     13   12   16   10   15

<u>H</u> <u>O</u> <u>U</u> <u>S</u> <u>E</u>
12   14   17   11   15

204 Chapter 8 Addition and Subtraction Facts to 20

Student Book A p. 204

Problem of the Lesson

Mom has 13 eggs in a basket.
She breaks 5 eggs into a bowl.
How many eggs are left in the basket?

Solution

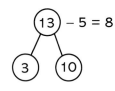

(13) – 5 = 8

(3) (10)

Answer: 8 eggs are left in the basket.

Differentiated Instruction

English Language Learners

The direction line on page 204 contains the term *riddle*. Explain that a riddle is like a problem. Riddles often ask a question. Help children find the answer to the question: 'Where does the President of the United States live?' Read the question and have children follow along, pointing to each word. Tell children that the answer to each subtraction problem is also one of the numbers below. When they find the number below, they write the letter that is next to that number above. Demonstrate with the first problem if necessary.

Best Practices Many children will be able to break numbers into tens and ones without visual or physical models. Others may still need support. Have available counters, ten frames, base-ten materials or any other manipulatives that will help children act out the subtraction strategies in this lesson.

Check for Understanding
✔ **Guided Practice** (page 204)

1 and **2** Check that children write the number bonds with the correct positions of the 10 and ones before they subtract.

3 Write the first subtraction sentence on the board and show children that they can subtract without drawing the number bonds, by looking at the ones digit in the two numbers. Guide children in completing the solution to the riddle.

For Advanced Learners You may want to suggest that groups of children use their state, city, or school names to make up a similar riddle to share with the class. Children would then work backwards to write the corresponding number sentences for the letters in the answer.

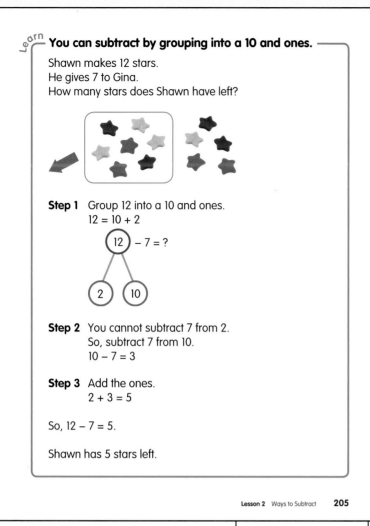

Learn You can subtract by grouping into a 10 and ones.

Shawn makes 12 stars.
He gives 7 to Gina.
How many stars does Shawn have left?

Step 1 Group 12 into a 10 and ones.
12 = 10 + 2

(12) – 7 = ?

(2) (10)

Step 2 You cannot subtract 7 from 2.
So, subtract 7 from 10.
10 – 7 = 3

Step 3 Add the ones.
2 + 3 = 5

So, 12 – 7 = 5.

Shawn has 5 stars left.

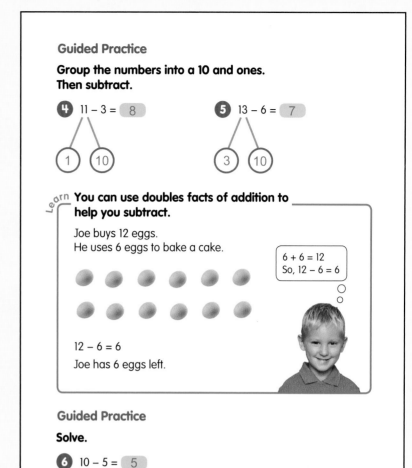

Guided Practice

**Group the numbers into a 10 and ones.
Then subtract.**

④ 11 – 3 = 8   ⑤ 13 – 6 = 7

(1) (10)   (3) (10)

Learn You can use doubles facts of addition to help you subtract.

Joe buys 12 eggs.
He uses 6 eggs to bake a cake.

6 + 6 = 12
So, 12 – 6 = 6

12 – 6 = 6
Joe has 6 eggs left.

Guided Practice

Solve.

⑥ 10 – 5 = 5

⑦ 14 – 7 = 7

Learn

Subtract by Grouping into a 10 and Ones
(page 205)

In this section, children learn to subtract from the 10 in the number bond of the minuend.

• Show two different subtraction problems: 17 − 3 and 12 − 7.

• Ask children to state the difference between the two problems. Help them by writing the number bonds for 17 and 12 with 10 on the left and the ones on the right. Explain that while they can subtract 3 from 7, they cannot subtract 7 from 2.

• Reverse the positions of 10 and 2 in the 12—10-2 number bond and show children that they can subtract 7 from 10 now.

• Show children the next step of adding the ones to give the answer.

✓ **Guided Practice** (page 206)

④ and ⑤ Check that children write the number bonds with the 10 after the ones. Guide them to subtract from 10, before adding the ones.

Learn

Subtract Using Doubles Facts of Addition
(page 206)

Children learned about fact families in Chapter 4. They can apply addition facts to solve subtraction problems.

• Draw 12 eggs on the board arranged in two rows, with 6 in each row.

• *Ask:* Can you make a doubles fact from this picture?
(6 + 6 = 12)

• Read the word problem in the Student Book, and explain how the doubles fact of addition can be used to find the answer.

✓ **Guided Practice** (page 206)

⑥ and ⑦ Ask children to provide the doubles facts for 10 and 14 before they subtract.

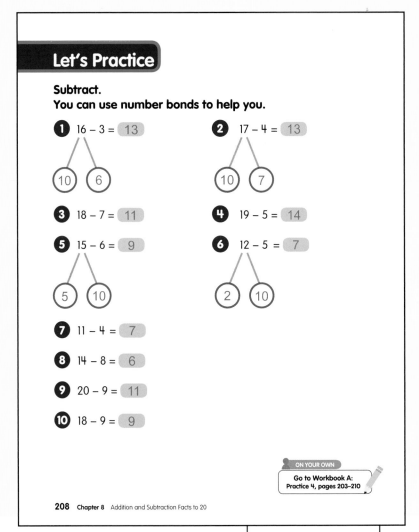

Teach See the Lesson Organizer on page 203 for Day 2 resources.

 **Game:**

Spin and Subtract! (page 207)

This activity provides additional practice subtracting 1-digit numbers from 2-digit numbers.

- Arrange children in groups of three and give each group **Spinner A and B** (TR14).

- Explain the steps in the Student Book. Check that children can evaluate the number sentences correctly.

Let's Practice (page 208)

This practice reinforces the use of different subtraction strategies to solve problems. Exercises ❶ to ❹ require children to subtract the ones after grouping into 10 and ones.

Exercises ❺ to ❾ require children to subtract from the 10 of the minuend.

Exercise ❿ can be solved by grouping into 10 and ones or by using a doubles fact of addition.

Common Error
Some children may have incorrect answers because they use the wrong operations. After breaking down the 2-digit number into a ten and ones, they *subtract* the ones. Then they *add* the difference to 10. Some children may subtract from 10 thinking that it is a subtraction problem. Review the correct procedure with children who make these errors.

ON YOUR OWN

Children practice the different subtraction strategies to subtract 1-digit numbers from 2-digit numbers in Practice 4, pp. 203–210 of **Workbook 1A**. These pages (with the answers) are shown on pages 208A and 208B.

Differentiation Options
Depending on children's success with the Workbook pages, use these materials as needed.
Struggling: Reteach 1A, pp. 137–142
On Level: Extra Practice 1A, pp. 125–130

Practice and Apply

Workbook pages for Chapter 8, Lesson 2

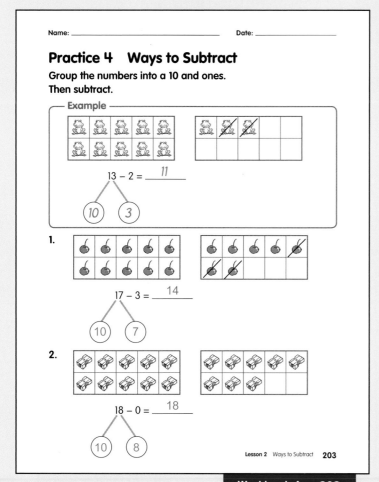

Name: _____   Date: _____

Practice 4   Ways to Subtract

Group the numbers into a 10 and ones.
Then subtract.

Example

13 – 2 = ___11___
(10) (3)

1.

17 – 3 = ___14___
(10) (7)

2.

18 – 0 = ___18___
(10) (8)

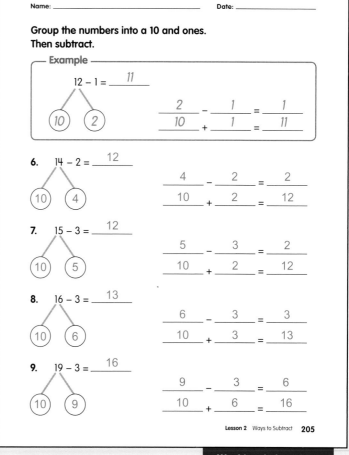

Name: _____   Date: _____

Group the numbers into a 10 and ones.
Then subtract.

Example

12 – 1 = ___11___
(10) (2)

2 – 1 = 1
10 + 1 = 11

6.   14 – 2 = ___12___
(10) (4)

4 – 2 = 2
10 + 2 = 12

7.   15 – 3 = ___12___
(10) (5)

5 – 3 = 2
10 + 2 = 12

8.   16 – 3 = ___13___
(10) (6)

6 – 3 = 3
10 + 3 = 13

9.   19 – 3 = ___16___
(10) (9)

9 – 3 = 6
10 + 6 = 16

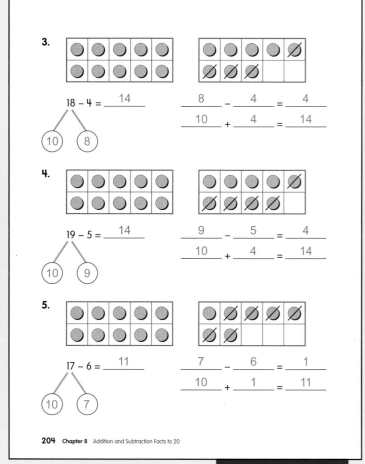

3.

18 – 4 = ___14___
(10) (8)

8 – 4 = 4
10 + 4 = 14

4.

19 – 5 = ___14___
(10) (9)

9 – 5 = 4
10 + 4 = 14

5.

17 – 6 = ___11___
(10) (7)

7 – 6 = 1
10 + 1 = 11

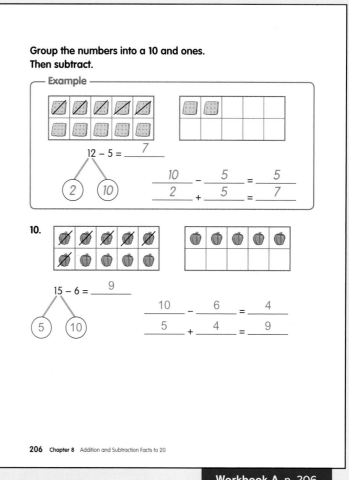

Group the numbers into a 10 and ones.
Then subtract.

Example

12 – 5 = ___7___
(2) (10)

10 – 5 = 5
2 + 5 = 7

10.

15 – 6 = ___9___
(5) (10)

10 – 6 = 4
5 + 4 = 9

Workbook A p. 207

Name: _____ Date: _____

11.

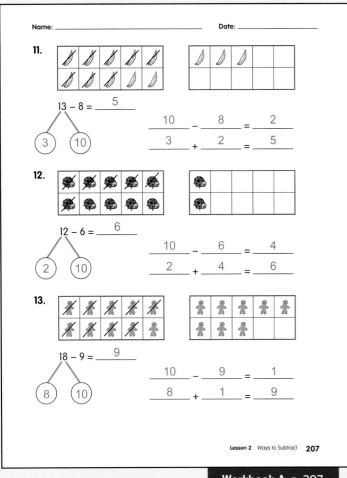

$13 - 8 = \underline{5}$

3   10

$\underline{10} - \underline{8} = \underline{2}$

$\underline{3} + \underline{2} = \underline{5}$

12.

$12 - 6 = \underline{6}$

2   10

$\underline{10} - \underline{6} = \underline{4}$

$\underline{2} + \underline{4} = \underline{6}$

13.

$18 - 9 = \underline{9}$

8   10

$\underline{10} - \underline{9} = \underline{1}$

$\underline{8} + \underline{1} = \underline{9}$

Lesson 2   Ways to Subtract   **207**

Workbook A p. 207

Workbook A p. 209

Name: _____ Date: _____

Complete each subtraction sentence.

17.

$\underline{15} - \underline{6} = \underline{9}$

5   10

18.

$\underline{11} - \underline{5} = \underline{6}$

1   10

19.

$\underline{13} - \underline{8} = \underline{5}$

3   10

Lesson 2   Ways to Subtract   **209**

Workbook A p. 209

Workbook A p. 208

Complete each subtraction sentence.

14.

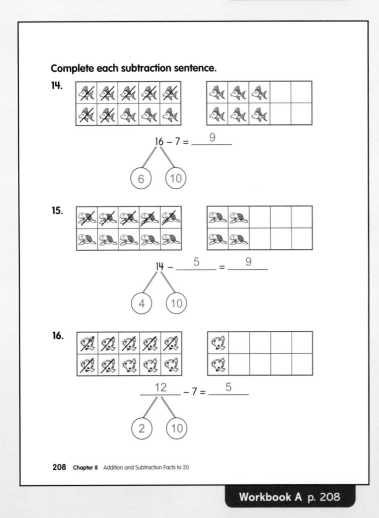

$16 - 7 = \underline{9}$

6   10

15.

$14 - \underline{5} = \underline{9}$

4   10

16.

$\underline{12} - 7 = \underline{5}$

2   10

208   **Chapter 8**   Addition and Subtraction Facts to 20

Workbook A p. 208

Workbook A p. 210

Complete the number bonds.
Subtract.

20. $16 - 6 = \underline{10}$

10   6

21. $14 - 7 = \underline{7}$

4   10

Solve.

22. Which number fell into the number machine?
Write the number in ◯.

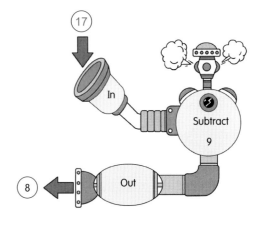

17

In

Subtract
9

8

Out

210   **Chapter 8**   Addition and Subtraction Facts to 20

Workbook A p. 210

208B **CHAPTER 8: LESSON 2**

3 **Real-World Problems: Addition and Subtraction Facts**

LESSON OBJECTIVE
• Solve real-world problems.

TECHNOLOGY RESOURCES
• *Math in Focus* eBook
• *Math in Focus* Teaching Resources CD
• *Math in Focus* Virtual Manipulatives

DAY 1 Student Book 1A, pp. 209–214
Workbook 1A, pp. 211–212

MATERIALS
• 20 connecting cubes (10 of each color) for the teacher
• A copy of Puzzle Grids (TR15) for each child

DIFFERENTIATION RESOURCES
• Reteach 1A, pp. 143–146
• Extra Practice 1A, pp. 131–132

 5-minute Warm Up

Explain to the children that you will read some problems aloud, and they have to tell you whether to add or subtract to solve.

(a) There are 3 fish in a fish tank.
Tony puts in 5 more fish.
How many fish are in the tank now? (add)

(b) Mia has 3 pet hamsters and 8 pet goldfish.
How many pets does Mia have in all? (add)

(c) There are 8 children on a bus.
4 children get off.
How many children are left on the bus? (subtract)

(d) There are 5 boys and some girls at the park.
There are 9 children at the park.
How many girls are at the park? (subtract)

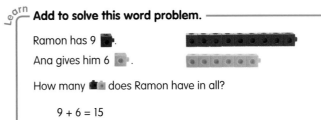 **3** **Real-World Problems: Addition and Subtraction Facts**

Lesson Objective
• Solve real-world problems.

Add to solve this word problem.

Ramon has 9 .
Ana gives him 6 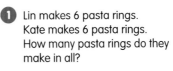.

How many does Ramon have in all?

9 + 6 = 15

Ramon has 15 in all.

Guided Practice

Solve.

1 Lin makes 6 pasta rings.
Kate makes 6 pasta rings.
How many pasta rings do they make in all?

6 + 6 = 12

They make 12 pasta rings in all.

Student Book A p. 209

DAY 1 # Teach

Add to Solve Word Problems (page 209)

Children have learned to add numbers within 20. In this section, they apply that knowledge to solve real-world problems.

• Join **connecting cubes** to make two number trains, one of 9 and the other of 6.

• Use the number trains to illustrate the concept of adding required in the problem on the page.

• Write the addition sentence.

• Encourage children to add using the counting on strategy and by making a 10 first.

Check for Understanding
✓ **Guided Practice** (page 209)

1 Have children write the addition sentence from the problem. Lead children to recognize that the two groups have the same number 6, so they can use a doubles fact to add.

Subtract to solve this word problem.

Ali has 16 clay shells.
He gives Mani 5 clay shells.
How many clay shells does Ali have left?

$16 - 5 = 11$

Ali has 11 clay shells left.

Guided Practice

Solve.

2 George has 11 paper clips.
3 paper clips are blue.
The rest are red.
How many paper clips are red?

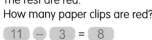

11 − 3 = 8

8 paper clips are red.

Let's Practice

Solve.

1 Terry picks 8 tomatoes.
Nan picks 8 tomatoes.
How many tomatoes do Terry
and Nan have in all?

8 + 8 = 16

They have 16 tomatoes in all.

210 **Chapter 8** Addition and Subtraction Facts to 20

Student Book A p. 210

Problem of the Lesson

Breanne has 14 coins. She drops some
coins into a box. She has 6 coins left.
How many coins does she drop into the
box?

Solution

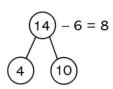

$14 - 6 = 8$

Answer: She drops 8 coins into the box.

Differentiated Instruction

English Language Learners

Remind children of common addition and subtraction
situations and discuss words that are often associated
with each situation. Some subtraction problems involve
taking away and use language such as *How many are
left?* Other subtraction problems compare two groups
that make one whole. Addition situations involve joining
groups and often ask *How many are there in all?*
Provide an example of each situation.

Best Practices You may wish to put children in pairs or small
groups to complete the word problems in the lesson. Make sure
each pair or group has at least one strong reader. Encourage
groups to identify the needed facts, discuss the operation that
should be used, and write the appropriate number sentence.
Mingle among groups and provide assistance.

Subtract to Solve Word Problems

(page 210)

Children have learned to subtract a 1-digit number from a
2-digit number. In this section, they apply that knowledge to
solve real-world problems.

• Read the problem in the Student Book.

• Guide children to recognize that this problem requires taking
away, or subtraction.

• Have children subtract the ones to find the difference.

✓ Guided Practice (page 210)

2 Read the problem. Explain the part-whole concept
related to the problem and lead children to write the
subtraction sentence from the problem and discuss which
subtraction strategy to use. (group into a 10 and ones,
subtract from the tens)`

Let's Practice (page 210)

This practice reinforces the use of different addition
and subtraction strategies to solve real-world problems.
Exercise **1** makes use of a doubles fact to add.

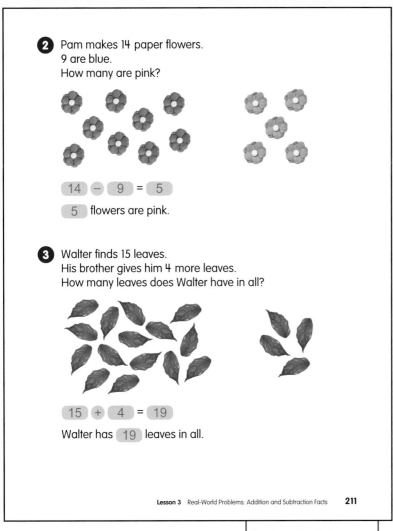

2 Pam makes 14 paper flowers.
9 are blue.
How many are pink?

$14 - 9 = 5$

5 flowers are pink.

3 Walter finds 15 leaves.
His brother gives him 4 more leaves.
How many leaves does Walter have in all?

$15 + 4 = 19$

Walter has 19 leaves in all.

Student Book A p. 211

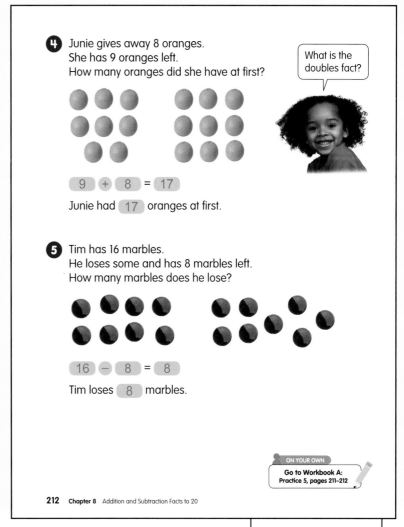

4 Junie gives away 8 oranges.
She has 9 oranges left.
How many oranges did she have at first?

What is the doubles fact?

$9 + 8 = 17$

Junie had 17 oranges at first.

5 Tim has 16 marbles.
He loses some and has 8 marbles left.
How many marbles does he lose?

$16 - 8 = 8$

Tim loses 8 marbles.

ON YOUR OWN
Go to Workbook A:
Practice 5, pages 211–212

Student Book A p. 212

Let's Practice (pages 211 and 212)

Exercise **2** uses the part-whole concept and requires subtraction from the 10 of the minuend.

Exercise **3** requires children to add by grouping into a 10 and ones.

Exercise **4** checks that children can apply the suitable doubles plus one fact.

Exercise **5** checks that children can apply the addition doubles fact to subtract.

For Advanced Learners Have children draw two groups of objects and write a pair of related addition and subtraction number sentences. Tell them to use the sentences to make up addition and subtraction story problems to share with classmates.

For example,

- Sal has 5 yellow balloons and 8 red balloons. How many balloons does he have in all? (5 + 8 = 13)

- Sal has 13 red and yellow balloons. He gives all 8 red balloons away. How many yellow balloons does he have left? (13 − 8 = 5)

Common Error Children may have trouble deciding which operation to use when they see pictures of two groups of objects. Remind them of the part-part-whole relationship. Suggest that they ask themselves what the whole is, and what the parts are. Then children can use the pictures to help decide where the parts and whole belong in the number sentence.

ON YOUR OWN

Children practice using the different addition and subtraction strategies to solve real-world problems in Practice 5, pp. 211–212 of **Workbook 1A**. These pages (with the answers) are shown on page 213.

Differentiation Options Depending on children's success with the Workbook pages, use these materials as needed.
Struggling: Reteach 1A, pp. 143–146
On Level: Extra Practice 1A, pp. 131–132

Practice and Apply
Workbook pages for Chapter 8, Lesson 3

Name: _____ Date: _____

Practice 5 Real-World Problems: Addition and Subtraction Facts

Solve.

1. Mandy has 5 toy bears.
   She also has 5 toy dogs.
   How many toys does she
   have in all?

   $5 + 5 = 10$

   Mandy has ___10___ toys in all.

2. 6 children are on the
   merry-go-round.
   6 more children join them.
   How many children are
   there now?
   $6 + 6 = 12$

   There are ___12___ children now.

3. Sam has 8 marbles.
   Lamont gives him 9 marbles.
   How many marbles does Sam
   have now?

   $8 + 9 = 17$

   Sam has ___17___ marbles now.

Workbook A p. 211

---

4. Sue has 13 green ribbons
   and red ribbons.
   5 ribbons are green.
   How many red ribbons
   does Sue have?

   $13 - 5 = 8$

   Sue has ___8___ red ribbons.

5. Malika makes 12 bracelets.
   She sells some bracelets.
   She has 4 bracelets left.
   How many bracelets does
   Malika sell?

   $12 - 4 = 8$

   Malika sells ___8___ bracelets.

6. Al makes 16 butterfly knots.
   He gives 9 butterfly knots to
   his friends.
   How many butterfly knots
   does Al have left?

   $16 - 9 = 7$

   Al has ___7___ butterfly knots left.

Workbook A p. 212

READING AND WRITING MATH
Math Journal

Look at the people around you.
Write an addition or subtraction story about them.
Use a number bond to help you.

Example

There are 12 children in my class.
3 children have blonde hair.
The rest have brown hair.
How many children have brown hair?

$12 - 3 = 9$

___9___ children have brown hair.

Chapter 8 Addition and Subtraction Facts to 20 **213**

Student Book A p. 213

READING AND WRITING MATH
Math Journal (page 213)

This journal activity provides children with the opportunity to identify and reflect addition and subtraction situations in the world around them.

- Read aloud the subtraction story in the Student Book and guide children to solve the problem.

- Encourage children to create an addition or subtraction story about the people around them. Have them share their story with a classmate and check each other's solutions. Their numbers should be within 20.

- Help children recall the different addition and subtraction situations including the concepts of part-whole, adding on, and taking away.

Let's Explore!
Make Fact Families (page 214)

This exploration leads children to experiment with different combinations of numbers within a given set to make number sentences and fact families. Encourage children to recall number bonds. Through this activity, children gain confidence in adding and subtracting numbers within 20.

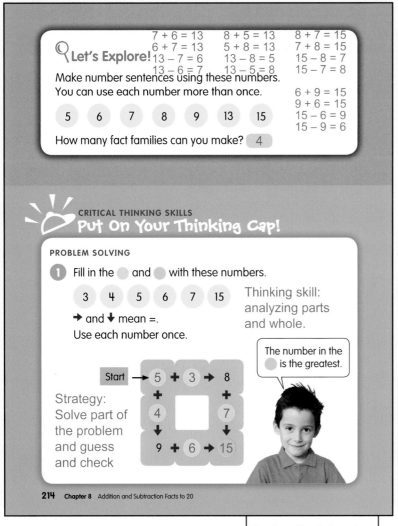

Let's Explore!

Make number sentences using these numbers.
You can use each number more than once.

5 6 7 8 9 13 15

$7 + 6 = 13$ $8 + 5 = 13$ $8 + 7 = 15$
$6 + 7 = 13$ $5 + 8 = 13$ $7 + 8 = 15$
$13 - 7 = 6$ $13 - 8 = 5$ $15 - 7 = 8$
$13 - 6 = 7$ $13 - 5 = 8$ $15 - 8 = 7$

$6 + 9 = 15$
$9 + 6 = 15$
$15 - 6 = 9$
$15 - 9 = 6$

How many fact families can you make? 4

CRITICAL THINKING SKILLS
Put On Your Thinking Cap!

PROBLEM SOLVING

1 Fill in the ⬤ and ⬤ with these numbers.

3 4 5 6 7 15

Thinking skill: analyzing parts and whole.

→ and ↓ mean =.
Use each number once.

The number in the ⬤ is the greatest.

Strategy: Solve part of the problem and guess and check

Start → 5 + 3 → 8
         +   +
         4   7
         ↓   ↓
         9 + 6 → 15

214 **Chapter 8** Addition and Subtraction Facts to 20

Student Book A p. 214

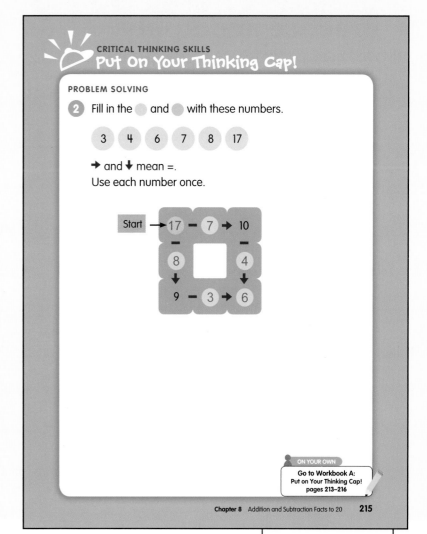

CRITICAL THINKING SKILLS
Put On Your Thinking Cap!

PROBLEM SOLVING

2 Fill in the ⬤ and ⬤ with these numbers.

3 4 6 7 8 17

→ and ↓ mean =.
Use each number once.

Start → 17 − 7 → 10
         −   −
         8   4
         ↓   ↓
         9 − 3 → 6

ON YOUR OWN
Go to Workbook A:
Put on Your Thinking Cap!
pages 213–216

Chapter 8 Addition and Subtraction Facts to 20 215

Student Book A p. 215

CRITICAL THINKING AND PROBLEM SOLVING
Put on Your Thinking Cap!
(pages 214 and 215)

Exercise 1 uses children's abilities to connect numbers that form addition facts and to use logical understanding.

- Arrange children in groups of 4. Give each child a copy of the **Puzzle Grids** (TR15).

- Read and explain the problem to children.

- Help children see that the orange circle should contain the greatest number, which is 15.

- Guide children to use number bonds for 8, 9, and 15 to solve the problem.

Exercise 2 provides an opportunity to connect numbers that form subtraction facts and to apply logical reasoning.

- Help children see that the orange circle should contain the greatest number, which is 17.

- Guide children to use number bonds for 9 and 10 to solve the problem.

Thinking Skill

- Analyzing parts and whole

Problem Solving Strategies

- Guess and check
- Solve part of the problem

ON YOUR OWN

Because all children should be challenged, have all children try the Challenging Practice and Problem-Solving pages in **Workbook 1A**, pp. 213–216. These pages (with the answers) are shown on page 215A.

Differentiation Options Depending on children's success with the Workbook pages, use these materials as needed.
On Level: Extra Practice, pp. 133–134
Advanced: Enrichment 1A, pp. 59–65

Practice and Apply

Workbook pages for Put on Your Thinking Cap!

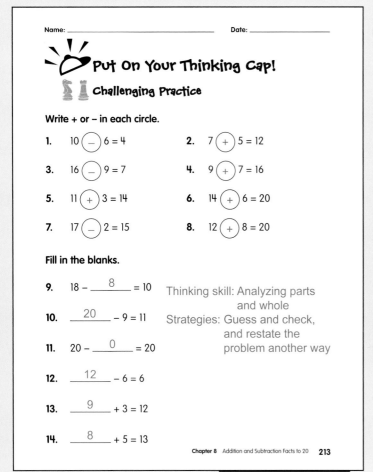

Name: _____ Date: _____

Put On Your Thinking Cap!
Challenging Practice

Write + or − in each circle.

1. 10 $\ominus$ 6 = 4
2. 7 $\oplus$ 5 = 12
3. 16 $\ominus$ 9 = 7
4. 9 $\oplus$ 7 = 16
5. 11 $\oplus$ 3 = 14
6. 14 $\oplus$ 6 = 20
7. 17 $\ominus$ 2 = 15
8. 12 $\oplus$ 8 = 20

Fill in the blanks.

9. 18 − __8__ = 10
10. __20__ − 9 = 11
11. 20 − __0__ = 20
12. __12__ − 6 = 6
13. __9__ + 3 = 12
14. __8__ + 5 = 13

Thinking skill: Analyzing parts and whole
Strategies: Guess and check, and restate the problem another way

Chapter 8 Addition and Subtraction Facts to 20 **213**

Workbook A p. 213

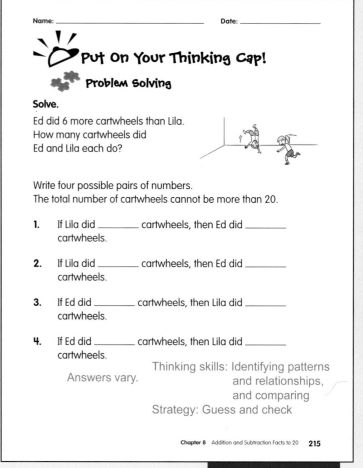

Name: _____ Date: _____

Put On Your Thinking Cap!
Problem Solving

Solve.

Ed did 6 more cartwheels than Lila.
How many cartwheels did
Ed and Lila each do?

Write four possible pairs of numbers.
The total number of cartwheels cannot be more than 20.

1. If Lila did _____ cartwheels, then Ed did _____ cartwheels.
2. If Lila did _____ cartwheels, then Ed did _____ cartwheels.
3. If Ed did _____ cartwheels, then Lila did _____ cartwheels.
4. If Ed did _____ cartwheels, then Lila did _____ cartwheels.

Answers vary.

Thinking skills: Identifying patterns and relationships, and comparing
Strategy: Guess and check

Chapter 8 Addition and Subtraction Facts to 20 **215**

Workbook A p. 215

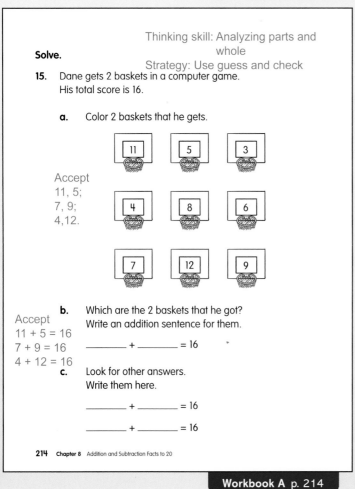

Thinking skill: Analyzing parts and whole
Strategy: Use guess and check

Solve.

15. Dane gets 2 baskets in a computer game.
His total score is 16.

a. Color 2 baskets that he gets.

11	5	3
4	8	6
7	12	9

Accept
11, 5;
7, 9;
4, 12.

b. Which are the 2 baskets that he got?
Write an addition sentence for them.

Accept
11 + 5 = 16
7 + 9 = 16
4 + 12 = 16

_____ + _____ = 16

c. Look for other answers.
Write them here.

_____ + _____ = 16

_____ + _____ = 16

214 Chapter 8 Addition and Subtraction Facts to 20

Workbook A p. 214

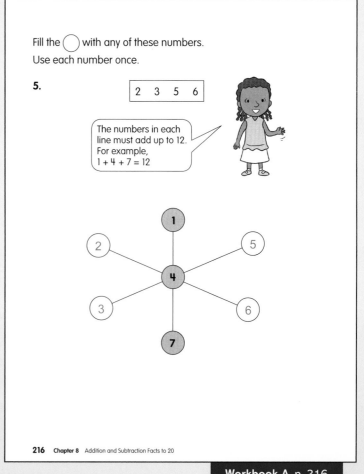

Fill the ◯ with any of these numbers.
Use each number once.

5.

| 2 | 3 | 5 | 6 |

The numbers in each line must add up to 12.
For example,
1 + 4 + 7 = 12

(Diagram: center circle 4, with spokes to circles 1, 2, 5, 3, 6, 7)

216 Chapter 8 Addition and Subtraction Facts to 20

Workbook A p. 216

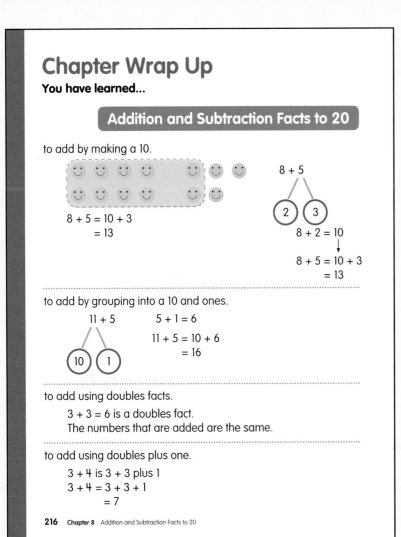

Chapter Wrap Up

You have learned...

Addition and Subtraction Facts to 20

to add by making a 10.

$8 + 5$

$8 + 5 = 10 + 3$
$\quad\quad = 13$

$8 + 2 = 10$

$8 + 5 = 10 + 3$
$\quad\quad = 13$

to add by grouping into a 10 and ones.

$11 + 5$

$5 + 1 = 6$

$11 + 5 = 10 + 6$
$\quad\quad\quad = 16$

to add using doubles facts.

$3 + 3 = 6$ is a doubles fact.
The numbers that are added are the same.

to add using doubles plus one.

$3 + 4$ is $3 + 3$ plus 1
$3 + 4 = 3 + 3 + 1$
$\quad\quad = 7$

216   **Chapter 8** Addition and Subtraction Facts to 20

Student Book A p. 216

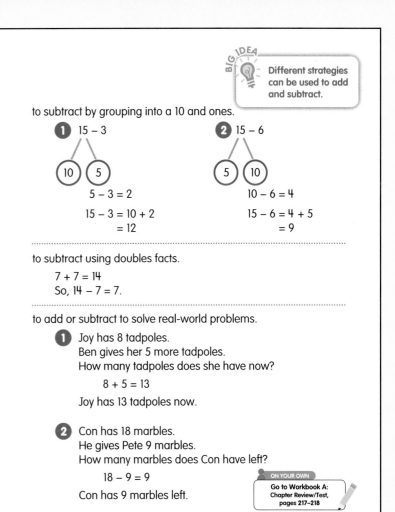

BIG IDEA Different strategies can be used to add and subtract.

to subtract by grouping into a 10 and ones.

1 $15 - 3$

10   5

$5 - 3 = 2$
$15 - 3 = 10 + 2$
$\quad\quad = 12$

2 $15 - 6$

5   10

$10 - 6 = 4$
$15 - 6 = 4 + 5$
$\quad\quad = 9$

to subtract using doubles facts.

$7 + 7 = 14$
So, $14 - 7 = 7$.

to add or subtract to solve real-world problems.

1 Joy has 8 tadpoles.
Ben gives her 5 more tadpoles.
How many tadpoles does she have now?

$8 + 5 = 13$

Joy has 13 tadpoles now.

2 Con has 18 marbles.
He gives Pete 9 marbles.
How many marbles does Con have left?

$18 - 9 = 9$

Con has 9 marbles left.

ON YOUR OWN
Go to Workbook A:
Chapter Review/Test,
pages 217–218

Chapter 8 Addition and Subtraction Facts to 20   **217**

Student Book A p. 217

Chapter Wrap Up (pages 216 and 217)

Review addition and subtraction strategies and facts to 20 with the examples on these pages. Help children recall that they can add two 1-digit numbers by making a 10, using doubles facts or doubles plus one. They can add a 2-digit number and a 1-digit number by grouping into a 10 and ones. Review subtraction strategies of subtracting by grouping into a 10 and ones, and using doubles facts. Help children recall that the position of the parts in a number bond depend on the magnitude of the subtrahend. As you work through the examples, encourage children to use the chapter vocabulary:

- group
- same
- doubles fact
- doubles plus one

ON YOUR OWN

Have children review the vocabulary, concepts and skills from Chapter 8 with the Chapter Review/Test in **Workbook 1A,** pp. 217–218. These pages (with the answers) are shown on page 217A.

Assessment

Use the Chapter 8 Test Prep on pages 60–63 of **Assessments 1** to assess how well children have learned the material of this chapter. This assessment is appropriate for reporting results to adults at home and administrators. This test is shown on page 217B.

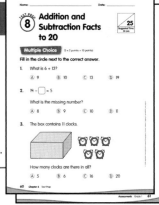

Assessments 1 pp. 60–63

Workbook pages for Chapter Review/Test

Name: _____ Date: _____

Chapter Review/Test

Vocabulary

Circle the correct answers.

1. Which numbers are the <u>same</u>?

   (4)   9   6   0   (4)

2. Which fact is a doubles fact?

   9 + 1 = 10   4 + 8 = 12   (9 + 9 = 18)

3. Which fact is a doubles plus one fact?

   (1 + 2 = 3)   3 + 3 = 6   9 + 2 = 11

Concepts and Skills

Fill in the blanks.

4. 6 + 5 = ___11___   5. 9 + 6 = ___15___

Complete the number bonds.
Then fill in the blanks.

6. 15 + 4 = ___19___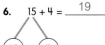

   (10)   (5)

7. 6 + 14 = ___20___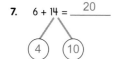

   (4)   (10)

8. 16 – 4 = ___12___

   (10)   (6)

9. 14 – 8 = ___6___

   (4)   (10)

Workbook A p. 217

Fill in the blanks.

10. 11 + 9 = ___20___   11. 12 – 5 = ___7___

Problem Solving

Solve.

12. Andy has 9 stickers.
    His sister gives him 5 more.
    How many stickers does
    Andy have in all?

    9 + 5 = 14

    Andy has ___14___ stickers in all.

13. Tia has 14 hair clips.
    She gives 7 hair clips to her sister.
    How many hair clips does Tia
    have left?

    14 – 7 = 7

    Tia has ___7___ hair clips left.

14. I am double 6 plus 1 more.
    What number am I?

    6 + 6 + 1 = 13

    I am the number ___13___.

Workbook A p. 218

Notes

Assessments Book pages for Chapter 8 Test Prep

Answer key appears in Assessments Book.

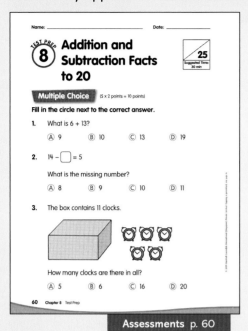

Name: _____ Date: _____

TEST PREP 8 — Addition and Subtraction Facts to 20

25 Suggested Time: 30 min

Multiple Choice (5 x 2 points = 10 points)

Fill in the circle next to the correct answer.

1. What is 6 + 13?
   Ⓐ 9   Ⓑ 10   Ⓒ 13   Ⓓ 19

2. $14 - \Box = 5$

   What is the missing number?
   Ⓐ 8   Ⓑ 9   Ⓒ 10   Ⓓ 11

3. The box contains 11 clocks.

   How many clocks are there in all?
   Ⓐ 5   Ⓑ 6   Ⓒ 16   Ⓓ 20

60   Chapter 8   Test Prep

Assessments p. 60

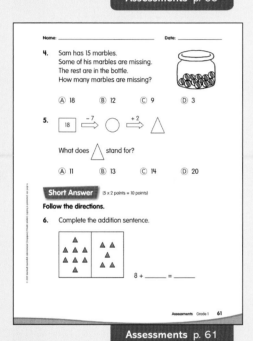

Name: _____ Date: _____

4. Sam has 15 marbles.
   Some of his marbles are missing.
   The rest are in the bottle.
   How many marbles are missing?

   Ⓐ 18   Ⓑ 12   Ⓒ 9   Ⓓ 3

5. $18 \xrightarrow{-7} \bigcirc \xrightarrow{+2} \triangle$

   What does $\triangle$ stand for?

   Ⓐ 11   Ⓑ 13   Ⓒ 14   Ⓓ 20

Short Answer (5 x 2 points = 10 points)

Follow the directions.

6. Complete the addition sentence.

   $8 + \underline{\hspace{1cm}} = \underline{\hspace{1cm}}$

Assessments   Grade 1   **61**

Assessments p. 61

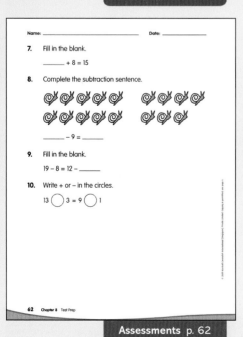

Name: _____ Date: _____

7. Fill in the blank.
   $\underline{\hspace{1cm}} + 8 = 15$

8. Complete the subtraction sentence.

   $\underline{\hspace{1cm}} - 9 = \underline{\hspace{1cm}}$

9. Fill in the blank.
   $19 - 8 = 12 - \underline{\hspace{1cm}}$

10. Write + or − in the circles.
    $13 \bigcirc 3 = 9 \bigcirc 1$

62   Chapter 8   Test Prep

Assessments p. 62

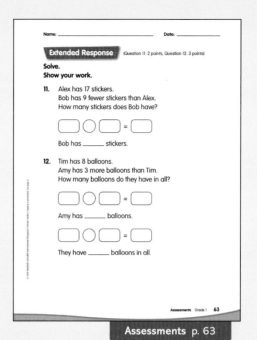

Name: _____ Date: _____

Extended Response (Question 11: 2 points, Question 12: 3 points)

Solve.
Show your work.

11. Alex has 17 stickers.
    Bob has 9 fewer stickers than Alex.
    How many stickers does Bob have?

    ⬜ ◯ ⬜ = ⬜

    Bob has _____ stickers.

12. Tim has 8 balloons.
    Amy has 3 more balloons than Tim.
    How many balloons do they have in all?

    ⬜ ◯ ⬜ = ⬜

    Amy has _____ balloons.

    ⬜ ◯ ⬜ = ⬜

    They have _____ balloons in all.

Assessments   Grade 1   **63**

Assessments p. 63

Notes

CHAPTER 9

Chapter Overview

Length

Math Background

As an introduction to measuring length, children compare the lengths of two objects both directly (by comparing them with each other) and indirectly (by comparing both with a third object), and they order several objects according to length. Their spatial awareness is exercised by having them recognize vertical length as height, when children learn to compare the length and height of objects in the classroom and the real-world.

As children progress to measuring length, the basic idea is to determine how many times a specific unit fits the object to be measured. The smaller the unit, the more precise the measurement. In this chapter, non-standard units are used to measure length. Measuring by laying multiple copies of a unit end to end and then counting the units by using groups of tens and ones supports children's understanding of number relationships. Children can compare the height and length of things by comparing the magnitude of the number of units used in measurement. It requires children to integrate their understanding of number, measurement, and geometry. This prepares children for measuring with standardized units and measurement systems.

Cross-Curricular Connections

Reading/Language Arts The first three lessons in this chapter focus on comparative and superlative vocabulary. Remind students that the *–er* ending means *more* and the *–est* ending means *most*. Take this opportunity to preview the vocabulary in the chapter (*tall, short, long* with *–er* and *–est* endings). Encourage children to name other comparatives and superlatives that they know.

Social Studies Point out the locations of mountains and rivers on a map of the United States. *Say:* Three *tall* mountains in the United States are Mt. McKinley (Alaska), Mt. Whitney (California), and Mt. Elbert (Colorado). Three *long* rivers are the Missouri, the Mississippi, and the Rio Grande. The mountains and rivers are listed in decreasing order. Use the terms *tall/taller/tallest* and *long/longer/longest* to compare these mountains and rivers.

Skills Trace

Grade K	Compare and order lengths and heights using non-standard units. (Chap. 15)
Grade 1	Compare the height and length of more than two things. Measure and compare using non-standard units. (Chap. 9)
Grade 2	Measure and compare length and height in metric and customary units. (Chaps. 7 and 13)

EVERY DAY COUNTS® Calendar Math

The January activities provide...

Review using the doubles and doubles + 1 addition strategies (Chapter 8)

Preview of picture graphs (Chapter 11)

Practice comparing quantities (Lessons 1 and 2 in this chapter)

Differentiation Resources

Differentiation for Special Populations

	English Language Learners	Struggling Reteach 1A	On Level Extra Practice 1A	Advanced Enrichment 1A
Lesson 1	p. 222	pp. 147–154	pp. 135–136	Enrichment pages can be used to challenge advanced children.
Lesson 2	p. 227	pp. 155–160	pp. 137–140	
Lesson 3	p. 232	pp. 161–162	pp. 141–142	
Lesson 4	p. 235	pp. 163–166	pp. 143–144	
Lesson 5	p. 241	pp. 167–170	pp. 145–150	

Additional Support

For English Language Learners

Select activities that reinforce the chapter vocabulary and the connections among these words, such as having children

- add terms, definitions, and examples to the Word Wall
- use sticky notes to label sets of objects with comparison terms
- play charades to act out and guess terms
- discuss the Chapter Wrap Up, encouraging children to use the chapter vocabulary

For Struggling Learners

Select activities that go back to the appropriate stage of the Concrete-Pictorial-Abstract spectrum, such as having children

- identify groups of students using comparison terms
- use manipulatives to act out and describe how to measure length
- draw pictures of estimated lengths, then check using non-standard units
- guess and check lengths of classroom objects using estimation and non-standard units

See also pages 228–229

If necessary, review:
- Chapter 1 (Numbers to 10)
- Chapter 7 (Numbers to 20).

For Advanced Learners

See suggestions on page 235.

Assessment and Remediation

Chapter 9 Assessment

Prior Knowledge

	Resource	Page numbers
Quick Check	Student Book 1A	p. 220
Pre-Test	Assessments 1	p. 64

Ongoing Diagnostic

Guided Practice	Student Book 1A	pp. 221, 222, 227, 228, 234, 235, 236, 240, 241, 242
Common Error	Teacher's Edition 1A	pp. 225, 230, 233, 238, 239, 244, 245
Best Practices	Teacher's Edition 1A	p. 227

Formal Evaluation

Chapter Review/Test	Workbook 1A	pp. 243–246
Chapter 9 Test Prep	Assessments 1	pp. 65–69
Cumulative Review for Chapters 7 to 9	Workbook 1A	pp. 247–252
Mid-Year Test	Workbook 1A	pp. 253–263
Mid-Year Test Prep	Extra Practice 1A	pp. 153–164
Mid-Year Test	Assessments 1	pp. 70–82

Remediation Options

	Problems with these items...		Can be remediated with...	
	Review/Test Items	Chapter Assessment Items	Reteach	Student Book
Objective	**Workbook 1A pp. 1–20**	**Assessments 1 pp. 65–69**	**Reteach 1A**	**Student Book 1A**
Use chapter vocabulary correctly.	1	Not assessed	pp. 148–170	pp. 221, 226, 231, 234, 240
Compare two lengths.	1	6, 12–13	pp. 148–154	Lesson 1
Compare more than two lengths.	2, 3, 7–8, 9	4, 7–8	pp. 155–160	Lesson 2
Use a common point when comparing lengths.	3		pp. 161–162	Lesson 3
Measure lengths using non-standard units, and understand that using different non-standard units may give different measurements for the same item.	4	1, 10, 14–15	pp. 163–166	Lesson 4
Use the term 'unit' to describe length and count measurement units in a group of ten and ones.	4, 5–8	2, 3, 5, 9, 11–15	pp. 167–170	Lesson 5

Chapter Planning Guide

9 Length

Lesson	Pacing	Instructional Objectives	Vocabulary
Chapter Opener pp. 218–220 Recall Prior Knowledge Quick Check *78*	*1 day	💡**Big Idea** Compare the height and length of things. Measure with non-standard units to find length.	
Lesson 1, pp. 221–225 Comparing Two Things *79*	1 day	• Compare two lengths using the terms tall/taller, long/longer, and short/shorter	• tall/taller • short/ shorter • long/longer
Lesson 2, pp. 226–230 Comparing More Than Two Things *80*	1 day	• Compare two lengths by comparing each with a third length • Compare more than two lengths using the terms tallest, longest, and shortest	• tallest • shortest • longest
Lesson 3, pp. 231–233 *81* Using a Start Line	1 day	• Use a common starting point when comparing lengths	• start line
Lesson 4, pp. 234–239 Measuring Things *82 83*	2 days	• Measure lengths using non-standard units • Understand that using different non-standard units may give different measurements for the same item	• about

*Assume that 1 day is a 45–55 minute period.

Resources	Materials	NCTM Focal Points	NCTM Process Standards
Student Book 1A, pp. 218–220 **Assessments 1,** p. 64			
Student Book 1A, pp. 221–225 **Workbook 1A,** pp. 219–222 **Extra Practice 1A,** pp. 135–136 **Reteach 1A,** pp. 147–154	• 20 connecting cubes (10 of one color) for the teacher • 40 connecting cubes (20 of one color) per group • 20 paper clips (10 of each color) for the teacher	*Number and Operations* Solve problems involving measurement and data	Communication Connections
Student Book 1A, pp. 226–230 **Workbook 1A,** pp. 223–228 **Extra Practice 1A,** pp. 137–140 **Reteach 1A,** pp. 155–160	• 40 connecting cubes (10 of each color) per group	*Number and Operations* Solve problems involving measurement and data	Reasoning/Proof Connections
Student Book 1A, pp. 231–233 **Workbook 1A,** pp. 229–230 **Extra Practice 1A,** pp. 141–142 **Reteach 1A,** pp. 161–162	• Fish Cut-Outs (TR16) for the teacher • Copy of Strips of Paper per child (TR17) • crayons • pair of scissors per child	*Number and Operations* Solve problems involving measurement and data	Problem Solving Reasoning/Proof Communication
Student Book 1A, pp. 234–239 **Workbook 1A,** pp. 231–234 **Extra Practice 1A,** pp. 143–144 **Reteach 1A,** pp. 163–166	• Copy of Strips of Paper (TR17) per child • 1 set of Strips for Measuring (TR18) per pair • 20 craft sticks per group • 20 paper clips for the teacher • pieces of paper • pair of scissors per child	*Number and Operations* Solve problems involving measurement and data	Problem Solving Reasoning/Proof Communication Connections

Chapter Planning Guide

Lesson	Pacing	Instructional Objectives	Vocabulary
Lesson 5, pp. 240–246 *84* Finding Length in Units	1 day	• Use the term "unit" to describe length • Count measurement units in a group of ten and ones	• unit
Problem Solving p. 247 *85* Put on Your Thinking Cap!	1 day	Thinking Skills • Comparing Problem Solving Strategies: • Act it out • Use a diagram	
Chapter Wrap Up pp. 248–249 *86*	1 day	• Reinforce and consolidate chapter skills and concepts	
Chapter Assessment *87*	1 day		
Review *88*			

*Assume that 1 day is a 45–55 minute period.

Resources	Materials	NCTM Focal Points	NCTM Process Standards
Student Book 1A, pp. 240–246 **Workbook 1A,** pp. 235–238 **Extra Practice 1A,** pp. 145–150 **Reteach 1A,** pp. 167–170	• 20 craft sticks per group • Measurement Table (TR19) • 20 paper clips per group • long umbrella for classroom demonstration	***Number and Operations*** Measure by laying multiple copies of a unit end to end and then count the units by using groups of tens and ones	Problem Solving Reasoning/Proof Connections Representation
Student Book 1A, p. 247 **Workbook 1A,** pp. 239–242 **Extra Practice 1A,** pp. 151–152 **Enrichment 1A,** pp. 66–74		***Measurement*** Solve non-routine length problems	Problem Solving Reasoning/Proof
Student Book 1A, pp. 248–249 **Workbook 1A,** pp. 243–246			
Assessments 1, pp. 65–69			
Workbook 1A, p. 247–252 **Workbook 1A,** pp. 253–263 **Extra Practice 1A,** pp. 153–164 **Assessments 1,** pp. 70–82			

Technology Resources for easy classroom management
• *Math in Focus* eBook
• *Math in Focus* Teaching Resources CD
• *Math in Focus* Virtual Manipulatives
• On-Line Web Resources

CHAPTER

9 Length

Chapter 9
Vocabulary

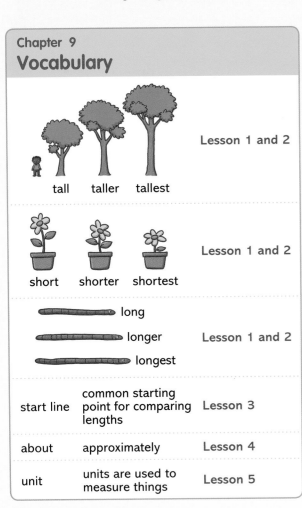

tall taller tallest	Lesson 1 and 2
short shorter shortest	Lesson 1 and 2
long longer longest	Lesson 1 and 2
start line	common starting point for comparing lengths	Lesson 3
about	approximately	Lesson 4
unit	units are used to measure things	Lesson 5

Student Book A p. 218

💡 Big Idea (page 218)

Comparing the height and length of things and measuring is the main focus of this unit.

• Children compare lengths and heights using terms such as *tall/taller/tallest, long/longer/longest,* and *short/shorter/shortest.*

• Children use common objects as non-standard units to measure and compare length.

Chapter Opener (page 218)

The picture provides a situation for children to observe and compare height and length. Children learned in Kindergarten to compare the length and height of up to three objects directly by comparing them with each other. Then they learned to measure height and length using non-standard units. Finally, they compared the length between two objects using non-standard units. In this chapter, these concepts will not only be reinforced, children will also be introduced to the concept of using units to measure length.

• Have children look at the picture and talk about what they see.

• *Ask:* How are the two girls alike? (same clothes) How are they different? (one is taller and has longer hair)

• Ask similar questions about the other pairs of objects in the picture: sunflowers, bones, houses, trees, spades, dogs' tails, and worms.

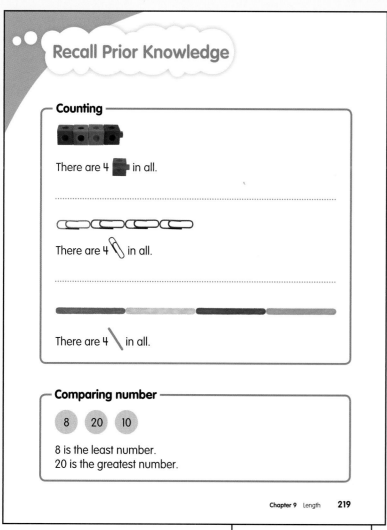

Student Book A p. 219

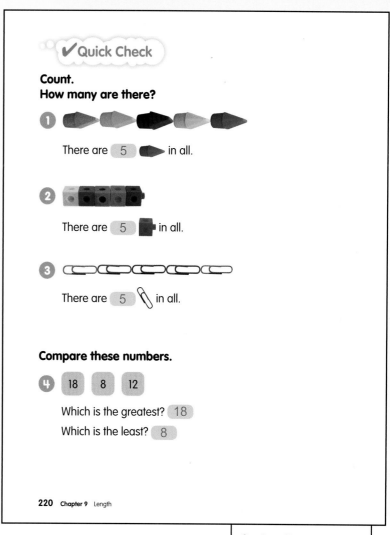

Student Book A p. 220

- Lead children to compare the lengths of the dogs and potted plants and *say:* They have the same length (height).

Recall Prior Knowledge (page 219)

Counting

Children learned in Chapter 7 to count to 20.

- Have children count the connecting cubes in the picture.

- Have children count the paper clips and craft sticks in the picture.

- Point out even though the number of each object is the same, the lengths are different. This prepares them for measuring length by counting non-standard units.

Comparing Numbers

Children learned in Chapter 7 to compare more than two numbers up to 20, using *greatest* and *least*.

- Write the numbers 8, 20 and 10 on the board.

- *Ask:* Which number is the least? (8)
Which number is the greatest? (20)

- Repeat with another set of three numbers, if necessary.

✔Quick Check (page 220)

Use this section as a diagnostic tool to assess children's level of prerequisite knowledge before they progress to this chapter. The exercise on this page assesses counting and comparing skills.

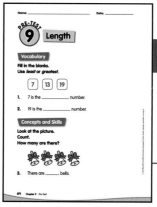

Assessments 1 p. 64

Assessment

For additional assessment of children's prior knowledge and chapter readiness, use the Chapter 9 Pre-Test on page 64 of **Assessments 1**.

1 Comparing Two Things

LESSON OBJECTIVE
• Compare two lengths using the terms tall/taller, long/longer, and short/shorter.

TECHNOLOGY RESOURCES
• *Math in Focus* eBook
• *Math in Focus* Teaching Resources CD
• *Math in Focus* Virtual Manipulatives

Vocabulary

tall	taller
short	shorter
long	longer

DAY 1 Student Book 1A, pp. 221–225
Workbook 1A, pp. 219–222

MATERIALS
• 20 connecting cubes (10 of each color) for the teacher
• 40 connecting cubes (10 of each color) per group of 4 children
• 20 paper clips (10 of each color) for the teacher

DIFFERENTIATION RESOURCES
• Reteach 1A, pp. 147–154
• Extra Practice 1A, pp. 135–136

 5-minute Warm Up

• Ask two volunteers to use **connecting cubes** to each make a number train of any number from 1 to 10.

• Put the two trains next to each other. Have children compare the two number trains and say which has more cubes.

• Now provide 20 paper clips, and have two volunteers make paper clip chains of any number from 1 to 10.

• Have children compare the two chains by putting them next to each other.

• Lead children to see that the *more* cubes or paper clips, the *longer* the train or chain.

---

1 Comparing Two Things

Lesson Objective
• Compare two lengths using the terms tall/taller, long/longer, and short/shorter.

Vocabulary

tall	taller
short	shorter
long	longer

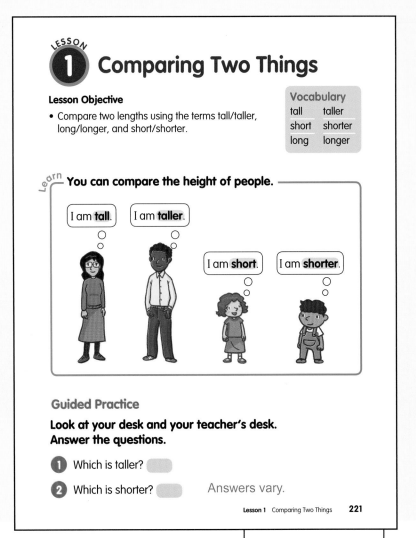

Learn You can compare the height of people.

I am **tall**. I am **taller**. I am **short**. I am **shorter**.

Guided Practice

Look at your desk and your teacher's desk.
Answer the questions.

1 Which is taller? [   ]

2 Which is shorter? [   ]   Answers vary.

Lesson 1 Comparing Two Things **221**

Student Book A p. 221

DAY 1 ## Teach

Learn
Compare the Height of People (page 221)

Children compare height using the terms *tall/taller* and *short/shorter*.

• Ask children what they understand by the terms *tall*, *short*, *taller* and *shorter*.

• Use the example in the Student Book to explain each term.

• Invite pairs of volunteers to the front of the classroom and have other children compare their heights. Model the following statements: (name) is tall. (name) is taller. (name) is taller than (name). (name) is short. (name) is shorter. (name) is shorter than (name).

• Explain to children that *tall/short* are relative terms and not labels, and that children grow taller at different rates.

Check for Understanding
✓ **Guided Practice** (page 221)

1 and **2** Guide children to see that *taller* and *shorter* are opposites when comparing the length of two objects.

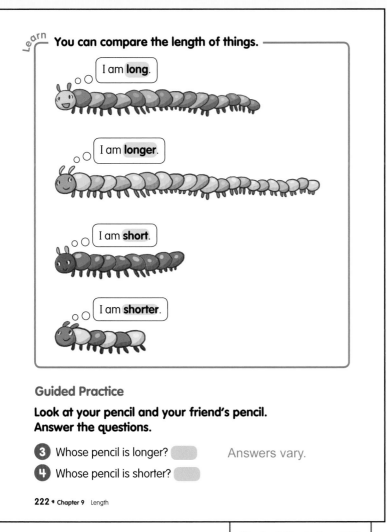

Learn **You can compare the length of things.**

I am **long**.

I am **longer**.

I am **short**.

I am **shorter**.

Guided Practice

Look at your pencil and your friend's pencil.
Answer the questions.

3 Whose pencil is longer? ▢   Answers vary.

4 Whose pencil is shorter? ▢

222 • **Chapter 9** Length

Student Book A p. 222

Student Book A p. 222

Problem of the Lesson

Which is shorter?
- (a) a tree or a branch
- (b) a house or a skyscraper
- (c) an adult or a baby
- (d) an onion or a carrot

Answers:
- (a) branch
- (b) house
- (c) baby
- (d) onion

Differentiated Instruction

English Language Learners

Some children may not understand the difference between *long* and *tall*. They might not realize that *short* is used as the opposite of both *long* and *tall*. Discuss these ideas with children and create a graphic organizer to reinforce the concepts visually. Draw a pair of different-length horizontal lines and label them *longer* and *shorter*. Draw another pair of different-length vertical lines and label them *taller* and *shorter*.

Learn

Compare the Length of Things (page 222)

- Children compare length using the terms *long/longer* and *short/shorter*.

- Make two different colored number trains using **connecting cubes** and have children compare the length. *Say:* The (color) train is long. The (color) train is longer.

- Remove some cubes to make the trains shorter, then compare the length using *short* and *shorter*. *Say:* The (color) train is short. The (color) train is shorter.

- Repeat using paper clip chains, if necessary.

- Talk about the examples in the Student Book to give children more practice using the terms *long/longer* and *short/shorter*.

✓ Guided Practice (page 222)

3 and **4** Guide children to see that *longer* and *shorter* are opposites when comparing the length of two objects.

Best Practices   The focus of this lesson is comparing two things. You may want to group children in pairs to complete the entire lesson. They can act out the concepts on pages 221 and 222. On page 223, partners can take turns constructing the towers as directed.

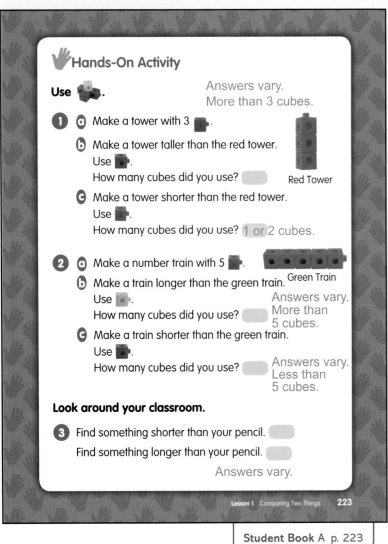

Hands-On Activity

Use 🧊.

Answers vary.
More than 3 cubes.

1. a) Make a tower with 3 🧊.
   b) Make a tower taller than the red tower.
      Use 🧊.
      How many cubes did you use? [   ]

   Red Tower

   c) Make a tower shorter than the red tower.
      Use 🧊.
      How many cubes did you use? 1 or 2 cubes.

2. a) Make a number train with 5 🧊.
   b) Make a train longer than the green train.
      Use 🧊.
      How many cubes did you use? [   ]

   Green Train

   Answers vary.
   More than
   5 cubes.

   c) Make a train shorter than the green train.
      Use 🧊.
      How many cubes did you use? [   ]

   Answers vary.
   Less than
   5 cubes.

Look around your classroom.

3. Find something shorter than your pencil. [   ]
   Find something longer than your pencil. [   ]

   Answers vary.

Student Book A p. 223

Let's Explore!

👥 **WORK IN PAIRS**

Papa Cat and Little Cat are sewing!
Talk about this picture with a friend.
Use these words.

Answers vary.

tall | taller
long | longer
short | shorter

> Little Cat's tail is long.
> Papa Cat's tail is longer.

Student Book A p. 224

✋ Hands-On Activity:

Make Towers and Number Trains with Connecting Cubes (page 223)

The activities in ① and ② let children use **connecting cubes** to vary the height of number towers or length of number trains. They help to show the difference between *tall* (vertical) and *long* (usually horizontal).

- Arrange children in groups of four and provide 40 connecting cubes each (10 of each color).
- Guide children through the steps in the Student Book. Explain that they may have different answers to the questions in ⓑ and ⓒ.

Find a Thing Shorter and Longer Than Your Pencil (page 223)

In ③, children observe the things around them and compare the length of different objects.

🔍 Let's Explore! (page 224)

Talk About a Picture Using Height and Length Words

- Arrange children in pairs.
- Encourage children to talk about the length and height of the various objects in the picture using the helping words given.
- Model the activity by giving one or more examples:
  - Papa Cat and Little Cat have long tails.
  - Papa Cat has a longer tail than Little Cat.
  - The blue hat is shorter than the purple hat.

Let's Practice

Look at the pictures.
Solve.

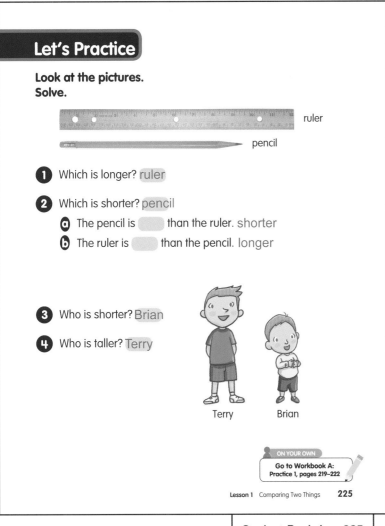

1. Which is longer? ruler
2. Which is shorter? pencil
   a. The pencil is ____ than the ruler. shorter
   b. The ruler is ____ than the pencil. longer

3. Who is shorter? Brian
4. Who is taller? Terry

Terry   Brian

ON YOUR OWN
Go to Workbook A:
Practice 1, pages 219–222

Lesson 1 Comparing Two Things **225**

Student Book A p. 225

Let's Practice (page 225)

This practice reinforces children's understanding of the concepts of *longer*, *taller*, and *shorter*. Exercises **1** and **2** use *longer/shorter* to compare length. Exercises **3** to **6** use *taller/shorter* to compare height.

Common Error If children confuse the terms *shorter* and *longer*, suggest that they write each term on a thin strip of paper. Have them place the "shorter" strip on the pencil and the "longer" strip on the ruler. As they complete the activity, the labels will help reinforce word meaning.

ON YOUR OWN

Children practice comparing two lengths using the terms *taller*, *longer*, and *shorter* in Practice 1, pp. 219–222 of **Workbook 1A**. These pages (with the answers) are shown at the right and on page 225A.

Differentiation Options Depending on children's success with the Workbook pages, use these materials as needed.
Struggling: Reteach 1A, pp. 147–154
On Level: Extra Practice 1A, pp. 135–136

Practice and Apply
Workbook pages for Chapter 9, Lesson 1

Name: _____   Date: _____

CHAPTER 9 Length

Practice 1 Comparing Two Things
Circle the correct answer.

— Example —
Which is longer?

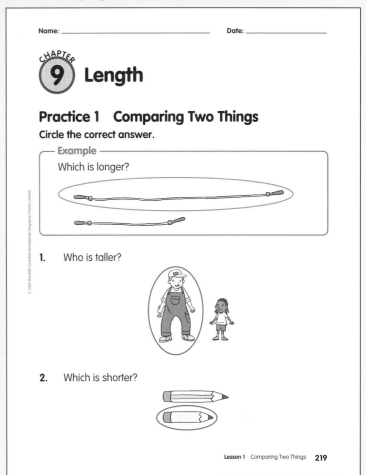

1. Who is taller?

2. Which is shorter?

Lesson 1 Comparing Two Things **219**

Workbook A p. 219

Fill in the blanks.

— Example —
Which is longer?
Which is shorter?

caterpillar   snake

The snake is _longer_ than the caterpillar.

The caterpillar is _shorter_ than the snake.

3. Which is shorter?
   Which is taller?

The giraffe is ___shorter___ than the tree.

The tree is ___taller___ than the giraffe.

220 Chapter 9 Length

Workbook A p. 220

Name: _____ Date: _____

4. Which is longer?
   Which is shorter

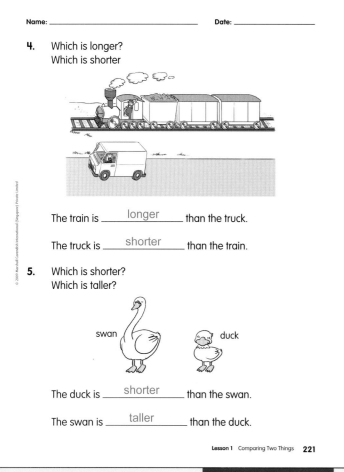

The train is ___longer___ than the truck.

The truck is ___shorter___ than the train.

5. Which is shorter?
   Which is taller?

swan   duck

The duck is ___shorter___ than the swan.

The swan is ___taller___ than the duck.

Workbook A p. 221

Draw.

┌─ **Example** ──────────────────────┐
│ a longer arrow   │
│ ───────────────▶   │
│ ──────────────────▶   │
└────────────────────────────────────┘

6. a shorter tree

   Accept all drawings of
   trees that are shorter.

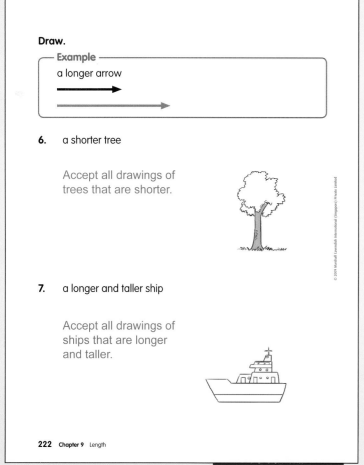

7. a longer and taller ship

   Accept all drawings of
   ships that are longer
   and taller.

Workbook A p. 222

Notes

Comparing More Than Two Things

LESSON OBJECTIVES

- Compare two lengths by comparing each with a third length.
- Compare more than two lengths using the terms tallest, longest, and shortest.

TECHNOLOGY RESOURCES

- *Math in Focus* eBook
- *Math in Focus* Teaching Resources CD
- *Math in Focus* Virtual Manipulatives

Vocabulary

tallest

shortest

longest

 DAY 1 Student Book 1A, pp. 226–230
Workbook 1A, pp. 223–228

MATERIALS

- 40 connecting cubes (10 of each color) per group

DIFFERENTIATION RESOURCES

- Reteach 1A, pp. 155–160
- Extra Practice 1A, pp. 137–140

 5-minute Warm Up

- Write three numbers on the board and ask children to compare them. Ask children to arrange the numbers from the greatest to the least.

- Draw three squares of different sizes, and name them A, B and C. Ask children to compare them by area and arrange them from smallest to largest.

Comparing More Than Two Things

Lesson Objectives

- Compare two lengths by comparing each with a third length.
- Compare more than two length using the terms tallest, longest, and shortest.

Vocabulary
tallest
shortest
longest

Learn You can compare the height of more than two people.

Chris is taller than Brandon.
Brandon is taller than Annie.
So, Chris is taller than Annie.

226 Chapter 9 Length

Student Book A p. 226

DAY 1 # Teach

Learn

Compare the Height of More Than Two People (page 226)

Children have learned to compare the height of two people. In this lesson, children will compare the height of more than two people.

- Read the example in the Student Book with children.

- Point out that they can compare the height of more than two people by comparing the height of any two at a time.

- Invite three volunteers to stand in front of the class, and ask children questions to model the situation in the picture.

- Apply the transitivity concept to the terms *short* and *shorter*.

- *Say:* Brandon is shorter than Chris. *Ask:* Who is shorter than Brandon? (Annie). Then, who else is Annie shorter than? (Chris)

Guided Practice

Fill in the blanks.

1

The red scarf is longer than the blue scarf.

The blue scarf is longer than the ▢ scarf. green

So, the red scarf is longer than the ▢ scarf. green

Learn **You can compare the height and length of more than two people or things.**

Annie   Brandon   Chris

Chris is the **tallest**.
Annie is the **shortest**.

Annie has the **longest** scarf.
Brandon has the **shortest** scarf.

Lesson 2 Comparing More Than Two Things **227**

Student Book A p. 227

Best Practices Throughout this lesson, children must correctly use the terms *tall* and *long*. You may want to precede the lesson with a review of the proper use of these terms. Identify objects in the classroom and point out that *tall* is used to describe things that are up and down. *Long* generally describes lengths of things that go left and right.

Check for Understanding

✓**Guided Practice** (page 227)

1 Guide children to deduce the answers to the third statement from the first and second.

Charlie is taller than Min.
Min is shorter than Leroy.
Leroy is shorter than Charlie.
 1. Who is the tallest?
 2. Who is the shortest?

Solution:

Charlie   Min   Leroy

Answers:
 1. Charlie
 2. Min

Differentiated Instruction

English Language Learners

Emphasize the difference between the *–er* and *–est* endings. Ask a child to stand next to you. Describe the situation using the terms *shorter* and *taller*. Relate that that there are two people being compared and the *–er* ending has two letters. Now have another child stand up and describe the situation using *tallest* and *shortest*. Point out that more than two people are being compared and the *–est* ending has more than two letters.

Learn

Compare the Height and Length of More Than Two People (page 227)

• Write the words *taller* and *tallest* on the board.

• Explain that when only two things are compared, *taller* is used. When more than two things are compared, *tallest* is used.

• Write *shorter/shortest* and *longer/longest* on the board, and explain the differences.

• Look at the picture and *ask:* Who is the tallest/shortest? (Chris/Annie) Who has the longest/shortest scarf? (Annie/Brandon).

Guided Practice

Look at the picture.
Answer the questions.

Pablo and Erin see some animals in the zoo.

2 Which is the tallest animal? giraffe

3 Which is the shortest animal? zebra

4 Which is the longest animal? crocodile

5 Which is the shortest animal? turtle

Student Book A p. 228

Hands-On Activity

Use 🎲.

1 Make four towers like this. Then place them in order. You may start with the tallest or the shortest tower.

2 Make a tower taller than the tallest tower. More than 5 connecting cubes tall.

3 Make a tower shorter than the shortest tower. One connecting cube tall.

Look around your classroom.
Find these things.

1 the longest thing

2 the tallest thing   Answers vary.

3 the shortest thing

Rearrange the letters to solve.

TEH   STAUTE   FO   LIEBRTY

Which is the longest word?
Liberty

Student Book A p. 229

✓ Guided Practice (page 228)

Exercises **2** to **5** Help children recall the difference between *tall* (vertical) and *long* (horizontal), then guide them to answer the questions. In Exercises **2** and **3**, children are comparing the *heights* of the animals (tallest/shortest). In Exercises **4** and **5**, they are comparing the *lengths* (longest/shortest) of the animals.

For Struggling Learners Children need to be able to identify all the animals in the illustration. You may want to read the names of all the animals (including the children's names) before children complete the exercises.

Hands-On Activity: 🎲

Make Towers with Connecting Cubes (page 229)

In this activity, children use **connecting cubes** to build towers of varying heights and then order the towers according to height.

• Arrange children in groups of four and provide 40 connecting cubes each (10 of each color).

• Guide children through the steps in the Student Book.

Find the Longest, Tallest, and Shortest Things in the Classroom (page 229)

• Ask children to complete **1** to **3** on their own first. They are likely to have different answers. Then have them compare their answers with other group members to reach a conclusion.

• Lead a discussion to compare the group's answers and decide together on the longest, tallest and shortest objects in the classroom.

• Have children solve the puzzle about the Statue of Liberty. Say that the Statue of Liberty is one of the tallest statues in the world.

Let's Practice

Compare.
Answer the questions.

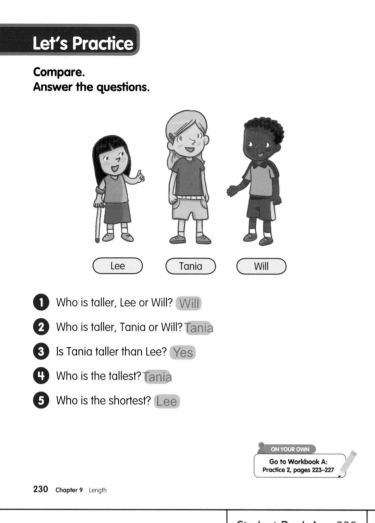

(Lee) (Tania) (Will)

1 Who is taller, Lee or Will? Will

2 Who is taller, Tania or Will? Tania

3 Is Tania taller than Lee? Yes

4 Who is the tallest? Tania

5 Who is the shortest? Lee

> **ON YOUR OWN**
> Go to Workbook A:
> Practice 2, pages 223–227

230 Chapter 9 Length

> **Student Book A** p. 230

Let's Practice (page 230)

This activity lets children practice comparing the height of more than two people. Exercises **1** to **3** require children to compare heights using *taller*, while Exercises **4** and **5** require children to compare heights using *tallest/shortest*.

Common Error If children have difficulty comparing the heights of the pictures of children, suggest that they align a ruler or other straight edge horizontally at the top of each picture. They can move the straight edge up and down to compare the heights.

> **ON YOUR OWN**
>
> Children practice comparing height and length in Practice 2, pp. 223–228 of **Workbook 1A**. These pages (with the answers) are shown at the right and on page 230A.
>
> **Differentiation Options** Depending on children's success with the Workbook pages, use these materials as needed.
> **Struggling:** Reteach 1A, pp. 155–160
> **On Level:** Extra Practice 1A, pp. 137–140

Practice and Apply
Workbook pages for Chapter 1, Lesson 2

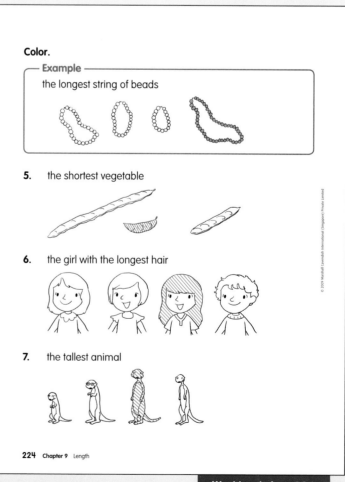

Name: _____ Date: _____

Practice 2   Comparing More Than Two Things
Look at the picture.
Fill in the blanks with the correct names.

Rolo   Lad   Biff

1. ____Lad____ is taller than Biff.

2. Biff is taller than ___Rolo___.

3. So, Lad is also taller than ___Rolo___.

Read.
Then draw the tails on the mouse and dog.

4. The mouse's tail is longer than the cat's tail.
   The cat's tail is longer the dog's tail.
   So, the mouse's tail is longer than the dog's tail.

Lesson 2 Comparing More Than Two Things **223**

> **Workbook A** p. 223

Color.

┌─ **Example** ─────────────
│ the longest string of beads
│
└───────────────────────────

5. the shortest vegetable

6. the girl with the longest hair

7. the tallest animal

224 Chapter 9 Length

> **Workbook A** p. 224

Name: _____ **Date:** _____

Fill in the blanks with *taller, tallest, shorter* or *shortest*.

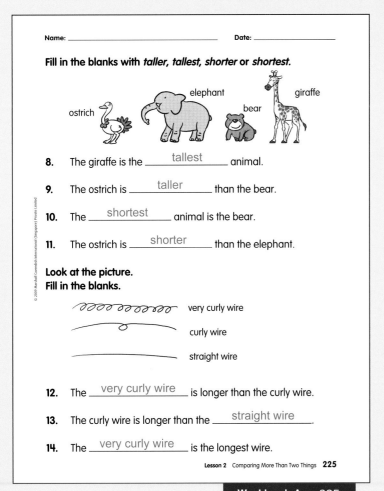

ostrich   elephant   bear   giraffe

8. The giraffe is the ____tallest____ animal.

9. The ostrich is ____taller____ than the bear.

10. The ____shortest____ animal is the bear.

11. The ostrich is ____shorter____ than the elephant.

Look at the picture.
Fill in the blanks.

very curly wire

curly wire

straight wire

12. The ____very curly wire____ is longer than the curly wire.

13. The curly wire is longer than the ____straight wire____.

14. The ____very curly wire____ is the longest wire.

Lesson 2   Comparing More Than Two Things   **225**

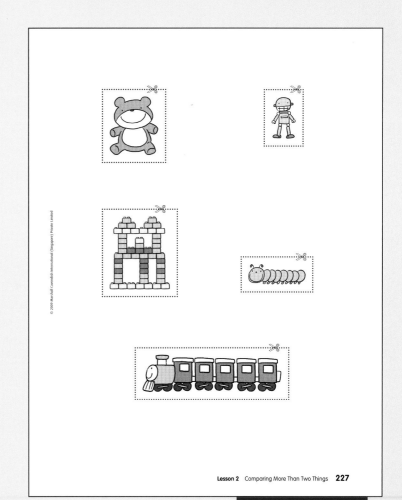

Lesson 2   Comparing More Than Two Things   **227**

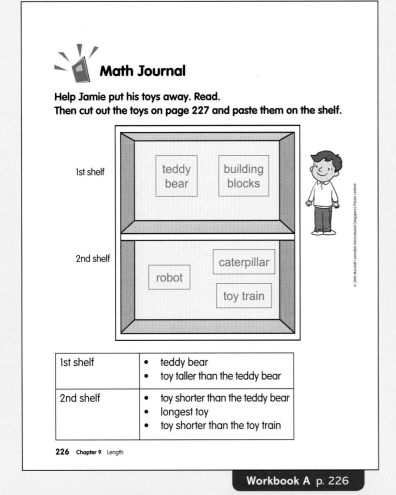

Math Journal

Help Jamie put his toys away. Read.
Then cut out the toys on page 227 and paste them on the shelf.

1st shelf — teddy bear / building blocks

2nd shelf — caterpillar / robot / toy train

1st shelf	• teddy bear • toy taller than the teddy bear
2nd shelf	• toy shorter than the teddy bear • longest toy • toy shorter than the toy train

226   Chapter 9   Length

BLANK

3 Using a Start Line

LESSON OBJECTIVE

- Use a common starting point when comparing lengths.

TECHNOLOGY RESOURCES

- *Math in Focus* eBook
- *Math in Focus* Teaching Resources CD
- *Math in Focus* Virtual Manipulatives

Vocabulary

start line

| **DAY 1** | Student Book 1A, pp. 231–233 |
| | Workbook 1A, pp. 229–230 |

MATERIALS

- Fish Cut-Outs for the teacher (TR16)
- copy of Strips of Paper per child (TR17)
- crayons of various colors per pair
- pair of scissors per child

DIFFERENTIATION RESOURCES

- Reteach 1A, pp. 161–162
- Extra Practice 1A, pp. 141–142

 5-minute Warm Up

- Ask for two groups of four volunteers. Tell them that the two groups are about to take part in a contest.

- Each child chooses one object in the classroom to form a line with other children in their group. The objective is for each group to make the longest possible line with objects found in the classroom. Give the children one minute to do this. Have the groups start at opposite sides of the room.

- Have the other children compare the length of the two lines and decide on the winning group.

- If it is difficult to tell which line is longer because they do not start at the same point, declare a tie, and proceed to the lesson on start lines.

Student Book A p. 231

DAY 1 Teach

Compare the Length of Things with a Start Line

(page 231)

Children have learned to compare the length and height of objects and people. Using a common starting point will help them compare the length of objects more accurately.

- Place the **Fish Cut-Outs** A, B, C, D, and E (TR16) on the board. Position them randomly as shown in the Student Book.

- Ask volunteers to order the fish according to their length, from the shortest to the longest. If children give different answers, accept them all for now.

- Then, draw a vertical line on the board and place the cut-out fish along the line, in random order. Now, ask children to order the fish according to their length again. Guide them to realize that it is easier now because of the start line.

- Have children look at the fish and the start line in the Student Book. Explain that the start line helps us compare the length of things more accurately when the difference in length is small.

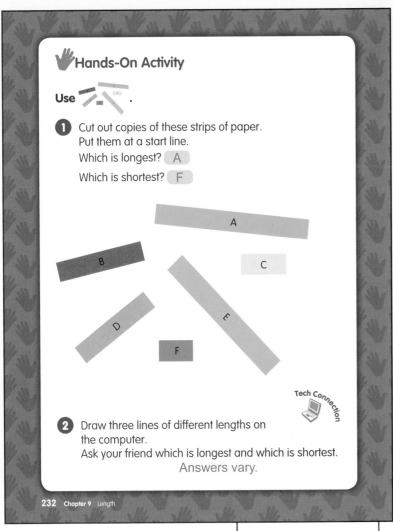

Hands-On Activity

Use .

1 Cut out copies of these strips of paper. Put them at a start line.

Which is longest? A

Which is shortest? F

2 Draw three lines of different lengths on the computer.
Ask your friend which is longest and which is shortest.
Answers vary.

Tech Connection

232 Chapter 9 Length

Student Book A p. 232

Hands-On Activity:
Compare the Lengths of Strips of Paper

(page 232)

This activity helps emphasize the importance of a start line when comparing lengths.

• Arrange children in pairs or have them work on their own. Provide each pair with a copy of **Strips of Paper** (TR17), scissors, and crayons.

• Have children cut out the strips and color them as shown on page 232.

• *Ask:* Which strip is the longest, What would help you to compare the strips?

• Have children draw a start line with a ruler on a blank piece of paper. Place the strips at the start line and compare the lengths.

• *Ask:* Which strip is longest? (A) Which strip is shortest? (F)

• Provide a place for children to keep the strips of paper for use in the Hands-On Activity on page 238 in Lesson 4.

Best Practices The Hands-On Activity requires making copies and cutting out strips of paper. You may want to have children work in pairs to complete this activity. Decide ahead of time how many copies you need to make and prepare a set of materials for each child or group. Include a ruler in each set of materials that children can use as the start line or to draw one.

Hands-On Activity:
Tech Connection
Draw Lines of Different Lengths on the Computer (page 232)

• Arrange children in pairs to use computers.

• Use a projector to model the activity in Exercise **2** on the teacher's computer.

• Have children draw lines on their computer and ask their partners to say which line is longest and which is shortest.

Let's Practice

Solve.

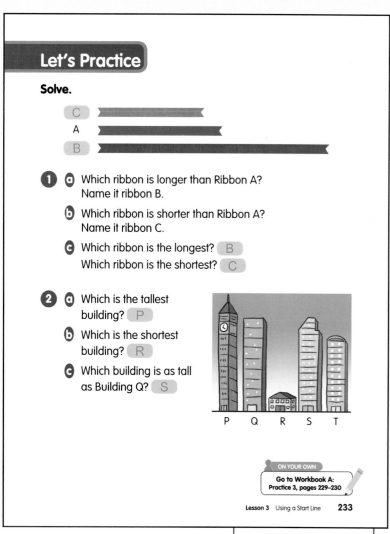

1. a. Which ribbon is longer than Ribbon A?
      Name it ribbon B.
   b. Which ribbon is shorter than Ribbon A?
      Name it ribbon C.
   c. Which ribbon is the longest? **B**
      Which ribbon is the shortest? **C**

2. a. Which is the tallest building? **P**
   b. Which is the shortest building? **R**
   c. Which building is as tall as Building Q? **S**

ON YOUR OWN
Go to Workbook A:
Practice 3, pages 229–230

Lesson 3 Using a Start Line **233**

Student Book A p. 233

Practice and Apply
Workbook pages for Chapter 9, Lesson 3

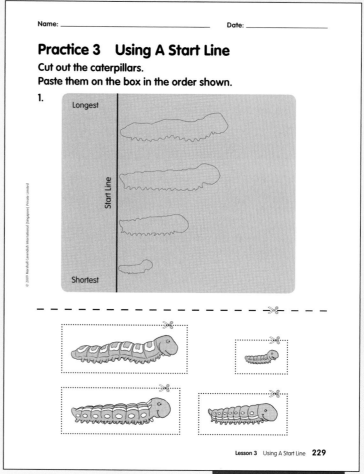

Name: _____   Date: _____

Practice 3   Using A Start Line
Cut out the caterpillars.
Paste them on the box in the order shown.

1.

Lesson 3 Using A Start Line **229**

Workbook A p. 229

Let's Practice (page 233)

In these exercises, children compare length and height using a start line. Exercise ❶ compares length from a start line while Exercise ❷ compares height, the ground being the start line.

Common Error Some children may not understand why a start line is used. Demonstrate by using three pencils of different lengths. Arrange the pencils so that they do not align on the left-hand side. Guide children to see that it is difficult to compare lengths if the objects are not aligned.

ON YOUR OWN

Children practice comparing length and height using a start line in Practice 3, pp. 229–230 of **Workbook 1A**. These pages (with the answers) are shown at the right.

Differentiation Options Depending on children's success with the Workbook pages, use these materials as needed.
Struggling: Reteach 1A, pp. 161–162
On Level: Extra Practice 1A, pp. 141–142

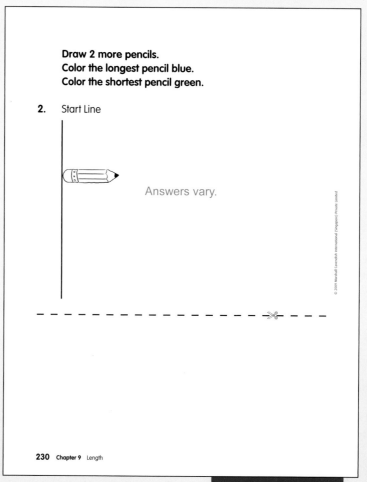

Draw 2 more pencils.
Color the longest pencil blue.
Color the shortest pencil green.

2.   Start Line

Answers vary.

230 Chapter 9 Length

Workbook A p. 230

4 Measuring Things

LESSON OBJECTIVES
• Measure lengths using non-standard units.
• Understand that using different non-standard units may give different measurements for the same item.

TECHNOLOGY RESOURCES
• *Math in Focus* eBook
• *Math in Focus* Teaching Resources CD
• *Math in Focus* Virtual Manipulatives

Vocabulary
about

DAY 1 Student Book 1A, pp. 234–237

MATERIALS
• 20 craft sticks per group of four children
• 20 paper clips for the teacher
• Copy of Strips of Paper (TR17) per child
• 1 set of Strips for Measuring (TR18) per pair
• pair of scissors per child

DAY 2 Student Book 1A, pp. 238–239
Workbook 1A, pp. 231–234

DIFFERENTIATION RESOURCES
• Reteach 1A, pp. 163–166
• Extra Practice 1A, pp. 143–144

 5-minute Warm Up

• Ask five volunteers of similar heights to form a human train in front of the class, with their hands on the shoulders of the child in front, arms outstretched. Have them turn to face the class.

• Lead children to notice that each child is evenly spaced from the children on either side.

• You join the line somewhere in the middle and have children adjust their positions.

• Lead children to notice that the space in front of you is longer than that behind you. Ask children why this is so.

• Explain that your arms, being longer than the other children's arms, kept you further apart from the child ahead of you.

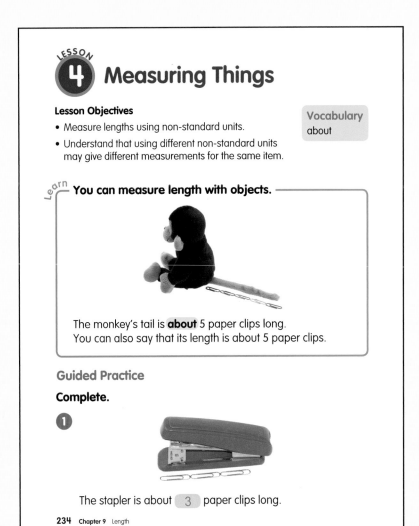

4 Measuring Things

Lesson Objectives
• Measure lengths using non-standard units.
• Understand that using different non-standard units may give different measurements for the same item.

Vocabulary
about

Learn You can measure length with objects.

The monkey's tail is **about** 5 paper clips long.
You can also say that its length is about 5 paper clips.

Guided Practice

Complete.

1

The stapler is about 3 paper clips long.

234 Chapter 9 Length

Student Book A p. 234

DAY 1 # Teach

Learn

Measure Length with Objects (page 234)

Children have not been formally taught to measure length. In this lesson they will learn to use objects as non-standard units to measure length, as an introduction to using standard units of measures later in Grade 2.

• One way to measure length is to compare the length to multiple copies of an object placed end-to-end.

• Ask children to look at the monkey's tail in the picture. Point out that paper clips are being used to measure the tail. Note that the paper clips are placed next to the tail one after another without overlapping. Ask children to find the length of the tail by counting the number of paper clips. (about 5)

• *Ask:* Why do we say *about* 5 paper clips? (it is not exactly the same length as 5 paper clips, it is longer)

Check for Understanding
✓ **Guided Practice** (page 234)

1 Have children count the paper clips. Lead children to observe the objects are placed end to end, without overlap or any gaps.

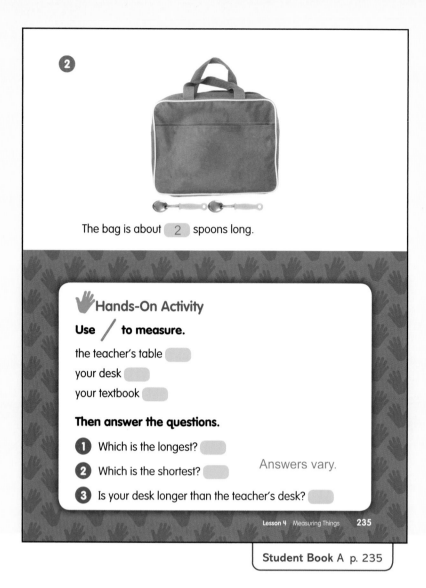

②

The bag is about ⟨2⟩ spoons long.

✋**Hands-On Activity**

Use / **to measure.**

the teacher's table ⬭

your desk ⬭

your textbook ⬭

Then answer the questions.

❶ Which is the longest? ⬭

❷ Which is the shortest? ⬭   Answers vary.

❸ Is your desk longer than the teacher's desk? ⬭

Lesson 4 *Measuring Things* **235**

Student Book A p. 235

✓Guided Practice (page 235)

② Have children count the spoons and fill in the answers.

Best Practices This lesson requires the use of several different manipulatives. Preview the lesson and make note of what you need. Gather the necessary materials and arrange them according to the activity in which they will be used. This will allow for the lesson to proceed smoothly and with little delay.

✋**Hands-On Activity:**

Measure Length with Craft Sticks (page 235)

• You may arrange children in groups of four or have them work on their own. Give each group or child 20 **craft sticks**.

• Ask children to measure the given objects using the craft sticks. Remind them to place the sticks end to end. Ensure they measure the length, which is the longer side of each object.

• Help children recall the terms *longer/longest* and *shorter/shortest*.

• Point out that using objects to measure length does not require a start line.

Problem of the Lesson

Alicia measures the length of her kitchen table using pens and pencils.
They look like this:

pen   pen   pencil pen   pencil

She says that the table is about 4 pens long.
Is she correct? Explain your answer.

Answer: No, she is not correct. She has to use the same item (pens or pencils), to measure.

Differentiated Instruction

English Language Learners

After gathering the materials needed for the lesson, introduce each item. Hold the item up, for example, a craft stick. *Say:* This is a craft stick. You will use it to measure a table, a desk, and a textbook. Point to a table, desk and textbook, if necessary. Continue with the other objects until children are familiar with the names of the materials they will use.

For Advanced Learners Give pairs of children a chart with a list of 4 or 5 other classroom objects such as the width of a door, or the height of a waste basket, and have them *estimate* (without measuring) about how many craft sticks long or high the objects are. Ask them to explain how they estimated each length before they check their estimates by measuring.

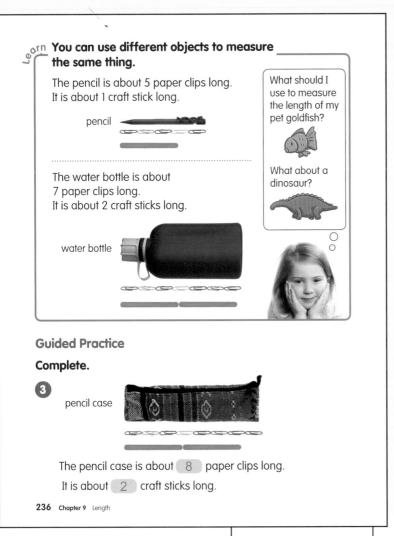

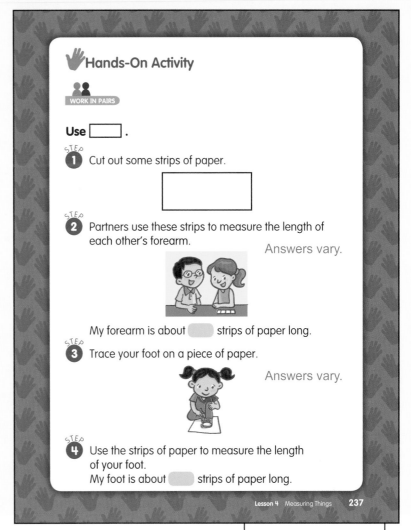

Use Different Objects to Measure the Same Thing (page 236)

Children use **craft sticks** and **paper clips** to measure the same object. They learn that there is a relationship between the length of a measuring object and the number of objects needed. They use this relationship to choose suitable objects to use for measurement.

- Ask a volunteer to measure his or her pencil using paper clips. Ask another volunteer to measure the same pencil using craft sticks. Write each answer on the board and *say:* The pencil is about ____ paper clips long. It is about ____ craft stick(s) long.

- Compare children's answers. Lead children to see that the first measurement is more than the second.

- Explain that this is because paper clips are shorter than craft sticks, so more paper clips are needed to measure the pencil.

- Emphasize that although the measurements obtained are different, the length of the object measured remains unchanged.

- Repeat the steps using a water bottle.

- *Ask:* What would you use to measure the length of a goldfish? (paper clips or something else small)

- *Ask:* What about a dinosaur? (cars, buses, or something else large)

✓Guided Practice (page 236)

❸ Have children count the paper clips and craft sticks to complete the exercise. Lead children to observe that by using craft sticks, the water bottle in the previous Learn box and the pencil case have the same length. But different lengths are obtained using paper clips. Explain that shorter objects can measure length more accurately.

✋Hands-On Activity:

Measure Length with Paper Strips (page 237)

- Arrange children in pairs. Give each pair a set of **Strips for Measuring** (TR18) and a pair of scissors.

- Read and explain the instructions in the Student Book.

- Have children discuss their findings. Lead them to realize that for many people, the lengths of their forearms and feet are about the same.

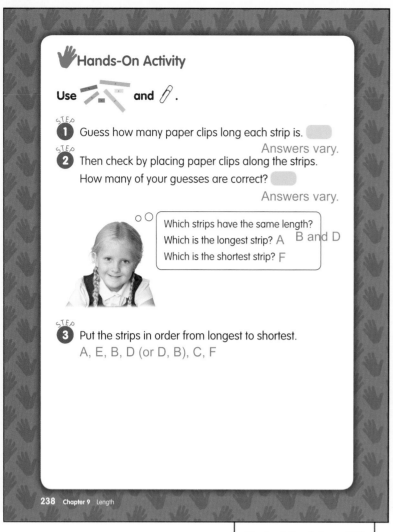

Student Book A p. 238

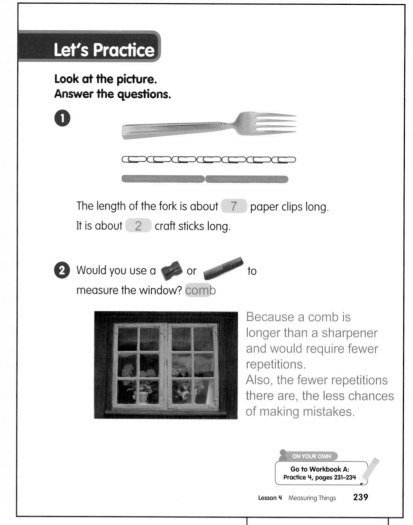

Student Book A p. 239

DAY 2 Teach

See the Lesson Organizer on page 234 for Day 2 resources.

Hands-On Activity:

Guess and Measure Length of Paper Strips with Paper Clips (page 238)

- Arrange children in pairs or have them work on their own. Ask each child to re-use **Strips of Paper** (TR17) that were prepared and used in the Hands-On Activity on page 232 in Lesson 3.

- Ask children to guess the length of each paper strip, before checking their answers using paper clips to measure.

- In **3**, explain that since Strips B and D are the same length, it does not matter in which order they are placed.

Let's Practice (page 239)

In these exercises, children practice measuring length using non-standard units. Exercise **1** uses different objects to measure the length of a fork. Exercise **2** checks if children can make a suitable choice of object to measure.

Lead children to see that although the pencil sharpener may give a more accurate measurement, more repetitions of the sharpener will be needed, so it may be easier to use the comb which is longer instead.

Common Error In Exercise **2**, ask questions to guide children to a decision. For example, **ask:** Which is shorter — the pencil sharpener or the comb? Would it take more time to measure the window with the pencil sharpener or the comb?

ON YOUR OWN

Children practice measuring length using objects as non-standard units in Practice 4, pp. 231–234 of **Workbook 1A**. These pages (with the answers) are shown on page 239A.

Differentiation Options Depending on children's success with the Workbook pages, use these materials as needed.
Struggling: Reteach 1A, pp. 163–166
On Level: Extra Practice 1A, pp. 143–144

Practice and Apply

Workbook pages for Chapter 9, Lesson 4

Name: _____ Date: _____

Practice 4 Measuring Things

Count.
Fill in the blanks.

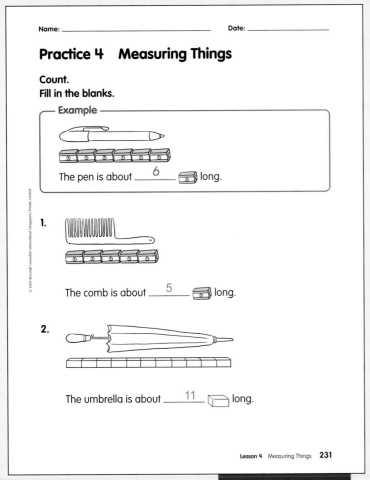

Example

The pen is about ___6___ long.

1.

The comb is about ___5___ long.

2.

The umbrella is about ___11___ long.

Workbook A p. 231

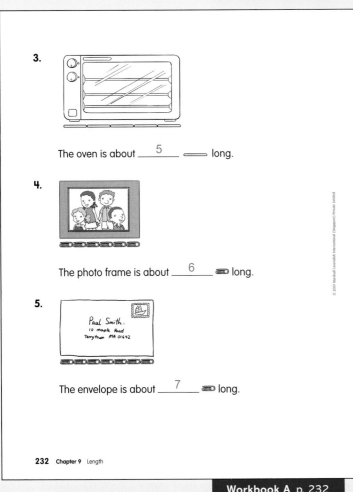

3.

The oven is about ___5___ long.

4.

The photo frame is about ___6___ long.

5.

The envelope is about ___7___ long.

Workbook A p. 232

Name: _____ Date: _____

Fill in the blanks.
What is the length of each tape?

Example

tape

buttons

pegs

The tape is about ___8___ buttons long.

It is about ___2___ pegs long.

6.

The tape is about ___11___ buttons long.

It is about ___3___ pegs long.

7.

The tape is about ___9___ buttons long.

It is about ___2___ pegs long.

Workbook A p. 233

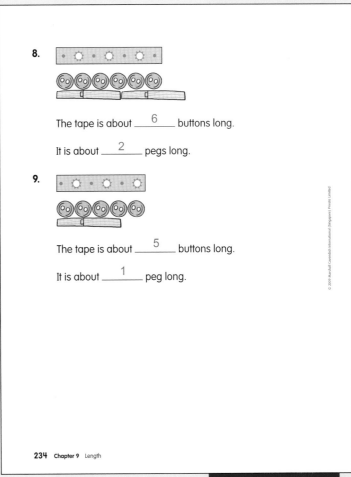

8.

The tape is about ___6___ buttons long.

It is about ___2___ pegs long.

9.

The tape is about ___5___ buttons long.

It is about ___1___ peg long.

Workbook A p. 234

LESSON 5 Finding Length in Units

LESSON OBJECTIVES
- Use the term "unit" to describe length.
- Count measurement units in a group of ten and ones.

TECHNOLOGY RESOURCES
- *Math in Focus* eBook
- *Math in Focus* Teaching Resources CD
- *Math in Focus* Virtual Manipulatives

Vocabulary

unit

DAY 1	Student Book 1A, pp. 241–246
	Workbook 1A, pp. 235–238

MATERIALS
- 20 craft sticks for each group of four children
- Measurement Table (TR19)
- 20 paper clips for each group of four children
- long umbrella for classroom demonstration

DIFFERENTIATION RESOURCES
- Reteach 1A, pp. 167–170
- Extra Practice 1A, pp. 145–150

 5-minute Warm Up

- Show children a long umbrella and a craft stick. Ask them to say which object they should use to measure the length of each of the following: a schoolbag, a child's desk, the classroom, a textbook, the chalkboard.

- Ask children to name other things they might use the umbrella or craft stick to measure.

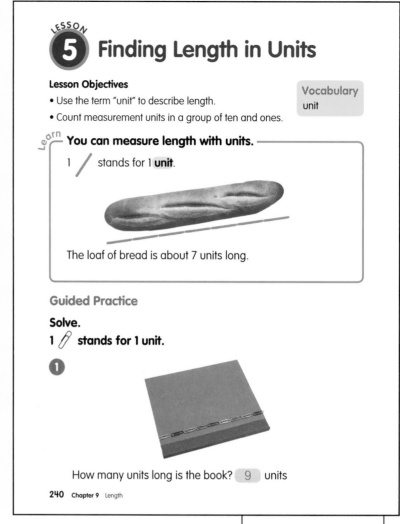

LESSON 5 Finding Length in Units

Lesson Objectives
- Use the term "unit" to describe length.
- Count measurement units in a group of ten and ones.

Vocabulary
unit

Learn **You can measure length with units.**

1 / stands for 1 **unit**.

The loaf of bread is about 7 units long.

Guided Practice

Solve.

1 / stands for 1 unit.

1 How many units long is the book? 9 units

240 Chapter 9 Length

Student Book A p. 240

DAY 1 Teach

Learn

Measure Length with Units (page 240)

Children have learned to use objects to measure length. In this lesson, they use the term *unit* to describe length. This prepares them to use standard units in higher grades.

- Ask children to look at the picture in the Learn box.

- *Ask:* What object is used to measure the length of the loaf of bread? (craft sticks)

- *Ask:* How many craft sticks are there? (7) *Say:* The loaf of bread is about 7 craft sticks long.

- Explain to children that the term *unit* can be used to replace *craft stick* and that 1 craft stick stands for 1 unit.

- *Say:* We can say that the loaf of bread is about 7 units long.

Check for Understanding
✓ **Guided Practice** (page 234)

1 Point out that 1 paper clip can also stand for 1 unit.

- Have children count the number of paper clips on the book.

- Lead children to see that 9 paper clips is the same as 9 units.

Student Book A p. 241

Measure Length With Units (page 241)

Children measure length using more than 10 units .

- Ask children to count the craft sticks used to measure the jump rope. **Ask:** How many units long is the jump rope? (14)

- Help children recall that 14 can be grouped into a 10 and 4. You may use the concept of number bonds or place value.

✔Guided Practice (page 242)

2 Have children count the craft sticks as units. Reinforce how the number of units can be grouped into a 10 and ones.

Problem of the Lesson 💿

1 ☐ stands for 1 unit.

A																		
B																		
C																		
D																		

1. Which is the longest strip? _____
2. Which is the shortest strip? _____
3. Which two strips have the same length? _____
   They are _____ units long.

Answer:

1. A
2. C
3. B and D; 13

Differentiated Instruction

English Language Learners

Explain that a *unit* is one of a whole group of objects. Each unit is exactly the same. Emphasize that *unit* is a general term that can be used to describe different objects for measuring. Flip through the pages of the lesson with children to point out the different items that are used as units. **Say:** A craft stick can be 1 unit. A paper clip can be 1 unit. A connecting cube can be 1 unit.

Best Practices This lesson begins with an example of counting measurement units in a group of ten and ones. You may want to precede the lesson with a review of place value. Show a tens rod and several single unit cubes. Invite children to tell how these materials can also be used to measure length.

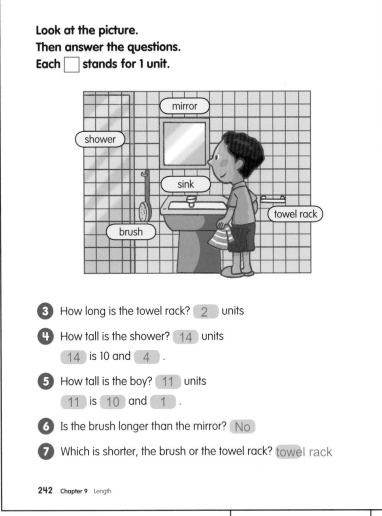

Look at the picture.
Then answer the questions.
Each ☐ stands for 1 unit.

3 How long is the towel rack? `2` units

4 How tall is the shower? `14` units
`14` is 10 and `4` .

5 How tall is the boy? `11` units
`11` is `10` and `1` .

6 Is the brush longer than the mirror? `No`

7 Which is shorter, the brush or the towel rack? `towel rack`

Student Book A p. 242

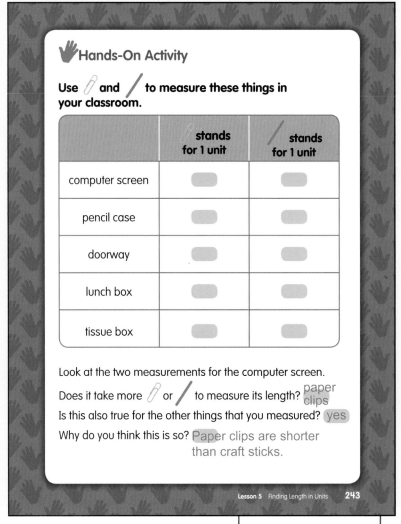

✋**Hands-On Activity**

Use and / to measure these things in your classroom.

	📎 stands for 1 unit	/ stands for 1 unit
computer screen	⬭	⬭
pencil case	⬭	⬭
doorway	⬭	⬭
lunch box	⬭	⬭
tissue box	⬭	⬭

Look at the two measurements for the computer screen.

Does it take more 📎 or / to measure its length? `paper clips`

Is this also true for the other things that you measured? `yes`

Why do you think this is so? `Paper clips are shorter than craft sticks.`

Student Book A p. 243

✔**Guided Practice** (page 242)

3 to **5** Be sure children can find the labelled objects in the picture. Have children count the measurement units required in the exercises. Guide children to group them into a 10 and ones when the length is greater than 10 measurement units.

6 and **7** Have children find and measure the brush and mirror in units before completing these exercises.

![WORKING TOGETHER]

✋**Hands-On Activity:**

Measure Things in the Classroom with Paper Clips and Craft Sticks (page 243)

- Arrange children in groups of four. Give each group a copy of the **Measurement Table** (TR19), 20 **paper clips** and 20 **craft sticks**.

- Ask children to measure the things listed in the table in the Student Book and record their measurements in their copy of the table.

- Use the completed tables to discuss children's findings as a class.

- Help children recall that more paper clips than craft sticks are required because paper clips are shorter than crafts sticks.

Let's Practice

Use 🖇 to measure.
1 🖇 stands for 1 unit.

The picture shows Chris's house, his school, and the playground.

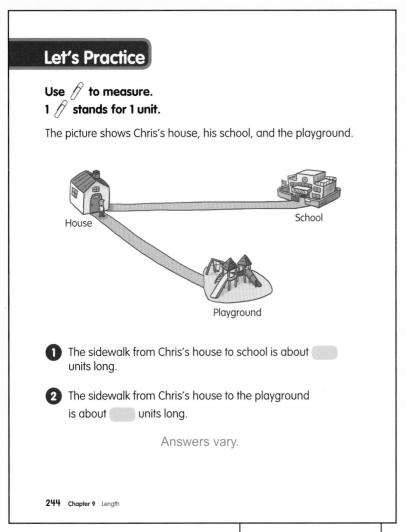

House

School

Playground

1 The sidewalk from Chris's house to school is about ⬜ units long.

2 The sidewalk from Chris's house to the playground is about ⬜ units long.

Answers vary.

Solve.

Snails A, B, and C crawl along the lines.

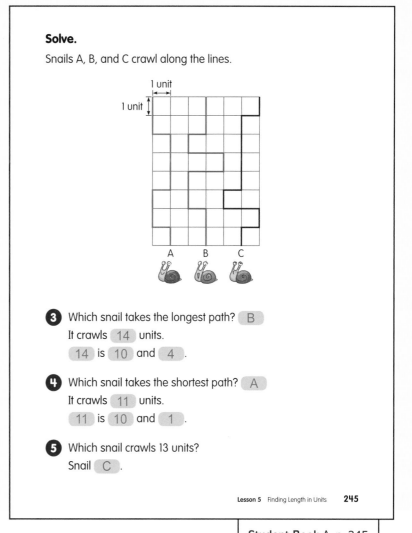

1 unit

1 unit

A   B   C

3 Which snail takes the longest path? (B)
It crawls (14) units.
(14) is (10) and (4).

4 Which snail takes the shortest path? (A)
It crawls (11) units.
(11) is (10) and (1).

5 Which snail crawls 13 units?
Snail (C).

Let's Practice (pages 244 to 246)

This practice reinforces children's learning to measure different kinds of paths using units. Exercises **1** and **2** require children to use paper clips as units of measurement. Tell children that the starting point for both sidewalks is the door in the front of the house. The sidewalks on page 244 are straight so children can position the paper clips along the sidewalks.

Exercises **3** to **6** use squares in a grid as units. The paths (lines) on page 245 are not straight lines. Children need to count units up as well as across in order to measure them.

Common Error Some children may be confused by the use of a grid square as a unit. Remind them that they are measuring length, and that the length of one unit is the length of any side of the square. Demonstrate how children can count the squares to determine the number of units.

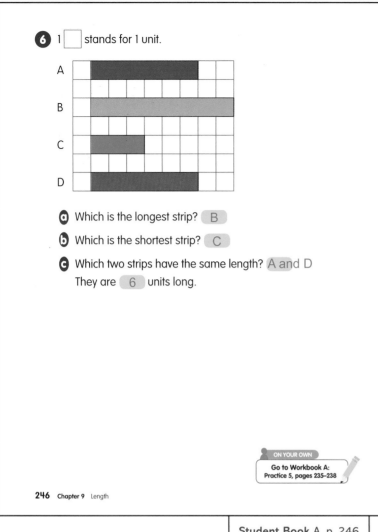

6 1 ☐ stands for 1 unit.

A

B

C

D

a Which is the longest strip? ⬚ B

b Which is the shortest strip? ⬚ C

c Which two strips have the same length? ⬚ A and D
They are ⬚ 6 units long.

ON YOUR OWN

Go to Workbook A:
Practice 5, pages 235–238

246 Chapter 9 Length

Student Book A p. 246

ON YOUR OWN

Children practice measuring length using units in Practice 5, pp. 235–238 of **Workbook 1A**. These pages (with the answers) are shown at the right and on page 246A.

Differentiation Options Depending on children's success with the Workbook pages, use these materials as needed.
Struggling: Reteach 1A, pp. 167–170
On Level: Extra Practice 1A, pp. 145–150

Practice and Apply
Workbook pages for Chapter 9, Lesson 5

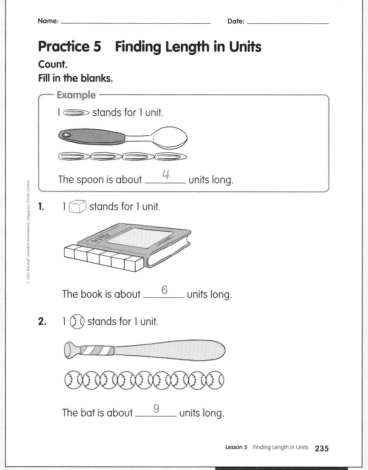

Name: _____ Date: _____

Practice 5   Finding Length in Units
Count.
Fill in the blanks.

┌─ Example ─────────────────────────────┐
1 🥄 stands for 1 unit.

The spoon is about ___4___ units long.
└───────────────────────────────────────┘

1. 1 ⬚ stands for 1 unit.

The book is about ___6___ units long.

2. 1 ⚾ stands for 1 unit.

The bat is about ___9___ units long.

Lesson 5 Finding Length in Units **235**

Workbook A p. 235

Look at the picture.
Fill in the blanks.

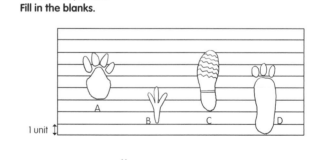

1 unit ↕

3. Footprint A is ___4___ units long.

4. Footprint B is ___3___ units long.

5. Footprint C is ___5___ units long.

6. Footprint D is ___6___ units long.

7. Footprint ___D___ is the longest.

8. Footprint ___B___ is shorter than Footprint A.

236 Chapter 9 Length

Workbook A p. 236

Name: _____ **Date:** _____

Look at the picture.
Fill in the blanks.

1 ☐ stands for 1 unit.

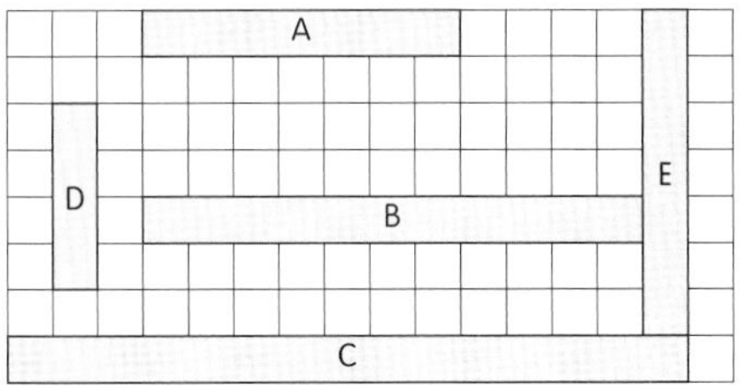

9. Strip ___C___ is the longest.
   It is ___15___ units long.
   The number of units is ___15___.
   This is ___1___ ten and ___5___ ones.

10. Strip ___D___ is the shortest.
    It is ___4___ units long.

11. Strip ___A___ is as long as Strip ___E___.

12. Strip ___B___ is shorter than Strip C but longer than Strip E.
    It is ___11___ units long.
    The number of units is ___11___.
    This is ___1___ ten and ___1___ one.

Lesson 5 Finding Length in Units **237**

Workbook A p. 237

Look at the picture.
Fill in the blanks. Use the words in the box to help you.

1 ☐ stands for 1 unit.

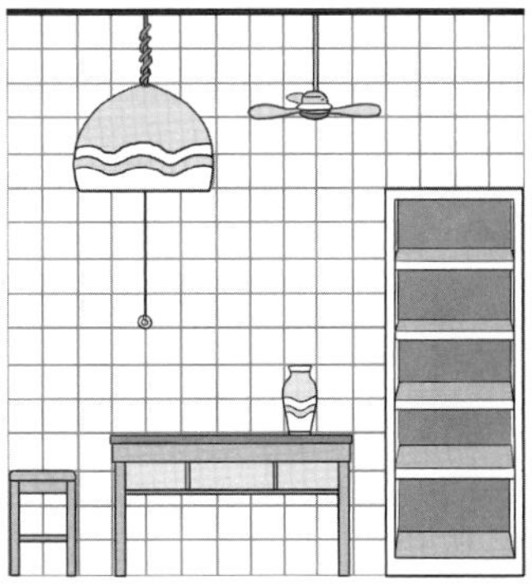

short
shorter
shortest
taller
tallest
longer
longest

13. The table is ___7___ units long.

14. The bookshelf is ___11___ units tall.

15. Look at the stool, the table, and the bookshelf.
    The bookshelf is the ___tallest___ thing.
    The stool is ___shorter___ than the table.

16. The vase is the ___shortest___ thing in the room.

17. The string from the light is ___longer___ than the pole of the fan.

238 Chapter 9 Length

Workbook A p. 238

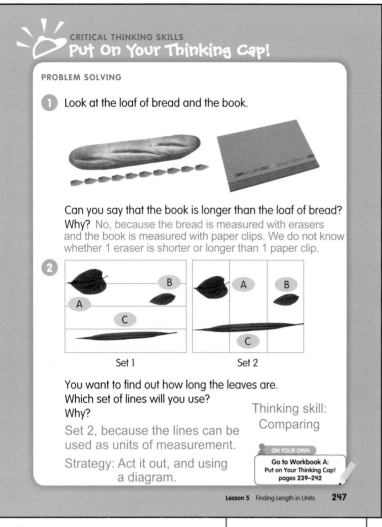

CRITICAL THINKING SKILLS
Put On Your Thinking Cap!

PROBLEM SOLVING

1 Look at the loaf of bread and the book.

Can you say that the book is longer than the loaf of bread? **Why?** No, because the bread is measured with erasers and the book is measured with paper clips. We do not know whether 1 eraser is shorter or longer than 1 paper clip.

2

Set 1   Set 2

You want to find out how long the leaves are. Which set of lines will you use? Why?

Set 2, because the lines can be used as units of measurement.

Strategy: Act it out, and using a diagram.

Thinking skill: Comparing

ON YOUR OWN
Go to Workbook A:
Put on Your Thinking Cap!
pages 239–242

Lesson 5 Finding Length in Units **247**

Student Book A p. 247

CRITICAL THINKING AND PROBLEM SOLVING
Put on Your Thinking Cap! (page 247)

PROBLEM SOLVING

1 This activity requires children to test inaccurate deductions.

• Ask children to say how long each object is. (the length of the loaf of bread is 10 erasers; the length of the book is 11 paper clips)

• Ask children to think about the question in the Student Book and explain their answers.

• Lead children to realize that they cannot say that the book is longer than the loaf of bread because they do not know the length of an eraser compared to the length of a paper clip. The units of measurement are not the same.

2 This activity lets children apply their learning in this lesson to a new situation.

• Ask children to measure the length of the leaves in each set using the units provided in the picture. Encourage children to answer the question in the Student Book. Have them explain their answers. Correct and explain any misconceptions.

• Explain that Set 1 has spaces between horizontal lines that can represent a non-standard unit. However, because the leaves are aligned horizontally, the spaces cannot be used as units for measurement.

• Set 2 has spaces marked with vertical lines that represent a non-standard unit. Because the leaves are aligned horizontally, the spaces can be used as units for measurement.

• Lead children to see that leaf A is about 1 unit long, leaf B is less than 1 unit long, and leaf C is about 3 units long.

Thinking Skills

• Comparing

Problem Solving Strategies

• Act it out
• Use a diagram

ON YOUR OWN

Because all children should be challenged, have all children try the Challenging Practice and Problem-Solving pages in **Workbook 1A**, pp. 239–242. These pages (with the answers) are shown on page 247A.

Differentiation Options Depending on children's success with the Workbook pages, use these materials as needed.
On Level: Extra Practice 1A, pp. 151–152
Advanced: Enrichment 1A, pp. 66–74

Practice and Apply
Workbook pages for Put on Your Thinking Cap!

Name: _____ Date: _____

Put On Your Thinking Cap!
Challenging Practice

Solve.

Mae moves the counters on a board.
The arrows show the moves.

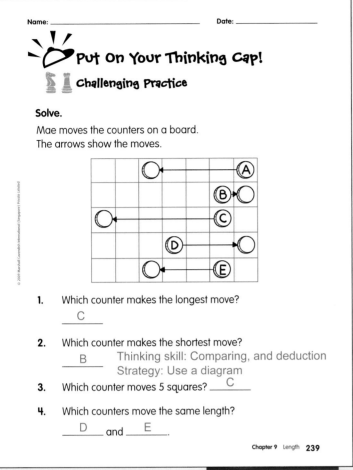

1. Which counter makes the longest move?
   _____C_____

2. Which counter makes the shortest move?
   _____B_____   Thinking skill: Comparing, and deduction
   Strategy: Use a diagram

3. Which counter moves 5 squares? ___C___

4. Which counters move the same length?
   _____D_____ and _____E_____.

Workbook A p. 239

Name: _____ Date: _____

Look at the picture and read.
Then draw.

🐛 stands for 1 unit.

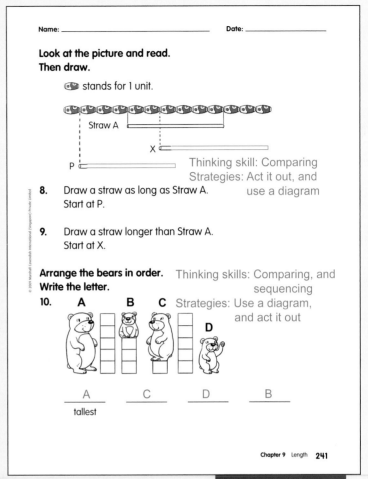

8. Draw a straw as long as Straw A.
   Start at P.

   Thinking skill: Comparing
   Strategies: Act it out, and
   use a diagram

9. Draw a straw longer than Straw A.
   Start at X.

Arrange the bears in order.   Thinking skills: Comparing, and
Write the letter.   sequencing

10.   **A**   **B**   **C**   Strategies: Use a diagram,
                                               and act it out
                            D

   _____A_____   _____C_____   _____D_____   _____B_____
   tallest

Workbook A p. 241

Three boys are lying on a mat.   Thinking skill: Comparing, and
                                                   deduction
                                   Strategy: Use a diagram

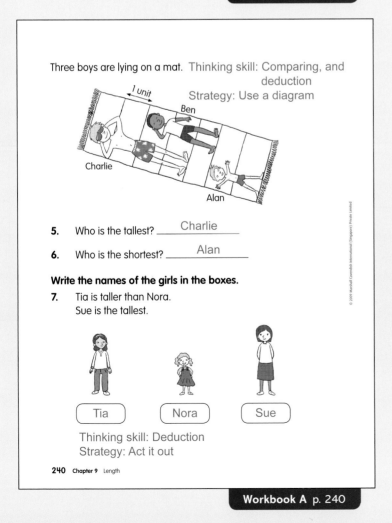

5. Who is the tallest? _____Charlie_____

6. Who is the shortest? _____Alan_____

Write the names of the girls in the boxes.

7. Tia is taller than Nora.
   Sue is the tallest.

   [Tia]   [Nora]   [Sue]

   Thinking skill: Deduction
   Strategy: Act it out

Workbook A p. 240

Put On Your Thinking Cap!
Problem Solving

Fill in the blanks.

1. Tim, Ella, Rosa, and Ling knit some scarves.
   Who does each scarf belong to?

   Scarf A   _____Rosa_____

   Scarf B   _____Ella_____

   Scarf C   _____Ling_____

   Scarf D   _____Tim_____

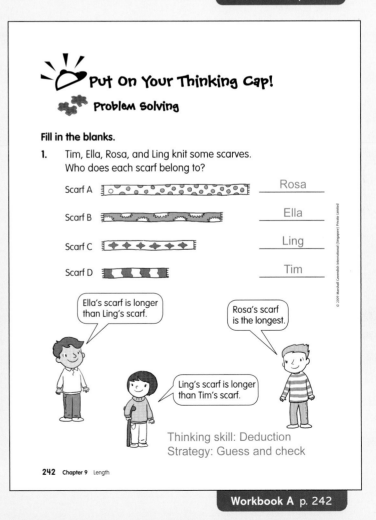

   Ella's scarf is longer than Ling's scarf.

   Rosa's scarf is the longest.

   Ling's scarf is longer than Tim's scarf.

   Thinking skill: Deduction
   Strategy: Guess and check

Workbook A p. 242

Chapter Wrap Up
You have learned...

Length

to compare two things.

tall | taller | short | shorter

long | longer

to compare more than two things.

Ally | Ben | Carlo

Ally is taller than Ben.
Ben is taller than Carlo.
So, Ally is also taller
than Carlo.

Ally is the tallest.
Carlo is the shortest.

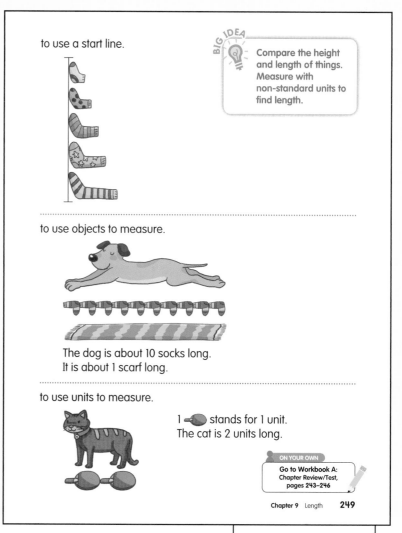

to use a start line.

BIG IDEA Compare the height and length of things. Measure with non-standard units to find length.

to use objects to measure.

The dog is about 10 socks long.
It is about 1 scarf long.

to use units to measure.

1 🦴 stands for 1 unit.
The cat is 2 units long.

ON YOUR OWN
Go to Workbook A:
Chapter Review/Test,
pages 243–246

Chapter Wrap Up (pages 248 and 249)

Review ways to compare length and height of two things and more than two things. Help children recall that they can use a start line to make comparing easier, and that objects and non-standard units can be used to measure length. As you work through the examples, encourage children to use the chapter vocabulary:

• tall	• tallest	• taller	• shortest
• short	• longest	• shorter	• start line
• long	• about	• longer	• unit

ON YOUR OWN

• Have children review the vocabulary, concepts, and skills from Chapter 9 with the Chapter Review/Test in **Workbook 1A**, pages 243–246. These pages (with the answers) are shown on page 249A.

• You may want to use the Cumulative Review for Chapters 7 to 9 from **Workbook 1A** pages 247–252 and the Mid-Year Review from **Workbook 1A** pages 253–263. These pages (with the answers) are shown on pages 249C–249G.

Assessment

• Use the Chapter 9 Test Prep on pages 65–69 of **Assessments 1** to assess how well children have learned the material of this chapter. This assessment is appropriate for reporting results to parents and administrators. This test is shown on page 249B.

• You may also wish to use the Mid-Year Test on pages 70–82 of **Assessments 1**. This test is shown on pages 249H–249J.

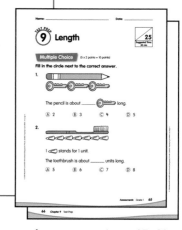

Assessments 1 pp. 65–69

Workbook pages for Chapter Review/Test

Name: _____ Date: _____

Chapter Review/Test
Vocabulary
Match.

1. short ●————————●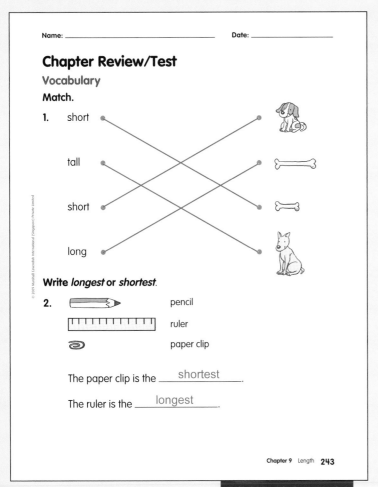

   tall ●

   short ●

   long ●

Write *longest* **or** *shortest*.

2. pencil

   ruler

   paper clip

   The paper clip is the ___shortest___.

   The ruler is the ___longest___.

Workbook A p. 243

Name: _____ Date: _____

Problem Solving
Solve.

1 ☐ stands for 1 unit.

Madison   Jimar   Patch

5. Madison is ___3___ units tall.

6. Patch is ___2___ units tall and ___2___ units long.

7. The longest balloon is ___3___ units long.

8. Who's balloon has the longest string? ___Patch___

Workbook A p. 245

Concepts and Skills
Draw a start line.
Read and color.

3. Color the longest ribbon yellow.
   Color the shortest ribbon blue.

   blue

   yellow

Fill in the blanks.

4.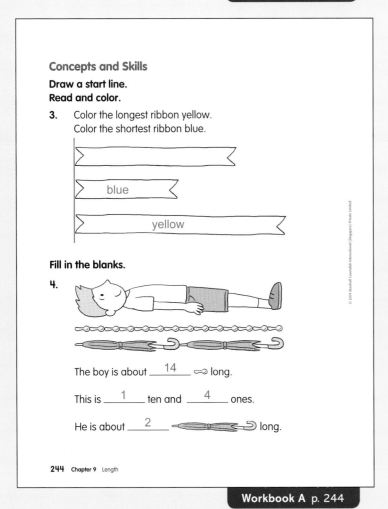

   The boy is about ___14___ ∽ long.

   This is ___1___ ten and ___4___ ones.

   He is about ___2___ ╱ long.

Workbook A p. 244

Solve.

9. Three children are on stage.
   Ben is taller than Ally.
   Charlie is shorter than Ben.
   Ally is the shortest.

   Who is the tallest?

   ___Ben___ is the tallest.

   Who is not the shortest and not the tallest?

   ___Charlie___

   You may draw a picture to help you

Workbook A p. 246

Assessments Book pages for Chapter 9 Test Prep
Answer key appears in Assessments Book.

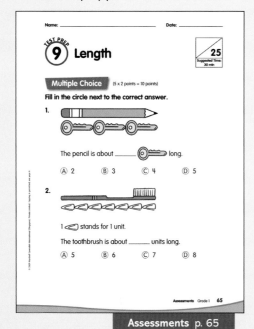

Name: _____ Date: _____

TEST PREP
9 Length

25
Suggested Time:
30 min

Multiple Choice (5 x 2 points = 10 points)

Fill in the circle next to the correct answer.

1.

The pencil is about _____ long.

(A) 2   (B) 3   (C) 4   (D) 5

2.

1 ◁ stands for 1 unit.

The toothbrush is about _____ units long.

(A) 5   (B) 6   (C) 7   (D) 8

Assessments Grade 1   **65**

Assessments p. 65

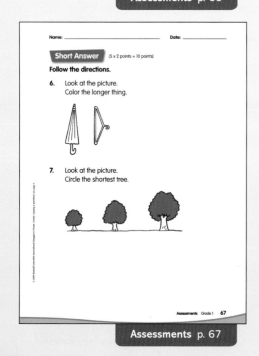

Name: _____ Date: _____

3.

1 ▷ stands for 1 unit.

The length of the toy jeep is about _____ units.

(A) 5   (B) 6   (C) 7   (D) 8

Look at the picture.
Answer Exercises 4 and 5.

1 unit

Paintbrush A   Paintbrush B

Paintbrush C   Paintbrush D

4. Which paintbrush is the longest?
(A) A   (B) B   (C) C   (D) D

5. Which paintbrush is about 2 units long?
(A) A   (B) B   (C) C   (D) D

66 Chapter 9   Test Prep

Assessments p. 66

Name: _____ Date: _____

Short Answer (5 x 2 points = 10 points)

Follow the directions.

6. Look at the picture.
Color the longer thing.

7. Look at the picture.
Circle the shortest tree.

Assessments Grade 1   **67**

Assessments p. 67

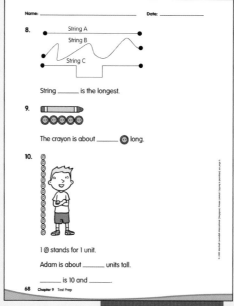

Name: _____ Date: _____

8.

String A
String B
String C

String _____ is the longest.

9.

The crayon is about _____ long.

10.

1 ◎ stands for 1 unit.

Adam is about _____ units tall.

_____ is 10 and _____

68 Chapter 9   Test Prep

Assessments p. 68

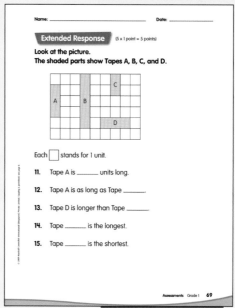

Name: _____ Date: _____

Extended Response (5 x 1 point = 5 points)

Look at the picture.
The shaded parts show Tapes A, B, C, and D.

Each ☐ stands for 1 unit.

11. Tape A is _____ units long.

12. Tape A is as long as Tape _____.

13. Tape D is longer than Tape _____.

14. Tape _____ is the longest.

15. Tape _____ is the shortest.

Assessments Grade 1   **69**

Assessments p. 69

Cumulative Review for Chapters 7 to 9

Workbook A p. 247

Name: _____   Date: _____

Cumulative Review
for Chapters 7 to 9

Concepts and Skills

Circle the ten.
Then fill in the blanks.

1.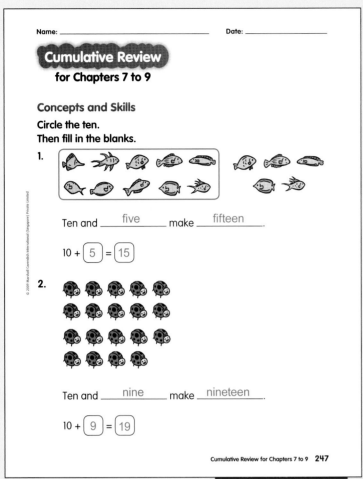

Ten and ___five___ make ___fifteen___.

$10 + \boxed{5} = \boxed{15}$

2.

Ten and ___nine___ make ___nineteen___.

$10 + \boxed{9} = \boxed{19}$

Workbook A p. 249

Name: _____   Date: _____

Complete each number pattern.

7. 9, 10, ___11___, 12, 13, ___14___, 15

8. 20, ___19___, 18, 17, ___16___, ___15___, 14, 13

Order the numbers from least to greatest.

9. | 12 | 17 | 16 | 8 | 11 |

___8___ ___11___ ___12___ ___16___ ___17___

Make a 10.
Then add.

10. $9 + 8 = $ ___17___ $9 + $ ___1___ $= 10$

$10 + $ ___7___ $= $ ___17___

Group into a 10 and ones.
Then solve.

11. $7 + 13 = $ ___20___   12. $15 - 8 = $ ___7___

Complete.

13. $7 + 7 = $ ___14___   14. $7 + 8 = $ ___15___

15. $16 - 8 = $ ___8___   16. $12 - $ ___6___ $= 6$

Workbook A p. 248

Show the number.
Draw ▯ for tens and ▢ for ones.

3.
Tens	Ones
10	

4.
Tens	Ones
18	

Write the number.
Then fill in the blanks.

5.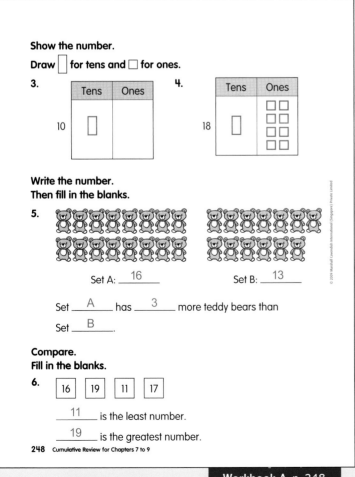

Set A: ___16___   Set B: ___13___

Set ___A___ has ___3___ more teddy bears than

Set ___B___.

Compare.
Fill in the blanks.

6. | 16 | 19 | 11 | 17 |

___11___ is the least number.

___19___ is the greatest number.

Workbook A p. 250

Fill in the blanks.
Use the words in the box.

| shorter | shortest | longer | longest | taller | tallest |

17. Rosa is ___taller___ than Lauren.

18. Lauren is ___shorter___ than Rosa.

19. Trey is ___taller___ than Rosa and Lauren.

So, Trey is the ___tallest___.

20. The tail on the white dog is ___longer___ than the tail on the spotted dog.

21. The tail on the black dog is ___longer___ than the tail on the white dog.

22. The tail on the spotted dog is the ___shortest___.

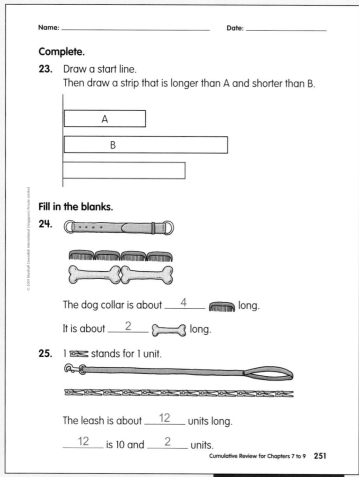

Complete.

23. Draw a start line.
Then draw a strip that is longer than A and shorter than B.

| A |
| B |

Fill in the blanks.

24.

The dog collar is about ___4___ 🪮 long.

It is about ___2___ 🦴 long.

25. 1 ▭ stands for 1 unit.

The leash is about ___12___ units long.

___12___ is 10 and ___2___ units.

Cumulative Review for Chapters 7 to 9   **251**

Workbook A p. 251

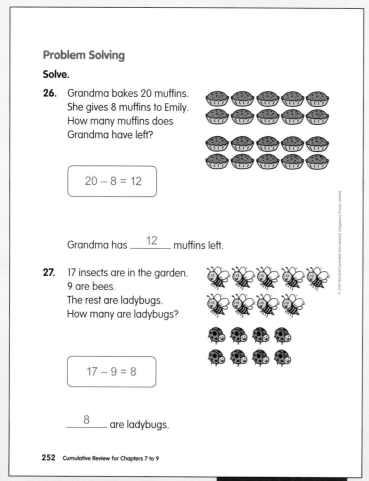

Problem Solving

Solve.

26. Grandma bakes 20 muffins.
She gives 8 muffins to Emily.
How many muffins does
Grandma have left?

| 20 − 8 = 12 |

Grandma has ___12___ muffins left.

27. 17 insects are in the garden.
9 are bees.
The rest are ladybugs.
How many are ladybugs?

| 17 − 9 = 8 |

___8___ are ladybugs.

252   Cumulative Review for Chapters 7 to 9

Workbook A p. 252

Notes

Mid-Year Review

Mid-Year Review
Test Prep
Multiple Choice

Fill in the circle next to the correct answer.

1. How many stars are there?

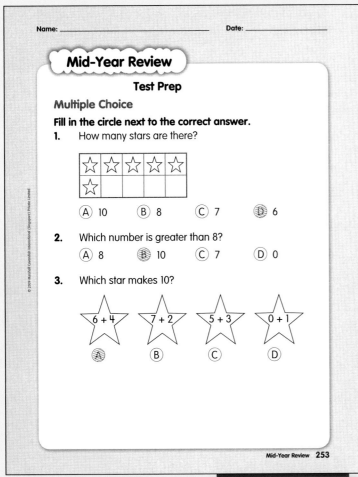

  (A) 10   (B) 8   (C) 7   (D) 6

2. Which number is greater than 8?

  (A) 8   (B) 10   (C) 7   (D) 0

3. Which star makes 10?

  6 + 4   7 + 2   5 + 3   0 + 1

  (A)   (B)   (C)   (D)

Workbook A p. 253

---

9. How are these shapes sorted?

  (A) shape

  (B) color

  (C) size

  (D) number of sides

10. Which solid shape can you roll <u>and</u> slide?

  (A) sphere   (B) cone   (C) cube   (D) pyramid

11. Complete the pattern.

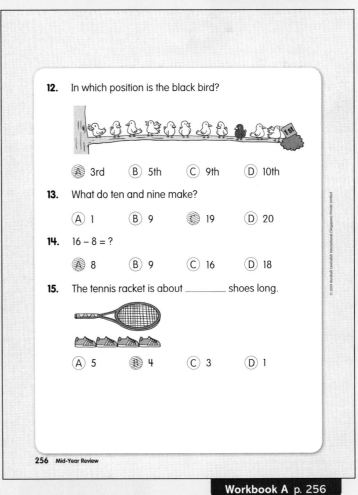

  (A)   (B)   (C)   (D)

Workbook A p. 255

---

4. Which star makes 1 less than 7?

  8 – 2   7 – 2   9 – 5   10 – 8

  (A)   (B)   (C)   (D)

5. Find the missing number.

$$\boxed{} + 9 = 10$$

  (A) 11   (B) 8   (C) 1   (D) 0

6. Find the missing number.

$$8 - \boxed{} = 4$$

  (A) 8   (B) 5   (C) 4   (D) 2

7. How many sides does a ◺ have?

  (A) 4   (B) 3   (C) 2   (D) 0

8. How many corners does a ◯ have?

  (A) 0   (B) 1   (C) 2   (D) 5

Workbook A p. 254

---

12. In which position is the black bird?

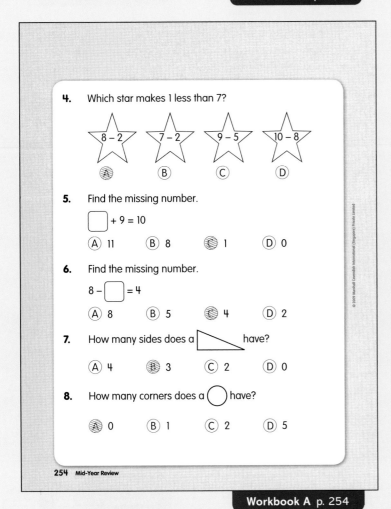

  (A) 3rd   (B) 5th   (C) 9th   (D) 10th

13. What do ten and nine make?

  (A) 1   (B) 9   (C) 19   (D) 20

14. $16 - 8 = ?$

  (A) 8   (B) 9   (C) 16   (D) 18

15. The tennis racket is about _____ shoes long.

  (A) 5   (B) 4   (C) 3   (D) 1

Workbook A p. 256

Short Answer

Read the questions carefully.
Write your answers in the space given.

Write the numbers in words.

16. 8 _____eight_____

17. 19 _____nineteen_____

18. 12 _____twelve_____

Complete the number patterns.

19. __0__ 1, 2, 3, __4__, 5

20. __18__, 16, 14, __12__, 10, 8 __6__

Add.

21. 7 + 8 = __15__

22. 20 − 7 = __13__

⑤ ②   ⑩ ⑩

Workbook A p. 257

Order the numbers from greatest to least.

23.

| 19 | 9 | 20 | 10 |

__20__ __19__ __10__ __9__

Look at the picture.
Circle the words for the shapes you see.

24.

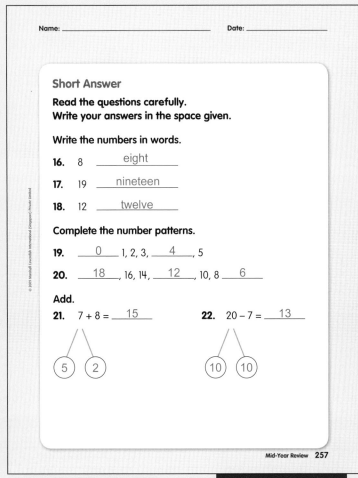

circle   (rectangle)   (square)   triangle

(sphere)   pyramid   (cylinder)   cone   cube

Workbook A p. 258

Look at the picture.
Then fill in the blanks.
Use the words in the box.

Maria Josh Liping Jamal

left	right
between	above
below	next to
first	second
third	second

25. Maria is last from the _____right_____.

26. Jamal is _____first_____ on the right.

27. Liping is _____between_____ Josh and Jamal.

28. The mouse is _____below_____ Josh.

Look at the picture.
Then fill in the blanks.

29. Building A is __9__ units tall.

30. Building B is __3__ units tall.

31. Building C is __12__ units tall.

32. Building __C__ is the tallest.

↕ 1 unit

A   B   C

Workbook A p. 259

Extended Response

Solve.

33.

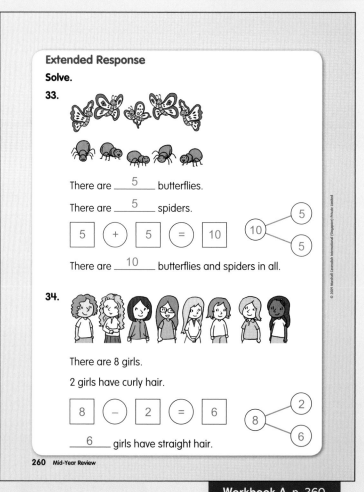

There are __5__ butterflies.

There are __5__ spiders.

| 5 | + | 5 | = | 10 |

⑩ ⟨ ⑤ / ⑤

There are __10__ butterflies and spiders in all.

34.

There are 8 girls.

2 girls have curly hair.

| 8 | − | 2 | = | 6 |

⑧ ⟨ ② / ⑥

__6__ girls have straight hair.

Workbook A p. 260

Show the number.

Draw ▯ for tens and □ for ones.

Then fill in the blanks.

35.

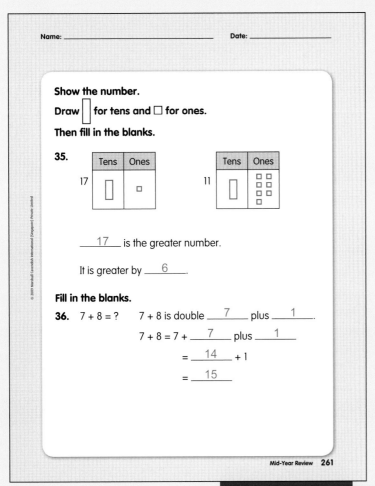

Tens	Ones

17

Tens	Ones

11

____17____ is the greater number.

It is greater by ____6____.

Fill in the blanks.

36. 7 + 8 = ?   7 + 8 is double ____7____ plus ____1____.

7 + 8 = 7 + ____7____ plus ____1____

= ____14____ + 1

= ____15____

39. Follow the directions:
First, draw a start line.
Next, draw a shorter arrow.
Then, draw an arrow that is longer than the other arrows.
Last, circle the shortest arrow.

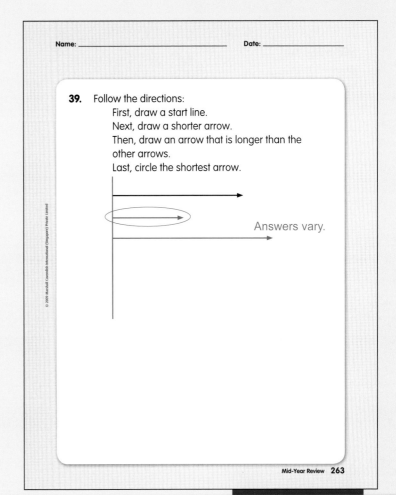

Answers vary.

37. Mom has 13 buttons.
She uses some to sew a dress.
7 buttons are left.
How many buttons does Mom use?

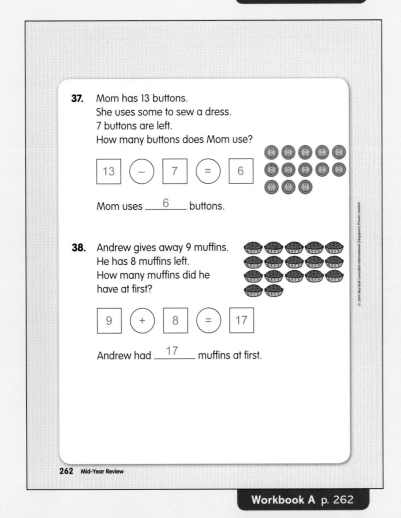

13	−	7	=	6

Mom uses ____6____ buttons.

38. Andrew gives away 9 muffins.
He has 8 muffins left.
How many muffins did he
have at first?

9	+	8	=	17

Andrew had ____17____ muffins at first.

BLANK

Assessments Book pages for Chapter 9 Mid-Year Test
Answer key appears in Assessments Book.

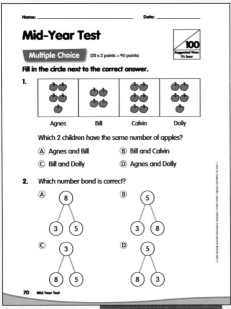

Assessments p. 70

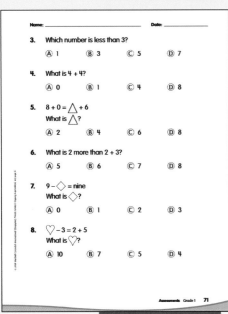

Assessments p. 71

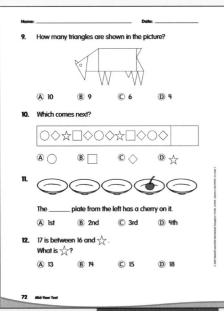

Assessments p. 72

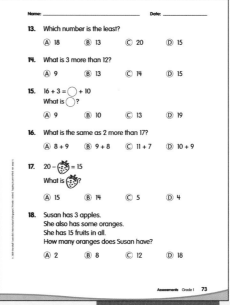

Assessments p. 73

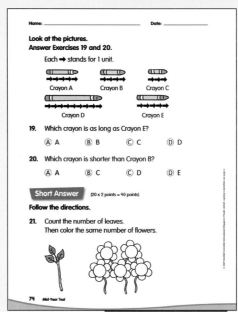

Assessments p. 74

Assessments p. 75

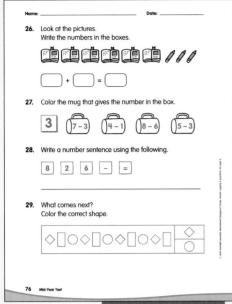

Assessments p. 76

Assessments p. 77

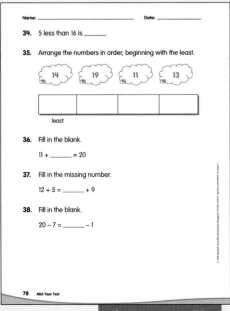

Assessments p. 78

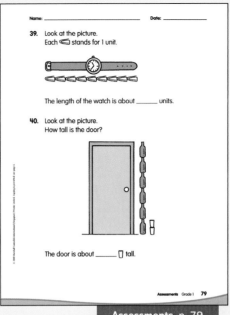

Assessments p. 79

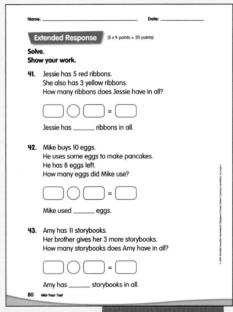

Assessments p. 80

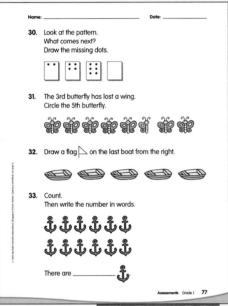

Assessments p. 81

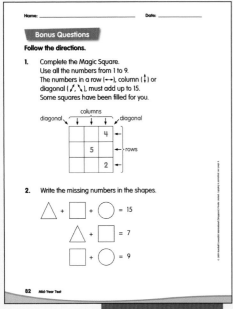

Assessments p. 82

Notes

Glossary

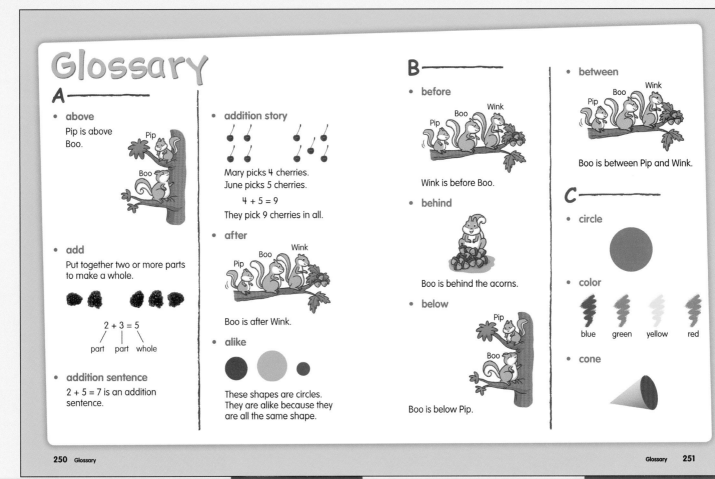

Glossary

A

- **above**
  Pip is above Boo.

- **add**
  Put together two or more parts to make a whole.

  $$2 + 3 = 5$$
  part part whole

- **addition sentence**
  $2 + 5 = 7$ is an addition sentence.

- **addition story**

  Mary picks 4 cherries.
  June picks 5 cherries.
  $$4 + 5 = 9$$
  They pick 9 cherries in all.

- **after**

  Boo is after Wink.

- **alike**

  These shapes are circles. They are alike because they are all the same shape.

B

- **before**

  Wink is before Boo.

- **behind**

  Boo is behind the acorns.

- **below**

  Boo is below Pip.

- **between**

  Boo is between Pip and Wink.

C

- **circle**

- **color**

  blue   green   yellow   red

- **cone**

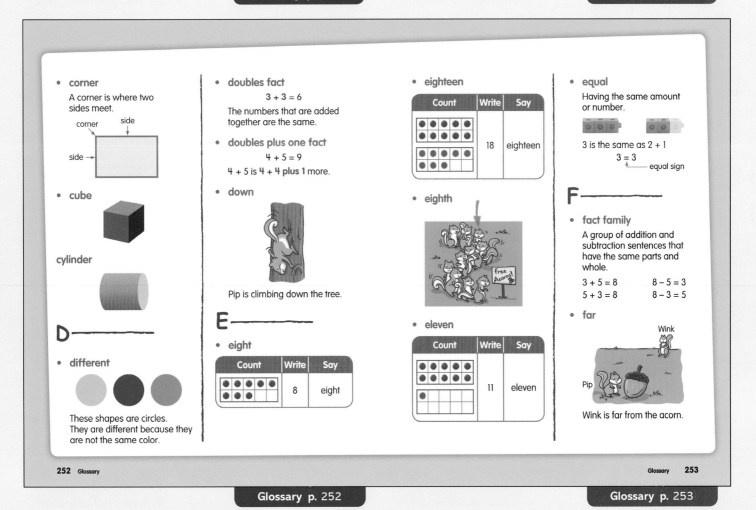

- **corner**
  A corner is where two sides meet.

  corner   side
  side →

- **cube**

- **cylinder**

D

- **different**

  These shapes are circles. They are different because they are not the same color.

- **doubles fact**
  $$3 + 3 = 6$$
  The numbers that are added together are the same.

- **doubles plus one fact**
  $$4 + 5 = 9$$
  $4 + 5$ is $4 + 4$ plus 1 more.

- **down**

  Pip is climbing down the tree.

E

- **eight**

Count	Write	Say
	8	eight

- **eighteen**

Count	Write	Say
	18	eighteen

- **eighth**

- **eleven**

Count	Write	Say
	11	eleven

- **equal**
  Having the same amount or number.

  3 is the same as $2 + 1$
  $$3 = 3$$
  equal sign

F

- **fact family**
  A group of addition and subtraction sentences that have the same parts and whole.

$3 + 5 = 8$	$8 - 5 = 3$
$5 + 3 = 8$	$8 - 3 = 5$

- **far**

  Wink is far from the acorn.

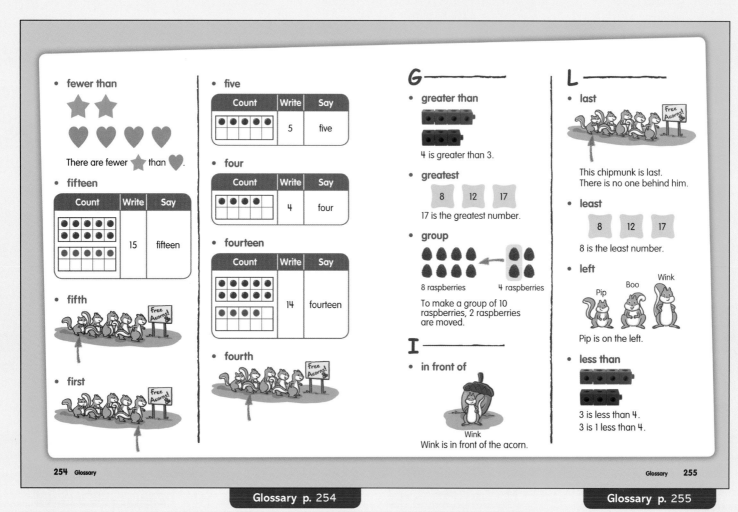

- **fewer than**

  There are fewer ⭐ than 💜.

- **fifteen**

Count	Write	Say
	15	fifteen

- **fifth**

- **first**

- **five**

Count	Write	Say
	5	five

- **four**

Count	Write	Say
	4	four

- **fourteen**

Count	Write	Say
	14	fourteen

- **fourth**

G

- **greater than**

  4 is greater than 3.

- **greatest**

  8 12 17

  17 is the greatest number.

- **group**

  8 raspberries   4 raspberries

  To make a group of 10 raspberries, 2 raspberries are moved.

I

- **in front of**

  Wink

  Wink is in front of the acorn.

L

- **last**

  This chipmunk is last.
  There is no one behind him.

- **least**

  8 12 17

  8 is the least number.

- **left**

  Pip   Boo   Wink

  Pip is on the left.

- **less than**

  3 is less than 4.
  3 is 1 less than 4.

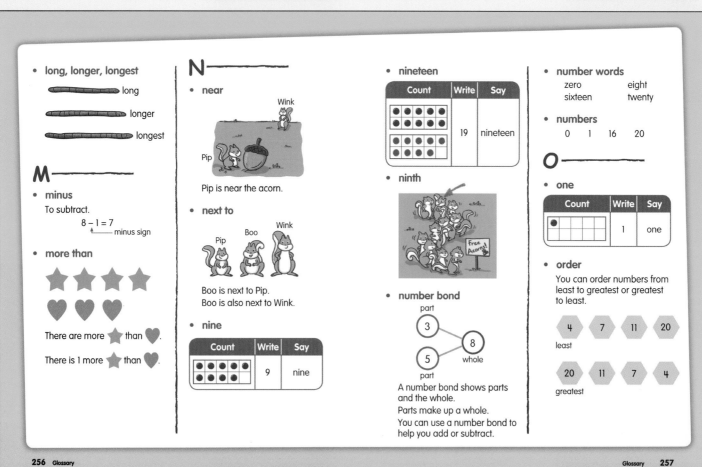

- **long, longer, longest**

  long
  longer
  longest

M

- **minus**

  To subtract.
  $8 - 1 = 7$
  minus sign

- **more than**

  There are more ⭐ than 💜.

  There is 1 more ⭐ than 💜.

N

- **near**

  Wink
  Pip

  Pip is near the acorn.

- **next to**

  Pip   Boo   Wink

  Boo is next to Pip.
  Boo is also next to Wink.

- **nine**

Count	Write	Say
	9	nine

- **nineteen**

Count	Write	Say
	19	nineteen

- **ninth**

- **number bond**

  part
  3
  5   8
  part   whole

  A number bond shows parts and the whole.
  Parts make up a whole.
  You can use a number bond to help you add or subtract.

- **number words**

  zero   eight
  sixteen   twenty

- **numbers**

  0   1   16   20

O

- **one**

Count	Write	Say
	1	one

- **order**

  You can order numbers from least to greatest or greatest to least.

  4 7 11 20
  least

  20 11 7 4
  greatest

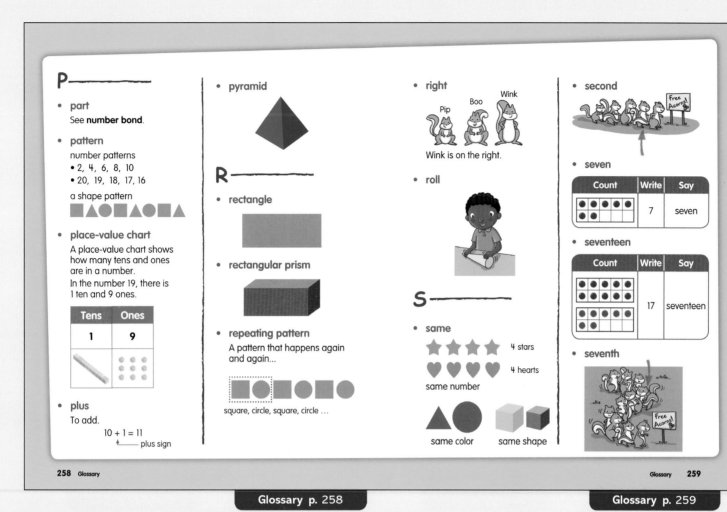

P

- **part**
  See **number bond**.

- **pattern**
  number patterns
  - 2, 4, 6, 8, 10
  - 20, 19, 18, 17, 16
  a shape pattern

- **place-value chart**
  A place-value chart shows how many tens and ones are in a number.
  In the number 19, there is 1 ten and 9 ones.

Tens	Ones
1	9

- **plus**
  To add.
  $10 + 1 = 11$
  ← plus sign

- **pyramid**

R

- **rectangle**

- **rectangular prism**

- **repeating pattern**
  A pattern that happens again and again...

  square, circle, square, circle …

- **right**

  Pip   Boo   Wink

  Wink is on the right.

- **roll**

S

- **same**

  ★ ★ ★ ★   4 stars

  ♥ ♥ ♥ ♥   4 hearts

  same number

  same color   same shape

- **second**

- **seven**

Count	Write	Say
	7	seven

- **seventeen**

Count	Write	Say
	17	seventeen

- **seventh**

258 Glossary

Glossary 259

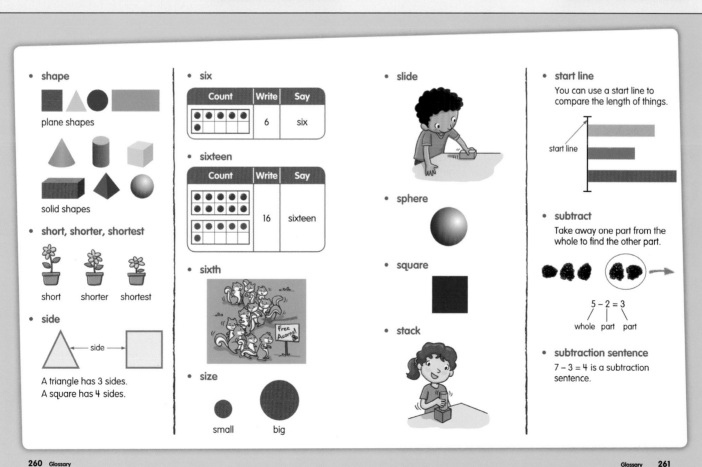

- **shape**

  plane shapes

  solid shapes

- **short, shorter, shortest**

  short   shorter   shortest

- **side**

  ← side →

  A triangle has 3 sides.
  A square has 4 sides.

- **six**

Count	Write	Say
	6	six

- **sixteen**

Count	Write	Say
	16	sixteen

- **sixth**

- **size**

  small   big

- **slide**

- **sphere**

- **square**

- **stack**

- **start line**
  You can use a start line to compare the length of things.

  start line

- **subtract**
  Take away one part from the whole to find the other part.

  $5 - 2 = 3$
  whole part part

- **subtraction sentence**
  $7 - 3 = 4$ is a subtraction sentence.

260 Glossary

Glossary 261

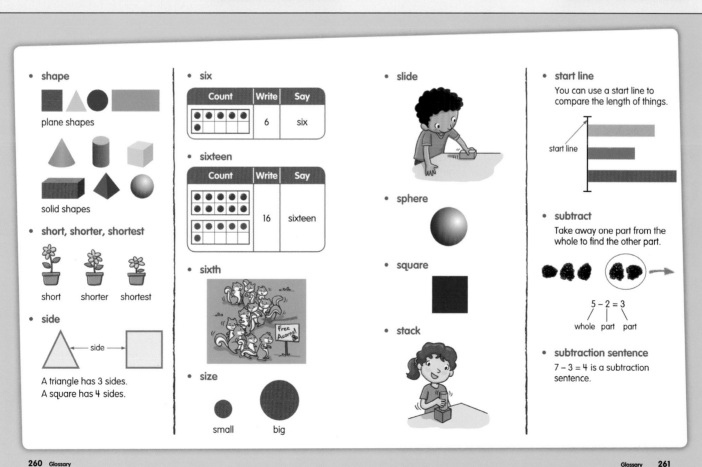

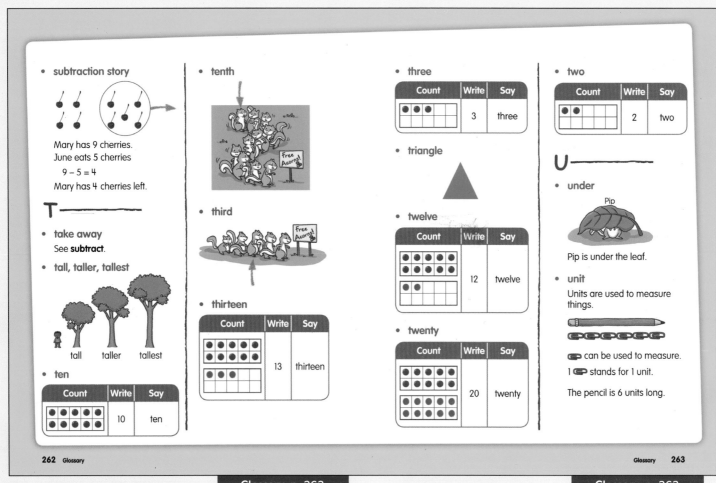

Glossary p. 262

- subtraction story

Mary has 9 cherries.
June eats 5 cherries
9 − 5 = 4
Mary has 4 cherries left.

T

- take away
  See **subtract**.

- tall, taller, tallest

tall taller tallest

- ten

Count	Write	Say
●●●●●●●●●●	10	ten

- tenth

- third

- thirteen

Count	Write	Say
●●●●● ●●●●● / ●●●	13	thirteen

Glossary p. 263

- three

Count	Write	Say
●●●	3	three

- triangle

- twelve

Count	Write	Say
●●●●● ●●●●● / ●●	12	twelve

- twenty

Count	Write	Say
●●●●● ●●●●● / ●●●●● ●●●●●	20	twenty

- two

Count	Write	Say
●●	2	two

U

- under

Pip

Pip is under the leaf.

- unit
  Units are used to measure things.

can be used to measure.
1 stands for 1 unit.

The pencil is 6 units long.

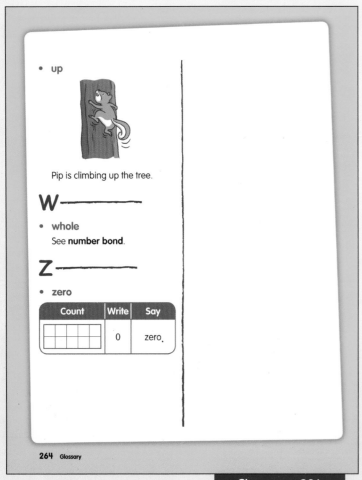

Glossary p. 264

- up

Pip is climbing up the tree.

W

- whole
  See **number bond**.

Z

- zero

Count	Write	Say
	0	zero

Program Overview

Teacher Resources

Professional Resources Bibliography

American Institutes for Research.® *What the United States Can Learn from Singapore's World-Class Mathematics System.* U. S. Department of Education Policy and Program Studies Services, 2005.

Chapin, Susan and Art Johnson. *Math Matters: Understanding the Math You Teach.* Math Solutions Publications, 2000.

Chapin, Susan, Catherine. O'Connor, and Nancy Canavan Anderson. *Classroom Discussions: Using Math Talk to Help Students Learn.* Math Solutions Publications, 2003.

Charles, Randall. *Teaching and Assessing of Mathematical Problem Solving.* Lawrence Earlbaum, 1989.

Copley, Juanita. *Mathematics in the Early Years,* National Council of Teachers of Mathematics, 1999.

Copley, Juanita. *The Young Child and Mathematics,* National Council of Teachers of Mathematics, 2000.

Gonzales, Patrick, Juan Carlos Guzmán, Lisette Partelow, Erin Pahlke, Leslie Jocelyn, David Kastberg, and Trevor Williams. *Highlights From the Trends in International Mathematics and Science Study: TIMSS 2003.* U.S. Department of Education, National Center for Education Statistics, 2004.

Hiebert, J., T. Carpenter, E. Fennema, K. Fuson, D. Wearne, H. Murray, A. Olivier, and P. Human. *Making Sense: Teaching and Learning Mathematics with Understanding.* Heinemann, 1997.

Fong, Dr. Ho Kheong. *The Essential Parents' Guide to Primary Maths.* Marshall Cavendish International, 2002.

Lee, Peng Yee, ed. *Teaching Primary School Mathematics: A Resource Guide.* Singapore Math Education Series, McGraw Hill Education, 2007.

Lee, Peng Yee, ed. *Teaching Secondary School Mathematics: A Resource Book.* Singapore Math Education Series, McGraw Hill Education, 2008

Ma, Liping. *Knowing and Teaching Elementary Mathematics.* Lawrence Earlbaum Associates, Inc., 1999.Martin et al. *TIMSS 2003 International Mathematics Report: Findings from IEA's Trends in International Mathematics and Science Study at the Eighth and Fourth-Grades.* Institute of Education Sciences, 2004.

National Council of Teachers of Mathematics. *Curriculum Focal Points for Prekindergarten through Grade 8 Mathematics,* 2006.

National Council of Teachers of Mathematics. *Principals and Standards for School Mathematics,* 2000.

National Mathematics Advisory Panel. *Foundations for Success.* U.S. Department of Education, 2008.

National Research Council. *Adding It Up: Helping Children Learn Mathematics.* Washington, D.C., National Academy Press, 2001

Ng Chye Huat, Juliana (Mrs.) and Mrs. Lim Kian Huat. *A Handbook for Mathematics Teachers in Primary Schools.* Marshall Cavendish International, 2003.

Polya, George. *How to Solve It.* Princeton University Press, 1945.

Richardson, Kathy. *Developing Number Concepts Books (Grades K-3): Counting, Comparing, and Pattern Book 1; Addition and Subtraction, Book 2; Place Value, Multiplication, and Division.* Dale Seymour Publications, 1998.

Stigler, James W. and James Hiebert. *The Teaching Gap: Best Ideas from the World's Teachers for Improving Education in the Classroom.* The Free Press, 1999.

Sullivan, Peter, and Pat Lilburn. *Good Questions for Math Teaching: Why Ask Them and What to Ask.* Math Solutions Publications, 1997.

Van de Walle, John A. *Elementary and Middle School Mathematics: Teaching Developmentally.* Allyn and Bacon, 2003.

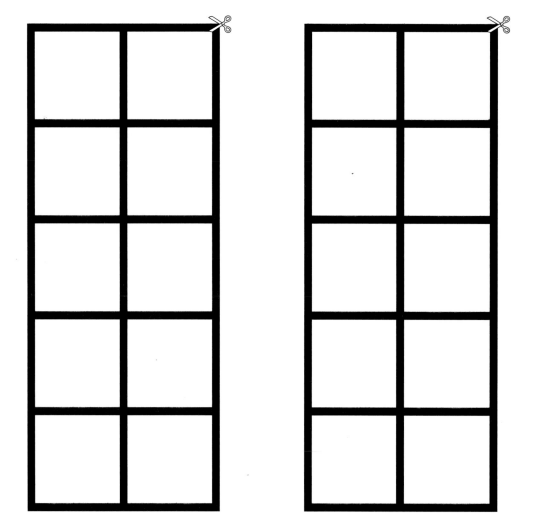

© 2009 Marshall Cavendish International (Singapore) Private Limited

Shoes and Socks Cut-Outs, and Horizontal Ten Frames　　TR02
Use with Student Book pp. 14, 17 and 24

© 2009 Marshall Cavendish International (Singapore) Private Limited

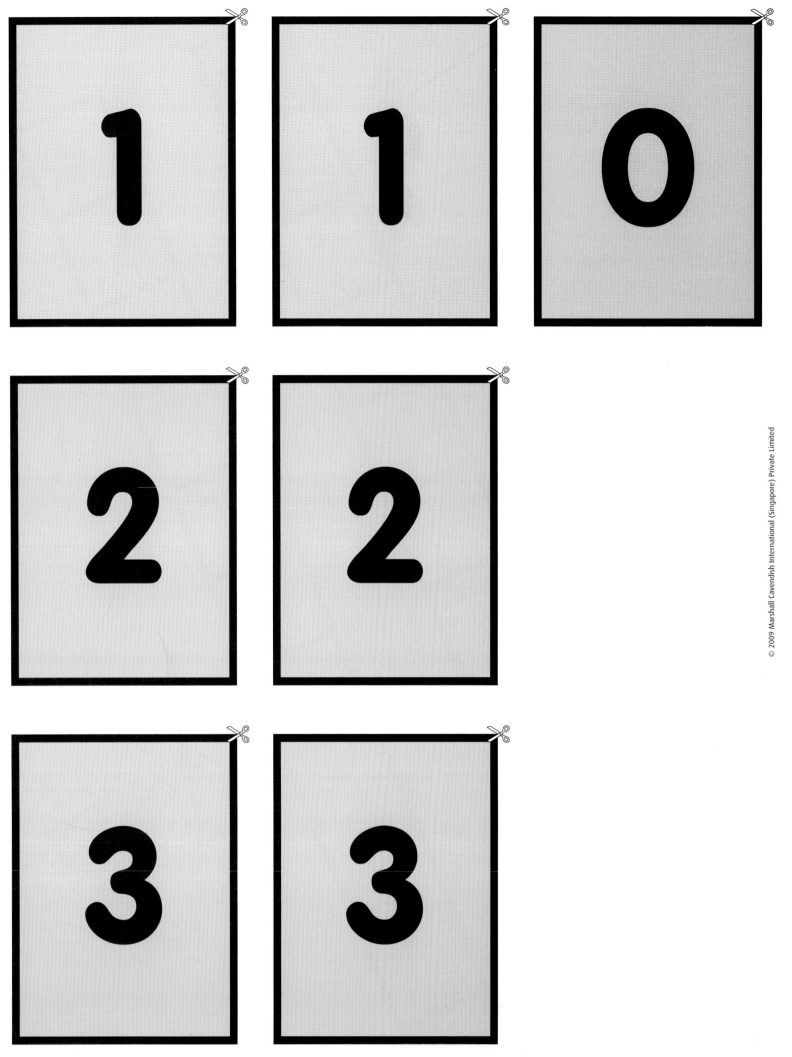

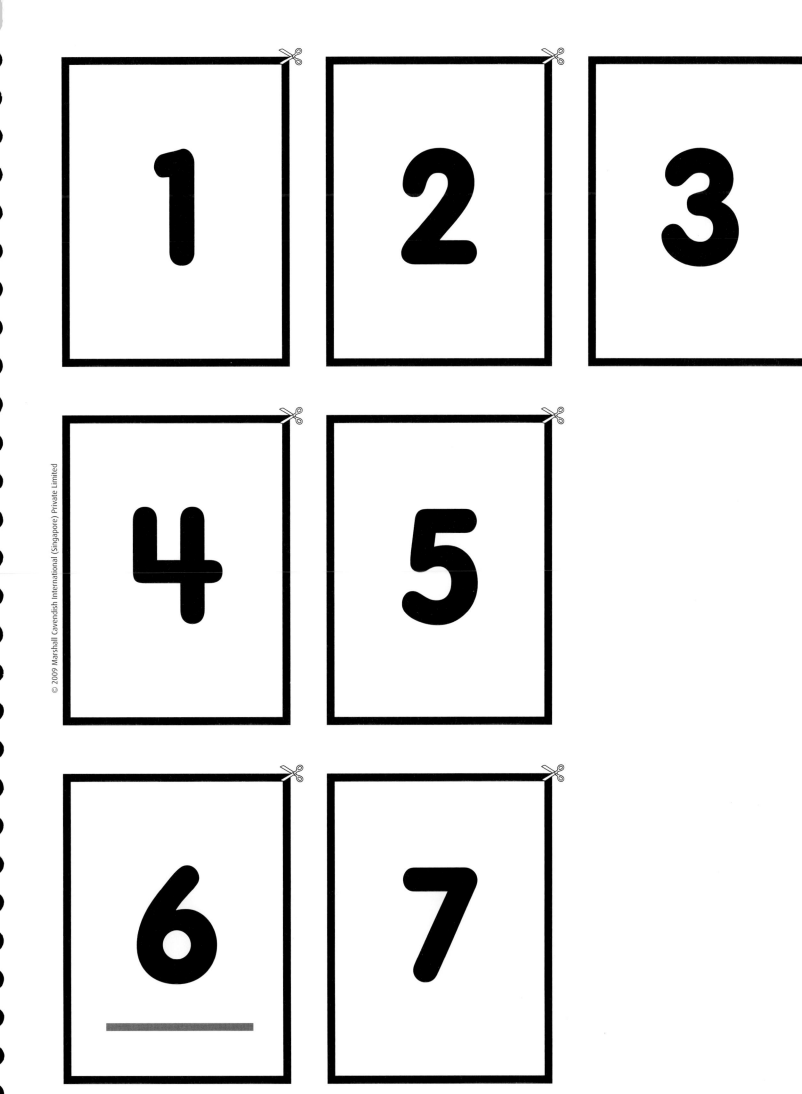

Number Cards: Pack Y   TR03
Use with Student Book p. 46

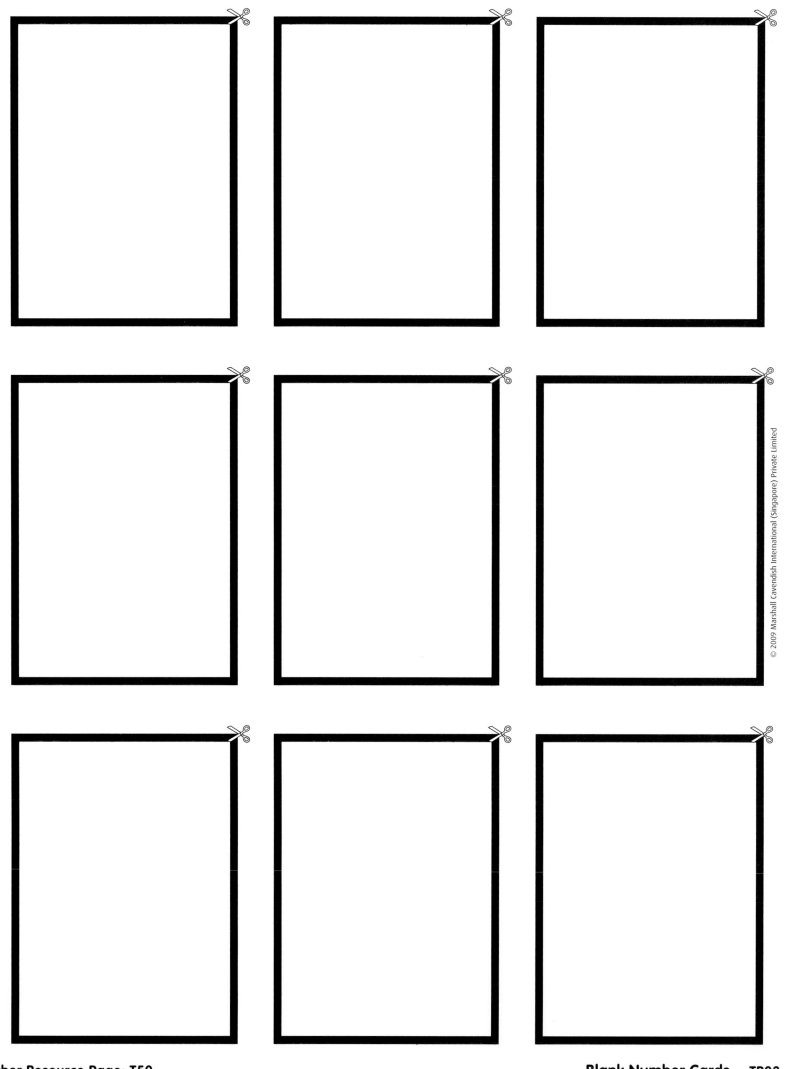

Blank Number Cards   TR03
Use with Student Book as necessary.

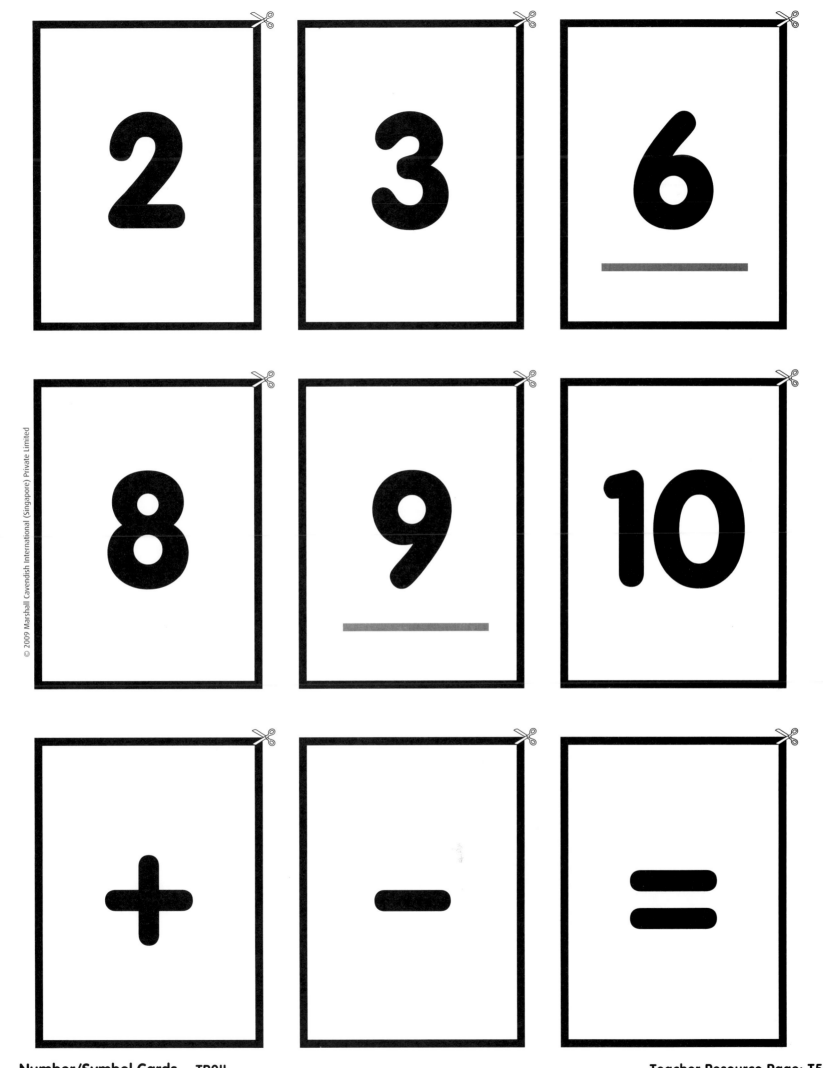

1.

Start →

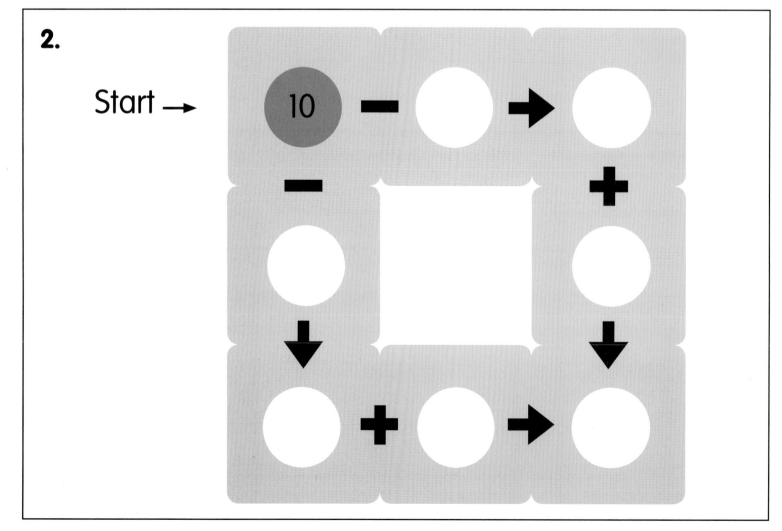

2.

Start →

Problem Solving Grids   **TR05**
Use with Student Book pp. 90 and 91

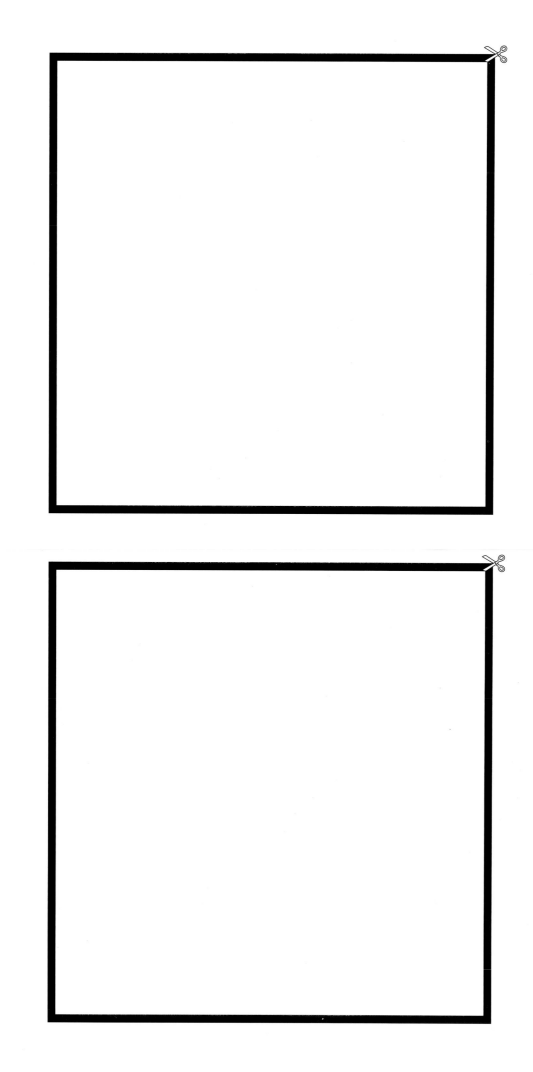

Squares to Fold TR06
Use with Student Book p. 107

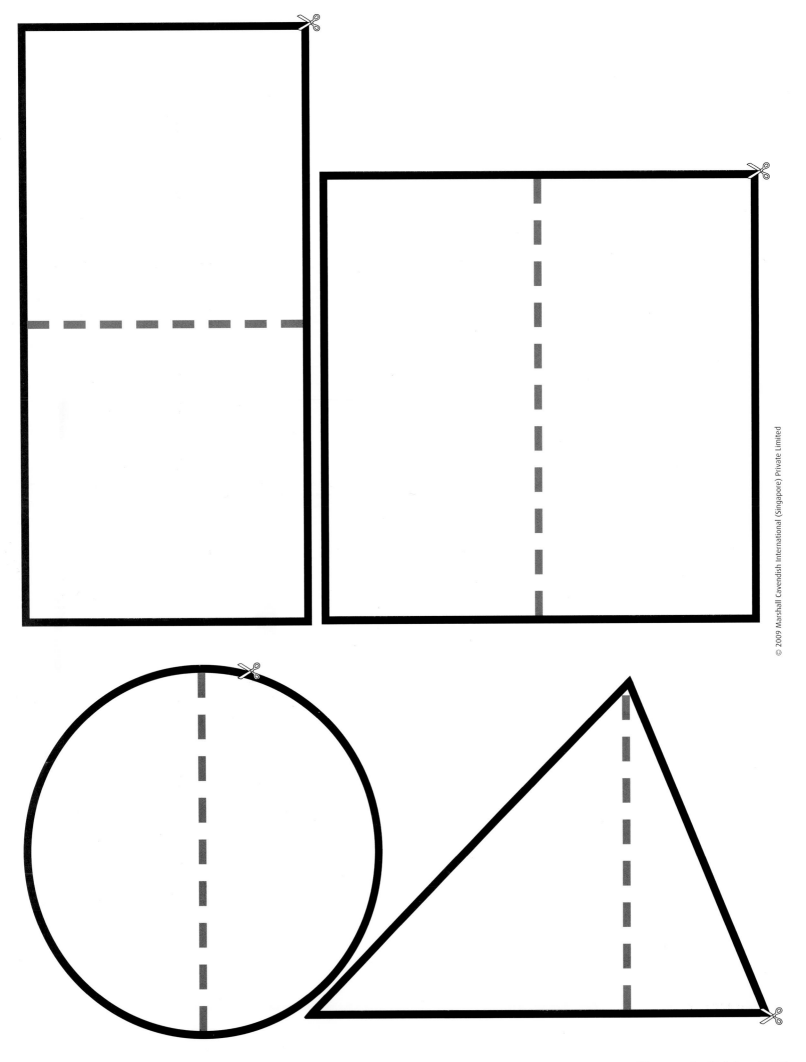

Shapes to Fold TR07
Use with Student Book pp. 108 and 109

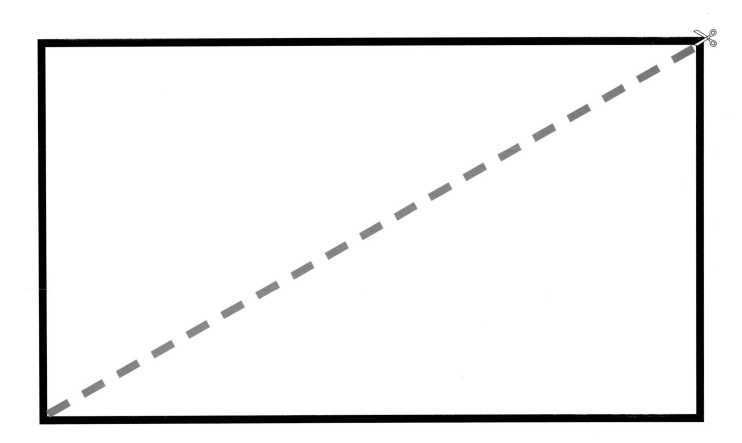

Shapes to Fold TR07
Use with Student Book p. 109

Solid Shape		Stack	Roll	Slide
rectangular prism				
sphere				
cube				
cylinder				
cone				

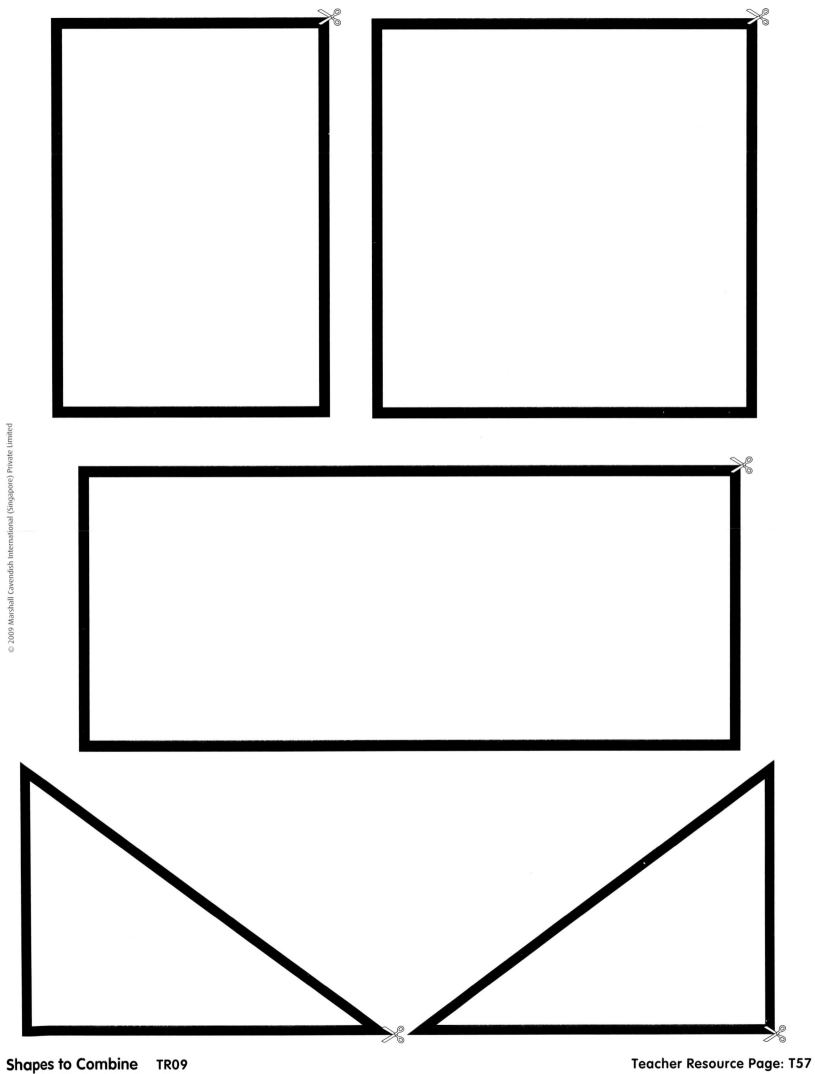

Shapes to Combine **TR09**
Use with Student Book p. 116

Shapes to Cut Out TR10
Use with Student Book p. 119 (Hands-On Activity)

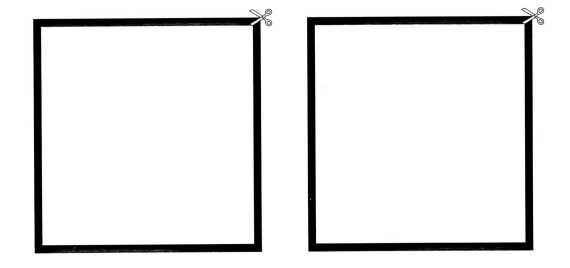

Shapes to Cut Out   **TR10**
Use with Student Book p. 119 (Let's Explore!)

Teacher Resource Page: T59

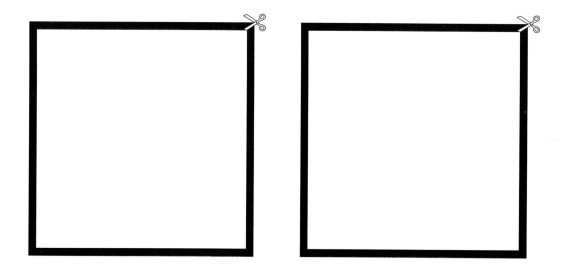

Shapes to Cut Out   **TR10**
Use with Student Book p. 119 (Let's Explore!)

Solid		How many?
cube		
sphere		
rectangular prism		
pyramid		
cylinder		
cone		

Position of the red cube from the Left	Position of the red cube from the Right	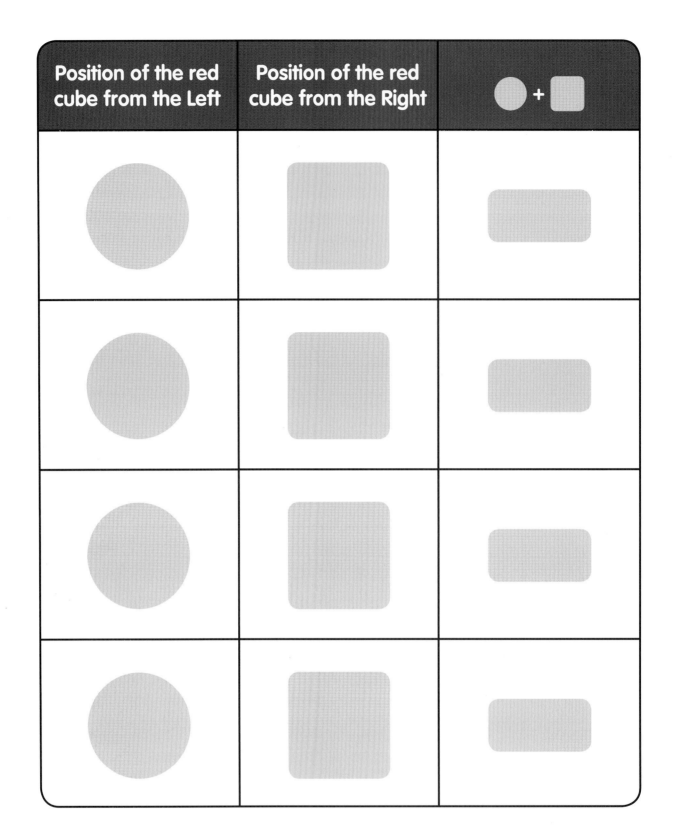 ◯ + ☐
◯	☐	▭
◯	☐	▭
◯	☐	▭
◯	☐	▭

Ones	Tens

Ones	Tens

Ones		
Tens		

Ones		
Tens		

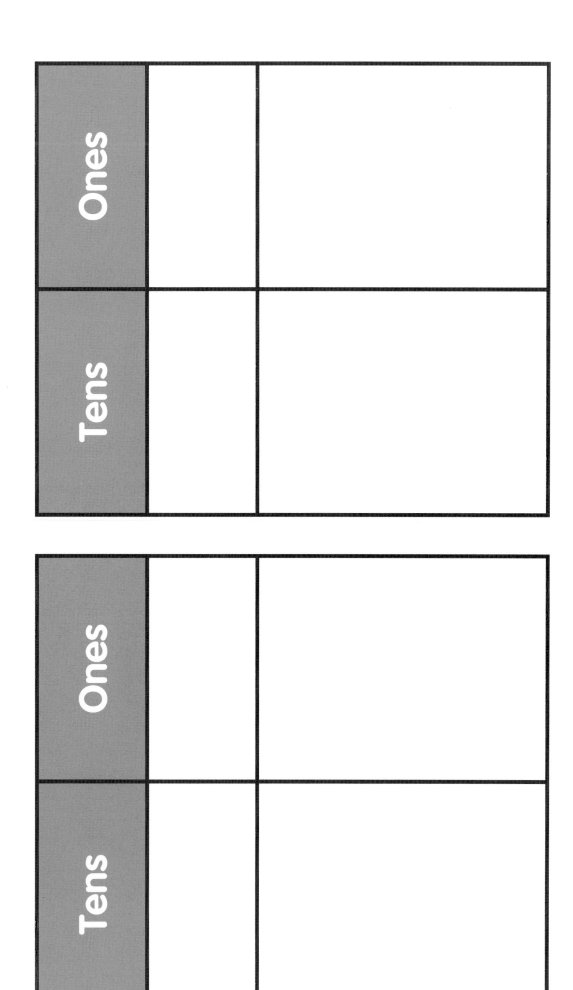

Place-Value Charts   TR13
Use with Student Book pp. 173, 177 and 179

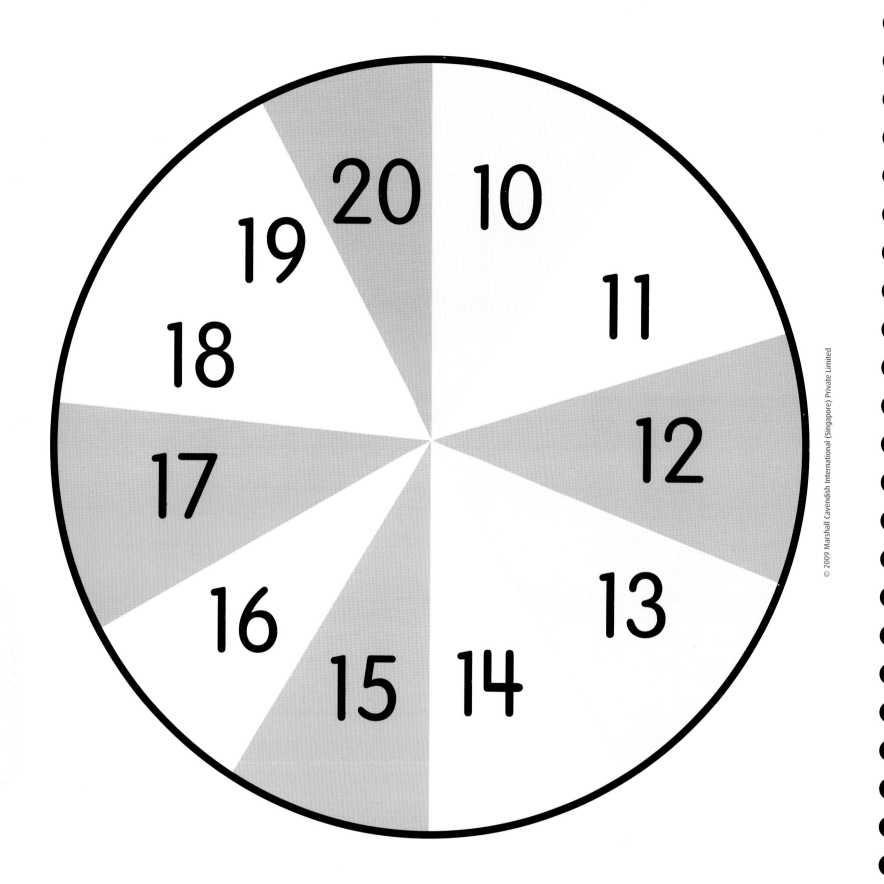

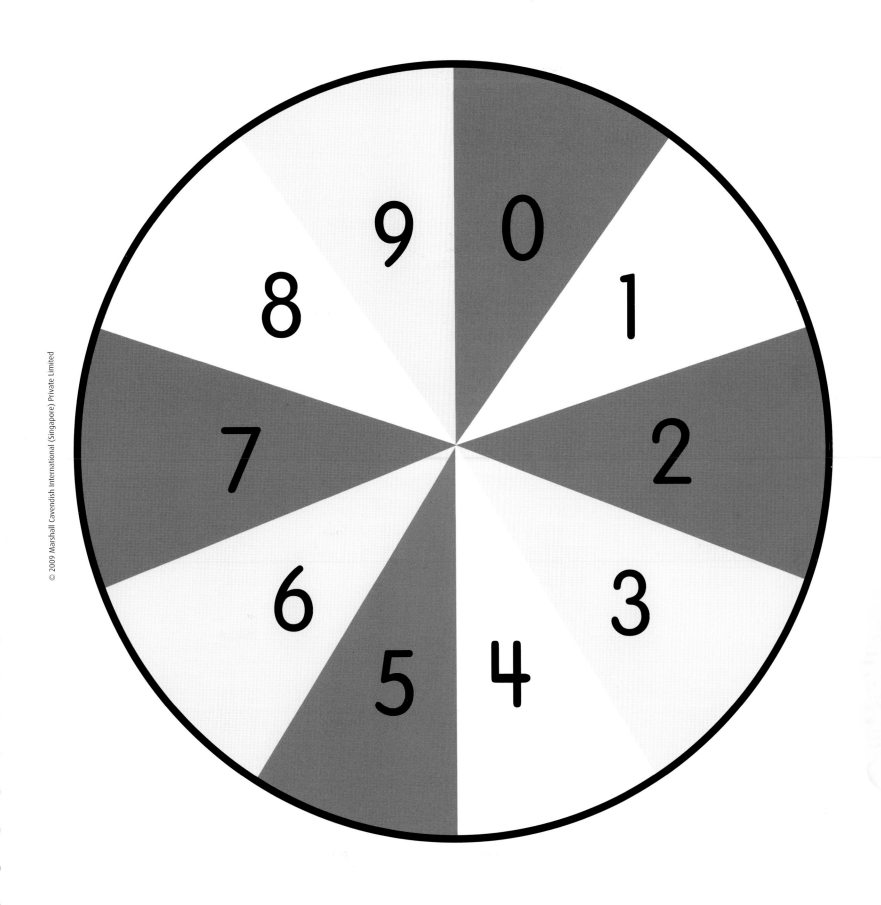

Spinner Bases (Spinner B)   TR14
Use with Student Book p. 207

1.

Start →

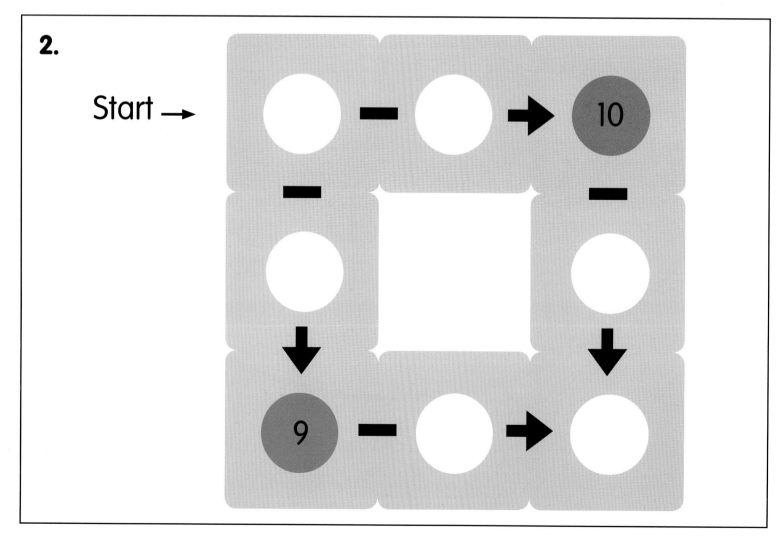

2.

Start →

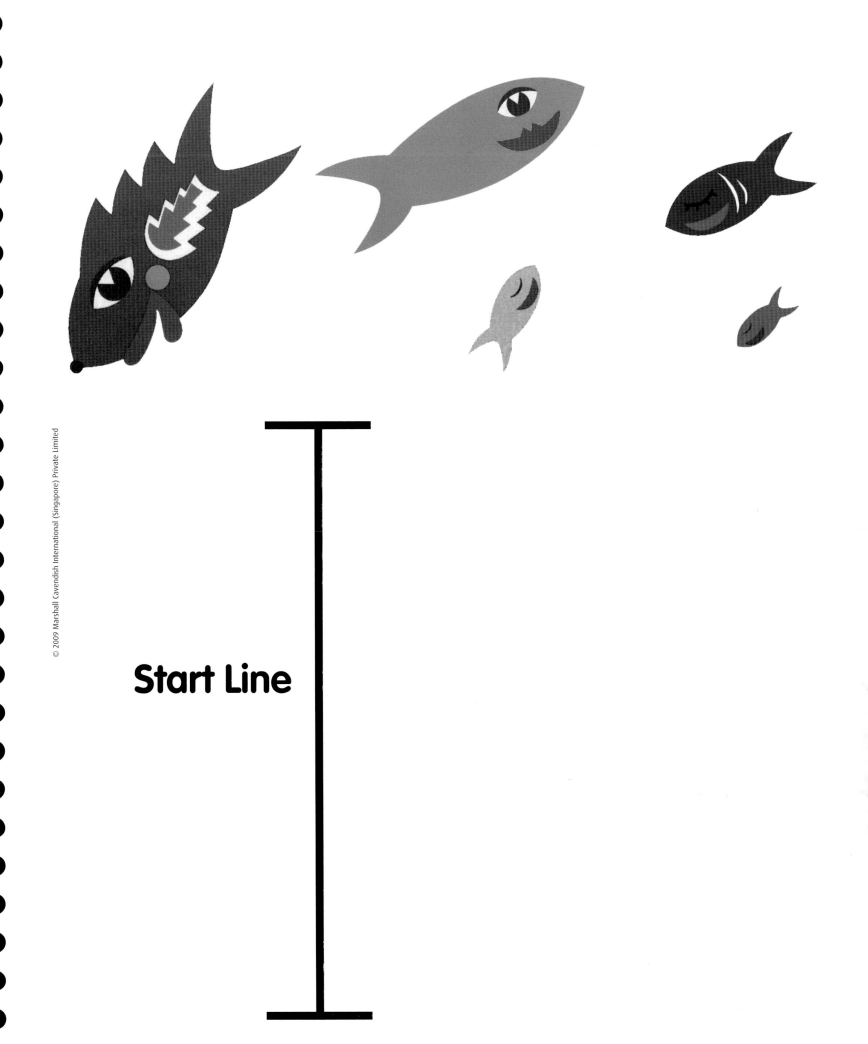

Start Line

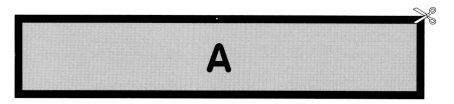

A

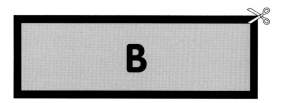

B

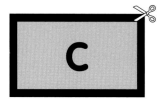

C

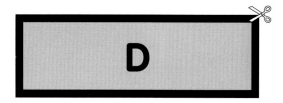

D

E

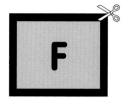

F

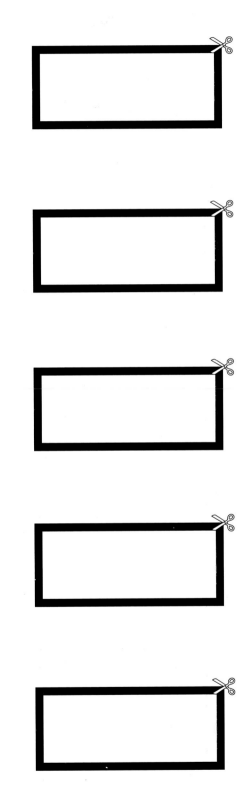

Strips for Measuring   TR18
Use with Student Book p. 237

	📎 stands for 1 unit	╱ stands for 1 unit
computer screen		
pencil case		
doorway		
lunch box		
tissue box		

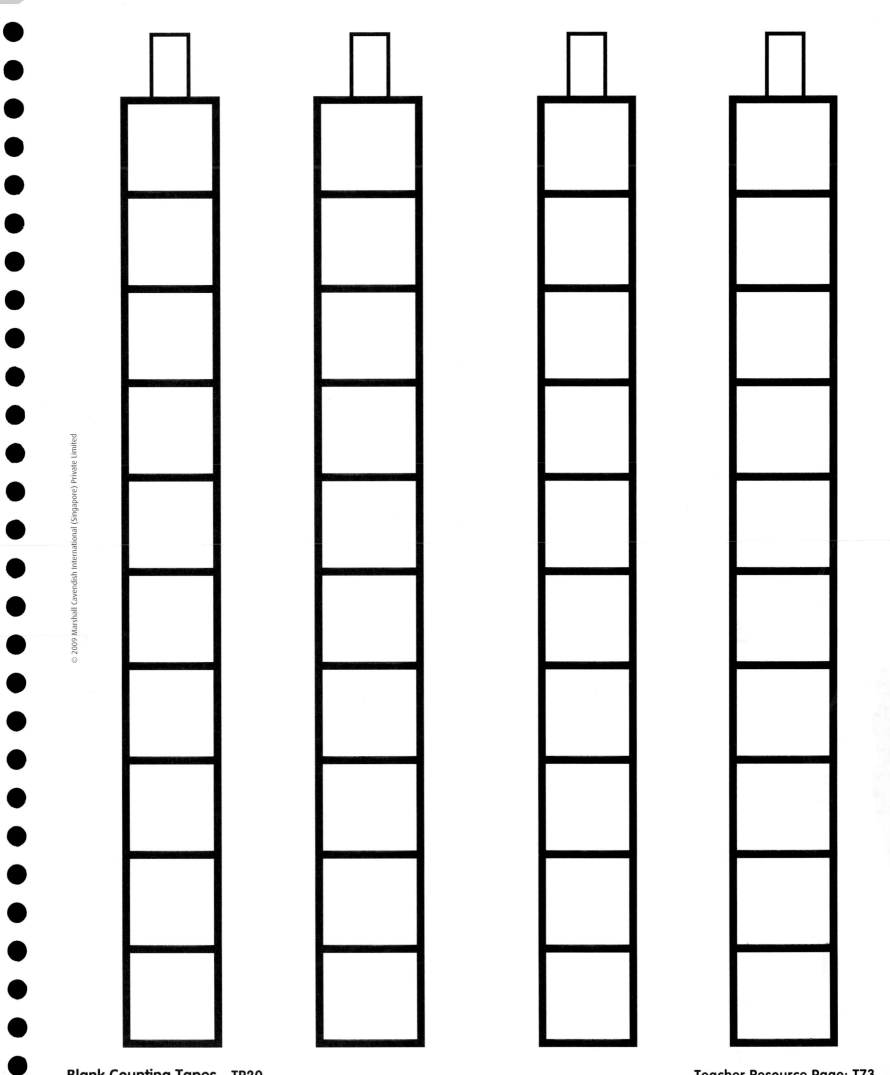

Blank Counting Tapes TR20
Use with Student Book as necessary.

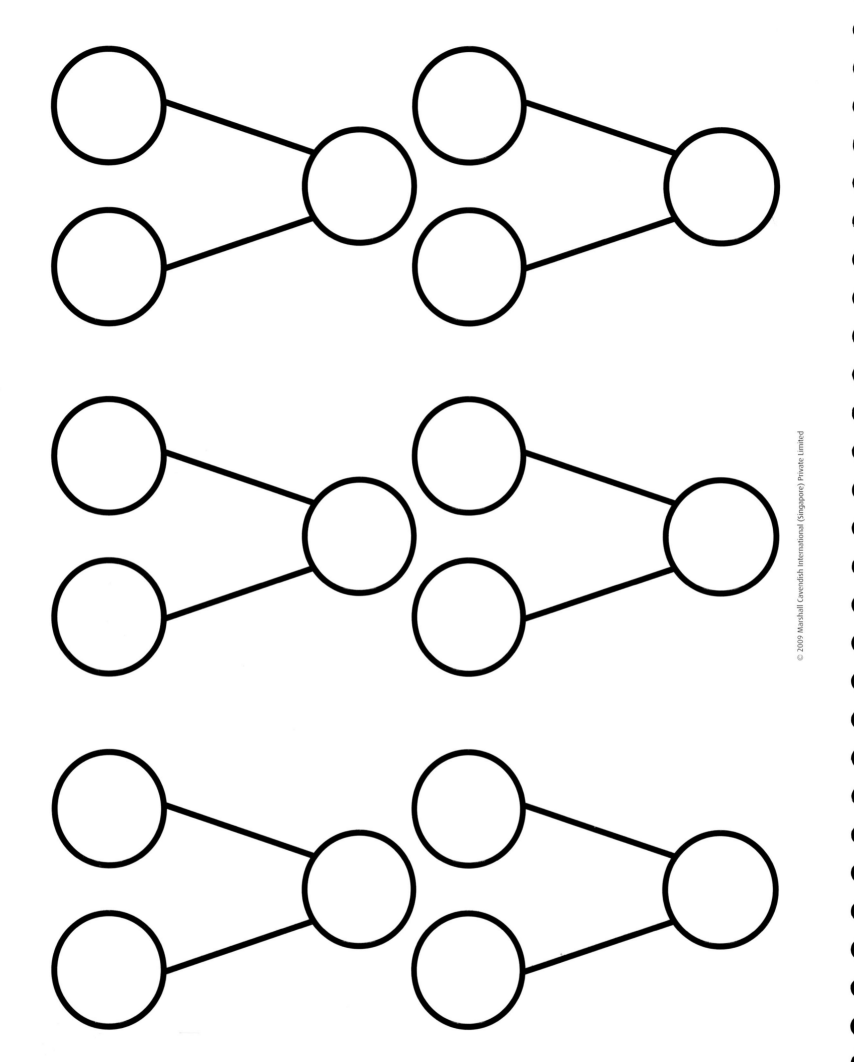

Number Bonds TR21
Use with Student Book as necessary.

Index

Pages in **boldface** type show where a term is introduced.

shapes, 129, 131, 131A, 132, 134-135, 137
  completing, 131, 134, 161C
  creating, 130, 131A, 133, 159A
  describing, 129, 132
  extending, 130–131, 131A, 133–135, 137A, 161D
  repeating pattern, **129**
ordering events, 159A
Put On Your Thinking Cap!, 26, 26A, 37, 37A, 61, 61A, 90–91, 135, 135A, 135B, 158–159, 189, 189A, 214–215, 215A, 247
sorting and classifying of geometric figures by attribute
  alike, **100**, 102–103, 105–109, 137A, 161C-161D
  color, **100**, 103, 105, 106, 137A
  different, **102**, 103, 105–106, 108–109, 161C
  number of corners, **101**, 102–103, 106–109, 161D
  number of sides, **101**, 102–103, 106–109, 161C-161D
  shape, **101**, 102–103, 105–109, 137A, 161D
  size, **101**, 102–103, 105–109, 137A, 161C-161D
strategies, *See* Addition, Problem Solving Strategies, *and* Subtraction
thinking skills
  analyzing parts and whole, 37, 37A, 57–58, 61, 61A, 90–91, 91A, 189A, 214–215, 215A
  classifying, 26, 26A, 127, 135A
  comparing, 26, 26A, 37A, 135B, 159A, 189, 189A, 215A, 247, 247A
  deduction, 37, 37A, 61, 61A, 91A, 157–159, 159A, 189A, 247, 247A
  sequencing, 157–159, 159A, 247A
  identifying patterns and relationships, 19A, 26A, 135B, 159, 189, 215A
  induction, 91A , 47
  spatial visualization, 135A, 135B

Recall Prior Knowledge, *See* Prerequisite skills

Rectangle, *See* Geometry

Rectangular prism, *See* Geometry

Remediation Options, 1C, 28C, 39C, 64C, 94C, 138C, 162C, 192C, 218C,

Representation
  addition models
    abstract, 57–63, 63A, 209–212, 217
    concrete, 43–45, 196–197, 200–202, 209
    pictorial, 42, 44–45, 48–55, 61, 63A, 171–174,177–179, 190–191, 195, 197–199, 201–206, 208, 213, 216–217
  addition sentences, **42**, 48–49, 57–58, 61, 62–63, 63A, 85, 87–88, 93, 93C, 195, 198, 200–201, 209, 216–217
  addition stories, **53**, 54–56, 56A, 61, 63A, 93C
  describing patterns, 20, 129, 132, 183
  equal sign (=), **42**
  geometric models, 103, 112, 120–123, 126, 133–134, 137
  Math in Focus Virtual Manipulatives, T21
  Number bonds, **30**
    addition, 48–49, 52–55, 52A, 57–59, 62–63
    part-part-whole, **30**, 31–35, 37–38, 37A, 38A, 38C
    related to fact families, 85
    subtraction, 74–78, 82–83, 92–93
  number machines (functions), 52A, 208B

number train, *throughout. See for example* 16, 23–25, 30, 35–36, 38
place-value chart, **171**, 172–174, 174A, 177–179, 181, 181A, 182, 190–191, 191A
subtraction models
  abstract, 73A, 76A, 77–81, 82–84, 81A, 85–86, 89–90, 93, 93A, 210–212, 217
  concrete, 68, 70, 73, 73A, 87, 93C
  pictorial, 68, 69, 72–76, 77–78, 81A, 82–83, 85, 92–93, 93A, 93C, 203–206, 208, 208A, 208B, 213, 216–217
subtraction number bonds, 74–76, 76A, 93A, 93C, 213, 217
subtraction stories, **77**, 78–81, 81A, 93, 93A, 93C
use a computer, 118, 130, 232
use a drawing/model, 61, 157–159, 247, 247A
use the +, -, = signs to represent addition and subtraction situations
  addition sentences, **42**, 48—49, 57—58, 61, 62—63, 63A, 85, 87—88, 93, 93C, 195, 198, 200—201, 209, 216—217
  subtraction sentences, **67**, 73, 73A, 75, 76A, 81A, 84, 89, 91A, 93A, 93C
writing numbers, 8, 27A, 191A

Research, T6

Reteach, *See* Remediation Options *and* Special Populations

Review
  Chapter Review/Test, 27, 27A, 38, 38A, 62–63, 63A, 92–93, 93A, 136–137, 137A, 160–161, 161A, 190–191, 191A, 216–217, 217A, 248–249, 248A–248B
  Chapter Wrap Up, 27, 38, 62–63, 92–93, 136–137, 160–161, 190–191, 216–217, 248–249

Right, *See* Position words

Science Connections, *See* Cross-Curricular Connections

Scope and Sequence, T24

Side, *See* Geometry

Size, *See* Geometry

Skills Trace, 1A, 28A, 39A, 64A, 94A, 138A, 162A, 192A, 218A,

Social Studies Connections, *See* Cross-Curricular Connections

Solid shapes, *See* Geometry

Sorting and classifying, *See* Geometry

Special Populations, *Found in each chapter in TE. For example*, 1B, 28B, 39B, 64B, 94B; *See also* Differentiated Instruction

Sphere, *See* Geometry

Square, *See* Geometry

Strategies, *See* Addition, Problem Solving, *and* Subtraction

Struggling Learners, *See* Differentiated Instruction

Notes

Notes

Notes